Rage & Roll

RAGE & ROLL

Bill Graham and the Selling of Rock

John Glatt

A Birch Lane Press Book
Published by Carol Publishing Group

A Birch Lane Press Book
Published by Carol Publishing Group
Birch Lane Press is a registered trademark of Carol Communications, Inc.
Editorial Offices: 600 Madison Avenue, New York, N.Y. 10022
Sales and Distribution Offices: 120 Enterprise Avenue, Secaucus, N.J. 07094
In Canada: Canadian Manda Group, P.O. Box 920, Station U, Toronto, Ontario M8Z 5P9
Queries regarding rights and permissions should be addressed to Carol Publishing Group, 600 Madison Avenue, New York, N.Y. 10022

Carol Publishing Group books are available at special discounts for bulk purchases, for sales promotion, fund-raising, or educational purposes. Special editions can be created to specifications. For details, contact: Special Sales Department, Carol Publishing Group, 120 Enterprise Avenue, Secaucus, N.J. 07094

Manufactured in the United States of America
10 9 8 7 6 5 4 3 2 1

Library of Congress Cataloging-in-Publication Data

Glatt, John.
Rage & roll : Bill Graham and the selling of rock / by John Glatt.
p. cm.
"A Birch Lane Press book."
ISBN 1-55972-205-3 (cloth)
1. Graham, Bill, 1931–1991. 2. Impresarios—United States—Biography. I. Title. II. Title: Rage and roll.
ML429.G69G6 1993
781.66'092—dc20
[B] 93-5138
CIP
MN

To my parents,
NOMAH AND LOUIS

Got to be a winner—trophy winnner
Got to hold your head up high up!
    Number one!

——Joni Mitchell

Contents

Acknowledgments

I am grateful to all those who agreed to be interviewed for this book, including: Michael Ahern, Peter Albin, Ellis Amburn, Sam Andrew, Mike Appel, Daniel Ray Bacon, Marty Balin, Barry Bell, Melvin Belli, Sid Bernstein, Lee Bloomer, Lynn Bowersley, Peter Brandt, Chris Brooks, Regina Cartwright, Irving Cohen, Jane Cohen, Neil Cohen, Robert Cohen, Michael Cohl, Richard Cole, Alex Cooley, Peter Coyote, R.G. (Ronnie) Davis, Dirk Dirkson, Jan Dodge, Thom Duffy, Frank Ehrenreich, Philip Elwood, Marc Eliot, Thomas Tesseny, Carl Freed, David Freiberg, Vinnie Fusco, David Getz, Herbert Gold, Arny Granat, James Gurley, Harold Guskin, Nick Gravenitis, Bob Grossweiner, Wavy Gravy, Jim Haynie, Jack Healey, Chet Helms, James Henke, Herbie Herbert, George Honchar, Thom Jenkins, Dan Johnson, Julius Karpen, Alton Kelly, Howie Klein, Michael Lang, Rabbi Josef and Hinda Langer, Carmen "Cuca" Leon, Jack Levin, Barry Levinson, Alex Ligertwood, Ben Liss, Jack MacDonough, John Morris, Larry Morse, Tom McConnel, Onnie McIntyre, Mike McNally, David Nadel, Daphna Noily, Tony Pirinjan, Joe Pipe, Adolph Ringen, Francois Rothstein, Frank Russo, Pete Sears, Dr. David Smith, Derek Taylor, Roger Trilling, Ken Viola, Matthew Walker, Joshua White, Michael Wilhelm, Wes Wilson, Steve Wozniak, Bill Wyman and Tim Yohannon.

This book could never have been written without the patience and inspiration of my agent, Susan Lee Cohen, who ignited the spark for this project.

I would like to thank my editor, Bruce Shostak, at Carol Publishing for his guidance and solid judgment throughout.

I extend my gratitude to Denise Childs, whose proven command of the English language and critical eye were invaluable.

I also owe an enormous debt to Pamela Dorman and Stuart Krichevsky who steered me on the right path at the beginning and were always there with advice and moral support.

Much thanks should also go to: Marion Collins, Paul Tharp, Roger Trilling, Robert Sites, Regina Cartwright, Ira Berger, Geri Chark, Tom Espey, Chet Helms, Judy Davis, Rita Ross, Christopher Bowen, Daniel Ray Bacon, Susan Comegys, Toni Reinhold, Norman Solovay, Alistair Duncan, Leo Greenbaum of YIVO, John Fromer of KRON-TV, Ian Kimmet, David Weitzman and Roger Hitts.

Prelude

Friday October 25, 1991, was a typical day for Bill Graham. After working a full day in his office in downtown San Francisco, he left at about 6:00 P.M. with his girlfriend Melissa Gold for the short drive over the Golden Gate Bridge to Sausalito. On his way out, he called his former lover, Regina Cartwright, to talk to their two-year-old daughter Caitlin, but there was no answer. They were en route to meet up with his friend, confidant, and personal pilot, Steve "Killer" Kahn, to fly to the Concord Pavilion, where he was presenting the final show in the Huey Lewis and the News Hard at Play tour. The pugnacious promoter had recently fallen out with Lewis's manager, Bob Brown, and wanted to go and make peace.

With the oncoming storm season, the weather was atrocious. As they took off in the red-and-white Bell Jet Ranger 206B, near-gale-force winds and driving rain made conditions so hazardous that Kahn was advised not to fly by local air traffic controllers. He was not qualified to fly using only instruments.

Kahn ignored the warning. The ride over was very rough, with the high winds tossing the tiny helicopter around like a feather, causing Gold to bruise her leg badly as she was slammed into the seat in front of her. Even Graham, wearing a jacket bearing the logo of Lynyrd Skynyrd, the Southern rock band which lost three members in an air crash in the early eighties, wanted to turn back. Kahn, who had flown the route many times before, said it was okay but agreed to alter course and fly around San Pablo Bay instead of across it, for extra safety.

When they landed in the Concord Pavilion car lot at about 8:00 P.M. all three were pretty shaken up. Graham told friends that it was one of the worst flights he had ever taken. During the ride to the pavilion, Graham and Gold both worried about the return flight and Graham urged Kahn to take the one-hour limousine ride back to his home, Masada, afterward. The pilot, feeling sure the weather was improving, was reluctant to leave the helicopter unattended all night in the car lot without security.

At the Concord Pavilion, Graham and Gold relaxed and began to enjoy themselves. During a backstage dinner with members of the band and their wives, Graham was in fine form, entertaining the table with hilarious tales of his early experiences with the heavy-metal outfit Metallica. The volatile promoter seemed unusually calm and peaceful and more interested in socializing than talking business. After dinner Graham spent an hour in Concord Pavilion general manager John Toffoli's office before going down to talk to the band who were preparing to go onstage. He repeated his fears about the flight back in the bad weather, admitting that he hadn't thought he would survive the flight over to Concord. News guitarist Mario Cippolina offered to drive him back for the one-hour journey to Masada if he waited until the end of the show, but Graham didn't reply.

As Huey Lewis took the stage at 9:20 P.M., Graham took a quick peek at the band before rounding up Melissa and Steve Kahn. Pavilion manager Mike McNally escorted the three down to the van on the lower level and bid them good night.

During the five-minute ride to the helicopter, all three were laughing and reminiscing about old times. The weather seemed calmer and the rain had almost stopped. Although it was still very windy, Kahn didn't foresee any problems, and Graham and Gold boarded the helicopter while the pilot walked around to untie the main rotor.

While he was making his final checks for the short thirty-minute fight to Gnoss Field in Novato, Kahn radioed the Oakland ATC Tower for weather conditions. He was again warned not to fly using visual flight rules because of fog, wind, and slashing rain. Ignoring the controller, Kahn took off at 9:39 P.M.

Three minutes later, the weather suddenly worsened and Kahn told Concord air controller Steve Ingebretson, "Well it's looking a little dark and gruesome over towards Martinez; we'll keep an eye on it." A minute later Kahn said he was having trouble seeing through the scuds—fast-moving, dark, patchy clouds.

Approaching Benicia Bridge, Kahn began chatting to Ingebretson about the dangers of not having red warning balls on electrical power lines as a warning to low-flying aircraft.

"It's, uh, just a real dangerous situation," Kahn said. "I've had PG and E guys up there and they say the neighbors complain too much they won't let them put balls on."

With hindsight, Ingebretson's reply was chilling; "Don't you always have to wait until somebody gets hurt or killed before they do anything."

As Kahn flew low over Benicia Bridge at 9:44 P.M., he asked Ingebretson if he could see the helicopter from the ground. The controller said he couldn't and then broke radio contact as Kahn flew out of his airspace.

With the storm gathering strength, Kahn decided not to go over San Pablo Bridge and flew toward Mare Island. With the low clouds and the driving rain, visibility was now so bad that Kahn dropped down to a couple of hundred feet so he could be guided by the car headlights going westbound on Highway 37.

As the helicopter plowed on through the menacing black clouds, Kahn found himself flying blind. In desperation, he took the Bell Ranger down even lower—to 100 feet—and dropped his speed to just 65 mph. With his blinking red anticollision lights on, Kahn followed the road. About a quarter of a mile from the Sonoma Creek Bridge, he saw a double set of power lines coming from his right, running parallel with the highway. Kahn maneuvered the helicopter over to the left, trying to steer clear of another power line that loomed overhead to his right.

Without warning, one of the rotor blades sliced through a low-slung 115,000-volt power cable as it crossed the road. The high-tension cable snapped and lassoed the helicopter furiously, sending it whiplashing the length of two football fields into a 225-foot-high electrical transmission tower. It exploded in a huge fireball. Graham, Gold, and Kahn were killed instantly, their bodies thrown to the ground as power blacked out 23,000 homes in the area and brought Huey Lewis's set to a halt.

Bill Graham had died as he lived—in an explosion of high-energy power.

Just a month earlier, Bill Graham had celebrated the fiftieth anniversary of his coming to America as a penniless refugee. All he owned were the ragged clothes on his back. In that time, Graham had achieved fame and fortune far beyond his dreams as the controversial Godfather of Rock—the man who had single-handedly turned rock 'n' roll concert promotion into big business.

Two weeks later on a warm summer afternoon Graham, looked back over his life at Masada, named after the ancient mountain top fortress where 960 Jews had committed suicide in A.D. 73, rather than be taken alive by Roman soldiers. In the tranquillity of the luscious Corte Madera Hills the sixty-year-old impresario, whose strength had been forged in the Holocaust of Nazi Germany, looked to the future with hope after a lifetime of turmoil and disappointment.

On the surface his turbulent life seemed at last to be on an even keel. He was about to announce his engagement to the new love in his life Melissa Gold and had just fulfilled his lifetime ambition by starring in a Hollywood feature movie playing Charles "Lucky" Luciano in *Bugsy*. And he was looking forward to flying to Los Angeles the following week to discuss an offer to become the Ed Sullivan of the 1990s with his own weekly television variety show.

He was also hard at work on the latest of a long line of his patented benefit concerts; this time to help the victims of the recent Oakland fire. All in all life had seemed sweet for the former immigrant who had pulled himself up from nothing to take his rightful place in show business history alongside titans Samuel Goldwyn, David O. Selznick and Florenz Ziegfeld.

Rage & Roll

1

Beginnings—Getting to the U.S.A.

Bill Graham was born Wolodia Grajonca in Berlin on January 8, 1931, during the beginning of Hitler's rise to power. The youngest child of engineer Jacob Grajonca and his stunningly tall wife Frieda (née Grass), Wolodia was just two days old when his father, who had fought for Russia in the First World War, was killed in a construction accident.

After Jacob's death, Frieda was forced to go out to work as a dressmaker to support Wolodia and his five elder sisters, Rita, Evelyn, Sonja, Ester, and Tolla. Life was a constant struggle for the Grajonca family, who were so poor they were forced to live in two rooms and a kitchen in Wedding, the roughest slum section of Berlin.

Scraping together a meager living by making artificial flowers and costume jewelry to sell in the market, Frieda could not afford to support her six children and had to send the two youngest, Wolodia and Tolla, to an orphanage to be looked after properly. But on the weekends they would all be reunited in the family home on Alte Jacobstrasse, where all five girls slept in the same bed next to Wolodia's crib.

When Wolodia was six, he was sent with Tolla, who was two years older, and the other orphan children, on a short vacation to Denmark. The little boy loved Denmark, most of all the delicious Danish cooking.

As the Nazis tightened their grip on Berlin, it became increasingly dangerous being a Jew as Hitler's anti-Semitic propaganda started being accepted by the German people. At school the Grajonca girls were expected to salute Nazi-style and say "Heil Hitler" whenever a teacher entered the classroom. And they were constantly mocked by the other schoolchildren who had enthusiastically enrolled in the Hitler Youth movement.

Living in the orphanage, Wolodia was sheltered from the anti-Jewish feeling. His favorite part of the week was coming home on weekends to be with his mother and sisters. To the little boy his sisters lived an exotic bohemian life-style, full of wonderful dancing and music. Rita and Evelyn, now pretty teenagers, were rebellious and sought independence in these tough times. Staying out late at night with boys led to constant arguments with their worried mother as she attempted to rein them in. Wolodia carefully followed the exotic adventures of his eldest sister Rita, who left home for Shanghai with her boyfriend and became a dancer in a coffeehouse. He was particularly impressed that she was earning $150 a month.

Wolodia was seven years old when the Nazis took their hatred of Jews to new heights in the infamous Kristallnacht (Night of Broken Glass) on November 9–10, 1938. Loyal party members and Hitler Youth throughout Germany and Austria went on an orgy of destruction, indiscriminately beating up Jews and attacking their businesses. In the aftermath of Kristallnacht, Frieda became more and more worried about her children's future and survival in Berlin, especially after the compulsory introduction of special "Juden" identity cards used to isolate Jews. But the hardworking mother did not have enough money to move her family out of Germany.

On June 5, 1939, before Hitler invaded Poland and plunged Europe into full-scale war, Wolodia and Tolla were among forty children sent off to Paris as part of a two-week Jewish exchange program with a French orphanage. His mother and sisters Ester and Evelyn went to the train station to see them off in an emotional farewell. It would be the last time that the two youngest Grajonca children would ever see their mother.

Eight-year-old Wolodia left Germany grasping a case which held everything he owned in the world, including his yarmulke, Jewish prayer book, and a picture of his parents. Tolla attempted to up keep his spirits, telling the frightened little boy that the family would soon be reunited to live happily ever after.

During the two weeks that Wolodia and Tolla were in Paris, the Nazis slammed the door shut on Jewish immigration, and the possibility that his mother and sisters would reach safety in France was gone. The orphans dared not return to Germany. They were stranded.

Far away from the turmoil and uncertainty of Berlin, Wolodia and Tolla passed the next year in the peace and tranquillity of the Chateau de Quincy, a beautiful old, spacious, tapestry-filled mansion outside Paris. Wolodia loved the vastness of the high-ceilinged chateau, which was run by its owner, a former French army officer. He was enrolled at the public elementary school at Quincy at the Chateau de Chaumont, where he loved the routine and stability after the uncertainty of Berlin.

For Wolodia, life at the chateau was idyllic. He ran around in a gang with other orphans, joining in their daring games and exploits, like stealing expeditions to the local shops, where they often got caught red-handed. To Wolodia, life at the chateau revolved around lunch, the main meal of the day, which was always the locally caught rabbit, cooked differently each day for variety. In class, Wolodia was a good student. He soon learned to speak fluent French and impressed his teachers with his love of nature.

When the Germans invaded France in May 1940, Wolodia, Tolla, and the other children were evacuated to another chateau located southeast of Paris. Wolodia disliked his new home and especially hated having to help the local townspeople build air-raid shelters outside the chateau as the German army marched on Paris. When German warplanes started circling Paris and the bombing raids commenced, the petrified children had to hide for safety in the deep rain-filled trenches. Night after night Wolodia lay in the wet air-raid shelters, terrified of the "little eel-shaped things" he could feel moving all over him. One night, while hiding in the trenches during an air raid, he was attacked by a snake—a nightmarish experience which left him with a lifelong terror of snakes.

When the German army neared Paris, a mass exodus was organized. An International Red Cross representative was sent to the chateau to escort the Jewish children south to safety, and Wolodia and Tolla were among the sixty-four child evacuees.

One night at the farm the children hid for their lives when fully armed German soldiers burst in, their fingers on the trigger in search of French soldiers, luckily failing to spot the children.

"This group of children has seen the Battle of Paris," wrote their Red Cross escort, "and lived through all the dangers, discovering certain cruel aspects of fighting which perhaps have left marks on their character. In the case of [Wolodia] Grajonca, however, I dare say with certainty that the moral damage is not serious."

"Everybody moved south," Graham remembered almost fifty years later. "There were sixty-four children between the ages of eight and sixteen. My sister and I were among these. We walked, got on buses, on trains, on carts and ate what we could. When a country is invaded, that's what happens. All hell breaks loose."

Traveling south from Paris, the children hid by day and walked 40 kilometers (25 miles) every night under cover of darkness, often scrambling for safety as German planes launched air attacks. They witnessed the horrors of war firsthand and became used to seeing dead bodies littering the highway. They lived on berries and anything they could find growing wild; they all suffered from malnutrition. Wolodia's sister Tolla, who was frailer than the others, contracted pneumonia during the journey. One day, just outside Lyon, as she was walking hand in hand with her brother, she dropped to the roadside, dead. Inconsolable, little Wolodia cradled Tolla's head in his lap and refused to be separated from his beloved sister. With the Germans nearly snapping at their heels, the Red Cross escort did not dare to stay behind long enough to bury Tolla and had to drag Wolodia off his sister's body, leaving it lying by the side of the road. From Lyon, the children walked to Marseilles.

On August 19, 1941 orphans were issued temporary passports by the American consulate. Little Wulf (Wolfgang) Wolodia Grajonca, as he was listed, wore a brave smile in his photograph. He was 4 foot 6 inches tall and weighed a mere 55 pounds. From Marseilles the group took a train to Toulouse and crossed the Pyrenees into Spain, traveling through Barcelona to Madrid.

"I was living in a convent with eleven children," Graham remembered later. "A stray bomb . . . next to us hit the building that I was in. Three of the children did not leave the building."

From Madrid the surviving children traveled to Lisbon. On September 10, Wolodia and the ten other children, all that remained of the sixty-four who originally left Paris, boarded the ocean liner *Serpa Pinto,* bound for the safety of America.

After a brief stopover in Casablanca to pick up more refugees, the *Serpa Pinto* set off across the Atlantic for the two-week voyage to New York. During the crossing they were stopped and boarded by both a U-boat and a British submarine, much to the horror of the forty Jewish children and regular passengers on board.

The *Serpa Pinto* docked at Ellis Island on Wednesday, September 24, 1941. Ten-year-old Wolodia Grajonca landed on American soil still undernourished and weak from his harrowing journey. Walking across

Europe and witnessing the loss of his sister and the horrors of the Nazis proved so traumatic an experience for the boy that he eventually blocked much of his early childhood from his memory.

At the dockside to meet him and the other children was Lotte Marcuse, director of placements for New York's German Jewish Children's Aid, Inc., who would be directly responsible for Wolodia until he came of age at twenty-one. As soon as the refugee children landed, they became the responsibility of a network of Jewish welfare organizations. After receiving a thorough medical examination by seven physicians and a team of Red Cross nurses, they were fully documented by the authorities.

Wolodia's first American meal was a kosher one, and after being given fresh clothing, the children were sent out to relatives and care facilities throughout the country. Wolodia and four other children from the *Serpa Pinto* were assigned to stay in New York State and put on a bus for a two-hour drive upstate to Pleasantville Cottage School, which served as a refugee reception center. On arrival at the barrackslike camp, Wolodia was first taken to a dormitory and given an orientation lecture on his new home before being bathed and put to bed for his lonely first night in the strange new country.

Wolodia's first day consisted of being examined and handled by strangers who spoke a language he could not understand. During his first interview, using a translator, Wolodia's caseworker was impressed by how well he had survived his ordeal.

"Interviewed Wolodia, who is a blond, stocky youngster with a mature and self-reliant air about him," wrote the caseworker in the official report. "He responded intelligently to my questioning. Wolodia has a good deal of poise about him and although he is not a very attractive child, he has a pleasant manner and intelligence which expresses itself in a cooperative attitude and willingness to participate in whatever chores the group is expected to do."

In the course of his interview, Wolodia insisted that he had an American aunt called Schneider, whom his mother told him to contact upon arrival. He could not say which state she lived in and the bureau was unable to trace her.

During his first few days, there was a marked deterioration in Wolodia's behavior as he began to realize the utter helplessness of his new situation. There was a strict routine at the converted school which served as a halfway house for the young Jewish refugees. Each week the children would be put on show for prospective foster parents who filed by the children, who desperately tried to win them over with their smiles.

When no one claimed Wolodia, he became intensely frustrated and went wild, attacking both staff members and children. His behavior so alarmed Miss Marcuse, who had started taking a personal interest in the boy, that she requested his transfer from Pleasantville to a New York City care center so she could keep a closer watch on him.

"Wolodia is one of the children who is extremely insecure and 'cries' for individual attention," wrote Miss Marcuse two weeks after his arrival. "His reaction in the group, to children and to adults alike is a most destructive one. He scowls most of the time and carries with him the expression of the bullying urchin. He is filthy and has no standards of cleanliness. He won't accept group action and has no feeling about disturbing adults and children alike.

"Yet yesterday, when I watched a group of children, Wolodia came along—and he had a smile, a really normal smile on his face. He had been told that in America, people 'keep smiling' and that this is a slogan that he must accept if and insofar as he wants people to like him. And Wolodia has a great need to be liked."

Yet few people saw that ingratiating side of Wolodia. His bad manners and stubborn behavior had so alienated him from the Pleasantville staff that Miss Marcuse grew concerned about his chances of ever finding a foster home and wrote:

> Wolodia is very thin, almost emaciated looking. He has a voracious appetite and atrocious table manners. The people who have lived with him do not consider him bright, and his fund of information is inferior to that of the other children of his age group. He should not be placed in a foster home in which there are children near him in age, either slightly older or younger.

For three long weeks, Wolodia was rejected by all the families who arrived at Pleasantville seeking to adopt a refugee. He felt like an unwanted animal in a pet shop as he was viewed, examined, and then returned to the crate. One by one the other children left Pleasantville to begin new lives, but Wolodia always remained behind until the next batch of would-be parents arrived.

Night after night, Wolodia, lonely and isolated, sank into the depths of despair, worrying about the fate of his mother and sisters. He could trust no one, and those terrible first days would haunt him for the rest of his life. He desperately yearned to make a future for himself in America, feeling intense frustration at having to place his fate in the hands of Lotte Marcuse, whom he did not trust and with whom he could not even communicate.

Finally, on October 10, Wolodia was claimed by Alfred and Pearl Ehrenreich, who thought his fluent German and French could help their son Roy in his studies. Wolodia's new home was 1635 Montgomery Avenue in the Bronx. Right from the beginning, Alfred Ehrenreich, an insurance salesman, was somewhat cold to Wolodia, who felt much closer to his new foster mother Pearl. The kindly woman immediately renamed him Billy and began fattening him up with plenty of American home cooking and rubbing him down daily with olive oil for his skin allergies. In return for providing a home for Billy, the Ehrenreichs received $25 a month from the Foster Home Bureau, and for a long time Billy suspected the money was the real reason they fostered him.

Billy immediately felt he was not being treated as well as their natural son, Roy, who was two years older than he and always received the best cuts of meat and more attention. This developed into an escalating rivalry between the two for their parents' attention, almost forcing the Foster Home Bureau to step in and remove Billy from the family.

Two months after Billy went to live with the Ehrenreichs, America entered the war, and the Bronx was plunged into a patriotic fervor. There were so many new things to comprehend. After the bleakness of war-torn Europe, the Bronx was a colorful explosion of patriotic red, white, and blue, vivid war posters pasting every wall.

Pearl Ehrenreich enrolled Billy Grajonca in P.S. 104, where he was placed in a class of seven-year-olds because he did not speak English. His fellow pupils were obsessed with playing war games and the skinny German boy, now officially designated as an Alien of Enemy Nationality, was immediately cast as the evil "Nazi." He was stoned as he walked to and from school and, once there, insulted cruelly and bullied by the other children who called him "fuckin' Jew" and a "Yid bastard."

"To them I wasn't a Jew, I was a German," he explained later. "I spoke German, I was a Nazi. And I used to get in more fights than I like to think about." Roy felt sorry for Billy, and one day, when the neighborhood kids were mocking his German accent, Roy stepped in and joined Billy to fight off the bullies, an event which marked a turning point in their relationship.

Roy realized that the only way for Billy to get the bullies off his back was to learn to speak fluent English and lose his thick German accent. Every night, in the bedroom they shared, Roy would make Billy read the day's newspapers out loud in front of the mirror, helping him to master English. The lessons paid off: nine months after his arrival in America, Billy spoke fluent Bronx English.

Although outwardly appearing to have adapted to life with the Ehrenreichs, internally Billy was deeply worried about the fate of his mother and sisters. He was very insecure, had developed a nervous twitch of his eyelids, and was plagued with allergies and hay fever.

On D day, June 6, 1944, all the schools in the Bronx closed early to mark the major Allied offensive, and Billy attended a special afternoon service in his synagogue to pray for the safe return of U.S. servicemen.

By mid-November, the U.S. Committee for the Care of European Children had given up hope of ever finding Billy's mother and sisters alive. Billy was heartbroken. Pearl Ehrenreich often found him crying hysterically in his room. As he became more depressed, he became more difficult to deal with. Feeling unwanted and uncertain, he refused to have anything to do with Roy, with whom he was constantly competing for the love of their parents. At school he also competed with his classmates for the teacher's attention, and when he didn't get it, he would throw a tantrum.

"We are planning to have Billy see the agency psychiatrist so that we will be better able to understand the anxiety and nervousness he is showing," wrote his new caseworker, Marjorie Davis, in June 1943. "We want to determine whether or not he is in need of psychiatric treatment at this time."

The psychiatrist who examined Billy found he didn't need psychiatric treatment but described him as "an insecure, immature child with a fear of aggression and with hostility in his associations," his bad behavior at school being caused by "personality difficulties."

Over the next few months, as his concern about his family's fate increased, Billy's behavior deteriorated still further. He was afraid to be left alone, and when he was, he would start crying uncontrollably. He also began neglecting his personal hygiene and his appearance, hardly ever washing or combing his hair.

Citing his "peculiar personal habits," his "secretive ways" and "extreme antagonisms with Roy," his caseworker advised taking him away from the Ehrenreichs and placing him under the care of the authorities.

But Billy was opening up to his caseworkers and starting to build trust by confiding his problems.

When Billy was expelled from P.S.104 for kicking a teacher who told him he would be deported if he didn't become right-handed, his behavior improved. He liked his new school, Macombs Junior High School (P.S. 82), and the Foster Home Bureau decided to let him remain with the Ehrenreichs, whom he now called "Mother and Father." Although Billy was developing close bonds with Pearl and Roy, Alfred Ehrenreich distanced himself from the boy and showed little warmth. In turn Billy considered the hardworking-but-dull insurance salesman a failure and avoided him as much as possible. The only time the family went out together was on the Jewish holidays, when Alfred took them to the synagogue.

As he grew into a lanky teenager, Billy became more and more attached to his new life in America and worked hard at becoming a typical New York street kid. His main drag was University Avenue, in the West Bronx, just down the hill from Montgomery Avenue, where he went to the children's morning shows at the Park Plaza Theater. Often managing to sneak in for nothing, he delighted in the program, which usually consisted of five cartoons, a Dick Tracy–type action serial, and a double feature. During the rest of the week, he hung out with the neighborhood kids, playing stickball or half-court basketball before spending his pocket money at Al's Candy Store.

He found his role models among the older street kids—from them he picked up street smarts and lessons in survival. He learned to live off his wits, mastering every hustle he needed to make a little money for candy and movies. The street became his classroom and taught him a strong moral code.

"I think that's what formed my character," he explained much later. "It's having to live by the book of unwritten rules, starting early on. What are the rules of life, the basic survival instincts? I didn't think about it then but now I realize there have always been certain unwritten rules."

At sixteen Billy joined his first gang, the Pirates, who proudly wore green-and-yellow jackets and met in a basement clubhouse. It was a matter of honor for a Pirate to have a girl by his side at the weekend meetings, and Billy, not wanting to be left out, always managed to find a local girl for a date.

Later, looking back on those happy days, he explained, "I loved to be outside and touch people and play and compete and cajole and just get out there and kick some ass and have a good time."

His wild behavior horrified Pearl Ehrenreich, but, surprisingly, it was Alfred who backed him up and even encouraged him to go out.

Billy's life changed forever when he was asked to bring pictures of his family to the Hebrew Immigrant Aid Society (HIAS) in Manhattan for their possible identification among the concentration-camp survivors.

Unknown to him, in Europe, his eighteen-year-old sister Ester, liberated by the Americans from the Spandau concentration camp, had begun trying to reunite the family. After finding her sister Evelyn in Budapest, she went on foot to Austria and located Sonja. As yet there was still no news of the fate of their mother, who, as was later discovered, had perished during the journey to Auschwitz concentration camp.

Ester got a job at the Hanover, Germany, branch of HIAS and persuaded her new boss, when he traveled to a New York conference, to look around for her young brother, Wolodia. A few days later, she received a telegram with the news that he had been found. Overjoyed, Billy began writing to all three sisters in Europe, and Rita, who was still in China, although there were no plans for an immediate reunion.

Knowing they were alive and safe produced a remarkable change in Billy, bringing him closer than ever to his foster family.

"The child is a really absorbed member of the foster family," wrote his new Foster Home Bureau caseworker, Elaine Steinman. "He is included in all family planning, and considers himself a member of the family."

With a new outlook on life, Billy enrolled at DeWitt Clinton High School, a far less prestigious school than that of Roy, who was already in his second year at the Bronx High School of Science. His first reports lauded his excellent academic work, and he was so popular at his new school that his classmates elected him class vice president. He was accepted on the school swimming team and showed a keen interest in all school athletics.

He had also discovered a new independence by making money doing odd jobs. His first job delivering the *Bronx Home News* made him \$5 a week which he spent on school expenses and movies. He enthusiastically took on extra jobs delivering groceries and meat and was soon giving the Ehrenreichs \$10.50 a week toward his board, in addition to the \$55 a month they were now receiving from the Foster Home Bureau.

Although he would later claim to have worked, starting at the age of fifteen, for two summers at the Catskill resorts, his Jewish Foster Bureau papers show that his first full-time summer job was in 1948, working as an office boy and messenger earning \$27.50 a week. Now a seventh-term honor-roll student at DeWitt Clinton, he planned to work and attend night college after his graduation.

It was during his senior year that Billy discovered his love of live music. He began to frequent the Apollo Theatre in Harlem to see Cab Calloway, and the Palladium at 53d Street and Broadway to hear his favorite Latin American stars like Xavier Cugat, Tito Puente and Esy Morales. Every Wednesday night he and a few friends would dance until three or four in the morning, but he never allowed the late nights to interfere with his schoolwork. On his graduation day, Billy received a glowing progress report from his social worker.

"Billy has grown from a distrustful, sly, underhanded, frightened little boy to a tall, good-looking, outgoing, secure, warm and friendly young man with a fine sense of humor," said the report. "He has many friends and varied interests, including school, all sports, reading and socializes with other boys and girls.

"The warmth and interest of the foster family, their intelligent handling of him, as well as the casework help given both, have helped Billy to grow into this well-rounded, likable young person."

Eager to obtain U.S. citizenship, he officially Americanized his name to William Graham, using the surname directly preceding Grajonca in the Bronx telephone book. It was Lotte Marcuse, his unseen guardian angel since the day of his arrival, who formally filed his change of name with the U.S. Department of Justice on April 13, 1949.

The 1949 DeWitt Clinton High School yearbook shows a smiling William "Bill" Graham, listing him as a member of the swimming team, a color guard and a one-term contributor to the school's *Magpie* magazine. To become a physical education instructor/coach is his given ambition and his graduating message by the side of his photograph is the simple toast: "To Graham."

2

Going Off to War

Early in 1950, William Graham was a strapping six-foot-tall youth ready to achieve the American dream. His only problem was that he was flat broke and embarrassed to have a part-time job in a neighborhood tailor shop paying only $10 a week. The $300 in scholarship money, which he had been awarded to study engineering at Brooklyn College, had already been spent on clothes. To help him survive, his foster parents grudgingly reduced his board to $10 a week. The real success story in the Ehrenreich family clearly was Roy, who had recently graduated Phi Beta Kappa from the University of Pennsylvania and found a job in journalism as a magazine rewrite man.

Fed up with not being able to afford to buy the stylish Harlem clothes he loved or go out nightclubbing every evening, Billy decided to take a semester off from Brooklyn College and get a full-time job that really paid. The word on the street was that there was big money in the Catskill Mountains some two hours north of New York City, working in one of the many Jewish hotels that dotted the beautiful countryside. Once there, he soon found a job as a busboy at Grossinger's Resort Hotel, one of the Catskills' two finest hotels. Popular with the other staff, he worked his charm on the female guests he served at the tables, ensuring good tips at the end of their stay. But after the summer season finished, the work ran out, and he returned to New York City.

Deciding not to return to Brooklyn College to become an engineer, Billy found work as a shipping boy at Davidson & Sons Jewelry Co. on

West 47th Street, which paid a respectable $45 a week. He impressed his superiors with his enthusiasm and was soon promoted to assistant foreman, learning the jewelry business with a particular emphasis on precious metals and stones. He liked the job, finding it stimulating, and seriously considered a career as a jeweler.

Now settled in a regular job and with his American citizenship imminent, Billy began making plans to reunite his natural family and bring them to America. However, the Korean War changed his life when he received his draft notice in late 1950, with orders to report to Fort Dix in New Jersey. His workmates at Davidson's were sorry to see him go and threw him a going-away party where they presented him with a huge gold ring bearing his initials, *BG*. His foster brother Roy had already been drafted into an army public-relations unit. Once again Billy came in a second as a regular private.

After passing his physical, Billy was assigned to Camp Chaffee in Arkansas for basic training. Once there, his hatred of authority and his rebelliousness soon alienated him from his corporal. One day, after getting a pinched nerve, he wasn't able to put on his backpack for the daily ten-mile hike. When the corporal ordered him to put on the pack, Graham's reply of "Fuck you, Jack!" was enough to win him a summary court-martial for insubordination.

After completing basic training, Graham was sent to Japan on a huge troop ship. Making the most of his Catskills training, he volunteered for kitchen duty, which entailed carrying food from the kitchen to the sick bay for the entire two-week voyage. Once at sea, Graham enthusiastically joined in on the nightly crap game and soon discovered that the players got hungry during the late-night games and were prepared to pay for extra food. The entrepreneurial young soldier immediately set himself up as the game's restaurant-delivery service, charging $1.50 for sandwiches and 25 cents for fruit he had stolen from the kitchens during the day. Business was brisk, and he was soon selling more than a hundred sandwiches a night, hiring another soldier to help him prepare the food. He left the ship with a huge profit of $3,700, which he soon lost in a crap game.

En route to Korea, Graham's company was assigned to a Japanese base to prepare for action. The aggressively outspoken young soldier soon upset another corporal by applying for his citizenship papers and creating extra paperwork for him.

"It was a corporal who really had it in for the big-city guys," Graham remembered. "Didn't like big-city guys and didn't like Jews, and he and

I got into it one day and he nailed me for insubordination."

The corporal made army life so tough for Private Graham that he volunteered out and was sent to the Korean town of Taegu for active duty as an artillery forward observer. As part of a two-man team, Graham had to venture out into no man's land to sight out the enemy and then report its positions on a radio telephone. On one early morning mission, Graham's reconnaissance team was attacked by four North Koreans who shot one of his friends and beat up another. Out of ammunition, Graham attacked one of the enemy soldiers and knocked him unconscious. Then, under full enemy fire, he carried his injured friend on his shoulders 300 yards to safety. Graham was later declared a hero and awarded a Bronze Star. Yet, within three days he found himself in serious trouble, facing a full court-martial for refusing a direct order under fire.

"The captain sent us on a suicide mission to lay some communication lines," Graham remembered. "It was obvious to us that if we carried it out, we had a ninety percent chance of ending up dead, as the enemy had all the high positions. It was the equivalent of the enemy sitting in the grandstands at a baseball game in full armor and machine guns. There's nobody on the field, and you asked me to round the bases and go for home plate. I refused a direct order because I knew it would be suicide."

With only days before the official presentation of his Bronze Star Graham was in a strong position; it was within his rights to refuse a suicide mission. When he threatened to fight the court-martial and prove his case, the captain backed down and withdrew the charges.

"He was one of those guys, shiny boots, khakis," said Graham. "A Missouri guy who wanted to be a major. He was one of those gung-ho schmucks, and about a month later he was going up the side of a hill, gleaming, and the enemy just popped him."

A few days after receiving his Bronze Star and a citation for holding the lines under enemy fire, Pearl Ehrenreich fell seriously ill, and Alfred requested immediate compassionate leave for his foster son. The army denied his request, but when a second telegram from the Red Cross arrived soon after, with the news she was on her deathbed, Graham was allowed to fly home.

He arrived too late and walked into the Montgomery Avenue apartment to find his foster father and brother in mourning for Pearl, who had died two days earlier. Grief-stricken, Alfred began rambling and unintentionally revealed the well-kept family secret that Roy was also not their natural child, but was an adopted "doorstep baby."Graham was stunned, realizing that his long-held belief that Pearl and Alfred had always favored Roy over him as their natural child was a complete fallacy.

"All those years passed before me. All the hundreds of times I said, 'Well, you did this to me because I'm not yours,' " Graham remembered many years later.

"All those years that she just swallowed what she wanted to say. That did it. That's probably the most meaningful thing that's ever happened to me. Judging people, blaming people. How can we ever know?

"Whatever positive things I have in me I owe to my foster mother. I was not an easy child to bring up. I was very angry at the world. And as I grew older I became quite bitter, and it was this woman who got me closer to the neutral than anybody else. She helped take away some of the bitterness."

"Bill idolized Pearl," said his foster uncle, Frank Ehrenreich. "He was very upset when she died."

When his thirty-day emergency leave came to an end he still had six weeks' combat duty to serve, and the U.S. Army insisted that he return to Korea. But when Alfred Ehrenreich had a heart attack, leaving no one to look after him except Graham, his foster brother started a campaign to stop his having to go back to Korea by writing to the *Bronx Home News* and the *New York Post,* which resulted in Graham's eventually winning a hardship discharge.

Soon after Pearl's death, Alfred Ehrenreich remarried and split the family in two.

"The boys didn't get along with my brother's new wife," said Frank Ehrenreich. "They used to come over to my house complaining that she made them feel very unwelcome and there was never food in the house. I felt sorry for them and gave them dinners."

It didn't take their new stepmother long to persuade Alfred to tell both boys to leave home. Amidst much bad feeling, they moved out and found an apartment together in Manhattan.

When Graham originally went off to war, he hadn't bothered to inform the Jewish Foster Home Bureau, which resulted in a worried Lotte Marcuse bombarding him with letters.

"I guess you did not know that I am one of the few people who met you on the day you arrived in this country," she wrote on October 31, 1950. "I have been hearing about your progress, however, since that time and I still have certain responsibilities for knowing where you are and how you are getting along with your plans."

Finally, on June 21, 1951, Graham was officially released from state care with absolutely no one to answer to but himself.

On leaving the army, Graham was determined to become a financial success and enrolled in the City College of New York, majoring in business administration. But he was restless and soon quit, again heading north to the Catskills to make real money. He found a job at the Concord Hotel near Monticello as a busboy in its ornate Empire Dining Room.

Serving breakfast, lunch, and dinner seven days a week, Graham soon became fast friends with Jack Levin, a young waiter who was a couple of years older and already married.

"Billy was a skinny little kid and he was a funny boy," remembers Levin, who four decades later is still working at the Concord as assistant maître d'. "In those days he wasn't as serious as he was later. When he was younger, he was full of life."

Once they had finished the evening shift, Graham and Levin would go out on the town in Monticello. Every hotel in the Catskills had its own nightclub which was strictly off-limits to lowly hotel staff, who were discouraged from mixing with the guests. Graham's favorite Latin music was the most popular music in all the Jewish resorts, and the two friends always managed to find ways to talk themselves into the clubs so they could hear the music and dance with the many available female guests.

"Billy was a real ladies' man and we wound up doing a lot of things off-color," Levin remembers. "He loved Tito Puente and Machito and was a fairly good samba dancer."

On their days off the two waiters went gambling at Saratoga Racetrack and whatever Graham won was usually lost later the same night in one of the local crap games. Graham loved gambling and soon realized the great potential in running games at the Concord for the staff and guests.

"I always had an ability to deal with groups of people," Graham explained. "In the army it was the guys I was in the army with. In the mountains it was the other waiters.

"I organized the greatest crap games, but I made more money from shill games. I was twenty-three years old, and I loved action, from the flea races in Canada to the dog races in Miami."

His first games were so successful that he rented out a ground-floor room in the hotel, which he turned into his first-ever club. As a sideline he also started a check-cashing service for Concord employees, where he cashed the checks but kept the change. He averaged around $200 a week from the Concord's 400 employees.

"Billy used to do very well," says Levin. "We'd start the game at ten in the evening and finish up about four, five, or six in the morning and then go right back to work. Everyone from the hotel used to go there and play. Billy used to take a cut and make some money on the dice. He supplied all the cards and he had food—often hot—for everybody and some beer or coffee. He'd provide whatever was needed."

On a good night, Graham could make up to $500; but, more often than not, he'd end up joining in the game in the small hours of the morning and lose his night's earnings.

"He didn't keep money too long," says Levin. "When he put it in his pocket, all of a sudden it became very, very hot and bored a hole right through. Billy was very good at losing, very good at losing. Winning . . . well, you know."

Graham's crap games were never dull and attracted many of the Concord's star performers like calypso star Harry Belafonte, who once played a few hands at Billy's cabana after his show. It also drew various people from the outside who were looking for action.

"We had a girl, an older woman, who used to shoot craps with us just wearing a bra and slip and nothing else," said Levin. "And while she was shooting dice every other word she used was an off-color one. She'd be cursing the dice and carrying on. Billy used to grab her by the ass as she threw the dice and she would scream. And if she made the numbers, she'd say, 'Grab my ass again, please.' And Billy would say, 'Imagine what would happen if I grabbed her titties.' It became an ongoing thing with them."

Billy told Levin and the other Concord staff that he was saving his money to enroll in stage school so he could become an actor. "He talked about it constantly. That was his first love," Levin said.

While he was at the Concord, Billy fell in love with Patricia Kern, a waitress from the station adjacent to his, who was working her way through Pennsylvania State University. Patricia became his steady girl for a couple of years and helped him organize the food for the crap games.

Whenever he had a weekend off, Graham would take the late Friday-night bus to New York to hit the Latin music clubs and party. He'd arrive back at the Concord early Monday morning, bleary-eyed, having been up for forty-eight hours. Somehow he always managed to snap back into cheery action for the breakfast crowd.

During its off-season, the Concord hosted many business conventions, and Graham delighted in testing out his acting routines on the guests. As the Concord's waiters were badly paid and relied on tips, the enterprising Graham always made an effort to relate to his guests individually. He would deliberately arrive early to scan the morning newspapers so he could converse on any news items that he knew they would be interested in.

"Billy was very smart," Levin said. "When we'd have conventions, he would size up the different types of businesspeople and would come up with a different manner for each. He'd say, 'I know you're here for seminars, so I'm gonna feed you, and I want you to get outta here fast.' He'd do it in a kidding way, and they always took it in the right spirit."

But by the evening, Graham would liven things up with his own brand of entertainment.

Levin remembers, "He'd walk over to the table with a load of dinners and start hitting them with a James Cagney, a Charles Laughton or an Edward G. Robinson routine complete with a cigar.

"He would go up and say, 'My name is Bill. I'm your waiter. I'm a future movie star, and you'll soon see my name in headlines in every marquee in the country.' The guests loved Billy and always asked for him when they returned the next time."

As the Concord's resident practical joker, Graham's repertoire of tricks amused his fellow waiters, often at their expense. Once, when a waiter was carrying twelve dinners piled high on a big tray, Graham removed the tray stand, leaving him with nowhere to put them down. Another favorite trick of his was to cut a long-stemmed rose in two near the top. He'd then hold it together and march over to the best-looking woman in the restaurant and gallantly offer it to her. Feeling flattered, she'd grab the bottom stem, and he would walk away with the rest of the rose to the delight of the other guests.

Jack Levin remembers one night in Monticello when Graham, having had too much to drink, mooned a couple of pretty girls as they drove past them on their way back to the Concord.

"Billy was capable of anything," says Levin. "He wasn't afraid of anyone."

Graham's unpredictable humor and the sheer force of his personality endeared him to the guests and often made up for his shortcomings as a waiter.

"Billy could come in for a table of eight and bring in ten dinners, and out of those six would be wrong," Levin says. "He would have to make four trips to a table when he should've made one because he had to keep coming back to get the things he had forgotten. He wasn't the greatest waiter, but he got the job done. No question about it."

One person who was not amused with the Billy Graham show was Concord maître d' Irving Cohen, whom Graham often compared to Captain Bligh. Graham had an uneasy relationship with Cohen during his three years at the Concord, and was eventually fired after he tried to get the staff unionized.

"He was a hippie," said Cohen, who is still the maître d' at the Concord after almost fifty years of service.

"He was one of the few people that I had working for me that had long hair. That was the beatnik years, and they all had long hair. We're conservative. Bill started to grow his hair long and I said to him, 'Bill, you do me a favor, will you. Cut your hair.' He said, 'Mr. Cohen, that's my style. I can't help it.' He was one of these characters. Everybody wore an earring, he wanted to wear an earring. If they wanted long hair, he wanted long hair. He was always in style with whatever they did. And he acted that way.

"You know what he once told me. He said if he wants to know about men's clothes two years from now, he goes to Harlem. He said black people are two years ahead of us here. He looks in the stores in Harlem.

"When he came here he had short hair. All of a sudden, he said, 'Oh, the style is long hair, I want long hair.' And he had long hair, believe me, to the point where his hair went into the food on the tray because it was so long. It's not healthy. It's unsanitary. I said if you're not going to cut your hair, then I can't use you here. So he says, 'Okay.' "

Returning to New York, Graham got a job as a waiter at the Town and Country Nightclub in Brooklyn, working bar mitzvahs and weddings and making a good living on the side by running crap games in the back of the kitchen. He moved into a Greenwich Village apartment on Waverly Place and became a regular player at the pickup games on the basketball courts nearby.

On January 11, 1954, Billy Graham officially became an American citizen and immediately began to apply for his sisters to come to the United States. His oldest sister Rita was the first to arrive a few months later with her husband Eric. They stayed in New York only a short time before deciding to settle in San Francisco. A year later, he fulfilled his dream of having his favorite sister, Ester, come to America, and was there to meet her when she stepped off the plane with her seven-year-old son Avi. His two other surviving sisters, Evelyn and Sonja, decided to remain in Europe.

Still ambitious to become an actor, Graham started going to every audition and casting call he could find, but he had little success. These two years were frustrating for Graham as he got used to accepting rejection after rejection. Bored with waiting tables and longing for adventure, Graham decided to drive cross-country to visit his sister Rita and her husband, Eric Rosen, in San Francisco.

It was love at first sight when Graham saw San Francisco. Adoring its unique beauty and freedom, he decided to stay and found a job through his brother-in-law at Pacific Motor Trucking. But after a year he returned to New York for another crack at becoming an actor.

He moved into a studio apartment on Christopher Street in the West Village and found a night job as a taxi driver. He spent his days working as a waiter at the Brooklyn nightclub and trying to get acting roles.

For the next few years, Graham became a wanderer, shuttling constantly between New York, San Francisco, and Europe. Still wanting to be an actor, he joined Equity, using the stage name Anthony Graham (there was another actor named William Graham). He appeared off-Broadway in *Guys and Dolls,* had a tiny part in the movie *Breakfast at Tiffany's,* and performed in a string of long-forgotten B movies. To improve his technique, he enrolled in Lee Strasberg's Actor's Studio, studying in the same class as Marilyn Monroe, but his inability to remember his lines stopped him from finding acting jobs.

As he approached his thirtieth birthday Graham found himself in a crisis, lacking direction and with no steady job or way of gaining the acting success he so craved. In one final make-or-break attempt to become a movie star he moved to Los Angeles to be nearer Hollywood and found himself an agent. Unfortunately, the nearest he got to becoming a celebrity was waiting tables in a Rodeo Drive restaurant, serving celebrities like Charles Laughton, David Niven, and Lee Marvin.

After nearly six months of going on fruitless casting calls, Graham was finally called back to audition for the role as second lead in a new TV series called *The Law and Mr. Jones* starring James Whitmore. His luck appeared to have changed when he was called back three more times, as one of four actors considered for this key role. When Graham was chosen for the high-visibility part he was ecstatic; it was the big break he had worked so hard to achieve. But his chance of stardom was nixed by Whitmore, who having final approval over his costar, worried that Graham's strong rugged looks would overshadow him.

Graham was floored by the rejection—which had nothing to do with his acting ability—and could not believe he had lost his one big opportunity because of his looks.

"He could not take not being in control," explained Hollywood acting coach Harold Guskin, who later would befriend Graham. "He quit acting there and then. It was a crushing blow to him."

Sinking into a deep depression and feeling himself an utter failure, Graham fled to Europe to rethink his life and decide where to go next.

3

The San Francisco Mime Troupe

In 1963, after a year of bumming around Europe, Bill Graham decided to settle down in San Francisco. He found himself a job as regional manager for Allis-Chalmers, a company which specialized in making heavy industrial equipment, and was soon making a big impression at the head office and on the fast track to promotion.

Responsible for San Francisco, Los Angeles, Seattle, and Denver, he had proven himself by streamlining his two offices into one and cutting back his staff from forty-seven to twenty-one—he was able to get the most work out of his staff while keeping morale high. Helped by his secretary and girlfriend Bonnie MacLean, Graham ran his office with astonishing success.

During his two years at Allis-Chalmers, he was given free rein to develop the management skills which he would later turn to great advantage in the music business. But although he was on the fast track, making a good wage of $21,000 a year plus a bonus, Graham felt creatively unfulfilled and itched to have his own business and not have to answer to anyone. The catalyst for Graham to realize his ambitions and combine the two diverse worlds of business and theater came in the shape of a radical group of actors called The San Francisco Mime Troupe.

Founded in 1961 by R. G. (Ronnie) Davis, the vagabond theater company, which cast itself in the role of a medieval traveling show, performing updated Italian Renaissance commedia dell'arte, was creating quite a stir in San Francisco with its experimental political plays featuring nudity and vulgar language. The left-wing group played for free in the parks in and around San Francisco, and by the mid-sixties the troupe had evolved into a group of colorful revolutionaries with a large following. Its Howard Street loft had become headquarters for the new colonies of poets, musicians and hippies which were springing up all over the city. Surviving on their wits and handouts from wealthy admirers in San Francisco society, the members of the troupe, who each received $5 a show, made a motley crew, traveling from neighborhood to neighborhood in an old truck full of threadbare costumes and props.

"We'd steal and swindle and do what we had to," said former Mime Troupe actor Peter Coyote.

Davis had ambitious plans for the troupe's growth by performing in parks where they could keep a high profile. But an ancient Park Commission regulation forbade any group to perform more than twice a year in the city parks. So, by the summer of 1963, Davis had adopted a new role as politician to try to lobby the ultraconservative San Francisco Park Commission into changing the rules so the troupe could perform whenever it wanted. Won over by Davis's persuasive charm, and the heartfelt appeals from the troupe's influential supporters, the Park Commission agreed to waive the regulations on condition it approved each show prior to performance, an option which nobody—temporarily, at least—bothered to exercise.

Free to embark on its ambitious schedule, the troupe played fourteen park performances of the comedy *Ruzzante's Maneuvers* in the summer of 1963. At the end of his most successful season even, Davis decided the company was ready to start touring throughout the Northwest.

"It was obvious that we needed a promoter/business manager who would handle the various complicated arrangements," Davis said.

Troupe bookkeeper Sandy Archer suggested that Davis might want to check out an energetic young executive she knew named Bill Graham. Taking Archer's advice, Davis tracked Graham down to his apartment, where they discussed theater and business over a meal of chopped liver. The two men had a lot in common, having both worked as busboys and waiters at the Concord Hotel in the Catskills, and they hit it off immediately.

Davis, impressed with Graham's fast-talking confidence and his obvious talents as a salesman, offered him the job as Mime Troupe business manager. Graham accepted on the spot with the proviso that he could bring his devoted girlfriend/secretary Bonnie MacLean along with him. The invitation to join the troupe was a heaven-sent opportunity for Graham. It provided the perfect combination of his two great loves: theater and business. The only drawback was the wages: the hard-up Mime Troupe could offer him only $1,400 a year, a far cry from his salary at Allis-Chalmers.

"I decided I'd still rather be in the world of theater even if I weren't performing," Graham told *Billboard* journalist Jack McDonough for his book *San Francisco Rock.* "So for the next two years I looked for gigs at schools and little theaters, made the deals, printed the posters, drove the truck, put up the lights and carried the spear."

Members of the troupe remember Graham hustling around San Francisco on his 1956 Lambretta motor scooter in a three-piece suit aggressively promoting the Mime Troupe. He was all business and quickly distanced himself from their radical political stance and communal lifestyle. But Davis valued Graham's aloofness, as it made him the perfect straight frontman and spokesman for the otherwise bohemian troupe.

"Bill Graham was just phenomenal, very high energy," said Peter Coyote. "He was very, very different from the rest of us. Not real long on revolutionary content but incredibly smart, energetic and ambitious."

Under Bill Graham's management, the Mime Troupe adopted a more professional approach. Shows started on time, and for the first time in the Mime Troupe's history there was some real organization. Graham ran the troupe from his desk phone hidden at the back of the troupe's loft, where he directed operations with almost military precision. There was even a brass nameplate on his desk bearing the name of his hero, the famous Russian impresario Sol Hurok.

The *San Francisco Chronicle* theater critic, the late John Wasserman, was very impressed with Graham. "I was working in the Theater Department and Bill would come bustling in every few days with pictures and releases and keep us up to date on the troupe's schedule," Wasserman said in a 1972 KSAN–Radio interview. "It is the only time the Mime Troupe has ever been run with any vestige of organization. Bill wasn't making any money at all, and he was spending money out of his own pocket for the Mime Troupe."

But Graham's need for control soon brought him to loggerheads with Davis when he tried to influence the artistic side of the troupe. Davis says Graham once even went behind his back to give the troupe's black actors from *A Minstrel Show* money out of his own pocket so he could direct them in an unofficial rehearsal and ensure a performance more to his liking.

"Bill was more or less a hustler and an opportunist," said Davis. "We never let him direct anything. He wasn't capable. What Bill was good at was getting us publicity in the *San Francisco Chronicle.*"

Later, in the *New York Times Magazine,* Graham criticized Davis's abilities as a director, claiming he had been continually "frustrated" by the troupe's "disappointing" performances and had been given no artistic control. But even if Graham's artistic hopes for the troupe weren't being realized, he was determined to make sure the show went on at any cost. Comedian Howard Hesseman, then stage manager for the comedy group The Committee, first met Graham while he was trying to get a large piano off The Committee's stage, where the troupe were giving a performance of *A Minstrel Show.*

"There were several doorways and a series of halls to get through, and the piano wasn't fitting," Hesseman said. "There were three or four of us trying to scrape the piano through the last doorway, and it got stuck. The manager of The Committee showed up, saw what we were doing, and told us to stop, as the piano was getting scarred up in the door frame.

"Bill was saying, 'It's not important. It's not going to hurt the piano. It will still play. We'll have it retuned, and everything will be all right.' Our manager was saying, 'You can't do that, you're going to ruin the piano.' Finally Bill stopped cold, became very logical and stopped shouting, looked the manager dead in the eye, and said, 'All right, if the piano is ruined, just get me a saw. We'll take the front legs off and that will get it off the stage.' "

Although the troupe had to respect Bill's get-it-done-at-any-cost attitude, his tough, abrasive New York business manner grated on the sensibilities of many. Graham isolated himself even further by declaring himself the troupe's impresario and insisted that "Bill Graham Presents" appear on the Mime Troupe's posters and handbills in the tradition of Barnum and Bailey. This marked the start of Graham's long-term strategy to turn his name into a household word in San Francisco.

Inevitably, Bill Graham's ego soon led to major conflict with Davis. Mime Troupe actor Jim Haynie says they argued daily over everything.

"They were quite a show," said Haynie. "They used to sit about three feet apart and yell at each other all day. Nobody wanted to stay in that room for long. They were both extremely loud and extremely pugnacious, and they did not get on well."

The hyperactive Graham, who always liked to be on the move, was more than a little frustrated by the troupe's frequent late-night meetings to discuss its socialist identity and political ideology.

Exasperated, Graham staged a coup d'état to take over control of the Mime Troupe.

"Bill and his secretary Bonnie wanted to take over the company," Davis said. "He had the company take a vote on whether he should become leader. He got two votes out of fifty. It was a stupid kind of showdown because he wasn't capable of doing it."

During the leadership battle, Graham and Davis were temporarily reunited when they had to respond to the Parks Department, which had finally decided to exercise its right to ensure that the Mime Troupe's plays were suitable for the good citizens of San Francisco.

In the summer of 1965, Davis and Graham started off the new season in the parks with a specially adapted version of *Il Candelaio* by Giordano Bruno, deliberately playing up the play's brutality and violence and throwing in a few swearwords for good measure. Realizing that the controversial nature of the new play was bound to attract attention, Graham cunningly decided to invite the park commissioners to the performance so there would be no surprises later which would jeopardize the show.

Before issuing the invitation, Graham shrewdly took the precaution of inviting two civil-liberties lawyers from the American Civil Liberties Union to view the performance. The ACLU representatives thought it brutal but not obscene, and the troupe's attorney, Marvin Stender, fired off a letter to Parks Commission chairman Walter Haas, warning him not to act as a censor. However, after seeing the play, the Parks Commission was appalled and revoked the Mime Troupe's permit after only three performances. Graham and Davis met with the Parks Commission to plead their case, but the meeting ended abruptly when Davis lost his temper and stormed out, shouting, "We will see you in the parks and in the courts."

Graham called a war council to plan the troupe's next move. As the company was flat broke, Graham saw the park ban as a golden opportunity to stage a spectacular public-relations coup and financially revive the company at the same time. He made an impassioned plea to stage a confrontation with police as a well publicized protest against the Parks Department. He argued that the Mime Troupe had a duty to protect First Amendment rights, not only for itself, but for the whole of San Francisco. His speech swayed the meeting, and he was given the go-ahead to publicize the showdown. Demonstrating his talent for public relations, Graham immediately called all his contacts in newspapers and television and persuaded them to come to Lafayette Park that Sunday afternoon to witness the Mime Troupe's public defiance of the Parks Department ban on the right to free speech. So the stage was set for the troupe's most spectacular show to date, *The Great San Francisco Mime Troupe Bust,* which finally cast Graham in his long-awaited role as director.

On the morning of Sunday, August 7, Graham and Davis led all fifty members of the Mime Troupe in full costume into Lafayette Park for the afternoon confrontation. At one o'clock the park began to fill up with police, Park Department officials and troupe supporters carrying large signs saying "Mime Troupe Si! Park Commission No!" Graham had done his job well and there were enough camera crews and reporters to cover a small war, as well as plenty of curiosity seekers.

Said Davis, "We had decided that I was to be arrested for this 'showcase spectacular.' We had prepared for years and it couldn't have been staged better—Sunday and a full house."

The show started with Graham, dressed in his familiar V-necked sweater, debating the ban with Davis and Park Department representative James Lang. Enter stage left: Stender, the troupe's attorney, followed by a contingent of police.

Then, clipboard in hand, Graham raised the curtain on Act Two by delivering an emotional address to the crowd outlining the events leading to the revocation of the permit. This was followed by Lang, who gave the commission's version, amid boos and hisses from the excited audience. By this time the cops were getting uneasy and tried to cool things down by asking all parties to be reasonable and come down to the station house to talk it out in a civilized manner.

"Graham and I got louder," remembers Davis. "We included the public in every statement while we tried to figure out what the police intended to do."

The tension was raised a notch when the Mime Troupe and their friends started singing and dancing around the performance area, to the delight of the growing crowd. Fearing a riot, Lang pleaded with the police to take immediate action. Suddenly everyone went quiet as Davis launched the final act by dancing into the performing area and, adopting the stance of a fairground barker, announced:

> Signor, Signora, Signorini
> Madame, Monsieur, Mademoiselle,
> Ladieeees and Gentlemen,

Il Troupo di Mimo di San Francisco
Presents for your enjoyment this afternoon . . .
AN ARREST!!!

On the word "arrest," Davis leaped in the air and into the arms of an astonished cop, who arrested him on the spot. Instantly, the whole park broke into an uproar. The cast, members of the public and even a reporter started attacking the cops by throwing grass at them and knocking their helmets off their heads. Davis and two other troupe members were arrested and driven off in the waiting police van. Two hours later, they were charged with performing in the public parks without a permit and released on bail.

"I think they arranged the bust to polarize the issue," Coyote said. "The idea of publicity would not have been lost on Bill, but I think it underestimates the serious intentions of both the Mime Troupe and Bill to reduce it to a political stunt. They were pressing the constitutional issues of it."

On November 1 Davis was found guilty after a four-day trial and pledged defiantly to "Fight until the parks are returned to their only 'owners,' the people of San Francisco." To raise money for legal expenses, Graham, the troupe's official fund-raiser, was appointed to organize an appeal party in the Mime Troupe's loft.

Graham had handbills printed to advertise the party, warning, "THE CREATIVE LIFE OF SAN FRANCISCO IS NOW DIMINISHED." The handbills also attacked Parks Department chairman Walter A. Haas for making his "good taste a matter of law." Using the issue of free speech as his clarion, Graham had no trouble enlisting the support of the San Francisco artistic community, which was greatly concerned about the enormous implications of the Mime Troupe Bust on censorship.

One of the first to offer Graham assistance was a new band with the unusual name of Jefferson Airplane, which rehearsed regularly in the Troupe's Howard Street loft. Poets, jazz musicians, and artists also rallied to the cause, and soon Graham had an impressive lineup for his Saturday, November 6, appeal.

As the pieces of the puzzle began to fall into place for Bill Graham, it is ironic that The Family Dog, a peaceful hippie commune whose members did not care about business, would provide the launching pad for his meteoric rise to success. The Family Dog nucleus comprised Luria Castell, a vivacious young woman whose long hair framed her Benjamin

Franklin wire-rim glasses and who liked to wear long granny dresses; Ellen Harmon, who had left her "straight" job in Detroit to come to the West Coast, and Alton Kelly, an artist who had retired from dealing marijuana when it became too risky. The three had formed a loose-knit company called The Family Dog, named in memory of Harmon's dog, who had been killed in a traffic accident. The group's simple aim was to brighten up San Francisco's dull nightlife and get people together to dance.

"Basically we want to meet people and have a good time and not be dishonest and have a profitable thing going on," Castell naïvely told *San Francisco Chronicle* columnist Ralph J. Gleason as she tried to enlist his support. "San Francisco can be the American Liverpool. There's enough talent here, especially in the folk-music field. We don't have any particular group to present, just a plan to get started, to acquire knowledge, information and have fun with a rock 'n' roll sound," Luria told Gleason.

Gleason, a hardened jazz critic with more than a decade of covering musical events in and around the city, was amazed by this new breed of hippie promoter and its infusion of fresh air into the stale San Francisco music scene. "These promoters were unlike any I had ever seen," he wrote in his book *Jefferson Airplane and the San Francisco Sound.*

The Family Dog's "Tribute to Dr. Strange" was held in the Longshoreman's Hall near Fisherman's Wharf two week's before the Mime Troupe benefit was scheduled. It was a runaway success and featured new groups like Jefferson Airplane, The Marbles, The Great Society, and The Charlatans. With an admission price of $2.50, it even made a tidy profit. The Family Dog joined in with the audience as participants and stopped dancing only to carry out running repairs on the sound system, help get the light show working, and to tell the security guards to stop being so strict with the kids. In fact, the audience was so well behaved that when the show finished at 2:00 A.M. many stayed behind to clean up the hall. Delighted with the success of their first dance concert, the Family Dog immediately announced a second one for a week later, to be called "A Tribute to Sparkle Plenty."

By now The Family Dog and its exciting new dance show was attracting attention, especially after Gleason penned an ecstatic review in his *San Francisco Chronicle* column.

Their second show, also held at the Longshoreman's Hall, featured the homegrown band The Charlatans and an up-and-coming New York band The Lovin' Spoonful, who were enjoying their first hit with "Do You Believe in Magic." The crowd from the first dance returned, bringing their friends, and the publicity from the first show attracted a much bigger crowd. At one point the members of a boogie band called The Warlocks, soon to become The Grateful Dead, wandered into the dance after taking a group LSD trip across the bay in Marin County. Bassist Phil Lesh was so impressed with the dance that he took Ellen Harmon aside, saying, "Lady, what this little séance needs is us."

The second dance was a greater success for The Family Dog. Realizing their dances were indeed filling a much-needed void in San Franciscan nightlife, they announced they would be holding them on a regular basis from now on.

Bill Graham's big breakthrough came when Family Dog members Alton Kelly and Luria Castell offered to help him stage his appeal for the Mime Troupe.

"We told Bill that we just wanted to help out the Mime Troupe because we had already been throwing dances," Alton Kelly said. "We offered to organize it ourselves in return for a mention on the poster. Bill listened carefully and then asked us about ourselves and what we were going to do next. We told him that we had found out that the old Fillmore Auditorium in the heart of the ghetto could be rented at only $60 a night and we were planning to put on dances there. He didn't seem overly interested, and when we left, he said he'd get back to us about helping him with the Mime Troupe Benefit."

But the ever-calculating Graham had been carefully taking mental notes during the conversation. The next day he tracked down the Fillmore's leaseholder, Charles Sullivan, a black promoter of R&B shows, and negotiated a four-year option for first rights to the auditorium whenever it was available. He even managed to get the large hall at the knockdown rate of $45 a night on a long-term option, borrowing most of the money needed for the down payment and using hardly any of his own.

"He just grabbed it and blew us right out of the water and out of business," Kelly said. "We didn't know any other halls we could rent in San Francisco for that price. Bill was very smart and he had seen what was happening with our dances. At just $45 a night for a four-year lease, he stood to get his money back in two or three weekends."

Meanwhile Graham kept quiet about his new Fillmore lease and put all his energies into organizing his benefit in the Troupe's loft. He even included The Family Dog on the poster, claiming, in what was later to be one of his favorite stories, that he was so green in the business he thought he was booking an animal act. Among the artists who gave their services were The Committee, Jefferson Airplane, The Fugs, Allen

Ginsberg, and Lawrence Ferlinghetti. A donation of at least $1 was requested for the appeal, which was scheduled to last from at 8 P.M. until dawn.

To publicize the event Graham rented a Cadillac convertible out of his $1,000 budget and covered it in banners. He packed the car with cast members in full costume and drove through downtown San Francisco handing out fliers to the lunchtime crowd. The traffic-stopping parade made the five o'clock television news and Graham was delighted.

Saturday, November 6, 1965, was a watershed in music history. Graham pulled all the divergent threads of the San Francisco underground scene together for that historic night. Three thousands hippies, beats, and radicals crowded into the tiny loft with a 600 capacity to witness the birth of a new era.

"The Mime Troupe benefit was, is and always will be the most exciting night of my life in theater," Graham said.

Under Graham's direction, the troupe members built a stage for the performers, painted the loft walls in bright colors and hung bunches of grapes and bananas from the ceiling. The walls were lined with giant sheets on which were projected endless loops of experimental 16-millimeter film. Graham bought cases of vodka at cost from a sympathetic merchant and mixed gallons of homemade punch with assorted fruits and orange juice in six huge steel drums.

The audience was welcomed with a tongue-in-cheek tariff at the entrance: $48 admission if you made over $80,000 a year; 16 cents entry for people living in a walkup apartment higher than the sixth floor; and if broke, people were asked to "leave having left something" or at the very least, help clean up afterward. Soon the crowd waiting to get in stretched around the block as people who had been to a Family Dog dance earlier that evening now arrived for the Mime Troupe benefit. The long line of people waiting outside on Howard Street attracted the attention of the police, who ordered Graham to shut down the party at midnight.

Jefferson Airplane's Paul Kantner remembers, "When I first met Bill, he was busy, simultaneously taking tickets, checking refreshments, mopping the floor and dealing with the SFPD, who had come to complain about the spillover of people from the loft."

Graham stayed calm, explaining to the officers that the crowd outside was awaiting the imminent arrival of Frank Sinatra, Liberace, and Rudy Vallee who were jetting in from Las Vegas especially to rescue the Mime Troupe. Whether or not the cops believed Graham's story, they were amused enough to agree to a compromise and ruled that the party could continue as long as Graham adhered to the Fire Department's legal occupancy limit of 600 people.

Taking the stage, Graham appealed to the people who had been at the dance since the beginning to leave. As a few grudgingly departed, the policemen took up positions at the entrance to the loft to make sure that the numbers of newcomers would equal those who left. What the police could not see was Bill Graham smuggling in extra people through a hidden freight elevator and grabbing their donations as he hurried them into the loft.

"We expected a few hundred people; thousands showed up," said Graham. "We raised $4,200, and the place was jammed. It was the first time I saw the undercurrents of San Francisco—long hair, short hair, pants, no pants, signs, tattoos, light shows, film. You turned over all the rocks, took all the worms, and put them in one place."

Although they didn't know it at the time, the people packing the small loft that night were pioneers of a new youth culture that would sweep the world within a year.

"Here were these filmmakers who met these poets for the first time," Graham said. "And jazz musicians and rock 'n' roll musicians. People were dancing with people they'd never met before. Men and women and kids were just dancing. And all of a sudden, it was six o'clock in the morning—it started getting light—and Allen Ginsberg was doing his mantra chants," Graham said.

By the end of the evening, everyone agreed that something was definitely happening in San Francisco. Although they couldn't tell where it was going to lead, nothing would ever be the same again.

"No one could have predicted the impact of Bill's Mime Troupe Benefit on both his own future and, indeed, the future of rock 'n' roll in San Francisco," Kantner said.

Brimming with confidence after the success of his appeal, Graham was finally prepared to ditch the Mime Troupe and start out on his own. He was ready to become the pied piper of San Francisco, producing musical events for the city to dance to.

"What I saw was an adventure," Graham said. "It was as if life filled out the form of how I could express myself. I didn't want to be an office manager and be behind a desk. I couldn't take regimentation. I had trouble in the army, and I wanted to be independent."

Playing down the importance of money in his decision to become a promoter Graham said later, "More than anything else it was a means of expression, being totally in charge." He enthusiastically announced a second Mime Troupe Benefit one month later at his newly acquired Fillmore Auditorium. This time, he promised, there would be more space for people to enjoy the show.

San Francisco Mime Appeal II was advertised by Graham as an event "For continued artistic freedom in the parks." Graham, had done his homework well and billed it as a dance concert. This was to sidestep Musicians Union rules which dictated that a preset number of musicians must always be paid at a music show even if they didn't perform. Exactly how many depended on the venue's capacity.

This time Graham limited the bill to music, booking Jefferson Airplane, The Great Society (which featured a model and singer named Grace Slick), The John Handy Jazz Quintet, and Sam Thomas and The Gentlemen's Band. Graham also hired a light show similar to the one at The Family Dog dance concerts. Graham saw a great opportunity to create massive free publicity for his benefit when Bob Dylan came to San Francisco for a concert. Dylan, who was riding high in his "electric phase" with the top-ten hit "Like A Rolling Stone," would be at a press conference at PBS television station KQED to publicize his show. Graham and Bonnie were there early with a bunch of posters and handbills. They sneaked into the studio and placed a handbill on every seat and then brazenly gave Dylan a poster when he arrived. Near the end of the interview, Dylan was asked about the poster he was carrying. Holding it up in front of the camera he replied, "Yeah. It's a poster somebody gave me. It looks pretty good—and I would like to go if I could, but unfortunately I won't be there." The enigmatic singer then proceeded to read off the complete poster on camera, giving Graham an incredible public-relations home run for his first Fillmore concert. This—Bill Graham's first meeting with Dylan—was immortalized in the movie, *Don't Look Back*.

Bill Graham, who was always superstitious, must have delighted to see a fireball light up the clear night as he opened the doors for his very first concert at the Fillmore. This time there was an admission charge of $1.50. By the time Graham opened the doors at 9:30 P.M., there were two lines of people running the length of the block. A total of 3,500 people came to the Fillmore that night to help Graham make history and a big profit at the same time.

Describing the scene in his column the following Monday, Gleason wrote: "Inside, a most remarkable assemblage of humanity was leaping, jumping, dancing, frigging, fragging, and frugging on the dance floor to the music of the half-dozen rock bands.

"The costumes were free-form Goodwill-cum-Sherwood Forest. Slim young ladies with their faces painted à la *Harper's Bazaar* in cats-and-dogs lines, granny dresses topped with huge feathers, white Levi's with decals of mystic design; bell-bottoms split up the side! The combinations were seemingly endless."

The Family Dog's Luria Castell, who was now heavily in debt after a recent run of failed dances, turned up at the Fillmore and was on her way up the stairs when she ran into Graham for what he later described as "the greatest confrontation I ever had." Pretending not to recognize her from their meeting six weeks earlier, Graham asked who she was.

"Luria Castell. You know, I ran the dances," replied the angry young woman.

Later, apparently still reveling in his cruel humiliation of Castell, Graham told Ralph Gleason he started out playing Mr. Nice Guy, giving her a free pass for the show. "I hadn't really become a professional yet at throwing people out," he explained. But when Luria started letting in her friends, he turned nasty.

"I became my real self!" Graham admitted. "I yelled, 'Fuck you!' and all this shit, and all of a sudden, she's standing on the stairs and she came up with the greatest remark that I ever heard in my life, the retort. She says, 'You stole my idea!' 'What was that?' I said. 'Throwing dances.' I looked at her and I said, 'That's four thousand years old. The Egyptians. You didn't start that.' "

The rest of the evening was more in keeping with the two large three-foot signs hanging at either side of the hall promoting the new buzzword of the sixties: "LOVE." Graham's sister Ester ran the kitchen upstairs, serving her matzo-ball soup and salad. As alcohol was unfashionable at that time and Graham did not have a liquor license, there was a "no booze" sign by the bar where volunteers were selling soft drinks. The wildly uninhibited dancing went on into the early-morning hours, and the one big question on everyone's lips was when the next dance was going to be held. Having made nearly $6,000 from this first Fillmore show, Graham could hardly wait for the next one.

Bubbling over with enthusiasm for these new dance events, Gleason also told his Monday readers, "The demand for dances is going to increase."

As 1966 dawned, the San Francisco in crowd of musicians, artists and hippie businessmen and women were throwing themselves on the dance-concert bandwagon. Graham finally severed his ties with the Mime Troupe and formed a company called Bill Graham Presents, realizing his dream to become a full-time impresario. He did, however, agree to hold one last benefit for the Mime Troupe on January 14.

Yet Ronnie Davis claims that the Mime Troupe was exploited by Graham and never saw any of the profits from the many subsequent benefits that were held at the Fillmore in its name.

"Bill ran away with the cash box," Davis said. "He used our reputation, and we never got any money. I don't think he was committed to anything but Bill Graham's ego and money in the bank. He was still using our name a year and a half after he left."

After the success of his two benefits, Graham stepped up his campaign to weave his name into the fabric of San Francisco consciousness. Soon his trademark "Bill Graham Presents" seemed to be everywhere around the city on posters, on the radio, and in the newspapers. He also branched out by hiring out his professional services to Ken Kesey for his three-day Trips Festival.

Kesey, the author of *One Flew Over the Cuckoo's Nest*, had been touring the country in a brightly painted van with his band of followers, The Merry Pranksters, in a kind of ongoing LSD experiment. Now back in San Francisco, he was keeping one step ahead of the police after getting busted for marijuana possession and being banned by a court order from attending his own festival. Giving the court the finger, Kesey defiantly drove the Pranksters' psychedelic bus straight to Union Square in downtown San Francisco. He then held a press conference to promote the Trips Festival dressed like a Marvel Comics character. The surreal world of the Pranksters did not lend itself to efficiency and organization, but who better to establish order out of chaos than Bill Graham, who was hired for a percentage of the profits.

After holding his third Mime Troupe Appeal at the Fillmore, Graham worked full time on the three-day Trips Festival, which was to be the most ambitious multimedia dance event planned to date. Scheduled to run for three days at the Longshoreman's Hall, the festival was billed as a "non-drug re-creation of the psychedelic experience."

The first night of the Trips Festival on January 21 was chaotic. Hundreds of people packed the Longshoreman's Hall to see the multimedia group America Needs Indians show slides in its teepee and the Open Theater stage a cabaret performance. The legendary LSD chemist and pioneer Owsley Stanley III arrived with a shopping bag full of his latest batch of acid and distributed it freely around the hall.

On Saturday night the music took center-stage with the newly formed Big Brother and the Holding Company, in only their second public appearance, performing in the first half of the show: "Options and Contracts." But it was The Grateful Dead, having recently changed their name from the Warlocks, who played the second half: "The Acid Test." The Dead's consciousness-raising music was accompanied by flashing strobes and ultraviolet lighting. The hall was awash in Day-Glo paint and pulsated with electric energy, and the freeform dancing got wilder and wilder. At one point a beautiful young woman ran up on the stage and stripped to the waist before she was led away by security.

In stunning contrast to the psychedelic mayhem, as if on another planet altogether, was Mr. Efficiency himself, Bill Graham, running around in his V-neck sweater with a clipboard, barking orders and screaming at anyone who got in his way. Future *Rolling Stone* writer Charles Perry, who was an observer, said that the word had gone out to keep Graham and Ken Kesey apart during the evening to avoid possible trouble.

"Kesey's costume was something between superhero and space suit, complete with a bubble helmet," Perry wrote in his book, *The Haight-Ashbury: A History*. "When he finally did run into Kesey, at the back door of the hall, where Kesey was letting in a bunch of Hell's Angels, he exploded, 'What the fuck do you think you're doing? Goddamn sonofabitch, I'm busting my fucking balls out here to make a dime and you . . .' Kesey simply closed his bubble helmet."

While Graham was still steaming at Kesey, Big Brother and the Holding Company's guitarist Sam Andrew unwittingly asked Graham for a free pass for the band's drummer, Chuck Jones.

"Bill started yelling and screaming and generally terrorizing us," said Andrew. "I just thought, 'What is he doing here? We're supposed to be in the Aquarian Age, and everything's supposed to be beautiful, and he's terrorizing everybody. So I leaned into Bill's ear and said, 'You're a motherfucker.' And he just exploded. I thought he was going to kill me. He was really violent.

"A couple of years later I was in London with Ken Kesey and he told me that right before my confrontation, Bill had exploded at him for letting fifty people through the back-door. So I was probably the last straw."

Later in the evening, when the LSD-laced ice cream had taken full effect and the dance was in full swing, Grateful Dead guitarist Jerry Garcia returned to the stage after a break in his set to find that his guitar bridge had been smashed and the strings were hanging limply.

"He was just staring at it and absorbing the news when a stranger wearing a cardigan sweater and carrying a clipboard showed up," Perry wrote.

" 'What's the matter?' he asked.

" 'Well, my guitar . . . the bridge . . . '

"Without another word, Bill Graham was down on the guitar with his customary furious energy, trying to fix the unfixable the same way he'd been trying to keep track of the incomprehensible all night."

At 2:00 A.M., when Graham closed the hall, there was still a line outside waiting to get in.

The final show on Sunday evening featured The Grateful Dead and Big Brother and the Holding Company, as well as various light-show artists, theater groups, and dancers. The master of ceremonies for the night was billed as "Pinball Machine." There was even a stroboscopic trampolinist who donned a ski mask to dive off the balcony onto a trampoline under a strobe light during the Grateful Dead set.

Graham must have been overjoyed when he sat down with Kesey after the festival to get his share of the $4,000 gross they had made over the three days from a gate of 6,000—not counting the hundreds who had got in for nothing.

"He found himself, quite accidentally, in a very fortunate position of financial opportunity and power in the newly developing San Francisco rock, blues and poster art world," said poster artist Wes Wilson.

But not everyone considered the Trips Festival to be a success. Jann Wenner a young student, who was writing his very first piece for the University of California at Berkeley's student newspaper, the *Daily Cal* under the nom de plume, mr. jones (sic), thought the festival a flop and singled out Bill Graham for special mention:

"The Festival's 'producer,' i.e., the man-who-was-in-charge-of-the-busy-work, was a total drag," wrote the student who would go on to found *Rolling Stone*. "Mr. Bill Graham, of the Mime Troupe, seemed opposed to having a good time, relaxation, and producing general ease. His extreme up-tightness put the rent-a-cops up-tight, and the rent-a-cops put quite a few other people up-tight."

After the Trips Festival, Graham began consolidating his position in the San Francisco music scene by setting up an organization. The nucleus of his team was three prominent San Francisco lawyers—William Coblentz, Brian Rohan and Michael Stepanian—who were hired to take care of his deals and contracts. He also recruited Mime Troupe actor Jim Haynie to manage the Fillmore once it opened on a regular basis as a concert venue.

"It was pretty obvious to me that Bill had, as my daddy used to say, a bird's nest on the ground, and it was going to make him a rich man,"

Haynie said. "He had a hall that would hold 3,000 people, and he only had to pay $45. What an opportunity."

At the end of January, Fillmore official leaseholder Charles Sullivan wanted out and offered Graham the opportunity to take over the Fillmore completely. Graham jumped at it but when he approached the owner, whom he described as a "little Jewish merchant," he was told, "Look kid, don't bother me. I'm going on a fishing trip for two weeks."

With his customary zeal, Graham replied by launching a frenzied letter-writing campaign which finally wore the owner down and made him sole leaseholder of the Fillmore. Graham's new career as a promoter was taking off faster than he had ever dreamed possible, but he still had many things to learn before he could take complete control of the San Francisco music scene.

4

Birth of the Fillmores

At the beginning of his career in the music business, Bill Graham always knew his limitations and was the first to admit them. Despite his rapid transition from organizing a one-time dance benefit to becoming a bona fide impresario with his very own venue, he was still an outsider in the close-knit San Francisco music community with few dependable contacts. Without a working knowledge of the music business or connections with any of the up-and-coming San Francisco bands, it soon became clear he that needed someone to teach him. The man who would unwittingly help Graham meet the bands and provide an entree into their world and the San Francisco scene was a young lanky Texan named Chester Helms, who had abridged his name to the hipper-sounding Chet.

Helms had been an integral part of the San Francisco scene since the early sixties, was now managing Big Brother and the Holding Company and would soon discover an electric new singer, Janis Joplin. An aspiring promoter, Chet joined forces with the Great Society manager John Carpenter and worked out a deal with Luria Castell under the Family Dog banner to stage their first dance at California Hall with Jefferson Airplane. But later, when Castell fled to Mexico after an emotional breakdown—and without booking the dates—Helms and Carpenter found themselves without a space to present the dance.

In desperation they decided to approach San Francisco's new hotshot promoter, Bill Graham. They met him during the second Mime Troupe Benefit at the Fillmore and presented him with an offer of free gigs from Big Brother and the Great Society. Their trump cards were prior commitments to play from Jefferson Airplane and out-of-town bands like Paul Butterfield, Love, and the Sons of Adam.

This meeting was a turning point in Graham's new career. Knowing little about the rock-music scene except that it held proven business potential, he was constantly questioning people around the Fillmore about new bands in town, asking, "What's their draw?" and "How many people do you think will come and see them?"

In Helms and Carpenter, Graham recognized a heaven-sent opportunity to learn from two men who were linked to the San Francisco music scene professionally and socially. He immediately offered them a partnership in the Fillmore. Explaining his wish to start organizing concerts on a regular basis, he admitted that he didn't have enough confidence or knowledge to support weekly concerts on his own and offered them the opportunity to stage shows at the Fillmore on alternate weekends. Impressed, Helms and Carpenter sealed the deal with a handshake over a Coca-Cola, agreeing to split all proceeds down the middle. When Graham asked what they were going to name themselves. Helms and Carpenter thought for a moment and then decided to continue with the name Family Dog.

The first Family Dog show at the Fillmore was the Tribal Stomp with Jefferson Airplane and Big Brother and the Holding Company on February 19, 1966. There was a $2 admission charge, and artist Wes Wilson was hired to do the poster. Wilson's black-and-white poster showing a Native American on a snow-white horse launched the beginning of the celebrated San Francisco poster era.

Although the first concert was a success, there was already friction between the Family Dog and Graham. "John and I busted our ass on the Tribal Stomp," said Helms. "The deal with Graham was that he would put up the money for the show and provide the Fillmore, and we would pay him for security and his running expenses. The proceeds were then to be split fifty-fifty."

Using his business expertise, Graham had arranged to cover his share of the expenses on credit, collecting half the gross when the proceeds from the show were split without having to lay out a cent. Helms and Carpenter were furious when they realized what he was doing and insisted on renegotiating Graham's share.

Helms said: "We told him, 'No way, Jose, we're not going for this. This is a rip-off because we did all the work and you're taking fifty percent for doing nothing.' "

Graham erupted into his usual tirade of screaming and cursing, finally agreeing to deduct 7 percent to provide essential house services. Other expenses like security would come off the top. In addition, Graham was to be paid a nominal fee for use of the Fillmore. This was one of the few times in his career that Graham ever backed down, and Chet Helms believed that he agreed only because he was still dependent on their contacts in the city's flourishing party scene.

"Graham still needed us to bring the bands and the audience to him," Helms said. "John Carpenter and I were, for lack of a better term, street people, and we had very good connections to the extensive word-of-mouth network of people in San Francisco."

Graham and The Family Dog maintained an uneasy truce for the next two months as each presented shows on alternate weekends. Although they pooled their resources for a time, with Carpenter and Bonnie MacLean both selling tickets or Helms emceeing some of Graham's shows, generally Bill Graham and The Family Dog were poles apart. It was only a matter of time before Helms's idealism and Graham's pragmatic business style would collide.

Buoyed by their success, Helms and Carpenter took a daring gamble on their third Fillmore concert by bringing in the then-unknown Paul Butterfield Blues Band from New York, paying them a record $2,500 for the weekend.

"You have to consider that we were paying Jefferson Airplane only $500 for a weekend at that time," Helms said. "It was very aggressive for us to pay $2,500 for three days for Butterfield, and Graham fought us a lot on that.

"He'd never heard of Butterfield, and he had no connection at all with the blues and no understanding of it in those days. But we told him we were locked into it. We had given our word. End of story."

A week before the show, Helms and Carpenter began to get apprehensive, having heard the Butterfield Blues Band only on record. So they decided to fly to Los Angeles to see the band play so they could gauge its drawing potential.

"We arrived at the club and there is the bartender, the Butterfield Blues Band, ourselves, and nobody else. We had agreed to pay $2,500 for an empty house. We were in a total panic," Helms said. "We came back to San Francisco and spent a whole week from dawn till dusk calling everyone we had ever known. We asked them if they were going to see Paul Butterfield at the Fillmore and the response was usually, 'Who's Paul Butterfield?' We implied that they had to be very square not to have heard of him."

Helms and Carpenter also did the rounds of Haight-Ashbury crash pads, sticking Paul Butterfield posters on refrigerators. Their tenacity paid off when 2,000 people each paid $2.50 on opening night, with a record attendance of 7,500 over the entire three nights. This meant a gross of $18,750, a huge sum in those days. The final show completed, Graham enthusiastically counted and divided the mountain of dollar bills with Helms and Carpenter, all three excitedly discussing future bookings for Butterfield.

However, Graham had other plans, and they did not include his two partners. On arriving home, he immediately set his alarm for 6:00 A.M., and placed a person-to-person call to Paul Butterfield's manager Albert Grossman in New York to secure all Butterfield dates for the next two years.

Helms and Carpenter were livid when they heard of Graham's scheme. They could not believe that their partner had gone behind their backs, acing them right out of the game. When they called him at the Fillmore, demanding a meeting to discuss it, Graham was unapologetic and told them, "Look, I get up early."

"Graham had this New York style of doing business where anything you can get away with is okay as long as you didn't break your word," Helms said. "If Graham sat in front of you, looked you in the eye, and made a deal with you, he would honor it until the death. His word was his bond. But it was all the things that were left unsaid. If you didn't say you were going to do that, that was okay. If he could figure out a way to screw you on paper, he would."

Summing up his brief partnership with Helms and Carpenter, Graham said, "We had unpleasant times . . . the whole freedom of drugs, we had a difference of opinion as to how it should be handled."

Graham finally dissolved the unhappy partnership a week before The Family Dog was due to fly the New York–based Blues Project in for a show. With the show already a sellout, The Family Dog moved fast, securing the Avalon Ballroom in Sutter Street, eight blocks east of the Fillmore, and staged their first concert with The Blues Project.

Now ready to establish the Fillmore as San Francisco's leading ballroom, Bill Graham found himself facing a wave of community hysteria, threatening him with immediate closure. In the wake of extensive national media coverage on the outrageous new-style dance concerts at the Fillmore came an immediate public backlash. Rumors of wild drug orgies on the ballroom floors spread like wildfire, and anxious parents began pressuring police to take action and root out this new evil corrupting San Francisco's youth.

The city had long been a magnet for teenage runaways, who now flocked to join the growing hippie scene in Haight-Ashbury. On weekends it was common to see groups of anxious parents scouring the streets in search of their lost children. The San Francisco Police Department was drawn into the controversy when it began receiving a barrage of complaints about the decadent behavior at the Fillmore. Columnist Ralph J. Gleason received many such letters himself and went to investigate. "I never could discover those naked males and females fornicating in the corners," he reported dutifully to his readers.

The Musicians Union was also muscling in on the Fillmore. Though Graham skirted their rules cleverly by billing his shows as dance concerts, the union nevertheless insisted that he still pay two weeks in advance for its required union quota of musicians per gig, the number of musicians depending on the size of the hall. On a bill of three bands with a total of fourteen musicians the union would demand he hire another ten of their members at full rate to simply stand around and do nothing, otherwise there would be trouble.

Alton Kelly believes there was a concerted effort by the police and the union, who both saw the Fillmore as a threat, to drive Graham out of business before he became too deeply entrenched. The founding Family Dogger, later to become a principal Fillmore poster artist, remembers a fierce showdown between Bill Graham and a deputation of cops and union leaders who tried to put the squeeze on him.

"When the cops and union people burst into the Fillmore, Bill held them off at the head of the stairs and really laid into them," Kelly said.

"Bill had an advantage because he knew that the Musicians Union was under federal investigation in Sacramento at the time. He told them that he'd come out of the Nazi concentration camps and he wasn't going to take any shit from them. He said, 'You guys want to fuck with me, we'll go to the investigation in Sacramento.' He played hardball, and that was the last we ever heard from the union."

Graham's confrontation with the San Francisco police was not resolved so easily. After twenty-eight local store owners signed a petition opposing Graham's application for a Fillmore dance license, it was presented to a city permit hearing by the local cop on the beat. Graham was denied the license.

Playing it straight, Graham put on a business suit and visited the opposing storekeepers one at a time. He explained that the Fillmore audience would bring extra business to the area and put more money in their pockets. His charm and persuasion won over each and every shop owner. At his next appeal, the only opposition came from the local cop and the a local rabbi who claimed that people were urinating on his wall.

In retaliation, the police stepped up the pressure by enforcing an obscure 1909 city ordinance which forbade minors to attend public dances unless accompanied by an adult. On Friday, April 22, the cops moved on the Fillmore for the kill during a Grassroots/Quicksilver Messenger Service concert, prompted by a Gleason editorial in the *San Francisco Chronicle* lending strong support to Bill Graham and the Fillmore. Accompanying the article, a cartoon depicted a policeman and dancers carrying the rather oblique caption "They're dancing with tears in my eyes."

Just after 10:00 P.M., Officer Ray Koenig arrived at the Fillmore with his partner, Officer Frank McCoy, and thrust a folded copy of the *Chronicle* cartoon into Graham's hands, saying, "This is a direct affront to me and my partner."

Outside, a paddy wagon drew up, waiting for the first signs of trouble. Seeing Graham deny four youths admission to the Fillmore for swearing at him, the cops moved into action, arresting the youths at the ballroom entrance. When Graham intervened to stop the arrests, Officer Koenig told him, "I don't feel I have to explain the law."

Later, explaining the arrests, his partner told reporters, "It's the voters. We're only a tool." Then the police moved onto the dance floor and started checking IDs. A young girl without ID was arrested. Screaming, she was carried downstairs to the paddy wagon, and thrown into the back with the drunken youths arrested earlier.

Graham himself was arrested at 3:00 A.M. for allowing minors into the Fillmore and thrown in jail, to be bailed out immediately by his lawyer, Brian Rohan. Facing the judge at his court appearance, Graham lost his temper, attacking the city fathers verbally for persecuting him, but was fortunately pacified by Rohan, who smoothed out the situation.

In the following day's *Chronicle,* Gleason denounced the police behavior, stating, "The only reason I would not allow my own teen-age daughters there without me now is for fear that they would be treated like criminals by the police for being under 18." The controversy over the Fillmore's dance license was finally resolved when a provision was introduced, legally allowing those under eighteen to attend dances where special rules prevailed. Exactly what the special rules entailed were never clarified. Nevertheless, a triumphant Graham got his permit, officially making him a dance-hall proprietor, and the Fillmore was saved.

Although in the beginning the Fillmore Auditorium was run more like a mom-and-pop operation than a business empire, Graham gradually began creating rules of operation that would form the blueprint for all future concert promotion. Rising at 6:00 A.M., he would arrive promptly at his desk in his Fillmore office at 7:00 A.M., in order to catch the New York agents when they arrived in their offices.

If Graham was the brains of the Fillmore, then his girlfriend, Bonnie MacLean, a quiet, conservatively dressed brunette who wore thick black-framed glasses, was its backbone. Graham claimed to have turned Bonnie down initially for the post of his secretary at Allis-Chalmers in 1963 after interviewing her and not liking her turquoise coat. After the employment agency told Graham how upset Bonnie was at not getting the job, he reconsidered, and she came to work for him in 1963. They soon fell in love and moved in together, Bonnie acting as his faithful girl Friday. To ensure that the business ran smoothly, she was in charge of securing all necessary permits from city hall and was responsible for scheduling, updating the blackboard regularly by drawing upcoming show listings in poster form.

Graham's antithesis, Bonnie was soft-spoken and reserved, looking more like a prim secretary in her buttoned-up-to-the-neck outfits than the first lady of Graham's thriving Fillmore operation.

San Francisco Examiner music critic Philip Elwood was a close observer of the early days of Graham's business. "He brought an organization in the midst of chaos to the Bay Area," Elwood said. "Bill had a lot of street smarts and a lot of savvy. I think he completely understood the astonishing power of that lost generation who had all the confusions of the Vietnam War and the Free Speech Movement piled on top of an increasingly popular drug culture. And those were the elements that turned out to be a multibillion-dollar music industry," Elwood said.

Graham pushed himself relentlessly now, working around the clock booking bands, putting on shows and publicizing his concerts in print and on the radio. Jim Haynie, the Fillmore's first manager, said Graham developed rules as he went along."

We didn't know what we were getting into," said Haynie, who is now a film actor in Hollywood. "Bill called me his right-hand man and gave me a number of hats to wear. In the early days Bill spent his time making deals with the bands, and I would make sure all the supplies were there for the weekend and that the technical stuff worked."

Haynie was made emcee and introduced the bands in the early days. He was also in charge of all concessions and the Fillmore's Sunday-afternoon auditions to find new local talent. It was Haynie who first discovered the young guitarist Carlos Santana.

Graham also introduced some clever innovations that helped establish the Fillmore's "caring" reputation. He placed a large barrel of apples at the top of the stairs with a sign inviting people to "Take One or Two," and he bought a large industrial vacuum cleaner to blow up hundreds of balloons which were put on the floor to give the audience something to play with when they arrived. A keen student of crowd control, Graham realized that turning the house lights on high at the end of a show did not clear the hall, so he ordered Haynie to turn the lights up only halfway, leaving the audience to file out peacefully to the calming strains of "Greensleeves" playing over the P.A. system.

"Bill was like hell on wheels around the place when we started," Haynie said. "He always liked to have control of everything, and he would come up and say, 'What are you doing? What's this?' and start yelling when he didn't like something or he wanted it to be different. He was picky, but you just got used to Bill.

"I remember screaming at him one time and saying, 'Fuck you, you motherfucker. Shut the fuck up. I'm tired of your shit.' I thought he might fire me, but he didn't. Bill didn't mind a little sass and spark as long as you were doing your job."

In the first weeks of operation, the Fillmore continued to stage shows every weekend featuring local bands but soon Graham began experimenting with eclectic combinations of musical styles for which he would later become famous. Jefferson Airplane was once paired with Russian poet Andrei Voznesensky, and Country Joe and the Fish with Howlin' Wolf.

Graham's profits were immediate, with an instant cash flow at every concert. In the beginning, headliner acts like Quicksilver Messenger Service or The Grateful Dead were getting only $200 to $300 for a show. With minimal outlay and practically no overhead, Graham could gross $25,000 in one weekend in tickets and concessions—more than he was earning for a whole year's work at Allis-Chalmers. And he didn't even have to worry about taxes. The Fillmore never issued tickets, which guaranteed untraceable income. After the show, Graham would hide the takings somewhere in the Fillmore, to be counted the next morning by a trusted staff member.

"Bill's profits were enormous," Haynie said. "We knew he was stuffing thousands of dollars away every week, and I thought he was sending it to Swiss bank accounts. I never knew for certain."

But one thing his staff did know was that they were not seeing much of the money.

"The people in the concession stand were getting only five dollars a night," Haynie explained. "I was always bitching and moaning to give them more money, but Bill would say, 'They'd be here anyway; they'd do it for nothing just to be here.' With Bill it was always business. Don't pay any more than you have to.

"He had the immigrant mentality and he said to me a number of times, 'Jimmy, this could all be over tomorrow!' So he was making hay while the sun shone."

With the legal fire department audience limit of 956 (a number displayed prominently at the entrance), Graham stood to make big profits charging $2.50 admission. Yet he wasn't satisfied and, skirting fire regulations, he would often pack the Fillmore with more than three times the legal number of people allowed. He played cat-and-mouse games with the San Francisco Fire Department for years and, as a result, it tried continually to catch him breaking fire regulations.

"Bill never paid attention to the regulations," Haynie said. "We used to pack them in and the honest truth is that we used to get between three thousand and three thousand five hundred people in on a good night.

"Bill had a great scam worked out that fooled them every time," Haynie said. "When the fire department arrived, they would shut down the box office and leave an officer at the door to stop anyone else coming in. Bill would tell me to show them around so they could count the house. That was pretty well impossible, as there were no seats or anything, and just a bunch of kids dancing. I would lead the officers on a little tour to the furthest corners of the place and into the darkest areas I could think of. I'd take them backstage and into the dressing rooms, which would have been cleaned out by our security so there were no drugs in the open.

"When they were safely in the back, I would give Bill the high sign, and he would start filtering people in through a side door. There would be a line of people waiting to get in outside the Jewish temple next door. Bill would pull them in off the line, hustle them up the fire escape, grab their money, and stuff it in a pasteboard box. We would be well over the limit, but Bill would just be pushing people in and getting their money while he could.

"The officer who was guarding the box-office line was totally unaware of what was happening. When the other fire officers finished checking out the dressing rooms, we would signal Bill that they were coming back, and he'd stop letting people in through the side door. It was beautiful and worked perfectly every time. The fire chief would then tell us only to let new people in as people leave and leave an officer to enforce it. But it was too late, as Bill had already got everyone in."

Philip Elwood, who regularly reviewed shows at the Fillmore Auditorium, and later the Fillmore West, said he was always worried about the dangers of overcrowding the second-floor auditorium. "I never understood what would have happened if there had been a fire there as the hall was upstairs and there was no access. There were huge windows all around and there were some fire escapes, but I always thought they would not be nearly enough if there was real trouble."

Jann Wenner savagely accused Graham in his *Daily Cal* column of ripping off the community: "These weekend dances at the Fillmore Auditorium are being promoted by a little man named Bill Graham," wrote Wenner as mr. jones. "When these things were originated by The Family Dog, they were meant to present local rock groups and generally provide everyone with a good time, as little hassle as possible, and just be a gas for the performers, participants, and spectators. Graham has turned these dances into money-making schemes first and foremost. Whatever fun one has is strictly incidental to, almost in spite of, Bill Graham. I think he believes he owns the whole scene, and this is wrong."

A month later, Graham defended himself in the *Daily Cal,* claiming he was being driven by a "maniacal frenzy . . . I'm proud of the Fillmore. I'm proud that we move, we swing, and that we wail."

Although Bill Graham was now making more money than he had ever thought possible, he maintained a frugal life-style, and still squired Bonnie around town on his old Lambretta.

Haynie remembers, "He never lived rich even when he had a shitload of money. He was not a guy to spend money on himself. It took him years before he even bought a decent car.

"He used to wear the same clothes all the time. Sweatshirts, jeans, baggy pants, and tennis shoes. That was Bill. It never varied. But he always had finely tailored suits from Vienna in case he had a business meeting where he had to dress up."

Graham also refused to do any repairs on the dilapidated old Fillmore building. "I used to beg him to do some plumbing in the bathrooms," Haynie said. "There were very crowded conditions, and they were overloaded. Bill never wanted to spend any money for repairs, and he'd only put a little paint in the place when he really had to."

Eight blocks down the road, Chet Helms was now at the helm of the Avalon Ballroom and running his weekend dances in direct competition to Graham. The Fillmore's large auditorium, which had been rented out for political meetings in its early days, strongly contrasted the Avalon, a former 1940s swing-dance hall with a sprung wooden floor, cloth ceiling, and elaborate draperies lining the sides—altogether more intimate and friendly. You didn't have to worry about getting your car broken into at the Avalon, for it was located in a far nicer part of town. Its greatest disadvantage was that it was much smaller than the Fillmore, with a legal capacity of 850.

"It was very competitive," said Helms. "I knew that Graham had as high as three thousand five hundred people through the old Fillmore in the course of one evening but I would never take the chances that he would with the physical well-being of my audience."

In an attempt to block Helms's access to bands and drive the Avalon out of business, Graham drew up restrictive contracts effectively blocking groups from playing the Avalon or any other San Francisco club for a full year after they played the Fillmore. Jim Haynie said that Graham used to arrange his exclusivity deals in cooperation with the booking agents. "If bands played for The Family Dog, he wouldn't hire them," Haynie said.

"If you played for Graham you couldn't play for a radius of several hundred miles around," Helms said. "He was very big on territory. Graham was very heavy about that right from the top. Graham put things on a very competitive basis. 'May the best man win' was his attitude. He didn't want to cooperate and work together for the common good."

Although Graham could usually tie up the out-of-town bands with his contracts, many of the local musicians refused to sign. "They didn't want to make exclusive arrangements with Graham," Helms said. "They liked to use us as a foil to negotiate a better deal."

Big Brother and the Holding Company was the house band at their manager's Avalon Ballroom, so they had no chance of ever playing at the Fillmore. "Graham would let us into the Fillmore for free, but he would never hire us in those days," said Big Brother drummer David Getz.

Graham and Helms soon emerged as the two top promoters in San Francisco, but their personal styles could not have been farther apart. It was the classic confrontation of the businessman and the hippie: Bill Graham, in his mid-thirties, hyperactive and continually on the move shuffling his legal pads of notes, always dressed scruffily in a T-shirt and jeans; Chet Helms, ten years younger, with long, flowing blond hair and Benjamin Franklin glasses, his San Francisco calmness withstanding any pressure.

Graham, the quintessential East Coast businessman, hated the hippie movement and all it stood for. Normally careful in voicing these views in community newspapers like the *Berkeley Barb* or the *Daily Cal,* he once let his true feelings slip out in the music trade bible, *Billboard,* in an issue that spotlighted the San Francisco music scene.

"I am not a freakout . . . I'm not a hippie . . . I don't sell love," Graham told *Billboard* magazine. "I sell talent and environment."

Graham classified himself as a "producer," proud of his art of "public assemblage" and crowd handling. On the other hand, Helms saw himself as a "cultural missionary" whose dance hall was a religious sanctuary where young people could come in safety to experience rites of passage.

"From my standpoint, we were more about cultural revolution than we were about money," Helms explained. "It wasn't just the bottom line. Graham was coming out of a fairly conventional business tradition, and his approach, which was basically a bottom-line one, didn't always result in the most exhilarating or inspiring shows.

"Graham always said he was a 'crowd engineer.' In a sense he had a mechanical model as opposed to a spiritual model of what a ballroom should be. He was a crowd engineer, and he was dealing with units, not human beings," Helms said.

From the start, Graham employed a black security force recruited from the Fillmore district to smooth out any possible trouble coming from the ghetto. Giving them a military presence, Graham issued them with green-and-yellow uniforms—the same colors as the Pirates gang he belonged to as a youth. And he ordered them to keep the audience in check and discipline anyone who got out of line, leading to accusations that he was running a private army within the Fillmore. Although Graham himself used drugs discreetly behind closed doors, he knew that if they were used openly in the Fillmore, the authorities would have cause to close him down, so he banned them from his shows. Playing schoolteacher, he confiscated any drugs that he found on the spot. Anyone caught smoking or selling drugs would be hauled into an office and confronted by Graham himself.

Manager Jim Haynie said that Graham's message was always the same. "Bill would say, 'You're fucking stupid. You're going to blow this for everyone. If you're going to have dope, I don't give a fuck, but keep it cool. Don't make it obvious.'

Graham later admitted that he used to punish drug dealers by taking their money as well as their dope. He'd ask them to name a charity for the money to be donated to and then send the offender home with ten dollars cab fare.

"They'd argue and yell and scream and I'd say, 'I'm not gonna give you your money back because then you're gonna do it again. I gotta punish you.' "

Graham and his security also had a special way of dealing with people having bad LSD trips and making a nuisances of themselves.

"In the old days everyone was taking acid and stuff and people would go crazy," said Electric Flag singer Nick Gravenitis who often headlined the Fillmore. "Bill Graham would put them in the back room all acided up and actually play games with these people while they were having a bad trip. He thought this was very amusing. I thought it was cruel."

Most of the confiscated drugs were given away to the staff and bands, with some even relying on the steady supply from Fillmore dope busts as a free source of illegal drugs. Graham admitted, "Early on in the 1960s, when there was a bad harvest in Mexico, and there wasn't any weed coming through musicians, managers and friends used to call me and say, 'Did you bust anybody tonight?' So they would come down and get it. We'd share it."

Bill Graham always liked to give the impression that even though he hadn't discovered Janis Joplin, he had nurtured her career and helped her blossom into the San Francisco legend she became. Like many Bill Graham stories, there is an element of truth, but it is far from the whole story. Originally in fact, he deliberately set out to destroy her career, having perceived her as a direct threat to his favorite first lady of San Francisco rock, Grace Slick, who recently had moved to Jefferson Airplane from The Great Society. Graham refused to book Janis—"that screaming witch,"—at the Fillmore and ridiculed her singing voice at every opportunity.

The first explosive confrontation between Janis and Graham occurred after the singer bad-mouthed the Fillmore during an interview to a small mimeographed newsletter called the *Mojo Navigator.* When the interviewer asked her to compare the Avalon and the Fillmore, Janis replied that the Avalon was the place where the San Francisco in crowd went to party and have a good time, while the Fillmore was where sailors went to get laid and was second-rate.

When Graham saw the article, he was so enraged that he cornered Janis one night when she arrived at the Fillmore for a B. B. King show.

She was flying high after having shot up crystal amphetamine.

"Bill met her at the top of the stairs and just pointed to the door and said, 'You're not coming in here,' " remembered Big Brother drummer David Getz. "Then he started screaming as he threw her out."

Janis burst into tears as a frenzied Graham ranted at her for insulting his Fillmore, a scene witnessed by scores of people waiting in line. Janis ran out into the road crying, inconsolable after her public humiliation. Her close friend, singer Nick Gravenitis, who was on the bill that night, heard what had happened and was furious.

"It totally freaked me out," said Gravenitis. "I thought that being an artist would make you immune from these kind of attacks by Graham. I was wrong. I really didn't mind when Graham would throw somebody out who was acting crazy or he had a personal vendetta against, but when he started throwing out artists, it was a threat to all of us. You don't humiliate artists like that."

Curious to know how the other artists were reacting to his attack on Janis, Graham hid in a closet in the backstage dressing room so he could eavesdrop.

"Bill Graham was the Sam Goldwyn of the rock 'n' roll business," said Gravenitis. "He was a strange guy with a lot of weird habits, and he would hide in places just to hear what was being said about him in his empire.

"I was in the back room when I heard Janis had been thrown out and I exploded. Went right off the handle. So here Bill is hiding in the closet with all these irate, pissed-off musicians putting him down using every conceivable epithet to describe his meanness.

"It went on for a long time, and he must have realized that it wasn't going to stop, and he was trapped in the closet. So all these people suddenly left the room and came out into the hallway, and I was ranting and raving about Bill Graham. Then he finally came out of the closet and was standing behind me where I couldn't see him. Michael Bloomfield pointed at the back of the room, and I turned 'round, and there was Bill. I knew that he had heard everything that I had said about him, so I continued, 'And Bill—that's not all, there's more!' I just cussed him up and down."

Graham didn't respond, but his eyes went cold and, giving Gravenitis an icy stare, he said, "I'll get you for this," and walked away.

But Graham's hostile attitude to Janis Joplin would soon change once she became a star and he needed her.

On September 27, 1967, heavy rioting broke out near the Fillmore after a white policeman shot a black youth in the nearby Hunter's Point ghetto. The word on the street was that the youth had been shot in the back. The result was a full-scale riot involving hundreds of black youths throwing rocks and setting fires. As the rioting spread, the National Guard was mobilized and a curfew was declared for all areas with a black population including the Haight. Concerned about the effects the rioting would have on his business, Graham made an urgent plea to the police chief to allow him to keep his dances going, claiming that they would help to keep the peace.

In fact, Graham had a blockbuster show planned for October 1 with Muddy Waters, Paul Butterfield, and Jefferson Airplane. Having originally booked the Winterland Auditorium, he decided at the last minute to stage it in the smaller Fillmore in case ticket sales were slow. At 8:30 P.M., as people arrived for the first show, the police had still not given Graham the go-ahead for the show; fearing trouble, Graham stationed his black security force outside the Fillmore to provide a menacing presence. Inside the Fillmore, Graham remained cool, kneeling at the top of the stairs blowing up balloons with an old hair dryer, beside him, the familiar tub of free apples beneath the "Take One" sign.

Just before 9:00, a police patrol arrived and an angry cop ran up the stairs, screaming, "What the hell are you doing opening tonight?" The sergeant then emphasized his point by prodding his cigar into the balloon Graham had been blowing up, saying, "I don't talk to guys that play with balloons." Keeping himself in check, Graham began reasoning with him for more than an hour, finally persuading the cop to call and ask his superiors to allow the show to start. It was a somewhat hollow victory for Graham: the 400 who attended the show marked the lowest attendance record ever for the Fillmore.

The new San Francisco music scene was now bursting out throughout the city in an explosion of colorful posters advertising upcoming concerts. Seductively eye-catching, these three-color posters began to plaster walls and doorways throughout the city as the Fillmore and the Avalon ballrooms started taking off.

Without question, the pioneer of this new art form was Wes Wilson, who did posters for both Graham and Helms. His distinctively flowing art nouveau style, which sublimated the poster information psychedelically right into the design, set the standard to follow for all future poster artists.

"I had complete control over what I did," said Wilson, who regularly designed the Fillmore posters for $100 a week. "Bill didn't really know anything about art directing, and I only had to do the poster and bring it to him on a Friday evening."

But Graham worried that Wilson's posters were often indecipherable and that potential Fillmore customers might not be able to read the concert information.

"I understood their desire, in this wonderful, childish, scheming way, to bury all the pertinent information underneath all the oozes and ebbs and flows and liquidy movement on the poster," said Graham. "I would say to Wes, 'Just watch people standing there, trying to read your poster!' "

As the popularity of the posters increased with the growing international interest in the San Francisco scene, they began to be viewed as art. Soon the posters were being ripped down the minute they were put up; so, to dissuade people from stealing them, Graham started giving them away at his shows.

After Wes Wilson and his work was featured in *Time* magazine and the *New York Times* in April 1967, the posters became incredibly lucrative, often bringing in more revenue to Graham than the box office. Initially, Wilson copyrighted his first forty-four posters, but soon stopped after Graham insisted that his own name and copyright be used instead. Unknown to Wilson, Graham had set up a new corporation called William Graham Posters, Inc., handling all the poster art, which soon developed into the largest grossing arm of his operation.

Graham offered to work out a deal with Wilson so they could both benefit. Wilson signed a contract drawn up by Graham's attorney, but was asked to return his copy for a "legal formality." That was the last time Wilson ever saw the contract. Later, after Graham boasted to the *New York Times* arts section that he had sold 100,000 copies of one of Wilson's posters at $1 each, Wilson demanded his fair share.

Said Wilson, "My agreement was that I got six cents on every dollar so I figured I should get $6,000 for that one poster. I went down to see Bill and said I wanted to see his books, which I had every right to do under our agreement. The only problem was they had never sent me my copy.

"Bill just freaked out when I brought up the matter to him. He made such a scene that a friend of mine who was in the room wanted to go out and have a fistfight with him there on the spot."

Later Wilson called Graham's office requesting his copy of the contract, but was told by an employee that it had been lost. Having never gained access to the contract, Wilson claims to have lost a fortune in royalties, as his posters have since become highly prized collectors items.

"Like others who naïvely took him at his word or trusted him to be honorable, I was lied to and cheated to by Bill about poster sales, poster copyrights, and royalties," said Wilson. "All the hype in the world can't erase that experience from my mind. It happened."

Yet revenge was delivered in the final poster he created for the Fillmore before quitting in May 1967. At the bottom he caricatured Bill Graham as a snake—a dollar sign between its teeth and a swastika on its forehead.

With the Fillmore firmly established and running smoothly, Bill Graham began looking for ways to expand into other areas of the San Francisco music scene. He decided to explore band management and sought a relationship similar to that of his rival Chet Helms and Big Brother. He reasoned that as a manager he would have more control over the musicians, enabling him to hire them whenever he wanted to. The only band he knew personally at the time was Jefferson Airplane, the undisputed premier band in San Francisco. The Airplane, which had played Graham's landmark benefit for the Mime Troupe, had now acquired superstar status within the city.

Jefferson Airplane was the creation of Matthew Katz, an eccentric man who had been in the music business for many years. Difficult to deal with and unable to communicate with the young musicians whose careers he guided, Katz's role in shaping the San Francisco music scene has been largely overlooked. Under his direction, Jefferson Airplane had become the first San Francisco band to secure a major record contract, with a $20,000 advance from RCA Victor. To promote their success and create a strong image, Katz dressed and groomed them and even transported them around town in limos.

Aware of the financial advantages in securing Jefferson Airplane as Fillmore regulars, Graham quickly arranged a meeting with Katz to settle on a figure before the band broke nationally.

Graham's aggressive business manner, complete with threats and intimidation, sharply contrasted with the low-key Katz, who came from the old school of Tin Pan Alley schmooze over three-martini lunches. When Graham arrived at Katz's home for the meeting, he was immediately ushered into his bedroom, as the manager was feeling under the weather. For some reason, which was never explained to Graham, Katz's insurance broker was also present.

"It was my first negotiation," Graham told Ralph Gleason. "I told him who I was, and I ran this place, and I'd like to deal for the group.

"He reminded me of the New York agents who are pretty schlock but would never say no to anybody. But in return for them considering you, you had to be one of their guys who hung around the office. This was the way Matthew dealt. 'Sit down, sonny. Oh, my back! If you only knew! Are you new in this business? Well, let me tell you . . . ' And now I heard his history."

Graham listened patiently as Katz played the seasoned old music pro, lecturing inexperienced youth on the business and offering advice on how to run the Fillmore. When Katz named an inflated price for Jefferson Airplane, which he called "the greatest band in America," Graham looked shocked, saying he didn't have that kind of money.

"I had a lot of chutzpah, already," boasted Graham, who was well used to the art of bluffing from his marathon poker sessions in the Catskills. At one point during the negotiations, Graham started to walk out of the room admitting defeat. Refusing to let him go, Katz ordered him back. It was at that point Graham realized that Katz just wanted a receptive listener; the money was just incidental. Finally, after four straight hours of holding court, Katz agreed to Graham's opening offer for Jefferson Airplane of $1,000 for a weekend, a nominal price for the most popular band in town.

Graham then embarked on a campaign to take over the management of the Airplane himself. Befriending band members, singer Marty Balin and rhythm guitarist Paul Kantner, he found out that they did not like Katz but felt they owed him some loyalty for securing their record contract.

Sensing the perfect opportunity, Graham took the band under his wing and became their unofficial confidant and adviser. His chance to oust Katz came when he discovered that it was improper for a manager to book his own band without going through an agent. Ruthlessly, Bill Graham took Katz to court, accusing him of soliciting gigs for Jefferson Airplane and his other bands, It's a Beautiful Day and Moby Grape, and had him defrocked as a manager in the San Francisco music scene. Ruined, Katz became enmeshed in a labyrinthine landmark case that took ten years to resolve, setting a precedent in entertainment law.

Assuming management of Jefferson Airplane was a major coup for Graham. It established him firmly as an important force in San Francisco music, dominating the city's largest ballroom and its top band. The relationship, however, proved not to be an easy one for Graham. The businessman hit a brick wall when he attempted to bring order and efficiency into the anarchic and drug-oriented life-style of the Airplane.

"We came from two different worlds," said Graham. "Theirs was the free-form revolutionary world, and mine happened to be a bit more realistic. I came from the business community, and it was my job to act realistically."

Graham took over management of the Jefferson Airplane directly after their triumphant appearance on the nationally televised "Bell Telephone Hour Special" featuring the San Francisco scene. Jefferson Airplane was featured prominently as the city's top band. Graham wanted to capitalize on the exposure by taking the band on a national tour. But he hadn't reckoned on the band's democratic process of decision making at group meetings with a show of hands. As the band's manager, Graham was allowed only one vote, and his passionate sermons for sanity fell on deaf ears. The Jefferson Airplane meetings tended to lapse into heated arguments, with Bill Graham the "administrative arguer" and Paul Kantner the "musical arguer."

"It's very difficult to act realistically and try to explain realities and practicalities to people who really didn't want to be tuned into that kind of reasoning," Graham admitted later. "It was very difficult, and there was a great strain between us sometimes."

"Bill Graham says we haven't paid our dues," said Kantner. "And for him he's right, but not for us. Graham always says that Duke Ellington gets off the plane feeling shitty, terrible, he goes there and does his thing, man, Otis [Redding] could do that. Well we can't do that. We have to be fairly comfortable mentally to perform like that. Those kind of performers do perform well under stress. They have a lot more discipline than the six of us, too. We're strictly undisciplined."

Even twenty-five years later Kantner still harbors some resentment towards Graham. "He always hated everything that we did, but then he wouldn't do anything for us."

In Paul Kantner, a former Golden Gloves boxing champion, Bill Graham found someone as stubborn and articulate as himself who would not be browbeaten into submission.

"I think over the years Paul's been the friendliest enemy I've had in rock 'n' roll," said Graham. "We've gone at it in battle royals many times."

Self-admitted spoiled middle-class brats, Jefferson Airplane turned its success into one long self-indulgent drug party. Singer Marty Balin said he was almost an outsider in the group, as he didn't do the same drugs or adopt their new arrogant superstar life-style.

"Everybody thought I was a dork," Balin remembers. "Everybody else was just living high on the hog. They all had entourages. Fifty people hanging around each guy. Me, I'd come—I've got nobody, just me. They got to be too big for me, even. You couldn't rehearse. Couldn't talk to them. Had to go through their entourage.

"I wasn't into the drugs, I just drank in those days. Everybody was on coke, and I couldn't communicate with anybody on coke in those days. I just got bored by it all."

Rock promoter John Morris was hired as tour manager for Jefferson Airplane as a final attempt by Graham to work with the band through a third party. Morris said, "Jefferson Airplane's whole thing was 'Yeah. Let's stay loose and stoned and high and have a great old time. But somebody's got to watch out for the business. Oh, Bill will do it.' "

But when Bill started saying, 'Oh, you're screwing up, you're doing this,' they didn't want to listen. That would frustrate the hell out of Bill and make it worse.

"Bill always adored Grace Slick. She was one of the most interesting, attractive, and wonderful people you could ever be around. She was also as crazy as a hoot owl when she wanted to be."

Morris recalls an incident on tour in Nashville when Grace announced that she was never going to sing the Airplane's most famous song, "White Rabbit," again because she was sick of it.

"I said, 'That's going to be a bit of a problem because to the whole bloody world you *are* "White Rabbit," and the audience is going to demand it.' So she just left it out of the next show, and the audience damn near tore the place apart. She finally had to sing "White Rabbit" during the encore. Afterwards she laughed about it, saying, 'Well, I tried.' I said, 'Yes. Your principles are intact.' "

The band was veering out of control, and members often went onstage perilously stoned. At one gig Grace, even turned on the audience, screaming and swearing at them for no apparent reason.

Finally, Spencer Dryden, the band's original drummer and Grace's boyfriend at the time, had a big argument with Graham before a show when Dryden was caught in the dressing room with a fifth of bourbon. Grace and Dryden were furious at their manager for daring to stop their fun and threatened to leave the band if Bill Graham wasn't fired. It was left to Balin to tell Graham that he was being replaced as manager by Bill Thompson, a friend of the band. Soon afterward, Balin and other band members decided to get rid of Dryden, offering Grace the ultimatum of leaving with Dryden or staying with the Airplane. Finally, her decision to stay left band members with the problem of who was going to look after the beautiful rock goddess.

"We had an election," Balin said. "We had a meeting to try and figure out who would go with Grace and take care of her because she always needed a guy to talk for her. Jorma [Kaukonen] didn't want the job, and [Jack] Casady had tried it and didn't like it, and I didn't want the job. Paul was actually elected—damned straight. The trouble with that band was that I never did sleep with Grace. That's a problem you know. If I'd slept with her she would have been a nice old lady. She's never had a good guy though."

When Graham and Jefferson Airplane split up, in early 1968 they were hardly on speaking terms, but both sides realized that it was mutually advantageous to keep working together.

"We've had some tough times," Graham said. "At the time, in '67 and '68, we both put out our long arms and said, 'Stay away from one another.' Since then we've learned that the world is big enough for both of us.

"I knew the potential and the abilities within the Jefferson Airplane. I think they made great music, but I think they could have made more of themselves. I think there's more than we've gotten."

As Bill Graham became increasingly successful and achieved celebrity status in San Francisco, he faced a growing hostility from many people who saw him as a capitalist pig growing rich on the backs of the Love Generation. Being branded as an exploiter hit a raw nerve; nothing could make Bill Graham angrier. Even the suspicion of that accusation behind his back would unleash a torrent of anger and abuse followed by an immediate ejection from the Fillmore, often at the hands of the sensitive impresario himself.

Whenever there was a problem with a band showing up late or not at all, it was Bill Graham who always got the boos and hisses from the angry crowd. Writer Ralph Gleason believed that Graham was badly misunderstood by his audiences. "The audience that evolved in San Francisco was in many ways a dependent audience and a rather immature audience," Gleason said. "Bill was blamed for everything that went wrong in the world of music."

And, as time went on, Graham's natural insecurity and paranoia was fed by the growing hostility from people throughout the San Francisco scene who distrusted his all-business approach and saw his success as a betrayal of their idealistic values.

Singer Nick Gravenitis saw many ambitious East Coast businessmen arrive in San Francisco to exploit the growing opportunities offered by the vibrant new music scene. "Inside a year their hair was real long, and they'd be smoking reefers and forgotten why they had come in the first place," said Gravenitis.

"Bill Graham was the exception, and he was really able to make the business transition to San Francisco. Bill was a good businessman, and he knew he had a hot thing going, but he was absolutely not part of the scene. He was outside it, and in fact he denigrated it.

"He thought we were kind of foolish and stupid, and he looked down on us in every way. He wasn't part of the hippie gang because he was a businessman."

5

The Summer of Love

By the start of 1967, disillusioned with the unfulfilled promises of the Kennedy era and thrust into the Vietnam War by Lyndon B. Johnson, the youth of America were finally ready to assert themselves. A tidal wave of anger and protest swept the country. With the unprecedented power of their discretionary income, young people were starting to flex their economic muscle in the American marketplace. And the first members of what would later be termed "baby boomers" were demanding nothing short of a new mass culture to mirror a total rejection of their parents' antiquated values. Rebellion was the name of the game. Overnight, film, television and music changed, reflecting a dynamic young market. The unifying thread of change was in the music voicing the frustrations, hopes, and dreams of the youth movement. For the first time, there was a medium of expression that could spread the message to the world.

Beatles George Harrison and Paul McCartney had both already visited San Francisco to give their seals of approval to the Peace and Love movement of Haight-Ashbury. Newspapers reported Beatles experimenting with LSD and the group's new single, "Strawberry Fields Forever," perfectly captured the hallucinogenic mood of San Francisco and carried it to willing ears everywhere.

The January 1967 Be-In in San Francisco, where 20,000 people flocked to celebrate peace and love, was a great success and the largest public gathering of the hippie tribes so far. This was soon followed by be-ins in New York and Los Angeles which captured national headlines. The media jumped on the hippie bandwagon and enthusiastically spread the word about the joyous hedonism of San Francisco where the beautiful people worshiped at the temple of Bill Graham's Fillmore. This publicity created an instant demand throughout the country for similar ballrooms where people could dance to the new acid-rock music. And there was no shortage of ambitious young entrepreneurs who tried to make their fortunes by setting up their own versions of the Fillmore, complete with psychedelic names, posters, and light shows.

A young deejay named Larry Magid opened the Electric Ballroom in Philadelphia. In Chicago there was the Kinetic Playhouse started by Aaron Russo. Boston kids flocked to the Boston Tea Party headed by Don Law, and George Popodopolus began the Psychedelic Supermarket in New York. In the Covent Garden fruit-market district of London, Middle Earth, a Fillmore-styled ballroom, opened with a big party attended by Chet Helms, flown in especially to provide a genuine link to the hippie Mecca that was San Francisco.

All the fledgling promoters recognized Bill Graham and his Fillmore operation as the blueprint for their own halls. There was no question in their mind that Graham was "writing the book" on the new concert-promotion business, and many regularly sent spies to check out the Fillmore so they could keep up with his latest innovations.

After only one year at the Fillmore, Bill Graham had gone from relative obscurity to undreamed-of wealth and power in San Francisco. Though many would have been content to coast for a while and enjoy the fruits of success, Graham launched himself into overdrive, stepping up his workload. In celebration of his first year at the Fillmore, Graham held the first of his legendary New Year's bashes with The Grateful Dead and Jefferson Airplane. With his natural flair for theatrics, Graham had his Fillmore manager Jim Haynie make a grand entrance at the stroke of midnight, cast as the New Year's baby.

"I was completely wacko-stoned," Haynie said. "I had taken my acid about an hour before, and I had been working all evening. I had made my own diaper and sparkly banner, and I had a wreath for my head and a basket of flowers."

At midnight, eight Fillmore guards hoisted him onto a litter hired for the occasion from a local prop shop. He was then carried ceremonially over their shoulders into the Fillmore, a procession greeted by a fanfare through the sound system.

"The one little spotlight they had on was searching around, and it finally found me at the back door," said Haynie. "As they carried me in, I looked around as if I was just waking up, and the crowd roared its appreciation. Then I got up on my knees, and there was another roar. When I finally stood on my feet rather unsteadily, they just about flipped. I was throwing flowers to people, and then, when we hit the stage Bill did his countdown to 1967 and The Grateful Dead started their set by playing 'The Midnight Hour.' "

Haynie became Graham's good-luck charm and was flown in annually to reprise his role as the Fillmore's New Year's baby. In later years, Bill Graham himself would join the tableau as white-bearded Old Father Time.

To help focus national attention on San Francisco, Bill Graham started a campaign of selling the new music scene to the national media. He confidently predicted to journalists that 4 million young people would flock to the city that summer. To make the most of this huge hippie pilgrimage to San Francisco, Graham enthusiastically announced plans to open the Fillmore six nights a week.

With a massive hippie invasion imminent, Graham was well aware that the conservative San Francisco city fathers would not be welcoming the rootless army of young people with open arms. In order to pacify the authorities and protect his investment, Graham developed his own social-welfare program, relieving city hall of the pressure.

With the San Francisco authorities doing everything within their legal—and sometimes not-so-legal—power to stem the hippie tide, Graham decided to set up a free legal-aid center, launching it in May with the HALO benefit. Working from an office based in The Grateful Dead's house, Graham's own lawyers, Michael Stepanian and Brian Rohan, were enlisted to advise on drug busts, army draft cases, and even music law.

He coopted the Haight-Ashbury Medical Clinic, which had been started by University of California Medical Center physician Dr. David Smith in June 1967, in direct response to the refusal of the government to provide health care to the hundreds of thousands of flower children now arriving in San Francisco.

"There was a lot of protest in San Francisco against delivering health care to the hippies," Dr. Smith remembers. "It was called the Summer of Love, and our motto was 'Love needs care, and health care's a right not a privilege.' The whole counterculture was evolving, and so society was in great turbulence, and there was protest against the hippies by the government and a lot of the citizens."

Dr. Smith assembled a squad of thirty volunteer doctors to provide a twenty-four-hour clinic for kids suffering from bad trips or venereal disease, or any other medical ailment. But, two months later after Monterey Pop, the clinic was broke and on the verge of closure.

"One day I received a call from Bill Graham out of the blue, and he came down to see the clinic," Dr. Smith said. "He told me his philosophy and then told me he thought I was doing good to help and he wanted to help us."

To raise cash for the clinic, Graham held a series of benefits at the Fillmore, rallying the support of Big Brother and the Holding company, Jefferson Airplane, Blue Cheer, and Quicksilver Messenger Service. At one of the benefits, comedian Bill Cosby turned up and jammed on the drums with The Charlatans. The concerts were highly successful, and the Haight-Ashbury Free Clinic survived, marking the beginning of a lifelong association with Graham and becoming one of the few lasting symbols of the Summer of Love.

Graham also raised cash for the anarchist band of political Robin Hoods known as The Diggers. Led by Emmet Grogan and former Mime Troupe actor Peter Coyote, the Diggers provided free food kitchens and created other effective community-action groups.

"We did incredible things at the Fillmore," Coyote said.

"The Diggers once held a party where we brought in a kilo of marijuana and threw it in a bucket filled with burning charcoal. We separated the room with an aisle down the middle and passed out huge cardboard mailing tubes and initiated a game we called 'Stone Your Neighbor.'

"To play, people blew huge clouds of smoke from the bucket from one side of the room to the other through these cardboard mailing tubes.

"Bill was out of his mind because he could have lost his license. I don't think he knew exactly what was coming, but he went along with us, knowing exactly what we were like."

Although he was not overtly involved at this time in the dope and sex side of the new hippie rock 'n' roll life-style, Graham was tolerant and never tried to force his employees to conform to his standards.

"Bill had a moral code that he went by and he respected everyone's rights to have their own life-style," Jim Haynie said. "He never fucked with my life-style in any way. I could come to work stoned as long as I did the work. He didn't give a shit. Bill stayed straight almost the whole time. Once in a while someone would slip him something, but I never saw him any way but straight. He would say to me, 'I love to go home and smoke a fat joint in a hot tub.' But never when he was working. Never."

Graham's new role as a charitable benefactor increased his power and social status in two ways. It provided him with extra leverage in dealing with the authorities, and it gave him a certain degree of prestige within the community, which he relished.

But Graham was not the only one seeking to capitalize on San Francisco's new status as hip world capital. Alternative businesses were springing up all over the Haight. New establishments called head shops catered to dope smokers, selling rolling papers, roach holders, and other drug paraphernalia. An alternative bookshop called Annex 13 Books opened along with a bead makers supply store with the peculiar name of Chickie P. Garbanza's Bead and Storm Door Co., Ltd. A hip diner sold Love Burgers for 25 cents and, in the spirit of peace and love, its striking female Iranian owner would even give them away free to "hard up" customers.

The conscience of the Haight was voiced in two alternative newspapers, the *Berkeley Barb* and the new *San Francisco Oracle,* the latter priding itself on being the world's only fully psychedelic newspaper with regular articles by acid gurus Timothy Leary and Richard Alpert and Merry Prankster Ken Kesey. The broadsheets, critiquing the scene and the personalities, soon become the mouthpiece and communications platform for psychedelic expression.

Jann Wenner, a young San Francisco mailman and part-time journalist, who had bitterly criticized Bill Graham in his column in the *Daily Cal* a year earlier, launched a new magazine, *Rolling Stone,* aided by his mentor Ralph Gleason. An early issue referred to the all-business promoter as "the burgeoning Howard Hughes of the dance scene."

Bill Graham's Fillmore Auditorium became central to the new alternative economy. Although the motto "Peace and Love" was everywhere, Graham was strictly business and dealt only in cash. Once a week he would do the rounds of the Haight head shops which served as his ticket agents, collecting a 10 percent commission on all tickets sold. As an added sweetener, he would often throw in a couple of extra free passes for the Fillmore. Oblivious to danger, the streetwise capitalist would always carry a large brown paper bag stuffed with thousands of dollar bills that he had collected.

In June 1967, The Beatles released their landmark album, *Sgt. Pepper's Lonely Hearts Club Band,* which changed the direction of rock music forever. The album embraced psychedelia and was a symbolic expression of the new age Aquarian life-style being pioneered in the Bay Area. Although less influential musically than *Sgt. Pepper,* a catchy song written by John Phillips, the leader of the Mamas and the Papas, called "San Francisco (Be Sure to Wear Some Flowers in Your Hair)," sung by Scott Mackenzie, became the hippie anthem, serving as an international "wish you were here" postcard. Ironically, it was the Los Angeles–based Phillips who was largely responsible for launching all the San Francisco bands into the big time together.

As national attention began focusing on San Francisco, a group of promoters decided to make a killing by holding a large pop festival 120 miles south of the city, in Monterey. It would be along the lines of the be-ins, but with a paying audience. When the original plan for Monterey Pop fell through, the festival was bought out by an L.A.-based consortium led by Phillips and record producers Lou Adler and Abe Somer. They planned to produce a West Coast version of the Newport Folk Festival and to celebrate the new San Francisco sound. To avoid charges of exploitation, the organizers put out a stream of press releases stating that Monterey would be a nonprofit event to help raise cash, enabling the Diggers to cope with the thousands of hippies now flowing into San Francisco. Highly skeptical of these claims, the San Francisco managers and bands, realized that all the free publicity would attract up to 100,000 people to a festival site equipped for only 20,000. They viewed it as an attempt by the slick L.A. music establishment to hijack and market the San Francisco sound for its own profit.

"There was a definite rivalry and antagonism between the L.A. and San Francisco camps. We had trouble even getting them to talk to us," John Phillips wrote in his autobiography, *Papa John*.

"Haight-Ashbury was becoming the universal hippie Mecca for both the drug and rock cultures. Musicians saw themselves as organic post-capitalist advocates of 'power to the people.' They wanted to co-opt—that was the word then—the event to feed 'their' people in the Bay Area."

Genial former Beatles publicity director Derek Taylor was hired as festival publicist and peacemaker, at a salary of $250 a week, and led a delegation to San Francisco to meet community leaders.

"The conscience of the movement was seen to be in San Francisco," Taylor remembers. "Bill Graham, Chet Helms, Ralph Gleason, and The Grateful Dead all had to be convinced that we were not charlatans. Bill was extremely hospitable when we met in his upstairs office at the Fillmore. During the meeting people kept running in and out to ask his advice, and there were a lot of comings and goings. He kept quite a salon and I was very impressed."

Later, when the organizers ran into problems raising cash and had contacted several major record companies for backing, Bill Graham, never missing a money-making beat, secretly invested $10,000 himself in the festival on the condition that the transaction stayed secret. He also acted as consultant, offering Lou Adler advice on the best way to deal with the San Francisco music community.

On June 11, Bill Graham married Bonnie MacLean after a concert cancellation at the Fillmore gave him a few hours' breathing space. Their relationship was in trouble and they saw marriage as a final attempt to patch things up.

"Bonnie used to constantly complain that Bill was just interested in business and would work all the time," Haynie said. "He was a workaholic, and they just did not have any personal time together."

Five days later, Graham left his new bride alone in San Francisco to spend a week in Monterey checking out the possibilities of this new festival phenomenon.

Bill Graham wasn't the only one with great expectations for Monterey. Word of the festival had reached New York, and representatives from every major record company, including Columbia Records Division president Clive Davis, flew to the West Coast armed with blank checkbooks to sign up new talent.

Albert Grossman, who managed a slew of top acts including Bob Dylan, The Paul Butterfield Blues Band, and Peter, Paul, and Mary, also jetted out to Monterey to see the available talent firsthand.

"The real action of Monterey took place backstage, in the makeshift green rooms and private bar areas where record companies made their deals," wrote Marc Eliot in his book *Rockonomics*.

It was backstage at Monterey where Bill Graham first really got to know Dylan's quiet but highly effective manager, Albert Grossman. A year earlier, Grossman had helped Graham by giving him sole rights on Butterfield, and Graham was only too eager to impress the big-time manager with his valuable knowledge of the San Francisco music scene.

"There was almost no power-tripping by anyone, but we had a few testy exchanges with Albert Grossman," John Phillips wrote. "He seemed to want to use Monterey as a showcase for his clout."

The three-day festival which drew 200,000 fans, soon turned into an auction, with the major record companies desperate to sign up as many new San Francisco bands as they could get their hands on. Organizer Lou Adler hired a film crew led by D. A. Pennebacker to shoot the festival and managed to sell the rights to ABC-TV for a network special at a purported price of $600,000.

Officially, Monterey remained a charity event, with none of the participating bands getting paid for appearing. The organizers ran into real trouble with the San Francisco bands which were asked to sign a release form, giving the filmmakers worldwide rights to the festival concert special. The idealistic bands and their managers were now convinced that they were getting ripped off, and it was only after much argument that the bands, with the exception of The Grateful Dead and Big Brother, signed the form.

On the Saturday night of June 17, Janis Joplin led Big Brother to an historic show-stopping set. It was clear to everyone that she was destined to be a major star. As Janis came offstage to tumultuous applause, Clive Davis moved in and offered Big Brother a major contract with Columbia on the spot. His face fell when she told him that Big Brother had signed with a minor-league independent record company for only $100 for airfare home, after getting stranded in Chicago. Explaining his dilemma to Grossman, the manager commiserated and told Davis he would see what he could do to help.

Grossman had more than just a passing interest in capturing a piece of Big Brother and was astonished when he found out that the band's present manager, former Merry Prankster Julius Karpen, had refused to let Janis's brilliant set be filmed for ABC. Grossman knew that by capturing Janis and Big Brother's riveting performance on a network show the band would be catapulted to instant stardom. Finding Janis celebrating backstage, Grossman took her aside and offered to make her a star if he could represent her. After finding large loopholes in the earlier record deal, Janis and Big Brother decided to cast their lot with the quietly spoken New Yorker. They also agreed to overrule Karpen and perform a second unscheduled set, which would be filmed, the following night.

Albert Grossman was on the roll of a lifetime. Before returning to Davis with the good news, he signed up Steve Miller and Quicksilver Messenger Service. He also agreed to buy out Big Brother's old contract for $100,000. With a superstable of bands under his wing, Grossman returned to Clive Davis, demanding a $100,000 advance for the entire package of Big Brother, Steve Miller, Quicksilver, and Electric Flag.

While Davis and Grossman were locked in heated discussions, Capitol

Records moved in slyly and bought up record rights to Quicksilver and Steve Miller for six figures apiece. Things were now moving so fast that Davis agreed to spend $50,000 for Electric Flag. With the demand that Janis was now creating from rival record companies, Grossman had upped her price to $200,000; outmaneuvered, Davis had no alternative but to accept.

During the remainder of the festival, Grossman also managed to sign up the festival's other big new find, Jimi Hendrix, for $100,000 and then sold off his record rights to Warner Brothers. Bill Graham quietly watched the action, awed by the dizzying speed of the big gun's financial firepower in buying up the San Francisco bands, while carefully taking mental notes for future use. When he went in afterward to congratulate Grossman on his coup, Grossman threw him a scrap, offering the Fillmore sole rights to his new stable of bands.

Graham was ecstatic. He was now one of the big boys in the music business. From now on, he would be playing in the major leagues.

When Bill Graham returned from Monterey he plunged into his work with a renewed vigor. The megadeals he had seen at Monterey inspired him to work all hours of the day and night overseeing the Fillmore, which was soon to open six days a week. In order to cope with the larger audiences, he now booked shows at Winterland Auditorium, four blocks away, for Fridays and Saturdays, returning to the smaller Fillmore for the remainder of the week. He drove himself relentlessly and expected his staff to keep up.

"Bill was a slave driver," Jim Haynie said. "When we started working this deal with Winterland, Bill and I would take down all the light-show screens off the walls of the Fillmore after the show, roll them up, and carry them on our backs to Winterland across Geary Boulevard in the middle of the night. We didn't have a crew so, we had to do all the heavy stuff ourselves.

"Then, at the end of Saturday night's show, we would take them down from Winterland and carry them back to the Fillmore and put them back up. I was always the guy who climbed the twenty-foot A-ladder trying to hang those things, and Bill would be down at the bottom telling everyone what to do.

"One night I was up there and he said, 'Jim pull it up!' and nothing happened. When he looked up, I was fast asleep, with my legs entwined in the ladder. Bill screamed at me, 'Jim, wake up. What the fuck's going on here?' I told him, 'Bill, we've been awake now working for twenty-eight hours. I'm fucking tired.' And he said,'Well we've still got to do it. Let's do it.'

"Bill later told me that was the first time he had ever thought about how many hours we were putting in."

Exhausted and burned out, Haynie finally quit just before the Summer of Love, preferring the relative peace of being on the road with the Butterfield Blues Band to working around the clock, six days a week managing the Fillmore.

Graham's biggest problem in staging the extra summer shows was finding enough acts to play. There were a limited number of bands in San Francisco, and importing out-of-town musicians was expensive.

Bob Grossweiner, New York editor of the concert promotion trade magazine *Performance,* says that prior to Bill Graham, promoters relied on the Alan Freed or Dick Clark touring revues, which showcased up to ten acts performing their latest hits.

"That was basically the era where Bill Graham came in. He saw that there was a potential to have a music show in a venue on a weekly basis, but in those days he didn't have enough acts to fulfill his vision," Grossweiner explained.

"So what Bill did was bring in jazz and blues and R&B and mix it with rock on the same package. After a while he didn't need the jazz because there were enough new acts coming out of Britain."

Graham favored booking the hardworking blues acts for the Fillmore. Although these black musicians were largely unknown to the white audiences, their material had been the inspiration for many of the superior new rock bands like The Rolling Stones, The Yardbirds, and Cream. Never seeing the vast profits their blues songs were making for the young white bands, these bluesmen eked out a meager existence, living out of station wagons, often playing more than 300 nights a year.

Albert Grossman and guitarist Michael Bloomfield of the Butterfield Blues Band encouraged Graham to start booking blues artists. Graham was only too happy. He liked the music; besides, he could get away with paying low wages. In the first half of 1967, he presented Jimmy Reed, Otis Rush and his Chicago Blues Band, B. B. King, Chuck Berry, Howlin' Wolf, and Bo Diddley.

"I met one through the other, and it was a chain reaction," Graham said. "I tried to bring in as many of them as possible but not for their draw. These are the artists that made a lot of today's artists possible. If it wasn't for Muddy Waters, there may have not been an Eric Clapton.

"Some of them have been around for so many years that they wanted to make it because they saw Hoochie Coochie and the All Stars, who can't really play very well, have a hit. And they say, 'Why not us?'

"I liked them and I thought it was authentic music, but I also felt the public would appreciate it. I would not have brought a lot of this music in if I didn't think the audience would like it. In other words, you can't cram it down their throat. The draw was Big Brother."

Rolling Stone bassist Bill Wyman felt that Graham should not be credited as the first white promoter to showcase the blues. "We brought the blues back with many other sort of small acts in England and then brought it over to America," Wyman said. "It then started to get a little bit of acclaim over there so I think Bill was a late runner in that and I don't think he can accept any great credit for it. The people he used were not the blues artists that we admired as much as some of the others. We were more into Elmore James, Slim Harpo, and John Lee Hooker. He was more into the sixties blues artists, where we were into the fifties blues artists from Chicago."

Another solution to the shortage of bands was to seek new talent. As the Fillmore took off, Graham became inundated with tapes and photos from hopeful new bands all over California. He realized the need to find the next Jefferson Airplane or Grateful Dead, and started to actively search for new blood. He stopped holding his Tuesday-night black community shows and began open auditions instead, charging a $1 entrance fee. The auditions were always preceded by a game of basketball on the court he had built backstage. Carlos Santana and Tower of Power were discovered among the hundreds of other acts, which included magicians, an accordion player, and even a chamber-music quartet.

Graham developed a strict hierarchy among the bands playing the Fillmore, splitting the acts into three parts: headliners, second on the bill, and third-line bands. Status was dictated by their popularity and drawing power and, like any business, new bands would start at the bottom and have to work their way up until they were able to sell out the Fillmore.

"When you get down to it, the draw is what it's all about," Graham said. "A group is paid on the basis of what you think they'll draw into your ballroom. There are many groups who sell many albums, but for some reason don't draw in person. And it works the other way, too."

Chris Brooks, who was the first Fillmore publicist, remembers going to Mel's Drive-in to wind down with Graham and the other musicians after the shows.

"Bill would always sit there without saying much until the discussion turned to bands, which it always did. And he'd say, 'Oh, so-and-so, that's a good band—what's their draw? What do you think?' Then he'd start taking notes."

Graham soon developed a sixth sense in knowing which bands would sell out the Fillmore or Winterland; he rarely booked an unsuccessful show. When it came to booking acts, he proved more than a match for the tough veteran agents of the music business and their dirty ways of doing business.

"I was a promoter that they'd never met before," Graham explained. "This is a very tough business. A very hard business. A very dirty business sometimes."

Graham loved the sport of negotiating terms with band representatives who would demand their money up front and fight for the length and number of sets the musicians would play.

"It's like a fifteen-round championship fight when you face someone," Graham said. "At the beginning it's tap tap, a little waltz, and then later on you wrestle. At the beginning it's feigning, throwing a little jab. You don't throw the heavy punches because you are feeling each other out, you're sort of on the curb, you know."

However, Graham didn't always win every fight. He emerged a loser when he first booked Ike and Tina Turner into Winterland as a last-minute replacement for Pink Floyd, which had missed its flight to San Francisco.

"At that time Ike and Tina Turner were making $400 or $500 a night and I agreed on a price with their manager on the afternoon of the concert," said Graham. "Then a very ugly thing happened. At seven o'clock that night, I'm in Winterland, and the manager comes over, and she says, 'There's a little problem.'

"I ask her what it is and she tells me it's the price. I said, 'We agreed on a price, and Ike's signed the contract.' She said, 'That ain't Ike's signature, baby. He didn't sign it.' I said, 'Hey, you're talking to a graduate of the New York streets. You don't play that game. How do you want it?' "

But Graham was outflanked—the audience was already arriving at Winterland for the show—so he paid up the extra money. He later got his revenge when Ike and Tina Turner heard what had happened and apologized to Graham saying their manager had acted without their knowledge.

Graham truly established himself on a national scale when he brought the English invasion of bands to the West Coast. By carefully researching the music scene across the Atlantic, he was able to open the floodgates of opportunity to new English talent by exposing them to receptive American audiences for the first time. Among those he presented in 1967 included The Yardbirds, The Who, Eric Burdon & The Animals, Cream, Donovan, Pink Floyd, and Procul Harum.

After Janis Joplin's triumph at Monterey and the founding of his business relationship with her new manager, Albert Grossman, Graham warmly welcomed Big Brother and the Holding Company into the Fillmore fold. Apparently forgetting he had ever called Joplin "that screaming witch" when he ejected her physically from the Fillmore, Graham acted as if nothing had happened, prompting Janis to remark, "Oh, he likes us now. He's good to any group that's made it."

Big Brother drummer David Getz commented that Graham's change of face didn't surprise him at all.

"Bill was really into power," Getz remembers. "And if he needed you, the power would be transposed into charm and graciousness and helping you. Bending over backwards. If, at some point, he just decided that he didn't need you, he could just cut you in ribbons and throw you away like a piece of garbage."

With Big Brother now arguably the biggest of the San Francisco bands, Graham needed them and wooed Janis like an ardent lover, focusing on her strengths and her weaknesses.

"She was a very independent modern rock woman," Graham explained in a KSAN radio interview. "I'd met her masculine counterpoint in sixty-five, sixty-six, but I'd never met a female. As I got to know her better Janis was streets. She could be a hard chick. She could be a very soft lady. Very raucous and very much a child. Most women are all these facets.

"From the very first day until the last day that I knew her, Janis was nervous when she got near that stage in the sense that she wanted things to be right. When the monitors didn't work, you got some choice words from Janis."

In those days, each band was expected to play two forty-five-minute sets a night. The first, for what Graham called "the bowling-game youth movement," started at 8:00 and the second show, for the "heads and the in people," kicked off at 11:30 P.M. with the headliners going on stage at 12:30 A.M. With a stationmaster's pride in having his trains run on time, Bill Graham was fanatical about his shows running to schedule. With three bands playing two sets apiece, all it took was one late musician to completely wreck the whole evening. The problem was that he was dealing with musicians who were often drugged out and oblivious, and did not share his serious, punctual approach to the business.

Graham's professional credo dictated that if a band signed a contract, they showed up and played. To the acid-dropping, laissez-faire musicians of San Francisco, being on time didn't seem all that important compared to all the alluring distractions of being stars during the Summer of Love.

Bill Graham saw both the positive and negative effects of LSD and told Peter Stafford of *Crawdaddy* magazine that it had made musicians more serious about their music, but at the expense of professionalism.

"What's happened is that they've lost what we—say the straight man—consider discipline," he said. "With or without acid, the younger generation—of which I consider myself a part—we want to break away, we want to revolutionize, we want freedom, we want more expression. We don't want to look at clocks—but yet I have to stick with one thing because I'm involved with the other side. I'm the one who takes the person's money when they come to the box office.

"And so when the schedule says nine o'clock and eleven o'clock, at nine o'clock I want that musician on the stage. Not with a whip—there's a piece of paper, a contract. And they say, 'Why do we have to have a contract?' Well, I'm sorry we have to have paper, but it's for a guy like you who's irresponsible. Because you're serious about your music once you're onstage, but you may be at home watching a B-movie and going on your trip—and that may be more important than the audience.

"What the new musician refuses to admit is that he's a professional entertainer. They don't want to say that. They want to tell you, 'I'm an artist looking for myself. I'm searching for the truth, for reality. I want to share and relate to the audience.' 'Well, it's ten o'clock, baby, and the man says eight o'clock—and what are you relating?'

"So there's a need for responsibility—and what acid has done for some people is poof and joy and happiness. From where I sit, one of the tragedies of life is that you are never totally free."

If a musician was late to a gig, Bill Graham would get so emotionally worked up that he would start pacing up and down outside the Fillmore, waiting for the offender to arrive. When the tardy musician finally rolled up, Graham would throw a tantrum, chastising him in front of whoever happened to be around. Then the angry promoter would literally kick the poor man straight onstage to play.

"It took me years to realize that the man went onstage a nervous wreck," Graham said. "Then I finally found a simple solution. No matter how late they were, I'd wait for them but swallow my anger, and I'd say, 'Hello. Please can you get onstage as soon as possible?' But when they got off the stage, I'd let them have it."

The worst offenders were The Charlatans, a group of psychedelic cowboys and one of the first San Francisco bands. Led by George Hunter and Dan Hicks, the happy-go-lucky band had a love/hate relationship with Bill Graham.

At one Fillmore benefit, The Charlatans were to open the show, followed by Jefferson Airplane and Quicksilver Messenger Service. One by one, the band members casually drifted in. The last to arrive was George Hunter, who strolled in thirty minutes late, smoking a marijuana joint and walked straight onstage to the delight of the audience, before Graham could stop him.

"He took a puff and gazed at the audience, checking out the scene," Graham said. "At that time I was concerned with the law because they were trying to close us down by whatever means they could find. I ran onto the stage and said, 'George, are you crazy?' His reaction was so insane, and I saw that he was beyond reality, beyond any form of sanity.

"He just looked at me and said, 'What is it?'

"I said, 'Do you know where you're standing? You'll be discovered.'

"He looked at me and said, 'Oh.' Then he took the longest hit I've ever seen anybody take, dropped it on the floor, and put it out the way John Wayne did in his Westerns. Then he exhaled and walked off the stage."

Charlatan guitarist Mike Wilhelm said that Graham was always firing the band and telling them they would never work again. "Two weeks later, he'd forgotten all about it and was rebooking us," said Wilhelm.

If Graham took a schoolteacher approach at the Fillmore, there were many band members who enjoyed playing the role of brats, goading him deliberately to watch him explode. One of the worst offenders was Butterfield Blues Band guitarist, the late Michael Bloomfield, who had a unique relationship with the inflammable promoter, providing the perfect foil to Graham's histrionics.

"We thought he was demented when we first saw him running about and screaming and going crazy," Bloomfield said. "We thought it was a stagehand run amok and left to his devices.

"But gradually I realized this was his pattern. This was how he conducted himself. How he got off his steam. When you first see Bill do his thing, you think he's nuts. Then you realize that it's drama. It's heavy drama. It's studied. Bill was an actor, and this is his drama."

Bloomfield loved sitting in the dressing room at the Fillmore rolling up joints while Graham looked on disapprovingly.

"The idea was to get him crazy," Bloomfield said. "I would say something to piss him off, and he'd go crazy from just a little provocation. I'd stay completely unruffled and give him a little more. Then we would really start screaming. It was a sort of Jewish verbal gymnastics. We were arguing to argue. To fight. My fondest memories are of fights that I had with him. They were never serious, but an observer seeing it would think that there was real hate going on."

The hippie musicians were weary of Graham's sober-minded business approach to concerts; but when the big money began rolling in from record companies, they suddenly found themselves stars, having risen above the local community that spurned them.

"This thing had started off as this very free-form collective dance where there were no primary focus," said Chet Helms. "Jerry Garcia would lean offstage and say, 'Hey Joe, I haven't seen you in a couple of weeks. How's the old lady? Are the kids okay? It was that casual. Later you got the spotlight on Jerry Garcia's hand while he played his solo."

Helms compares the changes to early Greek theater, which started off as collective, free-form spiritual celebrations, but soon the audience was separated from performers by a high stage or proscenium arch, representing a window to Olympus through which the mortals observed the gods.

"Rock 'n' roll followed the same course," Helms explained. "When we started, rock 'n' roll was free-form, and it was not unusual for big snake dances with hundreds of people to spontaneously happen. As the stages got higher with their huge towering columns of speakers on either side, we re-created the Greek proscenium arch.

"All of a sudden we mere mortals are down here on the floor looking up to a six-foot stage to watch the gods perform. I liked low stages at the Avalon because they were more intimate, but Graham's stages just got larger and grander."

San Francisco–based writer Herbert Gold also saw the Fillmore audience change during the Summer of Love.

"The first people who went to the Fillmore were doing something original and expressing themselves freely," Gold said. "The second generation was following a lead, and the musicians became canonized. It became a pilgrimage, and you don't dance when you're visiting the saint's chapel. A lot of the fun went out of rock music."

As the stages got bigger, so did the egos of some of the bands who, using their new exalted status as stars, started becoming arrogant and demanded special treatment.

When The Yardbirds came to play the Fillmore in July, guitarist Jeff Beck announced that he was going to play only one set although their signed contract had been for two.

"I'll go on record as saying he's the only musician I ever touched physically," Graham admitted. "I had a major problem with Jeff Beck. He had that image of a superstar, and he acted that way. I was at the airport to meet him, and he said a few choice words. He just didn't want to do two sets."

Later, in the dressing room, Beck refused to do two sets and, as he was walking out of the dressing room with his guitar to go onstage, he called Graham a Yankee bastard.

"I just put him against the wall and said, 'Would you care to repeat that?' I told him,'If you don't do two sets, you can walk right now, and I'll tell the public exactly what the situation is. Why there's no show.'

"It was a game of bluff. He went to the top of the stairs and he changed his mind because he knew I was going to go ahead with it. He did the two sets."

By August the Summer of Love was in full swing. The Beatles took peace and love to a global level by recording their new single, "All You Need Is Love," in a London studio, witnessed by millions of satellite TV viewers all over the world. Jefferson Airplane had also broken through internationally with "White Rabbit," their thinly disguised ode to psychedelia, while thousands of people, seeking utopia, arrived in San Francisco each week.

A *Time* magazine reporter sent to San Francisco to investigate what was going on literally ran into Bill Graham while trying to gain free entrance to the Fillmore for his story. Lawyer Brian Rohan was outside the box office to witness the confrontation.

"The guy says, 'I'm from *Time* magazine,' and whips out his card," said Rohan.

"Bill Graham took the card, holds it up, and does his best John Garfield stare at the thing. He tears it down one side. He turns it over and tears it down the other side. He throws it over his shoulder and says, 'I don't give a fuck who you are, man. Go back to the end of the line.'

"I said, 'Bill, it's *Time* magazine.' He says, 'Who needs *Time*—they need us.' "

As the summer wore on, the spirit of the Haight developed sinister overtones as the hippies moved from marijuana and LSD into harder drugs like methedrine and heroin. More than half the hippies in Haight-Ashbury were now reported to be shooting methedrine and then softening the comedown with heroin. To finance their expensive new drug habits, many turned to crime. Not long after one LSD dealer killed another in an argument over a drug deal, guns became standard tools of survival in the Haight drug culture.

On September 8, after six sold-out nights at the Fillmore by the English supergroup Cream, Bill Graham wound up his six-nights-a-week summer program and returned to weekends only. A month later, the chief of the State Narcotics Bureau personally led a raid on The Grateful Dead's house at 710 Ashbury. They busted Bob Weir, Pig Pen, and other members of the Dead family. The message from the authorities was loud and clear.

On October 6, 1967, the first anniversary of the law making LSD illegal, community leaders organized a special ceremony called The Death of Hippie, declaring the flower-power movement a failure.

Bill Graham, too, decried the "negativity," "defeatism," and "bitterness" that had crept into the San Francisco scene.

"The flowers wilted and the scene changed," Graham said with more than a hint of cynicism. "People reverted back to a way of life that always was before the disappointment by the flower generation."

6

Getting Down to Business

The Summer of Love may have been declared officially dead and buried in San Francisco, but elsewhere it was still very much alive. There was a demand in many other cities to re-create the San Francisco experience and, as a result, many hip young capitalists heeded the call, eager to seize the opportunity.

In the fall of 1967, Graham was hired by the O'Keefe Center in Toronto to stage a full week of San Francisco dance concerts, giving Canada its first taste of acid rock. To help stage the show, featuring The Grateful Dead and Jefferson Airplane, Graham hired Sensefex, a small New York–based company run by a group of former drama students. Their only previous experience in the concert business had been designing disco dances and fashion shows, complete with strobes and flashing lights. On arrival in Toronto, Sensefex lighting director Joshua White and his partners John Morris and Kip Cohen met with Bill Graham for a briefing.

"I thought Bill was the most insane human being I had ever met in my life," Morris remembers. "The first thing I remember is his face, which is not the most beautiful thing in the world. But the strength and passion of that face. They literally locked Bill and me into a room with each other for forty-eight hours and just had us talk. We understood each other instantly, although we were total opposites. I had been involved in a lot of theater in New York and knew production. Our love of the theater was the basis of our relationship in the beginning."

The big problem facing White and Morris was how to transform the formal O'Keefe Theater, with its seats, balcony, and stage, into a replica of the much smaller and more intimate Fillmore Ballroom. The Sensefex team discovered they were to work alongside Headlights, the Fillmore's resident light show operated by Jerry Abrams and Glenn McKay, who were there to demonstrate their new psychedelic art form.

"I thought all those people from San Francisco were supposed to love each other, but the fact is that these two guys hated each other and were feuding," White said. "We befriended Glenn McKay, who was this big, wide-open hippie with a ponytail, because he didn't treat us like we were 'those uptight' New York people."

"At that time there was this ridiculous rhetoric that music should be free and anyone with long hair was good and anyone with short hair was bad and cops were pigs. It was a very paranoid and highly ritualized time, and much less loose than people think.

"Bill Graham was free of that and was not caught up in the scene. He understood the music and how to put on a wonderful show, and he did. He was not wrapped up in the rhetoric. He was older, and he had a clear vision of what was good. He had wonderful instincts, and as a showman, he was a genius."

To publicize the O'Keefe concert, Graham helped Morris organize a free concert in a Toronto park for Jefferson Airplane and The Grateful Dead. It drew 52,000 people, an event which marked their first collaboration.

After working with Graham and seeing him weave his magic in the O'Keefe Theater, the Sensefex team decided to change direction and leave disco behind forever.

"I was just sucked in," White said. "I was sucked into the music of the Airplane and the Dead. I was sucked into the light show. I looked at it and said, 'This is good, but I could do this better.' And all the people who were part of my disco company felt the same way."

After the last show, Graham invited Morris back to San Francisco with him to help put the Fillmore Auditorium on a stronger business footing. Morris readily agreed and moved into Graham's Washington Street house for a few weeks, immersing himself in the financial tangle of the Fillmore operation.

"At that point, there was no organization," Morris said. "He didn't even have a DBA (Doing Business As—a business–tax license]. He was running it with cash out of his desk. I went to his lawyer, Bill Coblentz, and said, 'This is madness. There's no company. There's no corporation. There's no taxes. There's no nothing.' He agreed, but he couldn't get Graham organized, either.

"It was pass them in, pass them out. It wasn't done that way to bury tons of cash. It was done because that was the way it was done. Finally we hauled Graham into Coblentz's office and made him set up a business structure to form a corporation. He was delighted once we'd done it, and he left the office saying, 'Well, that was easy wasn't it?' "

During his stay on the West Coast, Morris became one of Graham's closest and most trusted associates, and they became firm friends. One particular night, the two men were walking home from the Fillmore, with Graham carrying the night's box-office takings in a plain brown paper bag, which he used to call his "Polish briefcase." Suddenly an attacker leaped out of the shadows brandishing a gun and demanded the money.

"Bill just told him, 'Fuck you, get outta here,' " Morris remembered. "Wouldn't even give the guy a quarter. The guy was stoned, and he just turned tail and ran. Then we went for a cup of coffee in a Zims and we had a really great waitress, like in *Five Easy Pieces*. It was about 3:00 A.M. and we had our coffee and breakfast, and we went back to his house to go to sleep.

"About an hour later, I'm awakened by Bill, standing stark naked in the doorway of my guest room shouting, 'John, have you got the bag? Oh, shit, I left it in the restaurant.'

"We got dressed at nine hundred miles per hour, hopped in the car and drove to Zims. The same waitress was there, and she pulls the bag out from behind the counter. She had no clue that there was about sixty thousand dollars in that bag. Bill was so relieved he pulled out a one hundred dollar bill and gave it to her."

After Morris finished whipping the Fillmore organization into shape, Graham asked him to stay on to become Jefferson Airplane's tour manager. He was put in charge of accompanying the anarchic acid-rock band on its first national tour. At this time, the only venues available for staging rock shows were the small clubs, college auditoriums, and the new ballrooms which were modeled after the Fillmore. There were no stadiums, and so far, few arenas had been used for rock concerts. It was during this tour that he first met the new breed of young promoters who were beginning to surface throughout America.

"It was an era of hip-capitalism," Morris said. "During that whole era, there were ballrooms and people trying to do ballroom-type things. The scale was much smaller than today, and we were playing two thousand to three thousand people. The interesting thing is that most of those early promoters are still there today."

In those pioneering days, the young promoters, some using proceeds from dealing dope as start-up money, began staking their territory in the new frontier of rock performance. Unintentionally, the young impresarios were dividing America into concert fiefdoms, a foundation which would enable future concert empires to generate untold billions of dollars over the next quarter century.

One such fledgling promoter was Larry Magid, a music-loving student at Philadelphia's Temple University who earned his concert-commission spurs booking bands for fraternity parties. Successful in booking concerts for his and other colleges, he readily quit Temple in his junior year when he was offered a job in New York by the General Artists Agency.

"To me, the American dream was getting paid for having fun," Magid told the *Philadelphia Inquirer* in 1988 in an interview celebrating his twentith anniversary in the music business. "This was a time when an act like Cream would get $1,750 to play a week at the Café Au Go Go in Greenwich Village. My company was so busy booking the big established acts that they weren't watching or understanding the new rock acts."

Like Bill Graham, Magid saw the enormous potential of staging ballroom rock concerts on a regular weekly basis. Late in 1967 he quit his job, returning to Philadelphia to start his own psychedelic ballroom, the Electric Factory, located in an abandoned tire warehouse. After painting the inside black and setting up a row of open coffins along one wall, the Electric Factory opened in February 1968 with a weekend of Chambers Brothers shows for which the group was paid $2,500 for seven sellout shows.

"Back then, concert promotion was a real hands-on business," Magid remembered. "We'd be out on the streets hanging posters, fielding phone calls, selling tickets from the office, and moving tickets between our outlets at boutiques and record stores," recalled Magid, who used a picture of Benjamin Franklin as the ballroom's official logo.

Five years earlier, in Washington, D.C., Jack Boyle, a federal government systems analyst, won $1,000 in a poker game and used the money to buy a share in a neighborhood bar. Within two years, Boyle owned three bars outright and in 1965 at the Cellar Door Bar staged his first concert with Fats Domino, thus launching his highly successful Cellar Door promotion company.

In Boston, ambitious university student Don Law was busy setting up his version of the Fillmore, aptly named the Boston Tea Party. Law had grown up in the music business; his father, Don Law, Sr., had produced Gene Autry's "Rudolph, the Red-Nosed Reindeer" as well as historic recordings by blues legend Robert Johnson and country stars Johnny Cash and the Carter Family. In the late 1960s Don Law began his reign as the king of Boston concert promotion; it continues to this day.

Rock 'n' roll may have made great inroads into the rest of America, but somehow, when bands went on the road, they ignored the South. A young Atlanta promoter named Alex Cooley, who loved the new acid rock coming out of the West Coast, decided to put the South on the American rock map.

Cooley, who had owned a pizzeria, started promoting doo-wop groups in the early 1960s, finding it more lucrative than selling pizza.

Cooley discovered acid rock when he attended the Miami Pop Festival, one of the many festivals to follow in the wake of Monterey Pop. Energized and highly impressed by the event, and in true '60s can-do fashion, Cooley decided to stage his own festival in Atlanta.

The result was the Atlanta Pop Festival, which featured Big Brother and the Holding Company, Led Zeppelin, The Grateful Dead, and Blood Sweat and Tears.

"We didn't know what we were doing," said Cooley, who persuaded seventeen of his friends to invest in the festival. "Looking back on it now, I'm dumbfounded that we pulled it off. It was a huge undertaking, and we borrowed and hocked and did anything we had to do to get the money to do it."

The Atlanta Pop Festival drew 100,000 people. After all the expenses were paid, Cooley and his friends made $16,000.

"Back in those days, it was bad karma to make money, so we turned around and did a free festival in a park with The Grateful Dead using money we had made from the festival," he said.

After Atlanta Pop, Cooley followed Bill Graham's example of staging the simpler and more manageable one-nighters in ballrooms around Atlanta.

Slowly but surely the American concert cake was carved up—the Midwest to the Belkin brothers, Jules and Michael, and Denver to Barry Fey. In the vital Los Angeles market, former William Morris agent Jim Rissmiller and his friend Steve Wolf started a concert promotion business covering Southern California called Wolf & Rissmiller.

Many of the future leaders of the music industry began their careers promoting college concerts in the late '60s, learning the ropes by trial and error. One promising entrepreneur was Howie Klein, a student at the State University of New York at Stony Brook. As chairman of the college's student activities board, Klein had his own radio show and was in charge of booking bands when they came to town. One of the first bands he promoted in the small college hall at Stony Brook was Jefferson Airplane. He booked them for a mere $1,200 before their price went sky-high with the success of their breakthrough album, *Surrealistic Pillow*.

"I was playing all these bands on my radio show that were considered really radical," said Klein, who is now vice president of Sire, Madonna's record label.

They were bands like Jefferson Airplane, The Grateful Dead, Country Joe and the Fish, Big Brother and the Holding Company, The Who, and Pink Floyd. The students hated them because they were very underground and avant garde. It was way before they became mainstream."

Klein met Bill Graham for the first time during the Airplane's Stony Brook concert. Klein had a great rapport with Graham and the Airplane members, and they invited him to see their show the following night at the Café Au Go Go. Klein decided to drop a tab of acid that had been given to him by LSD guru Timothy Leary, initiating his first trip at the Jefferson Airplane gig.

"I took it that night and saw the band play," Klein said. "Then I went out with Bill Graham and some of the members of the band to this Jewish delicatessen on Second Avenue. I was just totally stoned, and all these waiters were like old Yiddish theater actors, and there were several characters. I was just so blown out of my mind that I thought Bill Graham was just the greatest guy in the world. His brains were coming out of his ears at the deli."

A few months later, Klein went to San Francisco with his girlfriend and made a surprise visit to the Fillmore. Graham, who loved to keep his finger on the youth pulse to discover breaking trends, was delighted to see Klein and treated him like a long-lost friend. He showed him around the Fillmore and invited him to come to some shows.

"I maintained a friendship and a great respect for Bill ever after," said Klein.

This relationship was characteristic of Graham. One of Graham's great strengths was in recognizing and nurturing young talent. He would befriend and encourage many young men on the way up the music-business ladder, giving many their first break working at the Fillmore.

While many enterprising concert promoters had by now staked out their individual territories throughout the United States, New York, the center of the American music business, lay virtually unclaimed. Veteran promoter Sid Bernstein had been the Big Apple's leading promoter for nearly a decade, but by 1967 he was trying to emulate his hero Brian Epstein and move into management. Bernstein was already legendary in the music business for being the first to bring the Beatles to America, staging their historic Carnegie Hall concert in February 1964.

"When I brought the Beatles here first in 1964, I paid them six thousand five hundred dollars for two shows in one day," Bernstein remembers.

The following year I paid them one hundred eighty thousand dollars for just one show at Shea Stadium, which was the highest pay ever for a performer in the history of show business, and they only played twenty-eight minutes. When people saw the figures they realized it was suddenly a big-money industry, and the gold rush started.

"Prior to that, any kid fresh out of school could go in and hang up his banner to declare himself a promoter. Then it became a very money-oriented profit center, and a lot of the fun went out of it. The opportunities were no longer open for anyone who wanted to get in the field because alliances were made between promoters and agents and agencies. It became like a fiefdom. People were allotted territories to promote, and from there it all just fell into place."

Bernstein, who has observed the growth of the concert business for almost three decades, credits Bill Graham as the father of modern concert promotion.

"Northern California became his territory, and he earned it. He was a pioneer who started out in a very small way with his young secretary who became his wife. They carved out a niche for themselves in San Francisco and that became an important area. He nurtured it and was joined by this new group of entrepreneurs but he was always right there in the forefront."

In the mid-sixties Bernstein was the main promoter in New York, holding regular concerts at the Academy of Music on 14th Street, the New York Paramount, and Carnegie Hall. At the height of his promoting career he discovered a group called The Rascals and tried to turn them into "the American Beatles." Bernstein became totally involved in managing The Rascals and abandoned his position as New York's foremost promoter, leaving the city's lucrative concert scene wide open for the taking.

Among the several promoters eager to move in and claim the New York crown was Ron Delsener, who was strategically well placed as official promoter for Central Park's summer rock concerts.

"When I moved out, Delsener moved up," said Bernstein. "New York almost became his exclusive territory by virtue of the fact that he had Central Park as a venue," Bernstein said.

But Delsener's reign as the concert king of New York was short-lived once Bill Graham came to town.

After finishing the Jefferson Airplane's national tour, John Morris decided to remain in New York to investigate opportunities as a promoter. He hooked up with Joshua White and booked a week of shows in Mineola, Long Island, in December 1967 featuring Ravi Shankar, Frank Zappa, Vanilla Fudge, and the newly formed Joshua Light Show in a celebration of light and sound.

A month later White and Morris collaborated with the owners of *Crawdaddy* magazine to stage a series of rock shows at the Anderson Theater on Manhattan's Lower East Side. They all pooled their resources; Morris staged the shows, White ran the light show, and *Crawdaddy* booked the concerts. The only problem was that the Anderson Theater was financed by Tony Lech, a New Yorker who had no practical knowledge of the music business. Lech—who fancied himself as a "New York tough guy," owned a string of gay bars and reportedly kept a loaded gun behind his bar—operated the theater with his right-hand man, Jerry Pompili.

"It was a really hairy operation and done on a shoestring," John Morris remembered.

"At the shows we put on at the Anderson, everything that could possibly go wrong, did. So we had to fix it. We had tons of energy but very little money and an old disintegrating theater to work with. But we got the acts and drew people. It was East Village sixty-eight-anarchy."

Disillusioned with the lack of professionalism and stability in New York, Morris decided that what the city needed was the magic of Bill Graham.

"It was a constant campaign to get Bill into New York," said Morris. "I had found working with Bill was exciting and interesting and selfishly I wanted him to come to New York and set up a theater which I could run. Bill had a financial base in the Fillmore, and in those days most of rock 'n' roll did not have any money for investment. What we needed was cash and Graham's drive."

Insistent, Morris phoned Graham and his wife Bonnie again and again in an effort to persuade them to expand the Fillmore operation to New York. He emphasized that the city was wide open for a real concert scene, and tempted them with tales of big money to be made promoting shows. Turning the screws a little harder, he reminded the ex–New Yorker that the city was in his blood, and it was his duty to come back.

Faced with the real possibility of failure, Bill Graham was skeptical and more than a little fearful of extending his rock empire across the country. His dismal past experiences as a struggling actor in New York had been unpleasant and frustrating, and he questioned the wisdom of a move east, especially as things were going so well for him in San Francisco. But the gambler in Graham was restless, and little by little, as Morris increased the pressure, Graham became more and more interested.

Finally Graham agreed to fly to New York on a reconnaissance mission, with the prospect of leasing the Anderson Theater in mind. Morris and White arranged for him to attend a sold-out Big Brother and the Holding Company show at the Anderson Theater. To reel him in they staged a brilliantly planned stunt as the coup d'état of their campaign.

In order to keep the evening flowing and the audience amused during the interminably long set changes, the Joshua Light Show rear-projected a curtain of deep blue light onto the audience. The calming lights effectively masked the backstage set changes, although the audience was perfectly visible from the stage. That night, as Janis Joplin and Big Brother were preparing to take the stage, Morris led Graham out to the middle of the stage so he could see the packed New York audience hanging from the rafters.

"I think there and then he decided to come to New York," White said. "He realized it was doable."

A meeting was then hastily arranged between Graham and Lech at a Greenwich Village restaurant to discuss a possible partnership.

"I met Bill over a bowl of soup at the Tin Angel on Bleecker Street," remembers Jerry Pompili, who attended the meeting with Lech. "Tony had no idea who Bill was or what he wanted. Bill came in. We all shook hands. Bill ordered some soup, and he started talking. Tony never looked up from his plate."

After Graham put his cards on the table and proposed they go into partnership at the Anderson, Lech went berserk.

"Tony finished his soup, looked up at Bill, and started screaming, like he was doing a bad Jimmy Cagney impression from a third rate gangster flick," Pompili said. " 'Who da fuck do you think you are coming into town and telling me that we're gonna to do business together?'

"Tony went on like this for three or four minutes. He was making no sense whatsoever, but he was making a lot of noise. Bill never batted an eye. When Tony finished his outburst, Bill stood up, took all the papers and legal pads, and put them into the little leather case he used to carry and said, 'Hey, I'm sorry you feel that way. Thank you for your time.' He shook my hand very politely and said, 'Good-bye,' and he left.

"I turned to Tony, who was still ranting and raving, and said, 'Something tells me you just made a mistake dealing with this man the way you did.' Tony said, 'Fuck him. Who needs him?' "

Now that the Anderson was no longer a possibility, Graham's only other alternative was to set up his own theater. Morris suggested the semivacant Village Theater, across from the road from the Anderson. Formerly the Loew's Commodore East Movie Theater, in the 1930s it had housed the Yiddish Theater of New York and had also been used as a meeting place by radical political groups.

At this time, the Village Theater was used only when New York promoter Gary Kurfist, later manager of the Talking Heads and the B-52's, held occasional rock shows. The monstrously imposing corner building was run-down and in urgent need of repair. Yet, when Graham visited it, he saw a classically beautiful movie palace, similar to the ones he had loved going to every Saturday as a kid growing up in the Bronx. He marveled at the walls hung with red velvet, the mirrored walls, the double balcony graced by a huge chandelier.

The asking price for the Village Theater was $400,000. Working closely with John Morris, Graham set up a cartel of music-business investors to raise the cash, a partnership which included Albert Grossman and his partner Burt Block, promoter Ron Delsener and the broker for the building, Mike Rogers. Graham would hold 75 percent of the shares, dividing the remainder among the others.

"We had lots of meetings deciding how to do it," remembers John Morris, who already had been appointed general manager.

At one marathon investment meeting in Delsener's Upper East Side office, Bill Graham told the others in a highly emotional speech exactly how the new Fillmore East would operate.

Morris remembers: "Delsener was listening carefully but kept very quiet. Then in a very gentlemanly way he said, 'I have just come to a decision. I was here before you guys came with this project, and I think I will probably be here afterwards. So if nobody minds, I think I'll back out of my involvement.'

"I think Ron suddenly saw the egos involved were going to make his life miserable, and he stepped back from it. Now, every once in a while when I see Ron, we still laugh about that because he was dead on. He was there before and he is still there, and he has had a much easier life for not getting involved."

The remaining partners agreed to put up $40,000 each, leaving Graham to raise the rest. Later he would claim not to be able to remember where he had found the money for his share of the down payment.

By the beginning of February, the contracts were signed. White, along with most of the Anderson Theater staff, including Jerry Pompili, told Lech what he could do with his job and jumped ship over to Bill Graham. From then on it was a race against time to ready the theater for the March 8 opening night.

Leaving Bonnie in San Francisco, Bill Graham moved temporarily to New York to inspire his new troops with enthusiasm, standing over them doggedly as they worked around the clock cleaning, painting, and restoring the theater to its former glory.

"Bill held it all together and was the person that made you want to do it," White said. "We all knew that if we did our part, Bill was going to do his, which was to run it well. We knew he wasn't going to rip us off, and he never did."

Most of the newly hired staff were New York University teachers and theater majors as well as friends of White, Morris, and Cohen from their days at Carnegie Tech. Considering the sorry state of New York theater at the time, the graduates were delighted to be working.

"You had people with great theater skills and no theater to work in," says Joshua White. "So you ended up with a work force that was well skilled beyond what they were doing. I mean, playwrights and filmmakers were working as stagehands."

For his first New York show, Graham chose Janis Joplin and Big Brother and the Holding Company, with singer Tim Buckley and bluesman Albert King as support. He invited the cream of New York's music industry to attend, planning a show that would establish him as *the* New York impresario, like his hero Sol Hurok had been so many years before.

Just hours before the opening, Graham was forced to change the name of the theater, Bill Graham Presents at the Village Theater, after facing legal threats from the former owner. On the spur of the moment, he decided to name it Fillmore East.

On the grand opening night, Albert Grossman's newly hired accountant Vincent Fusco arrived early with his wife. Backstage pass in hand, Fusco noticed that the box office was still being painted; circling it nervously was Bill Graham.

While the couple awaited entrance to the theater, Graham suddenly announced that everyone, with the exception of crew, musicians, and pregnant women, was to vacate the premises immediately.

"He then aimed his flashlight right in my eyes, shouting, 'Who the fuck are you, my friend?' " Fusco recalled.

"Flushed in panic and not knowing if my capacity with Albert was of merit, I pointed at my wife, who was eight months pregnant with my son. Without missing a beat, he instructed the ushers and security people that we were okay."

The headlining Big Brother and the Holding Company, which was at the height of its success, was upset as Graham insisted on nickel-and-diming them by paying them the same as a second on the bill.

"We opened the Fillmore East and played a very significant part in him getting established in New York," said Big Brother's David Getz.

This was the biggest event in his career and was when he went from being just a Bay Area promoter to being a national figure. He always liked to get us for the most propitious concerts he would be doing and then pay us the least possible amount of money."

The opening night's concert was a sensation, acclaimed enthusiastically by the New York music establishment and the press. *Variety* gave the show a glittering review, saying that the New York rock scene had made a great leap forward. Bill Graham had returned to New York. Neither would ever be the same again.

During the next few weeks Bill Graham became truly "bi-coastal," shuttling between New York and San Francisco at least once every week to emcee as many of his shows as possible. He cultivated the image of the jet-setting impresario and even went to the trouble of having a double-dialed watch custom designed so he always knew the time at both his Fillmores. It was a symbol he loved showing off to reporters and soon became his personal trademark.

Inexhaustible, Graham reveled in catching the "red-eye" flight to New York and then putting in a full day's work. Functioning on pure adrenaline, he felt invincible, driving himself beyond the limits of a normal man, using prolonged periods of work like a drug.

"Everybody used to talk about David Frost, but Bill invented the shuttle and he loved every minute of it," said John Morris. "Whoosh . . . I'll be here one minute and there the next.

"The man's energy was phenomenal in good ways and bad. I believe Bill was a destructive person to himself."

Phil Elwood noted, "Bill was basically driven. I've known a few people in my life who almost took a pride in how much they drove themselves. He reveled in it.

"There were the Fillmores and Bill and his watch with East Coast and West Coast time. That was very much a part of his image then. I think Bill rather enjoyed his ascension into the deity of show business."

The *New York Daily News* visited the Fillmore East during its first few months to investigate what was happening to "a part of Manhattan that has always contributed more than its share of color to the New York scene" with its Jewish delicatessens and Ukrainian meeting halls.

"When a performer is working out at the Fillmore East, the whole place vibrates visually and physically like an earthquake under a light-bulb factory. Only those with strong stomachs and stronger eardrums can survive the exposure," the newspaper said.

The future of the Fillmore East looked to be in jeopardy when Martin Luther King, Jr. was assassinated in Memphis on April 4, 1968, sending a wave of sporadic rioting throughout urban America. There were fears that violence could flare up in the East Village. Graham, who was in San Francisco, left it up to John Morris to decide whether to go ahead with a scheduled Who concert the following night.

Morris called a meeting with Pete Townshend and The Who's management to discuss what action to take.

"We were of two minds," Morris said. "In the end, Pete said, 'I think we should go ahead. He swayed everyone and said the people need a place to let it out and a place to go."

During the meeting, Townshend spoke passionately about the stupidity of violence. Morris challenged him on The Who's violent stage act, in which instruments were smashed up and destroyed during the climax. The serious guitarist thought for a while and then announced that from then on he intended to cut out any stage violence, assuring a more peaceful performance.

That night The Who's amps were set up near the Fillmore's $6,000 rear-projection screen. Their set started on a restrained note, reflecting the tension in the air following the assassination. But that soon changed.

"I was standing in the wings, and all of a sudden Pete turned around and headed for the amps," Morris said. "He jammed his guitar into one of the amps and I just went, 'Oh, Jesus!' Then he dove in between the amps to save the screen. I started screaming, 'What are you doing?'

Then Pete started charging the amps and damned near took my hand off as he swung the guitar at the amps.

"I had to sit there behind those damn amps while he was attacking them and try and stop them going through the expensive screen. He was a performer, and that was it. When things hit a certain level, all of the nonviolence went right out the window."

After the King assassination, East Village nightlife ground to a halt during that long hot summer of 1968. Graham told his staff not to worry, saying he would ride it out. Due to lack of business that first summer, the Fillmore was seldom open. To the press, Graham accounted for the closures by claiming that he was taking a well-earned rest.

"Even during those dark days Bill never lost his vision," said Joshua White. "That was the key to the man. He had the bravery and the presence of mind, and the cash, to stay with it. And it made all the difference because by the following winter we were up and running, and it just got better and better."

7

Laying Down the Ground Rules

In the months leading up to the opening of the Fillmore East, Bill Graham had embarked on a campaign to establish himself as a major figure in the music business, using the trade press as his platform. Within that reactionary industry, Graham was now recognized as the driving force in the new hippie music capital of the world. He now possessed enough clout to air his views in the widely read music bible, *Variety*.

Under the headline "Rock Impresario Sez Concert Field Must Cast Off Disk Jockey Influence," Graham called for an end of the Dick Clark–style musical caravan tours. He raged at the current fashion of having amiable radio deejays emcee shows, saying they were an insult to good musicians and should be "barred from the concert field."

Flying directly in the face of the record industry, Graham advised groups to stop trying to produce hit singles and albums and instead to concentrate on creating real music. Graham's ongoing internal battle between his idealism and his craving for money came to the fore as he attacked the "chrome plating" and "commercialism" that seeped into the business while conceding that musicians needed money to survive. Urging them not to sacrifice music for wealth, Graham counseled, "Earnings will follow if good music is created consistently." In order to avoid pigeonholing himself as simply a rock promoter, Graham emphasized his current eclectic shows with jazz greats Count Basie and Charles Lloyd and the flamenco guitarist Manitas de Plata.

"He feels concerts with different groups help create wider audiences for each field," explained *Variety,* which noted admiringly that Graham did not need any radio or newspaper advertising to sell his shows. "His greatest reliance is on posters designed by his wife Bonnie. Posters of next week's bill are given out free, and they find their way all over the country."

Readers were also informed that Graham maintained a drug-free establishment. "As far as turn-ons are concerned they're not permitted," wrote *Variety.* "If a customer who pays $3 a head must indulge, there is a barrel of Golden Delicious apples in the lobby and customers may have as many as they wish."

But if Graham's California audience appreciated the free apples and the warm communal atmosphere of the ballroom, his grittier New York audience was much more demanding.

"The Fillmore East was theater with a capital T," said Joshua White. "Bill's creativity in New York was different than his creativity in California. In San Francisco it was very spiritual, and they would play basketball games and do wonderful things. In New York he channeled his creativity into showmanship."

To Graham, the Fillmore East symbolized a new world of potentials and the insight and teamwork of John Morris and Joshua White breathed life and form into his ideas.

"He knew that he could tell us what he wanted done and when he came back there it was ready for him," White said. "Then he could make those finite adjustments that are so beautiful when things are together."

There existed a keen rivalry with the West Coast staff who, lacking the theatrical training of their New York counterparts, possessed a much more laid-back attitude to deadlines.

"Their priorities were different," said White. "Bill was absolutely hands-on at the Fillmore Auditorium, but because we were good, he was able to be less hands-on with us.

"Once he wanted something special for the Airplane, and we suggested building a giant cutout of an airplane that takes off from behind the drums set and splits in half when it goes over the balcony. One half goes all the way to the back of the balcony while the other goes to the back of the orchestra, accompanied by bright headlights and giant sound effects. Bill loved the idea, and we made it happen."

In New York Graham began to fall under the influence of Albert

Grossman, who was starting to make his presence felt at the Fillmore East. Once Grossman even visited the Fillmore East behind Bill Graham's back, called the staff together, and told them, "This place is about money, not music."

Grossman, nicknamed "The Large Gray Cloud" for his long gray hair, great bulk, and understated—but at times menacing—presence, gave Graham a master class in the music business, at a price.

"Albert was a big cheese when Bill was just small fry," said singer Nick Gravenitis, who was a close friend of Grossman. "Bill had to be broken into the New York scene and Albert did that. I know that Albert always kept the upper hand with Bill, and whatever lessons he learned in business didn't come cheap. Business is business.

"I remember once we were talking about Graham and Albert said, 'Nick, I've got him so bad even you'd feel sorry for him.' Albert chewed Bill up pretty good when he came to the Fillmore East and I'm sure that he had to sign deals and make alliances that were not advantageous to him. He had no choice because he wasn't a big guy yet."

When in New York but not at the Fillmore East, Graham was most likely to be found hanging out in Grossman's office. "They were very close," said Lee Blumer, who was Grossman's secretary before she came to work at the Fillmore East. "Bill just went there to sit at the foot of the master and absorb everything he could."

Grossman's right-hand man Vinnie Fusco, whom Graham used to affectionately call "Albert Grossman's illegitimate son," claims that the promoter and the manager raised arguing to a science.

"Bill was good because he could get into tirades and bring in all this historical stuff," said Fusco. "He'd talk about German history, bringing in wars and battles and political events from two centuries ago to get his point over. Whereas every time Albert would want to back something up, he'd make up a college study on the spot to suit his purposes. They were quite a pair."

By taking over the Fillmore and providing New York with a regular rock music venue, Graham provided the last piece needed to create a coast-to-coast rock-touring circuit. As in the old days of vaudeville, bands toured America within an established circuit. This new network of promoters consisted of the Fillmore East in New York, the Kinetic Playground in Chicago, Philadelphia's Electric Factory, the Boston Tea Party, the Grande Ballroom in Detroit, the Fillmore Auditorium in San Francisco and a few college gigs to plug in gaps in between. According to *Performance* magazine editor Bob Grossweiner, "The booking agents and the record companies started to rely on these guys to help promote their acts."

Fusco, in charge of Albert Grossman's heavyweight stable of acts—including Dylan, Joplin, and the Butterfield Blues Band—said all the new promoters were also managing their own bands so there were reciprocal arrangements made through the circuit to package acts together.

"It meant that we had the clout of being able to trade off our acts and build them," Fusco said. "So if Bill Graham was managing Jefferson Airplane, Aaron Russo had It's a Beautiful Day and so on, we could set up tours between us and have a number of shows to offer."

But the man who pulled all the strings together and laid the foundations for the modern concert tour was balding, short and overweight Frank Barsalona, a man who did not fit any rock 'n' roll stereotype. Starting off in the music business as Sid Bernstein's assistant at G.A.C. (General Artists Corporation), Barsalona was one of the few people in the agency to recognize the potential of rock music. After helping organize Bernstein's Beatles tour, Barsalona became increasingly frustrated at his superiors' failure to take rock seriously. The older booking agents at G.A.C. and William Morris were more used to handling big bands and had no idea how to treat or package rock 'n' roll musicians. They would book a group in Carnegie Hall one week and then ship it out to San Francisco the next without any advance publicity or radio promotion.

"The way that the agency treated rock performers was a crime," said Barsalona. "If you were young and had a hit record, to them you had no talent; you were just lucky and manufactured, and they would treat you like that. Rock really was the asshole, it really was."

Rolling Stone Bill Wyman remembers the first two Stones tours as disasters. "It was all done through G.A.C. and those kinds of agencies and they weren't the right thing for us," said Wyman. "They were very established big organizations, so we believed that was the way it was done in America. But we learned our lesson.

"It was useless. We found ourselves booked into places who'd never heard of us. No promotion. Nothing. The local radio stations didn't know us or play our music, and it was a joke."

Finally Barsalona decided to strike out on his own and formed his own agency, Premier Talent, just in time to connect with the British rock invasion of the late sixties.

"Frank became powerful in the business because he was the first to sign the British acts and realize that they were going to be a big force in America," said Bernstein. "That was his great strength, and he was very creative in that area."

In the early days, Barsalona was the sole American agent specializing in rock. Among his first clients were Jimi Hendrix, Joe Cocker, and The Who.

"Premier quickly devised a simple but effective formula for large-scale rock success," Dave Marsh wrote in his book *Born to Run: The Bruce Springsteen Story.* "It involved frequent national tours, records released at well-spaced intervals (nine months to a year between LPs—anything shorter risked over-saturating the market, anything longer risked being forgotten), and a high degree of coordination between the act's management, record company and the various promoters."

When a band wanted to go on tour, its manager would hire a booking agent like Premier to set it up. The agents, who usually took 15 percent to 20 percent, were responsible for routing the tours, advising bands on what markets to play and, depending on their drawing power, whether to play clubs, arenas, or stadiums. Agents worked like real estate brokers: they didn't buy, but only sold, running no risk. The agent then negotiated with promoters like Bill Graham to fix a price for the band.

In the late sixties it was standard for a headline act to take 60 percent of the gross and be responsible for all the promoter's local expenses. Other promoters worked on a formula basis where they would pay a guarantee of $10,000 and then split the gross 60/40, with the band paying its touring expenses out of its share. Once the deal was signed, the promoter assumed all risk for the show and was responsible for newspaper and radio advertising and other promotions needed to sell seats. He also did the ticketing, hired the hall, if necessary, and organized security, medical services, and catering. As the band got a guarantee up front, the only party at risk if a show failed was the promoter.

"All promoters are gamblers," Grossweiner said. "When we have our annual summit conference, the highest rollers at the evening poker game are the promoters and they don't care if they win or lose. In the concert situation, the promoters are the only ones at risk. Everyone else has a guaranteed salary."

In order to survive, promoters had to know the sales potential of any given act and use it as a starting point in their negotiations with the agent.

Profits could be enormous. A typical Fillmore East program ran for two evening performances on Fridays and Saturdays. Tickets were $3, $4, and $5 and a full house for all four shows would gross Graham $45,000. Set against $13,000 in operating expenses including staff and maintenance, and $15,000 for musical talent, Graham could make $17,000 profit on a good weekend.

A top headliner like Santana or Paul Butterfield would receive $10,000 for four performances, but proven concert sellouts like Jimi Hendrix or Janis Joplin demanded up to 50 percent of Graham's net profit. In the early days of the Fillmore East, Graham's average net take for a weekend was $10,000. His later Fillmore West hall made him slightly less: $6,000. This gave him the potential to earn $832,000 a year from just staging concerts, without taking any other interests into account.

Yet, despite being a millionaire, Graham could still be a penny-pincher. Charlatan member Mike Wilhelm once saw him after a show scavenging for change which had fallen under the seats of the Fillmore.

"He'd be picking up all the coins and money that had dropped onto the floor and comment on how much he'd found," Wilhelm said. "He'd say, 'What a cheap crowd. I only got $5.98 today.' "

Jim Haynie remembers Graham regularly stealing paper clips and rubber bands from the Winterland office when they staged shows.

"It was unbelievable," Haynie said. "It was like the old Mime Troupe days when we were scroungers and scavengers. It was sort of silly because Bill had more money than he needed, but he did not like to part with any of it. That's for certain."

As the concert promotion business became more sophisticated, a complicated maze of relationships evolved among promoters, agents, and managers. These all-important alliances, often years in the making, became the oil that kept the concert machine running and generating money.

Over the years many young would-be promoters with stars in their eyes failed miserably without having even reached the first hurdle. In order to get a show off the ground, a promoter needed the cooperation of everyone, from the band and booking agents to the local radio station and the unions.

Bill Graham told journalist Roger Trilling how his Northern California empire was impregnable from attack of ambitious wanna-be promoters: "You might say, 'Well, I just graduated in marketing from Columbia or Stanford and I've chosen to get into business. My daddy gives me a couple of hundred grand, sticks it in the bank and I go down to L.A. and walk into the office and say, 'Listen, I want to book Elton John.' Well, Elton John works with Bill Graham in Northern California. 'Well I want to book Bruce Springsteen.' Well, Bruce Springsteen works with Bill Graham. 'I want to work with the Rolling Stones.'

"Then you go back and say, 'Daddy, I can't get ahead. That guy has a fucking monopoly up there.'

"No, we've been at it a long time. Were you involved with the band when they were nobody and maybe put them in a club and lost some money? And as they got bigger they stayed with that band. If you think it is as easy as going down to L.A. with a pocketful of money, every klutz in the world would do that. Who doesn't want to make a good living, be in the music business, live in the fast lane. If it was easy we'd have more yo-yo's in the business than we already do."

"Bill made it quite clear that he could tangle with the East Coast boys and win out," said *San Francisco Examiner* music critic Phil Elwood. "The combination of his experience out here [in San Francisco] and growing up in New York gave him a perfect position of leverage. Once the Fillmore East took off, it really established him as a national figure."

Premier talent agent Barry Bell went hand to hand with Graham for nearly two decades of tough negotiations. "Sometime you fight like cats and dogs. It's a battle," Bell said. "I remember one time I was going to put a particular band outside of San Francisco and he didn't want me to put this band in a particular place. Bill said at one point, 'If this is what's happening to the business, I might as well take my wife and retire. Blah, blah, blah.

"Let me put it this way; nearly every deal was a fight. It's never easy, but it got done. Bill was driving the bargain that he thought fair for himself, and we were driving a bargain that we thought was fair for the particular acts we were dealing with. But like I said, it always got worked out. I can't think of anytime it didn't."

Carlos Santana recalled: "He was a supreme shark dealing with sharks all the time on the phone with the other promoters or record-company owners or whatever, you know."

Nonetheless, Graham had a sense of humor about arguing and kept a clipping on his office wall called "How to Argue and Win." It advised: "Keep up a stream of illogical thinking. Employ fallacies, prejudices and if you find that doesn't work go heavy on emotionalism and inappropriate analogies. Be completely irrational and avoid facing the truth. This method so frustrates your opponent that though he may be completely right, you appear to have won. Signed Bill Graham."

Chris Brooks, who worked at the soon-to-open Fillmore West, says that Graham's telephone antics could bring the whole office to a standstill.

"A deal for Bill always came after an awful lot of yelling and screaming," she said. "You could hear him all over the place so there could never be any secrets because Bill's voice was too loud. His highs came when he closed the deal."

Clearly, the early rock tours were thrown together on an ad hoc basis.

The touring bands plugged their instruments into each venue's sound system and P.A. which would be rented along with an operator by each promoter. Therefore, there was little consistent sound quality from venue to venue, leading to endless complaints from musicians about bad mixes and shoddy monitors.

Vinnie Fusco remembers: "One day I'm sitting with Albert Grossman and he had the vision; 'Why don't we buy the sound system for each act and provide the operator and then rent it back to the promoter?'

Once we resolved what the plan was, I had to make it fly. So I got on the phone to several promoters and said, 'Okay, instead of you hiring the sound system and paying for it, we're going to provide it. You pay us the differential. In addition, the group ended up with a P.A. system as an asset.

"We started off with Bob Dylan and Janis, and then it just started rolling over to everybody, and when other managers saw what we were doing they copied us. So everything at this time was evolving on the spot."

As promoters began to realize that rock audiences were extending beyond the major cities, they recruited their friends to extend the touring circuit into secondary markets.

"It became a big buddy network," Grossweiner explained. "If no one was promoting in Kansas City or Dallas, the neighboring promoters found guys who were interested in getting into the business and set them up. This made some promoters extremely strong."

The new breed of promoters, although generally hip and the same age as the bands, were still distrusted by the musicians. Bill Wyman said that the Rolling Stones learned from bitter experience how promoters squeezed the extra dollar out of a band.

"You had to deal with the independent promoters in each city, and you found that they were fiddling," he said. "You know the guy in Chicago was doing deals. Buy a Rolling Stones ticket and you had to buy one for Billy J. Kramer or someone who was coming a month later. The same guy also arranged a fan-club meet where we sat down at a table and the fan club filed past. We'd sign autographs, and they'd give us presents and things like that. Afterwards we'd found out that the promoter had charged all the fan-club people ten dollars each to meet us. There were all these kind of scams going on which you had to keep stopping."

In the late sixties, being a promoter was virtually a license to print money. The profits were vast. When Bill Graham first promoted The Rolling Stones during its 1969 tour, he grossed nearly $250,000 for the three shows he put on in Oakland and San Diego. But it would be only a matter of time before the new superstar rock groups became aware of their true value and started demanding more and more money from the promoters.

In the months following the death of Martin Luther King, tension in the Fillmore ghetto increased between the blacks who lived there and Graham's Fillmore audience. The white middle-class rock fans became uneasy about crossing into the ghetto to see a show, and many preferred to remain home. Despite his efforts to maintain friendly relations with the neighborhood by staging community fund-raising benefits, Graham knew he had to secure a new auditorium in a safer part of town to survive.

"The Fillmore neighborhood became a battleground in the streets—black and white, racial issues—and I was ready to lose my business," said Graham, who himself narrowly escaped a beating at the time.

Graham seized his opportunity when the Carousel Ballroom became available. Ironically, The Grateful Dead and Jefferson Airplane had recently started staging their own shows at the Carousel in an effort to free San Francisco bands from Graham's stranglehold on the market. Due to inexperience and the amateur way it was run, the ballroom was losing money.

"All my competitors were running around trying to get the Carousel," Graham said. "The owner of that facility was an Irish businessman, and he was building a bunch of hotels in Ireland somewhere and wasn't expected back for months."

Knowing that his competitors would be bidding for the Carousel, Graham jumped on a plane to Ireland to make his offer in person to the owner, Bill Fuller. The tenacious promoter tracked Fuller down to a construction site near Shannon, and the two men hammered out a deal for the Carousel over breakfast and a bottle of bourbon. An overjoyed Graham left with a three-year lease on the Carousel just in time to catch the early plane back to the States. Not surprisingly, Graham's proactive maneuver was very unpopular among the San Francisco musicians, who regarded it as yet another example of his double-dealing.

The final show at the Fillmore Auditorium on July 2, 1968, was headlined by Creedence Clearwater Revival, coupled with Steppenwolf and It's a Beautiful Day.

"It was a historic gig," Graham remembered. "We formed a conga line between the two Fillmores. We were being a little tearful about leaving that place. We were still in the process of moving until the very last. It was very, very hectic and madness."

The Carousel, which Graham christened Fillmore West, opened the very next night with a sellout show headlined by the Butterfield Blues Band and Ten Years After.

A former ballroom turned car dealership, the Fillmore West building had a large parquet wooden dance floor where Graham soon resumed his beloved Tuesday-night basketball games. It was far bigger than the old Fillmore—it held 2,800 people—but Graham was soon up to his old tricks, packing them in way past the legal capacity. By now he was issuing tickets at the door for the sake of the fire marshals, but he had a new scam up his sleeve. At each show he personally collected the tickets in a small basket at the top of the stairs without tearing them. Then he would race back to the booking office and resell the same tickets so he could cover himself in the event of a raid by the fire marshals by claiming that he had sold the legal number of tickets.

Even while he was 3,000 miles away working at the Fillmore East, Graham still worried that his San Francisco staff wasn't cramming enough people into the Fillmore. Jim Haynie, having returned to the Fillmore after a year on the road with the Butterfield Blues Band, was left in charge the first weekend Graham spent in New York.

"Bill called me at least five times that night to see how many people had come to the show," Haynie said. "I told him the fire marshals had been round to check on us and were still on the premises to see that we didn't overcrowd. Bill got angry and said, 'Damn it. You've got to do better than that.' I told him not to worry and that I'd sneak more people through the side door when it was safe. Although Bill was 3,000 miles away, he still obsessed that we weren't getting everything we could. He was a strange guy."

San Francisco Examiner's Phil Elwood used to watch the shows at both West Coast Fillmores, perched high in the lighting platforms where he could count the audience. Once he triggered Graham's wrath after printing an estimated gate for the Fillmore West in his review of a Janis Joplin show.

"Bill read it and blew up," Elwood said. "Bill never liked anyone to make a comment like the place was sold out or overflowing or standing room only. I think he was very fearful that the law-enforcement people or the fire department would consider he was overfilling the hall.

"I remember he phoned me on a Friday morning and exploded at me, saying, 'Where did you get those figures?' It was one of the few times over the years that I was on the receiving end of one of Bill's intemperate screaming phone calls, and he let me have it. It probably made him feel better to blow off steam once in a while, although it didn't make me feel any better. It was an unnerving experience to be lambasted by Bill Graham for five minutes."

The late journalist John Wasserman walked into the Fillmore West offices one day to hear Graham's full force on the telephone.

"Bill was screaming like a maniac," Wasserman said. "He was screaming the most obnoxious, personal insults that I've ever heard anybody scream at anybody else. Just on and on. Challenging this person's right to exist, his ancestry, his morals, his appearance, his intelligence, his ethics—everything about him. I've never heard such a tirade in my life. And I thought who can this be. It must be Satan. I couldn't conceive who this villain must have been."

After overhearing ten minutes of nonstop high-octane abuse, Wasserman finally discovered that the unfortunate victim was none other than Graham's good friend and faithful lawyer Brian Rohan.

The harder Graham worked setting up his bicoastal empire, the more he neglected his wife Bonnie, who was now pregnant. He hardly ever came home to see her, as he had embarked on a passionate love affair with a young woman he had met at the Fillmore East.

"She was his East Coast girlfriend," remembers John Morris, who entertained Graham and his new lover at his secluded Virgin Islands retreat less than a month after the birth of Graham's son. "It was weird because Bill said, 'Can I bring her?' and we thought Bonnie was going to come. I remember my wife, Annie, didn't feel very good about it because we had socialized a lot with Bill and Bonnie.

"And Bill came down with her, and it wasn't done well. If Bill was going to have an affair, even if he was going to have it three thousand miles away from Bonnie, he didn't have the instincts, he didn't have the thoughtfulness. He didn't have whatever it took to keep it a really quiet and secret affair.

"Bill had an East Coast concert hall and a West Coast concert hall. He had a wife on the West Coast and he developed a girlfriend on the East Coast. To him that was basic logic."

When Bonnie went into labor with her baby in September, Graham stayed with his girlfriend in New York. His friends were shocked, believing his cold behavior to be a result of his miserable childhood.

"While she was giving birth to David, Bill was out here doing whatever it was that Bill did," Lee Blumer remembers. "The next morning,

Bill asked me if I had sent flowers to Bonnie. My mother had raised me right, and I knew how to send flowers. But I didn't think to send flowers for him. I assumed that he wanted to know if I had sent flowers. I had signed my name on the card and not his. That night his wife yelled at him for not sending her any flowers, so he almost killed me for that."

The very first time Graham saw his new son David was on the giant light-show screen at the Fillmore East. Joshua White had arranged to have a picture air-freighted to New York to show Graham during Saturday night's second show. Graham, ever the showman, was then led out onstage to share this special moment with his Fillmore East audience and receive their applause.

When he finally returned to San Francisco, Graham's marriage was in free-fall. Bonnie never forgave him for not being at her side when she needed him. She finally walked out on the marriage, taking David, after catching Graham in bed with a sixteen-year-old groupie in a seedy San Francisco motel room.

"My wife is a human being, and she finally went her way and I went my way," was his public explanation. "And I paid the price of success, or one of them, which is, here I am. Stuck with my business and no family."

John Morris believes that Graham's refusal to spend any time with his wife led to the collapse of their relationship. "They had fallen in love with each other and Bonnie had hitched onto his wagon," said Morris. "All of a sudden it became a jet and it just passed her by. She moved at one speed and Bill moved at another. And Bill's speed had afterburners to it. There was a demon pushing him.

"Basically over the years he just ran over her too many times. And timing and thoughtfulness were not among his characteristics. He hurt her in thousands of different ways he never even realized and wouldn't have done if he'd known it. I mean, I was constantly saying, 'Buy Bonnie a present. You've been away a week. Take something back to her.'

"I think in the end he lost her because he was Bill Graham. She was a normal, feeling, sweet and kind understanding person who lived with this whirlwind, and it became too much. She couldn't deal with him anymore, and she had to protect herself. I think losing her was a crushing blow to Bill. It was a tremendous failure for him."

To get over the loss of Bonnie and his newborn son, Graham worked even harder, often putting in eighteen-hour days and surviving on just three or four hours of sleep a night. But however late he may have been working the night before, he was always at his desk ready for work at 9:00 A.M.

But the intense pressures of juggling both Fillmores, 3,000 miles apart, ultimately forced the hands-on impresario to reluctantly start delegating authority to others.

"He was very nervous about doing it," Elwood said. "Bill was at his most tense at that time when he was racing back and forth across the country. After all, in only been three or four years, he suddenly had an empire, but he was still trying to find staff that he could work with."

Graham also needed more time to consolidate his sprawling operations so he could branch out into new areas of the music business. First he channeled all the cash coming from Fillmores East and West through his old poster company, William Graham Posters, Inc., which became his empire's biggest profit center. To shore up his operation, he funneled the rest of his concert profits, from the fifty additional shows he did a year at Winterland and other venues, into Bill Graham Presents, Inc. He then moved much of the money secretly out of the U.S. to his sister Evelyn in Switzerland who helped him buy real estate. In February 1969, Graham established the Fillmore Corporation, incorporated in Delaware, where the corporate laws were not as stringent as in California. The Fillmore Corporation became the umbrella for five subsidiaries: the Fillmore Management Company, his two record companies, the Fillmore Sound Company, the Fillmore Soundtrack Company, and his music publishing arm, the Fillmore Music Company.

He also set up two booking agencies, the Millard Agency, named after America's thirteenth President, Millard T. Fillmore, also known as "The Accidental President," and Fillmore Management, signing up eleven bands immediately. Five of the groups, including Cold Blood and Santana, were discovered at the Fillmore's special open-stage talent shows. Unlike other agents Graham only took 10 percent—a far lower percentage than other agencies charged. Graham claimed he made up for the loss by booking bands for twice as many gigs as rival agents and summed up his agent philosophy by saying, "When trying to make it, the groups call in for a gig: at the top, the calls come in *to* them." Aided by John Morris and Chip Monck, he formed FM Productions (Fillmore Millard) to handle the production side of his operation and began top-level negotiations with major record companies for his own label bearing the "Fillmore" logo.

The man who helped Graham get a foot in the record business was David Rubinson. Born in Brooklyn's Bedford-Stuyvesant in 1942, Rubinson was producing off-Broadway plays when he first spoke to Bill Graham about bringing the San Francisco Mime Troupe to New York.

The two stayed friends, and in 1969 Rubinson decided to throw in his lot with Bill Graham, selling off his business and moving his family to San Francisco. In a three-way partnership with Graham and Brian Rohan, he formed Fillmore Records, aligned to CBS, and San Francisco Records, linked to Atlantic Records.

"None of us were qualified to run a record label," Bill Graham told writer Jack McDonough in 1976. "And we've proved it to ourselves. Because now Rubinson is producing Santana, I'm managing them and Brian just negotiated their new contract."

The Fillmore Corporation was designed to orchestrate every part of an artist's career from a central point and to have complete control. The umbrella organization covered management, record publishing, and recording studios. Applying hard business to the San Francisco music scene would have been impossible during the Summer of Love, but things had changed dramatically. Rohan told *Billboard* that the local bands had moved away from love and peace to become more professional and businesslike.

"The city has developed a better-run music industry," said Rohan. "Musicians are not as paranoid today about record companies; they're more willing to give a record company a fair shake. The groups are more interested today in cooperating with the record companies."

But the "rock 'n' roll barrister" admitted that dope still played a large role in the business. "Grass alters your time perspection," he said. "And I think one reason why the kids are in the studio so much is they're stoned so much."

In the two years that Rubinson ran Graham's record company, he recorded Santana, Tower of Power, Cold Blood, and Elvin Bishop. Rubinson, equally hardheaded and manipulative as Graham, found himself clashing constantly with his partner over how the record company should be run.

"I've always had a great relationship with Graham, but neither one of us is psychologically suited for partners," Rubinson said. "Bill Graham is a typical Jewish refugee, a typical New York street fighter. He doesn't believe he's got something unless he's got it on his back or in his pocket."

Having gambled everything to come to San Francisco to start the company, Rubinson felt very vulnerable. To Graham, though, it was just a small part of his mushrooming empire.

"It wasn't the life-or-death struggle for Graham that it was for me," Rubinson said. "I didn't make enough hits, and Bill was busy tearing tickets. So I sold my stock to him and left."

Chris Brooks remembers the power play between the two master manipulators during their bitter final days together. "They used to fight a lot," Brooks said. "Bill would talk to David and let everyone listen in on the other line. It was a game, so you knew where your loyalty really lay, and that Bill signed the paychecks."

Channeling his energies into his growing empire, Graham relied increasingly on John Morris to run the Fillmore East and put employee Paul Baratta in charge of the Fillmore West. But there was never any real question of who called the shots. "Bill says I run the place, but it's all Bill," Baratta quipped at the time.

In truth, Graham often worked twenty hours a day running his extensive operation, rarely getting any sleep as he crisscrossed America, one year making a record thirty-nine round trips. His nonstop work schedule coupled with insomnia were taking their toll and he was becoming burned out and bad tempered. His staff was finding it increasingly difficult to deal with his frequent rages over the smallest things, and key employees could talk to him only in short, frustrating bursts between his incessant phone calls.

Graham himself even admitted that his organization at that period was a "dictatorship without time clocks or rules," adding, "I expect everybody to do their work. You do it, great. Don't, get out! If I was the S.O.B. everybody says I am, why do they all stay with me?"

Graham was also not above getting down on his knees to sweep the floors of the Fillmore or pick up rubbish. He was a perfectionist, frequently comparing his job as producer to that of a maître d'.

Although his regular temper tantrums scared many, Graham could also show great compassion and generosity to his employees in the tradition of the "Rock Godfather" figure he was fast becoming. When Chris Brooks's boss tried to fire her from the Millard Agency, Graham became her white knight.

"Bill called us both into his office and listened to Joe and then he listened to me," Brooks said. "He asked what I wanted to do, and I told him that I saw a need for publicity for the whole corporation. We had management, booking, a sound company, a publishing company, and we were planning a record company.

"Bill said he would give it some thought, and on the way out, as I was weepy and very upset, he put his arm around me and said, 'Don't worry, you're in good hands with a Jew.'

"I remember it was a Friday, and that afternoon Bill called me up and told me to report to my new office across the street on Monday morning.

I was stunned. I said, 'My office. What am I going to be doing?' He said, 'You are now national director of publicity for the Fillmore Corporation.' "

Graham maintained high morale and kept his finger on his organization's pulse by holding monthly "family meetings" where employees could bring up any problems.

Graham's innovative and highly effective management style complemented his genius for concert promotion, and his business grew rapidly. In his first major national profile in December 1968, Graham was described by the *New York Times* as a "two-fisted Jew battling for survival and hungering for identity." He was brimming with confidence when he told the *New York Times,* "I'm the best. It sounds so egocentric but it's true."

The profile introduced his new image of an unapologetic self-made music tycoon millionaire who still managed to retain a strong sixties ideology. "I've paid my dues; I deserve it," said Graham, who was compared to a Harold Robbins hero.

Although estranged from Bonnie, Graham still managed to paint a picture of marital bliss. He even boasted about taking his first vacation in three years, spent with Morris in the Virgin Islands, failing to mention that he took his girlfriend along instead of his wife and month-old son.

"It was *Holiday* magazine but real," gushed Graham. "I never knew that world existed. I never have time to discover those things. I work too hard making money to spend it. Those executives who work nineteen hours a day, then ride, play golf and sail for hobbies? I can't do it. Work is the whole shot."

Phil Elwood believes that Bill Graham's public image was vitally important to him and fulfilled a desperate need to be recognized for his accomplishments.

"Increasingly, Bill wanted to establish an image, which God knows he did," Elwood said. "I think as his life went along he was more and more interested in justifying his role in rock 'n' roll. He felt that it wasn't natural for a guy his age to be involved in all of that. He was, after all, the age of many of the parents of the kids in his audience."

Graham's generation gap with his audience became a real issue when he tangled with the radical New York community group, The Motherfuckers. The fuse was lit by the underground community newspaper the *East Village Other,* which became his tenants when he bought the Fillmore East. Soon afterward, the paper attacked Graham cruelly, saying it was a pity that he hadn't followed his parents into the Nazi concentration camps. Graham exploded and, storming into the paper's office, turned over the editor's desk, and threw him out into the street.

The Motherfuckers, who were looking for a cause, fixed their sights firmly on Graham. In the name of the people, the group demanded that the Fillmore be open to the Lower East Side community one night a week, drawing the battle lines of what would be a long and bloody confrontation.

Motherfuckers spokesman Ben Morea told *Rolling Stone* at the time, "The Fillmore's interests are not our interests, and that's the conflict. They're into making money and we're into living. They're somewhere else, which don't dig and which is bullshit."

Graham couldn't afford to take the Motherfuckers lightly, one wrong move could result in a community boycott and spell the end of the Fillmore East. In an attempt to calm the waters, Graham agreed to their demands to "liberate" the Fillmore for one free night a week, to be broadcast live on the left-wing radio station WBAI-FM. But all hell broke loose when the-avant garde theater group, The Living Theater, staged *Paradise Now* at the Fillmore as part of its benefit for student strikers at Columbia University.

At one point during the show, one of the actors suddenly announced that the people were going to liberate the Fillmore then and there. This immediately provoked Bill Graham to leap from his seat and dash onstage to defend his Fillmore against attack. Quickly overpowered, Graham was tied to a chair on the stage, where he remained for nearly six hours, arguing and screaming at the rioters.

"It was their drama and Bill's drama, but in retrospect it was hysterical," said Fillmore East employee Lee Blumer, who was hiding in the sound booth during the takeover.

"Bill battled the Motherfuckers," said Joshua White. "Bill stood up and fought for what he believed in and argued with everyone from the stage until four in the morning, when they went home. They were demanding that the theater should be free and accused us of stealing money from the community. Bill told them, 'It will be free when the musicians play for free and the airplanes fly them here for free and the limousines are free.' His argument was pretty tight."

The next day, an angry Graham told the *Village Voice* what he thought of the Fillmore mutiny. "Those rotten pieces of shit," he said. "I'm so sick and fucking tired of listening to that 'rip off the community' shit. I told those pieces of shit, 'You get the musicians, and you get the equipment and you pay my stage people, and I'll let you have this place on

Wednesday.' For all I care, this community can fucking shrivel up and die if they continue to let themselves be represented by that bunch of cheap-ass chicken-shit punks."

Yet, within a few days, Graham ate his words and agreed to let the Motherfuckers have use of the Fillmore every Wednesday night.

The first free Wednesday was a disaster, attracting Bowery bums, winos and speed freaks from St. Mark's Place who sprawled themselves all over the Fillmore getting stoned and vandalizing the hall.

The police soon stepped in and ordered Graham to stop the open drug taking at the Fillmore during the free nights and get tough or risk losing the Fillmore's operating license. Graham replied by hiring an expensive Manhattan public-relations firm to circulate an open letter to the community appealing for order, citing "Incidents of physical confrontation, and the blatant use, distribution, and sale of drugs on the premises—obviously illegal" and urging "intelligence, understanding and grace."

The Motherfuckers answered with an aggressively hard-hitting letter of their own. In the radical black-and-white rhetoric of the times it read: "Situation: Pigs and Bill Graham stop free night. Why? They say we smoke, they say we take dope, but we know it's because they are afraid of us. Afraid that we'll get together there to destroy their world and create our own. The pigs threaten to close Graham down unless he stops our free night. He doesn't have to worry about the pigs. We'll close him down. No free night, no pay night."

Graham replied by canceling the free nights and keeping the Fillmore closed Wednesdays. The situation exploded the day after Christmas, when the Motherfuckers threatened to burn down the Fillmore because Graham refused to give them hundreds of free tickets for an MC5 show. Even the radical band, whose patented battle-cry was "Kick out the jams Motherfuckers," refused to obey the Motherfuckers' order to disrupt the show, making it clear that they were there to play music.

"David Peel and the Lower East Side opened the program but the real show was the pressure and tension inside the hall," wrote *Rolling Stone* in a blow-by-blow account. "Although most of the seats were filled, the crowd outside the theater wanted in—and the people inside supported them with cries of 'Open the doors! Open the doors.' "

Graham, transported back to his childhood and the horror of the Nazis, prepared to defend his rock palace against attack. Fearlessly, he stepped out to face the angry mob head-on and shouted for order.

"They came into the lobby and said to me, 'You know we can come in by force,' " Graham remembered. "And I said, 'Well, I can't tell my staff to fight you, because that's not why they're hired, but I'm gonna stand in front of the building and if you try to come in, *I'm* gonna try to stop you.' "

The mob's vicious reply was a chain lashing across Graham's face, which broke his nose and started it pouring with blood.

"A strange thing happened," said eyewitness Kip Cohen. "The minute they saw the blood on Bill's face, there was a strong reaction from the crowd, and these hundreds of people who had been swarming on top of him, backed away."

Many people outside were disgusted by the chain attack on Bill Graham and left. But inside the Fillmore, the more militant Motherfuckers went on a rampage after the show, breaking an usher's arm with a metal bar and stabbing a young Puerto Rican boy. The asbestos stage curtain was slashed with a knife, and there were hundreds of dollars worth of damage to equipment. In the aftermath of the violence, the Fillmore's insurance company threatened to terminate the hall's coverage, and Graham gave the community one last chance, saying, "Look, when are you going to face up to the fact that you've blown it here?" He then offered the Motherfuckers several thousand dollars a month to leave him alone and to set up their own place, but they refused, still demanding the Fillmore. Eventually the group's violence lost them the support of the community, and they backed off from the Fillmore East.

While Graham tangled with the Motherfuckers outside, there was also a power struggle going on inside for control of the Fillmore. Kip Cohen, who had been brought into the Fillmore by his old college friends John Morris and Joshua White, had taken over bottom-end management, responsible for running the box office. A former theater manager, Cohen had been on the verge of dropping out when the Fillmore East started, and he had to be persuaded to join his friends and work for Graham. Now, seeing how successful the Fillmore East was becoming, he sought a higher position of power and management in the Graham organization. Blocking his path was John Morris, who not only was instrumental in bringing Graham to New York, but who played a key role in setting up the Fillmore East. Cohen made his bid for power while Morris was away organizing The Doors' and Jefferson Airplane's first European tour.

When Morris returned, Cohen had taken over.

"I was fired," remembers Morris, who was summoned to a meeting with Bill Graham and Kip Cohen at Ratner's Jewish Dairy Restaurant next door to the Fillmore. "Bill said, 'Look at it this way, John. You're a diamond cutter, and if I ever need a diamond cutter, I'm always going to come to you. But you're not an everyday, be-there, get-it-done, just-run-the-operation type guy.'

"Good night, good-bye, John. You're gone. I was flabbergasted and devastated. I was never a partner, although I'd helped organize the entire thing with all the investors. I was the chief honcho who ran New York, but Bill always controlled everything."

To this day, Morris is convinced that Cohen, now at A&M Records, was responsible for Graham's decision to fire him, and the two have not spoken since. Lee Blumer, who was Morris's assistant at the Fillmore, agrees. "John was not fast enough to see the boulder coming down the mountain," she said. "He got crushed."

AMERICAN FRIENDS SERVICE COMMITTEE
(QUAKERS AMERICAINS)
20 South 12 th Street PHILADELPHIA U.S.A.
HOWARD E. KERSHNER
29, Boulevard d'Athènes - MARSEILLE

N.B. - Ne rien écrire dans cet espace.

66

UATRE EXEMPLAIRES A LA MACHINE A ECRIRE
EXEMPLAIRES NOUS SERONT RETOURNÉS
ATRIÈME EXEMPLAIRE SUR LEQUEL SERA COLLÉE UNE PHOTOGRAPHIE AU COIN GAUCHE SUPÉRIEUR, ENTRE LES QUATRE FLÈCHES

Dix huit Aout 1941

I
NOM DE FAMILLE DU CANDIDAT Grajonca
PRÉNOMS Wolodia
SEXE masculin
DATE DE NAISSANCE, AVEC AGE EXACT huit Janvier mil neuf cent trente et un
LIEU ET CONTRÉE DE NAISSANCE Berlin
NATIONALITÉ LE JOUR DE LA NAISSANCE allemande
NATIONALITÉ EN CE MOMENT allemande
RÉSIDENCE ACTUELLE
DATE D'ARRIVÉE EN FRANCE Juin 1939

II
RELIGION israelite non

III
DEGRÉ D'INSTRUCTION DE L'ENFANT
Primaire ? primaire
Secondaire ?
QUELLES LANGUES L'ENFANT PARLE-T-IL ? français - allemand
DE QUELS TRAVAUX FACILES L'ENFANT EST-IL CAPABLE ?

IV
A
NOM ET PRÉNOMS DU PÈRE Jacob Grajonca
AGE, LIEU ET CONTRÉE DE NAISSANCE décédé
PROFESSION Ingénieur
NATIONALITÉ, RELIGION, DATE D'ARRIVÉE EN FRANCE
RÉSIDENCE ACTUELLE

B
NOM ET PRÉNOMS DE LA MÈRE Frieda Grajonca née Graus
AGE, LIEU ET CONTRÉE DE NAISSANCE
PROFESSION couturière
NATIONALITÉ, RELIGION, DATE D'ARRIVÉE EN FRANCE russe - israelite -
RÉSIDENCE ACTUELLE Berlin SW 68 Alte Jacob Strasse

N.B. - En cas de décès ou de disparition du Père ou de la Mère ou des deux prière de donner les indications suivantes :

C
NOM ET PRÉNOMS DU TUTEUR LÉGAL Parents absents : UNION O.S.E.
DEGRÉ DE PARENTÉ
DATE DE DÉSIGNATION
D'OÙ ÉMANE CETTE DÉSIGNATION ?
RENSEIGNEMENTS COMPLÉMENTAIRES

V
DATE DU DERNIER EXAMEN MÉDICAL DE L'ENFANT dix-neuf Aout 1941
JOINDRE 3 PHOTOGRAPHIES OU COPIES LÉGALISÉES DE CE CERTIFICAT MÉDICAL.
Joindre 3 photographies ou Copies légalisées du Certificat de vaccination Antivariolique.
(Ne doit pas remonter à plus de six mois.)
Joindre 3 photographies ou Copies légalisées du Certificat de vaccination Antidiphtérique.
Répondre par oui ou par non si l'enfant est atteint d'une infirmité ou d'un défaut physique; si oui en indiquer la nature. Non
INDIQUER ICI L'HISTOIRE MÉDICALE DE L'ENFANT

VI
L'ENFANT POSSÈDE-T-IL :
DES PARENTS AUX ETATS UNIS ?
DES AMIS AUX ETATS UNIS ? tante Mr. Schneider c/o Garber 2985 Ocean Parkway - Brooklyn N.Y. USA

VII
L'ENFANT POSSÈDE-T-IL UN PASSEPORT RÉCENT ? non
QUELLES PIÈCES D'IDENTITÉ L'ENFANT POSSÈDE-T-IL ?
Kinderausweis

VIII
ETATS UNIS ? pas pour l'enfant

IMPORTANT
A LIRE TRÈS SOIGNEUSEMENT ET A SIGNER A L'ENDROIT INDIQUÉ

Salomon André
Wolodia Grajonca
Wolodia Grajonca

TOUT DOSSIER INCOMPLET SERA REFUSÉ

dix neuf Aout 1941

EMPREINTES DIGITALES DE L'ENFANT
Pouce gauche — Pouce droit

SIGNATURE DE L'ENFANT

The temporary passport issued to ten-year-old German refugee Wolodia Grajonca in Marseille for his voyage to America in 1941. It bears one of his earliest known signatures.

Bill Graham in the 1950s, when he was in New York struggling to be an actor using the name Anthony Graham. (Courtesy Regina Cartwright)

The San Francisco Mime Troupe in action. Graham, who was the group's business manager, promoted his first show on November 6, 1965, as a benefit for the Troupe. (Gene Anthony)

The landmark weekend-long Trips Festival in January 1966, which Graham helped to organize. (Gene Anthony)

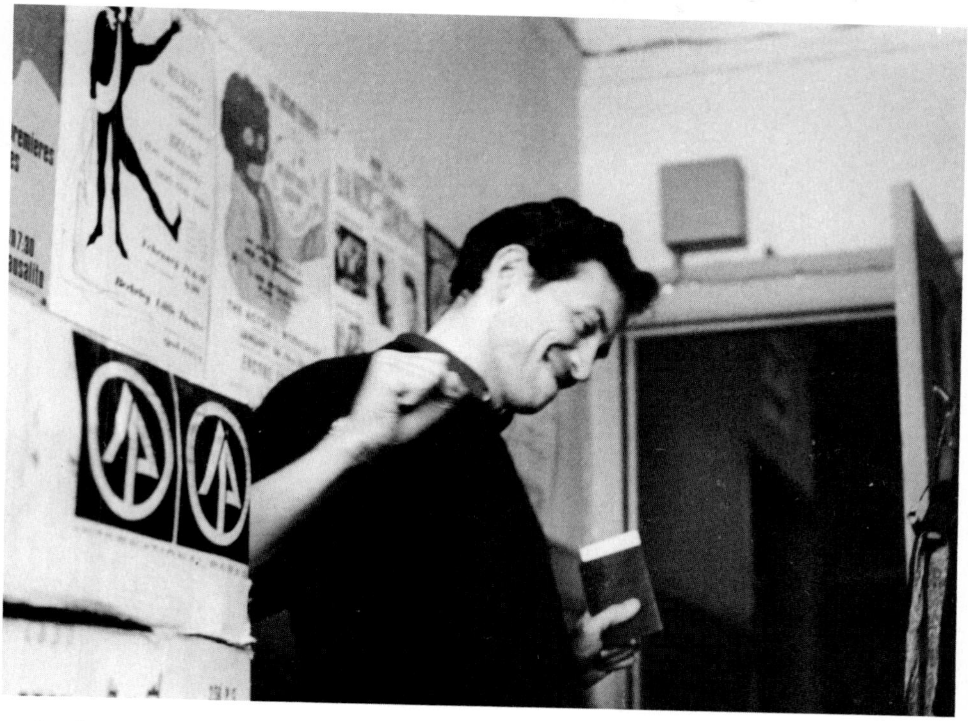

A triumphant Bill Graham at the moment he hears the news that the San Francisco Board of Supervisors has granted him a licence to run the Fillmore. (Gene Anthony)

Ever the maître d', Graham puts the finishing touches to the cake for a wedding during a concert at the Fillmore in 1967. (Gene Anthony)

Bill Graham surveys the ticket office at the Fillmore in 1967. The promoter was renowned for overcrowding the concert hall in a continuous cat-and-mouse game with the San Francisco Fire Department. (Gene Anthony)

The two queens of San Francisco rock, Janis Joplin and Grace Slick. Graham, who managed the Jefferson Airplane, tried to sabotage Joplin's career because he saw her as a threat to Slick. (Gene Anthony)

The Fillmore East's innovative Joshua Light Show on stage at Bill Graham's New York rock palace. (Amalie Rothschild)

The Grateful Dead, pictured here in 1966, were to play a vital part in Graham's career as he helped them gain superstardom in the 1970s and 1980s. (Gene Anthony)

The Fillmore East's manager, Jim Haynie, in action at the annual New Year's Eve concert. Bill Graham considered Haynie good luck and flew him into San Francisco regularly so he could be the New Year's baby. (Gene Anthony)

Hands-on promoter Bill Graham takes to the stage during a Jefferson Airplane New Year's performance at Winterland. Also pictured is Airplane bassist Jack Casady. (Gene Anthony)

The consummate bicoastal impresario, Bill Graham, pictured in his Fillmore East office, wore two watches so he always knew what the time was at both Fillmores. (AP/Wide World Photos)

Bill Graham's great San Francisco rival, Chet Helms, who ran the Avalon Ballroom. (Gene Anthony)

A serious-looking Bill Graham outside his Fillmore East after making the historic announcement in 1971 that he was closing both Fillmores because of the degeneration of the rock music scene. (AP/Wide World Photos)

Regina Cartwright, who became Bill Graham's receptionist in 1975 at age nineteen, became his lover a year later and began a torrid seventeen-year affair with the impresario. (Courtesy Regina Cartwright)

Bill Graham makes a strong point during an interview in his office in the early 1980s. (Jan Coor-Pender Dodge)

Rabbi Josef Langer of Chabad introduces Bill Graham from the stage during the annual Chanukah service, for which the Jewish impresario always provided the menorah. (Jan Coor-Pender Dodge)

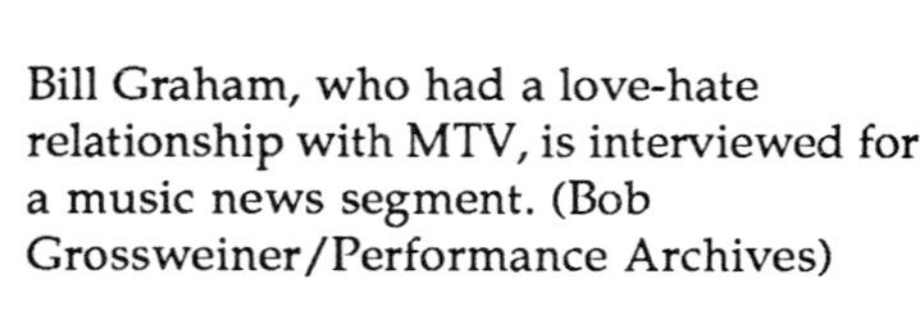

Bill Graham, who had a love-hate relationship with MTV, is interviewed for a music news segment. (Bob Grossweiner/Performance Archives)

8

Wall Street Goes Woodstock

By 1969 the *Wall Street Journal* was sitting up and paying close attention to rock 'n' roll. The paper hailed rock as a multibillion-dollar industry and cited Bill Graham as the major force in the business.

"Mr. Graham today can join the company of producer-impresarios in the tradition of Hammerstein and Hurok," wrote John J. O'Connor in his story "Pop Music Explosion: Rock and Bankroll." "He's tough, he no doubt can be impossible, but he also is honest and, in a tough business, he's respected."

The *Journal* reached the "inescapable conclusion" that the rock phenomenon was growing fast, "fed primarily by the more affluent young and in turn producing a new breed of youthful millionaires. It is upsetting traditions not only in the music business but in areas from fashion to lifestyles."

Yet Graham must have been upset that Alvin Cooperman, Madison Square Garden's executive vice president, took top billing as the concert kingpin of New York rock, having recently broken the magic $100,000 barrier for a single show for a Cream concert. The world-famous arena, seating 20,000, was Bill Graham's greatest single competitor in New York, placing him at a constant disadvantage by being able to pay acts up to six times what he could. In early 1968 The Doors were paid $50,000 for a single appearance at the Garden, causing Jim Morrison to phone Graham and taunt him.

The Garden's financial edge proved a real threat to Graham as more and more bands opted to play one Madison Square Garden show instead of six at the Fillmore for the same money. Saving face, Graham emphasized the intimacy and quality of the Fillmore, commenting in *Variety*, "Making money is of course an important thing in my business. But it isn't the ultimate reason. By playing in places they respect, in front of people they respect, using good equipment, good sound, good lights and good technical production, it's a sign to me that money is not the only reason they do this for a living."

Going on the offensive, Graham declared war on Madison Square Garden, drawing up contracts excluding bands from playing the Garden if they wished to play the Fillmore.

Although Graham faced tough opposition in New York, he felt confident that he had things pretty well sewn up in San Francisco. Chet Helms, his only serious competitor, was now more than $50,000 in debt, desperately trying to hold his own under Graham's hard-hitting restrictive contracts. The idealistic promoter fought for survival and was finally forced in early 1969 to move from the Avalon to the outskirts of San Francisco, where he opened a new venue called the Family Dog on the Great Highway. To cut down his expenses, he staged "free-form environmental theater" instead of big-name rock bands.

Graham was not magnanimous in victory. Whenever he ran into Helms socially, the successful impresario seemed to enjoy humiliating his vanquished foe.

"His attitude towards me in public was kinda like 'poor little Chet,' " Helms remembers. "He'd put his arm around me like it was a big joke and be very patronizing."

Graham liked to compare Helms to a missionary walking deeper and deeper into the jungle while being eaten by cannibals one limb at a time and waving his bleeding stumps at the cannibals, saying, "Bless you, my son."

"He would tell that story right in front of me, and all I could do was laugh," Helms said. "I never had the courage to ask him if he perceived himself as one of the cannibals."

Musicians felt sympathetic toward Helms, but in general they were too afraid to openly support him for fear of incurring the wrath of Graham.

"He screwed Chet. Screwed him forward and aft," said Michael Bloomfield, one of the few musicians brave enough to support Helms publicly. "He was a ruthless businessman. He was a cutthroat. The ruthlessness was the pleasure of his business. He left Chet broke."

Graham defended his actions, stating that he was merely exercising good business sense in the best American traditions. "Did I take advantage of a man who wasn't as businessy as I was?" he asked. "This is America. If we live in utopia, it's a different story. But we live in the United States of America, and everything that succeeds, succeeds like all hell and some.

"The kids made San Francisco into an international hip capital. Many of them resent it now because it has changed the scene so much and has made it pretty artificial; but it did something to San Francisco: it turned the city on! And that's something."

Yet financially things were not going so well for Graham. According to his first accountant, the boom years of the Fillmore were between 1965 and 1968. By 1969 his profits had started slowing down, in line with the national economy. The Fillmore audience had changed, too, and were less into music and more into hard drugs. If Graham was feeling a financial pinch, things were much worse for Chet Helms and the bands and artists involved in the original Haight-Ashbury scene who had all fallen into heavy debt. As the San Francisco scene began to disintegrate, hostility against Bill Graham intensified, and he became the scapegoat.

The bad feeling against Graham finally surfaced with the great San Francisco Light Show strike. It began with a letter to Bill Graham and Chet Helms from an anonymous group, signing itself Ma, who claimed to represent eighty-three light shows, although only twenty had ever performed in public. It demanded that light shows be paid $900 a weekend and share equal billing with the bands, or there would be picketing outside the Fillmore West, Winterland, and the Family Dog. Helms, who had been paying light shows $900 before he was forced to cut his budget, didn't take it too seriously until he arrived at the Family Dog on the Great Highway for a Grateful Dead benefit concert and walked straight into a picket line.

"They were trying to get Graham, but they saw me as vulnerable," Helms said. "They knew that if they pulled the same thing with Graham, he would have either called the cops or sent his bouncers out and it would have been physical."

While Helms was all peace and love, handing the demonstrators flowers and serving them tea and crumpets on the sidewalk, Bob Weir and Phil Lesh of The Grateful Dead drove up and clashed immediately with the pickets.

"There was a virtual fistfight," Helms said. "The Dead are a pretty physical bunch of people and there were a couple of punches thrown. Jerry Garcia showed up while this was erupting, and we both managed to calm things down and persuade the leaders to go across the street to the beach and talk."

Garcia, Helms and a delegation of strikers crowded into the back of the Grateful Dead equipment van to discuss the matter. They agreed unanimously and concluded that everyone on the scene, with the exception of Bill Graham, was in debt, and in order to survive it was necessary to forget any differences and work together for a common cause; towards this end they called a summit meeting at the Family Dog hall the following Tuesday.

Bill Graham was among the 300 people who packed the Family Dog hall for what Helms called "the common." The meeting began with Helms casting the I Ching as Graham, sitting with his head hunched over, looked bored.

Commencing the meeting, Helms admitted he was deep in debt and could not afford to pay the light shows what they demanded. He called for a new way to distribute "the few potatoes available."

Then Bill Graham stood up to speak, unaware of the high level of hostility toward him. He began by brushing off his old rival, saying, "Chet runs this place on a dream, a nice one, but he's having financial problems because although he understands the problems of the business, he has refused to meet them."

He then lashed out against the light-show members, who threatened to picket his Fillmore West that night, yelling: "You do not tell me what to do. If you don't like the way I conduct my business, why the fuck don't you get off your asses and do it? Where the fuck does the artist come to say, 'You the businessman must support *us*' when I personally think the light shows are not producing an income for me?

"The only way you can do this is to kill me and step over me. I will never have anyone tell me to what level I support an art, what I must pay a light show."

Self-appointed spiritual leader Steve Gaskin, then turned the meeting into a courtroom scene, with himself as Graham's prosecutor.

"When you started, you had to make a choice between love and money," Gaskin accused. "You've got our money, so you can't have our love . . . you've used dramatics today to fuck over a lot of heads with your emotional trips."

Shaken to his very roots and trembling with emotion, Graham attempted to defend himself, recounting his life during the Holocaust, his early days surviving in the Bronx, and his fight to run his own business.

Gaskin stood up, accused Graham of acting and announced to everyone that Graham was a fraud and had been quoting a speech verbatim from an Eli Wallach movie.

With tears in his eyes, Graham turned to Gaskin and said, "I apologize, motherfucker, that I'm a human being. I fucking apologize. Emotional—you're fucking right. Fuck you, you stupid prick! Do you know what emotions are? Stand up and have emotions. Get up and work. Get up and sing. Get up and act. You think I'm an actor? You're full of shit, man. I have more fucking balls than you'll ever see. You want to challenge me in any way about emotions? You slimy little man . . . you slimy little man."

After telling the meeting to fuck off, Graham then stormed out of the meeting trailed by an astonished *Time* magazine writer who was doing a profile on him. On the way out, a musician tried to calm him down. Seething with anger, Graham hissed, "Don't get peaceful with me."

Outside, a group of drunken surfers who happened to be driving by, hurled a brick through the Family Dog's plate-glass window at the same time Graham slammed the door shut, providing perfect punctuation to what Jerry Garcia later called "psychic anger."

Chris Brooks, who was at the meeting, said she was shocked to see how the whole community turned on Graham. "Bill had tears in his eyes. He hurt. He sat there while they called him a capitalist pig and kept attacking him. He kept trying to explain his position. He's a businessman. He's not a hippie."

Ralph J. Gleason also witnessed the spectacle. "It was one of the ugliest things I ever saw," Gleason said in 1972. "It was pretty awful the way it was finally laid down to him. That was a very tough and nasty and ungenerous way of expressing it, even though there may be an element of truth in it. Put that way to Bill, it really freaked him out."

Chet Helms still believes that Graham was playing to the gallery and giving an Oscar-winning performance. "Bill could play the victim better than anybody on the planet," he said. "He started going through his histrionics, pounding on his chest and crying, and he was so convincing he even had many people in the audience feeling sorry for him."

The next day Graham announced he was leaving San Francisco forever.

"This town has never stopped rapping an honest businessman for four fucking years," he told *Rolling Stone.* "I leave here very sad . . . I may be copping out, but your attitudes have driven me to my decision."

It wasn't the first or last time Bill Graham would threaten to pack up and leave San Francisco. The truth was that things were going too well for him in San Francisco to consider quitting his Fillmore gold mine. Later that year, when the Fillmore West building was purchased by the Howard Johnson restaurant chain, which planned to demolish it and build a hotel, Graham decided to move the Fillmore West to another location.

By this time the Fillmore West had become the best-known concert venue in the world and was *the* place to play. To cater for the legions of road-weary, out-of-town musicians, San Francisco reverted to its gold-rush mentality with every imaginable pleasure available for the asking. The finest drugs flowed freely, as did a growing army of sexy young groupies, with Graham applying his gift for organization to keep all this hedonism in control. There was always a good supply of marijuana and cocaine backstage at the Fillmore, and he appointed his new publicist Chris Brooks to ensure that the groupie scene ran smoothly.

"I was a pimp by virtue of the fact that I was publicist," says Brooks, then a twenty-nine-year-old mother of twins. "At the Fillmore, because of my seniority, I surrounded myself with a bevy of beautiful birds who I knew were clean and fun and would show the guys a good time on the weekend and not bother them later at home."

In 1969 Brooks, who used the nickname Sunshine, told *Rolling Stone* that the English groups called her "Mum" and she was their "mother confessor."

"I know I'm not beautiful, but I'm not self-conscious, either, and often I can get something going where the other girls would sort of hang back and wait for it to happen. I'm the front-runner."

Today Brooks lives in Los Angeles and looks back fondly on her days running the groupie scene at the Fillmore. "It was free love for everyone but me," she said. "I came from an older generation, and I couldn't behave like that if I wanted. I didn't have the guts. I don't sleep with strangers.

"When a guy is away from home and all of a sudden you've got beautiful girls—or not-so-beautiful girls—throwing themselves at you, you can indulge your wildest fantasies. I would like to know the man who could resist that one hundred percent of the time.

"Most of the bands I worked for were English and away from home. It would be a matter of Roger Daltrey saying, 'Chris, you know that Chinese bird over there with the big bristols?'

"I'd say, 'Yes, I do.'

" 'Could we have an introduction, please?' And they were always properly introduced.

"I introduced Glen Curnick of Jethro Tull to a woman he married because he asked me if I knew any Oriental girls. I said I know only one, and the next thing they were married."

According to Brooks, the English musicians were the most adventurous with the groupies. "English guys are not beyond two girls at a time," she said. "American guys are much more conservative. An Englishman at nineteen is as mature as an American at twenty-six or twenty-seven. There isn't an Englishman who doesn't know about amyl nitrate. Its medical use is for people who have heart attacks. Its legal at any drugstore. What they do is pop an amyl nitrate at the strategic moment in bed. It stimulates a climax, brings you up like a rocket."

Bill Graham amused many at the Fillmore West when he succumbed to the charms of a sexy young groupie, falling head over heels in love with her.

"At one point Bill was having a mad affair with this young groupie who was just turning him around and inside out," Brooks said.

One night Graham was devastated when he caught her having sex with a musician in the Fillmore dressing room.

"I remember Bill standing outside the door with his arms folded and his face getting redder and redder while she was in there screwing," said Brooks. "When she came out, the poor girl saw Bill, who gave her this wilting look. Then he turned on his heel and walked out."

But Graham was infatuated with the young groupie and his one-sided affair soon became the talk of the Fillmore.

"I think it was pure sex for Bill," Brooks said. "She was very young and very sexual and never wore underwear. She would flash him and do all sorts of things to get his motor running. We all felt sorry for him, as it was obvious that she was using him. He treated her like his mistress and paid her rent and things, but she wasn't faithful to him. She'd make it with bands right in front of him."

The backstage scene at the Fillmore West was not unlike a brothel, with dozens of girls packed into the cramped area trying to hook their favorite musician by eye contact as he walked by.

"Backstage is the battleground of groupie-dom," said *Rolling Stone,* describing the action. "They converge, colors flying, literally by the dozens when somebody like Jimi Hendrix or Cream are on, and the first obstacle is the guard at the backstage entrance. It's a real challenge getting by him, unless a chick is extraordinarily beautiful or special looking, or has some real business getting in there."

Brooks helped to arrange Led Zeppelin's legendary orgies after playing the Fillmore, although she never attended them. "Led Zeppelin were the least discreet of the bands," she said. "John Paul Jones and I would leave the room when we knew something heavy was going to come down. John didn't partake in those festivities, and I didn't want to watch.

At one Led Zeppelin orgy at the Villa Roma, where the main attraction was "live birds and squid in the bathtub," the most enthusiastic participant was one of Bill Graham's top executives.

"I had to baby-sit Bonzo [John Bonham] that night as he had the clap and didn't want to be tempted to join in. He said, 'Brooksy, stay with me please,' and he told me that the last time he had gone home with a dose and gave it to his wife.

"I once saw Bonzo heap a plate with potato salad, walk up behind this groupie, lift her skirt, and shove the whole plate between her legs. The poor girl went tripping out with potato salad dripping on the floor. Goes to the washroom. Washes up and comes back. That was the mentality of some of those girls. They demeaned themselves."

The concert promotion business came of age in August 1969, with three days of love and peace at Woodstock. The man responsible was Michael Lang, whose only previous foray into concert promotion had been the Miami Pop Festival the previous year. Preparing for the concert, Lang and his two partners began contacting agents and in the process angered Bill Graham by signing up the Fillmore East's complete summer schedule of bands. Graham had good reason to be alarmed, if Woodstock was a success, his shows would fold. The fans preferred to pay an extra $5 to see fifteen top bands on one bill instead of paying for separate Fillmore shows strung out over the summer.

"Bill called and threatened to pull the show," Michael Lang remembers. "He was trying to bully us. I said he can threaten all he wants, but I don't think anybody's going to budge. We have contracts. We've paid our money and we're in business here."

To avert a clash, Lang arranged to meet the powerful promoter at Ratner's deli for breakfast. He offered not to announce the acts for Woodstock until after they had played the Fillmore so ticket sales wouldn't be harmed. Graham agreed and even accepted an invitation to come to the festival.

"His parting comment to me after the meeting was 'I guess we both can't play God on the same day,' " Lang said. "Bill had one of the great egos of our industry, and Woodstock was something that was going to put him in the shadow. And it did."

After getting fired by Graham, John Morris went to work for Lang on Woodstock and recruited most of his old Fillmore staff to help him with the festival.

"Bill started putting Woodstock down from the very first minute," Morris said. "Bill thought Woodstock was taking a bunch of kids and putting them in a field. Bill hated the idea. Bill looked at festivals and outdoor shows as uncontrollable and unsafe to the audience. You can't hear as well. You can't see the music. You've got to remember that before the sun came up on that first day at Woodstock, the largest concert ever had been 55,000 at Shea Stadium for the Beatles. So the idea of 400,000 to 600,000 people was ludicrous."

Frank Barsalona played a key role in selling many of the acts for Woodstock to John Morris for prices that would skyrocket after the festival and the resulting hit movie and best-selling double album.

A breakdown of what the acts earned at Woodstock gives an insight into where the groups then stood in rock's hierarchy. Headliner Jimi Hendrix received $30,000; The Band, Janis Joplin, and Jefferson Airplane were paid $15,000; Sly and the Family Stone, The Who, and Crosby, Stills, Nash & Young all received $12,500; Joan Baez and Creedence Clearwater Revival each got $10,000; The Grateful Dead got $7,500; Ten Years After got $6,500; and Joe Cocker and Santana each played for a mere $2,500.

Graham was insistent that his little known protégés Santana play Woodstock as he knew the exposure would catapult them into the big time. He blackmailed Lang and Morris, threatening to pull The Grateful Dead from the show, if Santana didn't play. At first they were skeptical—Santana hadn't even released an album—but after hearing the band's infectious Latin rhythms, they were instant converts.

"I booked them into Woodstock as a favor to Bill and also because I thought they were fantastic," Morris said. "They were literally an add-on, and they took the thing over and kicked off an entire career because of it."

Morris sent his old friend a first-class ticket to fly to Woodstock and arranged a nostalgic stay at the Concord resort. Flying onto Max Yasgur's farm in New York's Catskill Mountains that first day, Graham found the Woodstock site in total chaos, with all his fears of disaster apparently realized.

"I was up to my ears in bodies and logistics," Morris remembers. "It was madness."

Morris and his staff were in a war zone with tens of thousands more kids than expected and with no basic facilities to accommodate them. In desperation, Morris appealed to Graham to help him sort out what he believed to be a life-or-death situation. Refusing to have anything further to do with Woodstock and have his name linked with a disaster, Graham demanded to be helicoptered out immediately.

"I had given it every single thing I could do," said Morris. "I went down on my hands and knees and begged him. I knew Bill was totally straight and wasn't going to do any drugs. He wasn't going to fall apart and go off into the ozone layer.

"He could have made a serious contribution to Woodstock. I let him sit there for ages waiting for a helicopter. I was just horribly disappointed in him. He just couldn't cope with it, for it was on a scale that his mind didn't compute. He let me down when I needed him, and I have always blamed him for that."

Eighteen months later, Morris had his reckoning with Graham during the premiere of the Woodstock movie. Without informing Graham, the producers had included footage of a revealing interview with Graham expressing his contempt for the festival. When asked in the movie how he would handle the enormous crowd pouring onto the site, he responded, "You have to have some control. You know, when you have those man-eating marabunta ants coming over the hill in South America, if they want to cut 'em off and stop them from coming, they make a ditch. They put oil in the ditch; they make a flame. I'm not saying they should put up flame to stop the people. There has to be some way to stop the influx of humanity."

John Morris, who helped in the film's production and knew exactly where the speech was, anxiously waited near Graham to see his reaction. "I came over and stood next to him for the sole purpose of being there when it came on. He was critiquing the Woodstock movie and taking notes on the whole film with a little pad and a pencil. When his speech about the ants came up, he snapped the pencil in half, and it shot out and hit somebody in the audience."

When the Rolling Stones started planning their 1969 U.S. tour it was only natural that they sought out Bill Graham, as the West Coat's number one promoter, to handle the San Francisco shows. But Graham's relationship with The Stones got off to a bad start when he received a forty-page rider for their 1969 tour, listing the band's demands for the three California shows in November. Most promoters would have been honored to be given a slice of the Stones' high-grossing action, but Graham felt insulted when he was summoned to meet with a tour representative to discuss the choice of menu and beverages he was expected to pay for.

"The rider itself was outrageous," Graham said. "That started the war on that particular Rolling Stones tour. So I called them in advance and said, 'Pray tell, if you arrive at my gig and you snap your fingers and you order pheasant on the glass for one hundred and four people and you want Dom Perignon champagne, is that what I give you and pay for?'

"And he said yes. I said, 'Well I have news for you. It's like visiting my home. If I invite you for dinner, let me present you with a spread. It's not à la carte. You're not in the Hotel Pierre here. You're in show business.' And we had an outrageous battle."

Throwing down the gauntlet, Graham completely ignored the rider and called out for a spread of hot dogs and hamburgers from Zim's.

On the other hand, The Rolling Stones first saw Graham as another dishonest promoter. "We weren't very impressed by him in those days," Bill Wyman remembers. "We just thought he was a bit of a wide boy and we didn't really trust him."

Things went from bad to worse at the first Oakland Coliseum arena show when thousands of people who had been dancing in the aisles rushed the stage in the middle of "Satisfaction," knocking over Graham's closed-circuit cameras.

"Graham jumped onto the stage and began bouncing around like a man trying to stamp out a nest of snakes, pushing kids away and giving orders," wrote *Rolling Stone* reviewer Jerry Hopkins. "Sam Cutler [the Stones' tour manager] asked Graham to leave the stage. Graham told Cutler to get the hell off *his* stage. Then Graham grabbed Cutler—and Cutler, having a fuse only millimeters longer than Graham's, grabbed back. They were going to kill each other. Five feet away the Stones were still playing 'Satisfaction.' "

After the fistfight was stopped, a raging Graham had to be removed from the stage before going backstage to sulk. After the Stones' first show, the backstage tension was intense. While Graham paced up and down fuming, a dozen black-suited security men were summoned to guard the Stones' dressing room in case of attack. Bill Wyman remembers the Stones taking their revenge later that night by trashing the dressing room and throwing fast food over the many Bill Graham posters and pictures on the wall. After seeing the damage, Graham snubbed the Stones and refused to pay his traditional dressing-room visit to wish them good luck before going onstage in San Diego later that week.

"He didn't come backstage and chat to us," said Wyman. "We'd heard that he said in the press that he didn't like us and we'd said in the press that we didn't like him. So he just did the promotion without even being in attendance and he didn't really appear."

At the San Diego Sports Arena, Graham directly challenged The Rolling Stones by appealing to the audience not to come up on stage after "three very serious physical incidents" at the recent Oakland shows.

"It was as if Graham were drawing a line and daring the Stones to cross it," wrote Hopkins. "The Stones crossed it."

Wyman says that at that time the Stones held Graham and the whole West Coast music scene in contempt. "What we really didn't like was the people he was promoting," Wyman said. "The San Francisco lot, the flower power and all that sort of stuff. It didn't really interest us. And all those acts that he had at that time weren't people that we admired. We thought most of the acts that were on then were a bit wet. They weren't our cup of tea. All the Buffalo Springfield and the Jefferson Airplane weren't the sort of music we were interested in."

Wyman added that at the beginning the band felt Graham had seriously underestimated them as businessmen. "That was something about him that upset us in the early days. I don't think he appreciated our attitude to the music business, as most people didn't. And he kind of underestimated us and he was a bit arrogant. We just thought he was a fly [shady] promoter and we couldn't give a damn who this guy was."

After the band left California for the rest of their U.S. tour, Graham pledged he would never again promote a Rolling Stones concert, although conceding, "Mick Jagger is the greatest fucking performer in the whole fucking world."

A few weeks later, Graham donated his Fillmore West crew to run the Stones' free concert at the Altamont Raceway on December 6 in exchange for being allowed to showcase his acts on the bill.

After the Stones had successfully used the Hell's Angels as security for its free concert in London's Hyde Park a few months earlier, the San Francisco chapter was invited to police Altamont. But the American Angels were a different breed than their more reserved British counterparts. The original San Francisco biker gang immediately stamped its authority on the proceedings by arriving early Saturday morning armed to the teeth with knives, chains and other weapons. For entertainment they brought a yellow bus packed with beer, red wine and a huge supply of LSD.

A few hours later the drink and drugs had taken hold and the Angels were running riot, attacking fans indiscriminately. The first real sign of trouble happened during Jefferson Airplane's set when singer Marty Balin was knocked unconscious after he jumped off the stage to stop an Angel beating up a fan.

By the time the Rolling Stones took the stage the Angels had taken over the show. Fast losing control, Mick Jagger stopped the show several times to appeal to the Angels to "keep it together." When the Stones started playing "Under My Thumb" an 18-year-old black man named Meredith Hunter suddenly rushed towards the stage brandishing what appeared to be a gun and was immediately stabbed to death by a Hell's Angel just 20 feet from Jagger.

After the tragedy Graham railed on his employees running the concert, calling them "murderers."

Using Altamont to focus national attention on himself, Graham offered Mick Jagger $50,000 to join him in a live coast-to-coast television or radio debate on Altamont. Publicly challenging the superstar singer, Graham patriotically wrapped himself in the American flag and demanded to know what right the Stones had to mock Uncle Sam and take $1.2 million out of the country.

Admonishing Mick Jagger, Graham said, "He's in his home country now somewhere—what did he leave behind throughout this country? Every gig, he was late. Every fucking gig, he made the promoter and the people bleed. What right does this god have to descend on this country this way? It will give me great pleasure to tell the public that Mick Jagger is not God, Junior."

Branding Altamont a "holocaust," Graham squarely laid the blame for the tragedy on the police, adding, "They should have taken Mister Jagger, twisted his fucking arms behind his back, put him in front of the radio and said, 'Mister Jagger, if we have to break your arms, call it off.' "

Bill Wyman believes that Graham's public challenge to the Stones was nothing more than a publicity stunt. "I think he used people to promote himself," said the Rolling Stone. "We thought he was more interested in extending his ego to his best advantage as opposed to doing his job and being a promoter."

9

Rock 'n' Roll Grows Up

After Woodstock the concert business grew up and would never be the same again. As the dust settled after the historic music festival, the musicians and their managers suddenly realized their new power and immediately started demanding a bigger slice of the profits from the promoters. The honeymoon between the promoters and bands was over. From now on it would be a rocky relationship.

"Woodstock was when everybody realized it was real," said promoter Vinnie Fusco. "It was both the beginning and the end because from that point on the bands changed position. If you want to target a point where the acts and their managers became wise enough to make the demands they made, it was after Woodstock. That's when we asked, 'Why did four hundred thousand people come?' Woodstock just told everybody, 'Maybe it's not Bill Graham the promoter, it's our acts.' And then eventually the artists assumed, 'It's me.' "

Three weeks before Woodstock, Fusco had organized the now-long-forgotten Atlantic City Pop Festival with the same lineup of bands as Woodstock and had been amazed by the response.

"We ran an ad in the *New York Times* which cost ten grand," Fusco said. "We had more money in the mail before we had even signed an act or paid a deposit, and it just built from there. Nobody realized what was happening. The audience that came to Atlantic City was from Canada, Iowa, Minnesota, and Wisconsin. What are they doing at the Atlantic City Racetrack? How did they even know it was happening? So there was a whole thing going on that was quicker than we, or anybody else, knew."

Bill Graham pulled no punches when he was asked about how Woodstock had changed the concert business. "It was a tragedy," Graham said. "Groups recognized that they could go into larger cattle markets, play less time, and make more dollars. What they've done is to destroy the rock industry."

Supergroup Led Zeppelin led the charge by demanding an unprecedented 90/10 split for their 1971 tour. "We were the most powerful band in America." said former Led Zeppelin tour manager Richard Cole. "No one else had ever done a ninety-ten."

Although publicly screaming "I will not do ninety-tens," Graham and his fellow promoters had no alternative and were forced to accept Led Zeppelin's demands.

"Bill had to take it or leave it," Cole said. "The thing was that if you advertised a Led Zeppelin date with a $200 ad in the newspaper, it would be a sellout on the day the tickets went on sale, whether it was five thousand or fifty thousand. There was absolutely no risk involved for the promoter."

Led Zeppelin's huge bearlike manager, Peter Grant, who looked more like the captain of a pirate galleon than a rock 'n' roll manager, also insisted on dispensing with the opening act.

"There really was no point having an opening act for Led Zeppelin because they played for two-and-a-half to three hours, and we would have had to go into overtime, which would have cut into our profits enormously," Cole explained.

The sheer sums of money involved were staggering. Grant liked Led Zeppelin to be paid in hard cash, so the band traveled with literally millions of dollars in ready money. Richard Cole remembers, "The gross for Zeppelin on Pontiac Stadium was $980,000. After you take out your expenses I'm sure we came up with seven hundred thousand dollars when ticket prices were six dollars. Imagine what it would be at today's prices."

But although the top rock stars were cleaning up, preaching noncapitalistic idealism while raking in the millions, audiences still regarded Bill Graham and the other promoters as the pinstriped capitalist bogeymen of rock 'n' roll. When bands forced up ticket prices or failed to turn up for a show it, was always the promoter who got the blame.

Jazz & Pop magazine columnist Patricia Kennely observed that while "it may be quite fashionable in certain circles to damn Bill Graham as a capitalist," he had contributed more to the music business than anyone else. "It is my personal observation that promoters as a group have been pretty badly mauled by people who ought to know better. It is all too easy to take a gratuitous swipe at Graham."

Kennely castigated groups who once were happy to play for "hamburger and beer money" but were now demanding $50,000 for a forty-five-minute set plus a percentage of the gross, asserting that they were directly responsible for driving up ticket prices.

"When the promoter who has to pay the band and cover overhead costs and staff salaries and often as not post a guarantee to the corporate owners of the hall or festival site and still hope to make a few bills for himself out of it all, gets *blamed* for all this, *then* I think change is due, and past due."

Joshua White observed the change in musicians' attitudes during this formative period of rock. "After Woodstock we all knew the Fillmore was doomed," White said. "All the managers figured their bands could play arenas and stadiums and eventually that's where they went. It was very hard to get the Airplane and the Dead on a bill together after Woodstock because they wanted to play those giant venues."

But Pete Townshend of the Who defended musicians, claiming it was impossible for a band to make a profit playing the Fillmore. "We've always been fond of Bill and have tried to be fair to him," Townshend said at the time. "So we used to go there for a third of what we can make on the road. We've always worked for him as cheap as we can, and for a man who's close to becoming a millionaire, it's a bit of a hard-luck story."

As the musicians quickly adapted to their new power in the rock business, a new arrogance set in. *Variety* condemned the increasing number of acts which were walking out on performances, noting their "shorter tempers and longer lists of demands." Comparing the egotistic protests to industrial wildcat strikes, *Variety* pointed the finger at Diana Ross for canceling a show after her pet dog died and Jimi Hendrix for storming offstage after breaking a guitar string. The trade paper singled out Jefferson Airplane as the group particularly feared by promoters for their bad attitude and instant cancellations.

In Bill Graham's eyes, this ungracious attitude was not only unprofessional, but showed a lack of respect for the profession.

"That's why the business isn't going to go where it should go," he said at the time. "They hold the weight. Jim Morrison holds the weight; Jimi

Hendrix holds the weight; Jefferson Airplane holds the weight. When Jim Morrison gets on the stage (I saw this in L.A.) and says to the public, 'You want music? You're not gonna get it now! I'm gonna read you some poetry!' What kind of poetry? Shit! And this man, who is God, Jr., in his opinion, gets on the stage and says to them, 'I'm gonna read it to you' . . . when he does it in Peoria and in Salt Lake City and Boise, he will get away with it until somebody goes up there and says, 'I'm gonna show you the real thing.' "

Although musicians may not have loved the unpredictable and outspoken promoter, they certainly respected him for his love of the music. Where Graham had once disliked rock music, he had now broadened his tastes from Latin music and could be seen at many of his concerts enthusastically accompanying the bands on his cowbell. He listened carefully to each and every note of the music and demanded the best performance out of his bands. If he thought a group hadn't delivered a good set, he would head off to the dressing room to critique. Like a manager of a basketball team, Graham would give his musicians a rousing pep talk, offering advice on how to better their performance for the second show.

Graham took Jimi Hendrix to task for playing a bad set during his 1969 New Year's Eve show at the Fillmore East when Hendrix introduced his Band of Gypsies. After finishing the first set to rapturous applause from the audience, a delighted Hendrix walked into Graham's office.

"Hendrix was a very quiet man, very shy," Graham said. "Jimi never asks, but he says, 'What'd you think, Bill?' And I didn't want to answer him, so I ask Kip and the others to leave the office. And I said, 'Jimi, you're the best guitar player I know, and tonight, for an hour-and-a-half you were a shuck. You were a disgrace to what you are.'

"And the guy's face just came down. He said, 'Didn't you hear that audience? They went crazy!'

" 'I know. You know what you did? You made the same mistake too many of the other great ones make. You subconsciously play what they want, you sock it to them. You did an hour-and-a-half of shuck and grind and bullshit, that you can do with your eyes closed lying down somewhere. But you forgot one thing. You forgot to play. And it's tragic for you because you can play better than anyone I know.'

"Well, the guy fell apart. 'Why are you telling me that?' 'BECAUSE YOU ASKED ME!' And we had a bad scene, pushing the furniture around, yelling. And Jimi's a quiet guy.

"And I said to Jimi, 'If I were you, and I'm dreaming, but if I could, one of the great ways to educate the public, to let them know that they've fallen into your shit, is to come out and say, 'Did I sock it to you?' 'Yeah!' 'Boogie woogie?' 'Did you dig it?' 'Yeah!' 'You're all full of shit, I apologize. Don't let me do that to you.'

"And Jimi said, 'You're right, you're right. I'm sorry.' And then we went down for egg creams, settled down. And what happened next is one of the warmest things that ever happened to me."

For the second show, Hendrix took Graham's advice to heart and delivered one of the greatest sets of his career, which was immortalized on his *Band of Gypsies* live album.

Graham recalled, "What followed, with respect to Carlos and Eric and all those others, was the most brilliant, emotional display of virtuoso electric-guitar playing I have ever heard. I don't expect ever to hear such sustained brilliance in an hour and fifteen minutes. He just stood there, did nothing, just played and played and played."

"He comes off the stage afterwards, a wet rag, and says to me . . . 'All right?' I said, 'Jimi, it was great.' And I hugged him and got all wet, and I asked him if he would do an encore. 'Yeah.' He goes out and does every conceivable corny bullshit thing he can do."

Years later, Graham gave The Rolling Stones a dressing-down after they played a bad show during their 1980 U.S. Tour.

Bill Wyman remembers: "He went into our dressing room and gave everybody a bollocking. He said, 'You call yourself fucking professionals? It's the worst I've ever heard you guys. That was a shitty show, and I think you ought to be ashamed of yourself coming off.'

"We were flabbergasted because no one talks to us like that and he got away with it. A band of our stature doesn't like criticism, you know. Well, we don't mind it from someone we admire, but not a promoter. Because you don't think of a promoter as someone who's really into the music, but Bill was. We accepted it and pulled our socks up, and we were all right after that. But I've never known any promoter to do that before and be admired afterwards instead of being kicked in the ass or something. I thought that was great. I really admired him for that. Putting himself on the line for no reason. He could have just collected the money and forgot about it. That's what most of them do."

Carlos Santana recalled how Bill Graham always demanded excellence from his musicians. "Bill was a very passionate man in the full sense of the word. He taught me that when you play, you should play the same way B. B. [King] plays or Miles [Davis] plays. Give it all your heart.

If you're gonna die, die on the line. Don't be jivin'. Don't play half-hearted. Bill couldn't stand musicians who in the middle of the set would look at their watch. That would drive him crazy."

One musician to feel the lash of the Graham tongue was jazz great Roland Kirk. After a dispute about one of Kirk's band members arriving late, Graham fired the band from a Led Zeppelin bill, yelling, "What do you think I'm running here, a fucking amateur hour?" Kirk responded by accusing Graham of patronizing black jazz musicians. "People feel that when they put us on a bill with rock groups they're doing us a favor—they're getting a lot of people there who never heard of you. Well, that's true, but it ain't no one-sided street. I don't stand up there with no tin cup playing for people. I'm giving them something. I'm giving them part of me."

Jazz legend Miles Davis also had a bitter confrontation with Graham. It happened after Columbia president Clive Davis ordered him to play the Fillmore East for exposure to white audiences, following the release of the trumpeter's *Bitches Brew* album. Graham offered him only $1,500 instead of his regular $5,000 a night. *New York Post* music columnist Alfred G. Aronowitz described the preshow Mexican standoff between Davis and Graham.

"You could see them bristling at each other," wrote Aronowitz. "Miles walking in through the stage door in his long white furry coat and Bill pacing back and forth in his shirtsleeves. They hardly spoke a word and yet they also hardly let a moment pass when they weren't in each other's sight. You kept finding them just off the wings backstage, Miles ignoring his dressing room, Bill ignoring his office, each ignoring the other."

Another time, Graham decided to teach the drummer of the English band Ten Years After a lesson he'd never forget following a weak drum solo.

"If there's anything I can't take in rock 'n' roll it's the extended drum solo," Graham said. "Very few can carry a drum solo.

I was determined to eliminate it the next time, and I went to Vegas and convinced Buddy Rich to come out with his band and be on the next show when this band hit town. We had an opening act, and then Buddy came on to play, and he was brilliant. At the end of his set, I went into the headliner's dressing room and put my hand on the drummer's shoulders and said, 'I can't wait for your solo tonight, baby.' "

At the end of 1969. Graham's trusted right-hand man at the Fillmore West, Paul Baratta, staged a coup to unseat his mentor as the king of San

Francisco rock. The former actor, hired to replace Jim Haynie at the Fillmore Auditorium, cut a deal with the owners of Winterland to jump ship and run concerts at the larger hall, where Graham had been staging them for years. On hearing the news, Graham acted fast and met with the owners of Winterland to stem the threat to his San Francisco empire. He managed to wrestle Winterland away from Baratta by guaranteeing $60,000 in rentals for the rest of the year in return for exclusive use. Only three weeks after quitting the Fillmore, Baratta had been effectively neutralized and was safely back in the Graham fold, heading up its new Southern California operation, aptly named Shady Management. Explaining his sudden about-face, Baratta admitted the deal had "smacked of underhandedness," but added, "sometimes working in a small room with Bill all the time can get to be trying after a while."

Ever hungry for new territory, Graham was now on the move across the Oakland Bay Bridge, where he had discovered a new cash cow—the 3,400-seat Berkeley Community Theater. By promoting three bands in a Fillmore West–type format, he was able to double his gross by charging $3.50 to $5 a ticket instead of the $3 Fillmore price. Quickly realizing the theater's potential, he attempted to lock up every available date for the next year to freeze out all competition.

Meanwhile, on the East Coast, Graham was suddenly hit by a series of setbacks. His much-touted Summer Music Series at the New York State Pavilion, on the site of the 1964–65 World's Fair in Flushing Meadows, Queens, was canceled after the city withdrew the permit. Then he failed in an ambitious attempt to market the Fillmore experience as a television special. "Fillmore at Tanglewood" was to be the first made-for-television rock special; the show, headlined by The Who and Chicago, was designed to re-create the excitement of the Fillmore while being filmed on location at the picturesque Tanglewood Music Barn in the Berkshire Mountains in Massachusetts. New York producer George Honchar was hired as technical director and the show was to be emceed by Graham.

"We filmed the shows, which included historic footage of the last time The Who ever played *Tommy* with Keith Moon," said Honchar. "The problem was that Bill had not finalized all the rights agreements with the acts. Unfortunately after the taping some of the acts could not reach agreements with Bill and the project had to be abandoned."

Furthermore, Graham's bold thrust into Southern California and the lucrative L.A. market had also gone sour. Police harassment pulled the plug on many shows and the American Federation of Musicians, who had been trying to clamp down on Graham for paying third string bands below union scale, now began investigations for unfair practices after hearing complaints against him from Little Richard, Country Joe and the Fish, and Roger McGuinn. With this series of failures, many music-industry observers saw Bill Graham on the ropes, fighting desperately to keep his empire together.

Later Graham admitted that dealing with the Fillmores alone had run him ragged, bringing him to the edge of a nervous breakdown.

"The economics got so it was madness," Graham explained, looking back a couple of years later. "They'd become a fifty-two-week job and they were three thousand miles apart and driving me mad because it was becoming more and more difficult to operate very small halls."

Now believing Graham to be vulnerable, Paul Baratta staged a second coup for Winterland. This time he was in a much stronger position, as Graham had not paid his $60,000 guarantee to Winterland. Angry with Graham, the owners decided to back Baratta, handing him Winterland on a plate. Baratta fired his first salvo by signing up Graham's favorite bands, including Jefferson Airplane and The Grateful Dead, for his first Winterland show. For the San Francisco bands, which largely owed their success to Graham, it was an ideal opportunity to start a bidding war among the promoters and drive their performance prices up.

"I think Bill's in for a fight," said a confident Baratta in *Rolling Stone,* revealing his plans to become the premier promoter in San Francisco. "Graham has never had any real competition. I know how to package a show as well as Bill. Winterland is the biggest hall in town and I know the market well enough to put the shows together so the people will come to see them."

Justifying his split with Graham, Baratta labeled Graham a heartless money-making machine. "I broke with Bill because of a growing disenchantment," he said. "At first what Bill did was good. He had heart. Then it began to seem like the bankbook was pumping blood through his veins. We just went our separate ways."

Watching the fight closely from the sidelines, *Rolling Stone* reported the action with the gravity of a world-championship boxing match and forecast that the seasoned pro could be expected to "fight a hard battle" against the young challenger.

Siding with Baratta, *Rolling Stone,* whose owner, Jann Wenner, had long been feuding with Graham, issued this warning to the hard-nosed promoter:

> You meet the same people on the way down as you did on the way up.
>
> Graham has made many enemies over the years. Now, at least

some of them are happy to see him get some real competition and will do all they can, including playing the Winterland affairs, to reduce Graham's overwhelming totalitarian position in the entertainment world."

During Baratta's first Winterland show came the sad news that Janis Joplin had died of a heroin overdose on October 4, 1970, this just one week after Jimi Hendrix's death. Baratta kept the news from Jefferson Airplane and The Grateful Dead, concerned that they might be too upset to play. But it was left to Bill Graham to give perspective to the drug deaths of rock's two great legends of the sixties, by telling *Rolling Stone* they had been unable to handle their meteoric rise to success:

"Janis, like anybody else in rock, I don't think ever knew how to handle success . . . I think it created problems for Janis—but it never spoiled her. It has always been questionable—does this kind of success include happiness? People have said to me many times, 'Look at you yelling and screaming all the time. With your money, are you happy?' That's for me to determine."

Now under threat from Baratta in his home territory, Graham hung tough, telling *Billboard* magazine that there was room for only one major promoter in San Francisco: "If one butcher shop does good business, but another opens up across the street, there won't be twice as much business. They will split the business. With two ballrooms an act can be offered $5,000 by me and then $6,000 by someone else. The act then comes back and says, 'Gee, Bill, we want to play for you. Just offer us $7,000.' Pretty soon the price is $10,000 and the person who gets the act goes out of business."

Three months later, Graham had recaptured Winterland and left Baratta out in the cold by securing exclusive use of San Francisco's largest venue for 1971 with options on the next two years. Taking aim at his critics, Graham told The English music paper *Melody Maker*, "After a time I get sick of being called a capitalist pig, the big rip-off, being talked about as though I were some kind of leper. In San Francisco they say I have a monopoly. Man, there are four to five halls in that city waiting for someone to make it happen. Isn't it just possible that someone is better than the rest at making it happen?"

After Paul Baratta left the Fillmore West, Graham, taking no chances hiring an outsider, replaced him with his old Concord Hotel buddy, Keeva Kristal. The two had met years before when Graham was a busboy and Kristal a waiter who had shown him the ropes. Without any advance notice to his staff Graham brought Keeva into the Fillmore West and introduced him as the new manager. Graham then disappeared for a few weeks.

Kristal was given a free hand in running the Fillmore West, and he soon made his presence known by coming down hard on the staff and issuing a flurry of pink slips. The Fillmore West staff disliked Kristal intensely. Graham, meanwhile, spent more and more time away on business.

Most of the key people in his organization indulged freely in drugs and were often high at work. But the drugs of choice were changing from marijuana and LSD to the harder-edged cocaine.

"The fish stinks from the head down," says Joshua White who disbanded his Joshua Light Show and left the Fillmore East in mid-1970. "Instead of getting stoned and getting mellow, they got stoned and mean. A lot of high-level management at the Fillmore were taking cocaine, which didn't have evil connotations at that time. In the Joshua Light Show I was dealing with people I loved, but they were making me crazy. When they smoked they would just get silly and mellow but then when they started taking cocaine they weren't silly and mellow anymore. I had to get out of the Fillmore because I was just scared of those people. I thought everybody was getting crazy here."

White says that cocaine was one of the main reasons he left the music business to move into television production. "The thing about coke is that you think you're being terribly organized. You have meetings and everything goes real fast and you just feel, like you can rule the world. And for a time you can. But when you crash, you lose it all."

As cocaine penetrated more deeply into both Fillmores, the audiences were graduating from marijuana and LSD to the unpredictable combination of downers and booze, which had a markedly bad effect on their behavior. To counter the increasingly combative audiences, the Fillmores' security force freely beat up troublesome fans in a reign of terror. This new drug-induced dark side of rock trickled down through the industry—from the music company executive at the top, down to the audiences at rock concerts.

By the beginning of 1971, rock's metamorphosis from childhood innocence to greed and decadence was alarming Bill Graham. Adopting the stance of a Bible-pounding preacher, Graham delivered a sermon to the music industry from the pulpit of *Variety,* predicting the death of rock 'n' roll unless honesty and decency were restored to the business.

"Right now there is a struggle going on between rock's essence and its decadent alter ego," warned Graham.

He then attacked promoters and artists for being corrupted by the huge sums of money rock was now generating and for sacrificing their art for the quick buck.

"The entire monetary structure of rock has greatly changed, meaning that many groups can play a few large arenas and pocket enough money to live in luxury. It is not uncommon to find a twenty-two-year-old earning up to $1,000,000 a year. This emphasis on playing the big halls, taking your money and running has had a bad effect on rock. Many groups have priced themselves out of the medium-sized concert market and lost respect for the audience.

Graham then proffered his favorite analogy: himself as theatrical maître d'. "We are in theater. You put a steak on a paper plate and it tastes all right, but you take the same steak and put it on china and it tastes different."

He then called for a return to standards in the concert industry, warning that rock could not afford to underestimate the taste of audiences by playing in huge arenas with no personal contact.

"The stars know that America is a fickle lady," he said. "Three-quarters of the groups around today are lousy. They just get out there and bang away to make a quick killing." When asked what was keeping rock alive, Graham replied contemptuously, "The idiot mass. A majority of the people don't eat what they want to eat, only what they are fed, or can buy. The groups today know they don't have to be good, just gimmicky—give 'em what they want. I book the bad ones into the Fillmores because of economics—an overhead of $30,000 a week—not including talent. We bring in the best groups we can and then the best of the worst."

Questioned by *Newsday* writer Prudence Brown in January 1971 about the hazards of putting on rock shows, the bitter promoter replied, "the highly probable chance that the producer will become neurotic and mentally disturbed."

Bill Graham was not the only promoter facing problems running small 3,000-seat auditoriums. The Aragon Ballroom closed its doors in October 1970, followed by Larry Magid's Electric Factory in December and the Boston Tea Party in January 1971, signalling the end of the "vaudeville" hippie ballroom circuit that dotted America. By the spring of 1971, Graham had overworked himself into the ground. His Fillmores no longer generated the enormous profits they once had, and Graham was worried. His insomnia had worsened steadily, and so had his tantrums. Always unpredictable, his terrible temper was now totally uncontrollable, and he would shout and scream constantly at his staff and colleagues during business negotiations, making him harder and harder to deal with. Old friends began to turn away from raging Bill, unable to handle his constant abuse.

Graham had also tied himself up in business knots by having gotten involved in many contradictory areas of the music industry. In addition to being a promoter, Graham now wore the hats of theater owner, agent, manager, and recording executive.

In effect, Graham found himself in the unworkable position of running a music industry within a music industry. As many of the areas were by nature adversarial, it inevitably led to his being in constant conflict with himself.

Graham realized that his only chance of survival in the seventies was to streamline his unwieldy music empire into a more efficient operation. He needed to exploit the opportunities offered by the new mega rock 'n' roll concerts. In a dramatic public relations masterstroke, Graham cleverly turned his weaknesses into strengths and set the stage for the next part of his career. He summoned the press to the Fillmore East and announced the closings of both Fillmores and his retirement from the music business. Sitting casually on the edge of the Fillmore stage with his usual V-neck sweater and rolled-up sleeves and wearing his trademark two-faced watch, the relaxed-looking promoter sent shock waves through the music industry with his announcement that the Fillmore East would close on June 27 and the Fillmore West later that summer. He delivered a seven-point indictment of the music industry, casting himself as the injured party, a victim of greedy bands, unscrupulous managers, and predatory agents. The timbre and nuances of the charges, embittered reprimands of each and every part of the music business, are pure Bill Graham.

> Ever since the creation of the Fillmores, it was my sole intention to do nothing more, nor less, than present the finest contemporary artists in this country, on the best stages and in most pleasant halls. The scene has changed and, in the long run, we are all to one degree or another at fault. All I know is what exists now is not what we started with, and what I see around me now does not seem to be a logical creative extension of that beginning. Therefore I am taking this opportunity to announce the closing of the Fillmores, and my eventual withdrawal from producing concerts.
>
> My reason are as follows:
>
> • The unreasonable and totally destructive inflation of the live

concert scene. Two years ago I warned that the Woodstock Festival syndrome would be the beginning of the end. I am sorry to say that I was right. In 1965 when we began the original Fillmore Auditorium, I associated with and employed "musicians." Now, more often than not, it's with "officers and stockholders" in large corporations—only they happen to have long hair and play guitars. I acknowledge their success, but condemn what that success has done to some of them. I continue to deplore the exploitation of the gigantic-hall concerts, many of them with high-priced tickets.

• I had always hoped to be able to present artists whose musical worth I felt was important; artists whose music was valid, whether commercially popular or not. There are fewer quality artists today; but many of those that do exist do not appear in public regularly. Therefore, in order to stay in business, I would be forced to present acts whose musicality fell far below my personal expectations and demands. I could do this, and in having to book 52 weeks a year it becomes tempting because it is so much easier to do. Thousands might even come to these concerts, but I personally would prefer not to present them. For who would gain?

• With all due respect for the role they play in securing work for the artists, the agents have created a new rock game called "packaging" which means simply that if the Fillmore wants a major headliner, then we are often forced to take the second and/or third act that the agent or manager insists upon whether or not we would take pride in presenting them, or whether or not such an act even belongs on that particular show. To do so would be to relinquish the essential responsibility of being a producer, and this I will not do.

• In the early days of both Fillmore East and West, the level of audience seemed much higher in terms of musical sophistication. Now there are too many screams for "more" with total disregard for whether or not there was any musical quality.

• The time and energy that is required for me to maintain a level of proficiency in my own work has grown so great that I have simply deprived myself of a family life.

• For six years, I have endured the abuse of many members of the public and press (in most instances people who did not know me personally). The role of "anti-Christ of the underground" has obviously never appealed to me. And when I ask for people to either judge me on some factual personal knowledge, or at least base their opinions on that which I produced and gave to the public, I was rarely answered.

• Rock has always been good to me in many ways, but the final and simple fact is that I am tired. The only reason to keep the Fillmore in operation at this point would be to make money. And though few have ever chosen to believe me on this point, money has never been my prime motivation; and now that it would become the only possible motivation to continue, I pass.

The Fillmore will become a thing of the past. I will remember with deep emotion and fondness the great and joyous moments of that past. I sincerely thank the artists and business associates who contributed to our success. But I warn the public to watch carefully for what the future will bring.

The rock scene in this country was created by a need felt by the people expressed by the musicians, and, I hope, aided to some degree by the effort of the Fillmores. But whatever has become of that scene, wherever it turned into the music industry of festivals, 20,000-seat halls, miserable production quality, and second-rate promoters—however it went wrong—please, each of you, stop and think whether or not you supported it regardless of how little you received in return.

I am not pleased with this "music industry." I am disappointed with many of the musicians working in it, and I am shocked at the nature of the millions of people who supported that "industry" without asking why. I am not assured that the situation will improve in the future.

When the astonished members of the press asked Graham why he was shuttering up the Fillmores, he explained his decision was made after his hero Sol Hurok had asked him to fill some free dates at the Metropolitan Opera House and the bands had wanted too much money for the project to be viable. The final straw had come when Jon Taplin, the manager of The Band, told him, "Bill are you trying to tell me that you want my act to play for [only] $50,000 a week?"

Graham's announcement hit the music industry with the full force of an earthquake and generated heated debate about whether rock was dead.

Clive Davis, president of Columbia Records, distanced himself from Graham and reassured *Variety* that rock was very much alive. "What is happening is that music is gradually changing in structure, in sound, in creativity, in appeal," Davis explained. "No, contemporary rock music is not dying. It is just weeding out the lesser lights by a process of elimination and the entrance fee is getting higher. But it is here to stay."

Davis also had some prophetic words of warning for Graham about abdicating his concert-promoting throne in New York. "If he stays away too long, we can be sure that others will come along to keep the musical fires burning with taste, style and dignity."

In the days following the press conference, Bill Graham became a national celebrity. He was interviewed by almost every major magazine and newspaper in the country and appeared on a slew of late-night talk shows, explaining his decision and discussing the future of rock 'n' roll. The showman in Graham loved the spotlight, and he came across well as an articulate and witty elder statesman of rock. To maximize the potential gold mine in the Fillmores' closings, Graham announced a final series of shows worthy of the legendary rock palaces.

Graham would not make it easy, however, for any aspiring promoters who hoped to step into his shoes after his retirement. Promoter Howard Stein, who ran the Capitol Theater in Port Chester, New York, which was essentially a clone of the Fillmore, found himself attacked bitterly by Graham after press speculation that he might take over the Fillmore East.

"I think Howard's become a promoter," Graham said, cynically emphasizing the difference between a mere promoter and Graham's self-appointed role as a producer. "A promoter is somebody who sells a product to a mass audience."

The venomous attack came after Stein promoted a badly organized Grateful Dead dance marathon at the Manhattan Center, prompting Graham to accuse his rival of staging a "planned, calculated rip-off."

Stein replied by asking why Graham was feeling "such hatred" against him and concluded that Graham was "elated" by the problems he had with the Grateful Dead show. "He called me up to scold me. How's that for self-importance," Stein said. "He called me up, screaming, 'I'm going to expose you because you knowingly robbed your audience!'

"I think he's such a vulnerable man. He puts himself up as God. He now is in his own mind the only concert producer in America. Everybody else is a promoter. But his great skills at being a good booker do not include being God."

On Memorial Day, Graham's careful plans to close the Fillmore West were thrown into disarray when someone spiked a water jug with LSD during a Grateful Dead show at Winterland, leading to the hospitalization of fifty fans with bad trips. Accusing San Francisco police chief Alfred J. Nelder of "overreaction" after he called for Graham's dance permit to be revoked, Graham railed, "What am I . . . some kind of fly-by-night slob? I've staged twelve hundred concerts for three million people, and this is the first incident like this. I don't think anybody took the acid by accident. Those who took a drink knew what was being passed around." The police and city reaction was so hostile that Graham decided to move up the closing of the Fillmore West to the week after Fillmore East's final show.

The final concert at the Fillmore East was by invitation only on June 27. The last bill was headed up by the Allman Brothers, Albert King (who had played on the first bill) the J. Geils Band, Mountain, The Beach Boys, and Country Joe and the Fish. The bands played in front of a banner reading "Graduation 1971," and the show was broadcast live on two New York FM radio stations WNEW and WPLJ. In an emotional moment at the end of the concert, Graham, who was emceeing, addressed his audience: "It's a strange feeling. If I can put it into little jars and put it on my shelf, I will be very happy." He then invited the entire Fillmore East staff to join him onstage and take a bow.

Behind the scenes there was great bitterness from many influential music-industry and press people who were not invited to the final show due to lack of space. Somewhat ironically, Graham later told Fillmore East press flack Pat Luce that he should have held the closing show in Madison Square Garden with all its extra room.

The following week the Fillmore West closed with five shows on consecutive nights culminating on July 4 with a billing of Santana, Creedence Clearwater Revival, and Tower of Power. In a well-coordinated plan to milk the final days of the Fillmore West for everything he could, Graham involved himself in producing a documentary of the closing week as well an all-star live double album of the final shows.

When the movie *Fillmore* was released the following May, with an R rating because of Graham's bad language, there was no doubt who was the star. Through shouting, screaming, cursing, and extracting every last drop of emotion for a full half hour of the 105-minute film, Bill Graham had finally made it to the silver screen in perhaps his best character performance—playing himself. Although the film was billed as a documentary, Graham was hailed by England's *Melody Maker* film critic for being "as riveting as Bogart or Cagney."

For a large part of the movie, Graham, looking more and more reptilian as he gets more and more excited, lambastes, browbeats, and argues with such stars as Boz Scaggs and Carlos Santana as he arranges the final Fillmore West shows. Later, his partner David Rubinson accused him of faking all the telephone scenes in the film, a charge which ex-actor Graham denied vehemently.

In the climax of the movie, former Charlatan member Mike Wilhelm arrives at the Fillmore to ask Graham to book his new band for the closing shows. When the promoter refuses, a frustrated Wilhelm ignites Graham's short fuse with the show-stopping line, "Well, I'd just like to say, 'Fuck you and thanks for the memories, man.' "

Graham then loses it and, in a torrent of abuse, marches Wilhelm out of the door raging, "The next time you say 'Fuck you' to me, I hope it's out there somewhere with no camera around. I'll take your teeth out of your mouth and shove 'em through your nose . . . Fucking animal."

Wilhelm remembers, "Graham certainly didn't stay angry with me. Soon afterwards I got a call from him, saying, 'That thing you pulled on me is the most exciting thing in the movie.' Bill wanted me to sign a release for them to use it, which I did, and I got royalties.

"But the vibe around town was that Graham and I had a feud and that made me untouchable as everyone thought I was on his out-list. As a matter of fact, Graham was friendlier to me after that than he had ever been before."

Obtaining a release from Mike Wilhelm was a picnic for Graham compared with the problems he had with The Grateful Dead. As the film had been shot at only a week's notice, the bands originally agreed to be filmed with the understanding that they would have total control over how they appeared in the final cut. It was Graham's job to try and get the Dead's members together in one place so they could vote on whether they liked their part of the footage. It took Graham a full seven months finally to get all the members of the Dead together to view the film; that was only after he sent some "nice goodies and toys" in a stretch limousine over the Golden Gate Bridge to collect them and take them to Francis Ford Coppola's Mission Street Studios for a viewing.

"I nudged them and grouched and chozzeried [sweet talked] them and just played the Jewish midwife," said Graham. "I think what they finally said was, 'Let's get him outta our hair.' It's like Charles Laughton in *Les Miserables* chasing Fredric March through the trenches of Paris because he stole a loaf of bread. And he's haunted for life. Well I think the Dead said, 'Let's get him outta here.' "

10

Going National

Bill Graham righteously claimed to be retiring from the music business when he closed the Fillmores, but he had already started carefully planning his ascent into the giant sports stadiums and arenas that were now fixtures in most American cities. Although he contemptuously referred to these new super venues, some of which held 80,000 or more spectators, as "cement factories," he owed his next period of expansion directly to them.

Variety estimated that rock audiences at auditoriums and arenas spent a total of $2 billion in 1971—nearly twice the amount that Americans spent that year going to the movies. Although top bands like The Rolling Stones or The Who could easily sell out the huge arenas in a matter of hours after box offices opened, many civic-arena managers refused to book rock concerts, frightened off by the music's outlaw image. The manager of Veteran's Memorial Hall outside San Francisco in Marin County placed a moratorium on acid-rock shows after fans at a Big Brother/Quicksilver Messenger Service concert caused $30,000 of damage.

"No upholstered place wants acid rock," manager Leon Kalimos told *Variety*. "It excites too much body movement. I don't blame the kids. If they have to sit still they feel cheated. So they start jumping up and down in the seats. I blame the promoters."

"We used to have to beg to get dates," explained Atlanta promoter Alex Cooley. "There was a tremendous amount of prejudice in those days. I remember hall managers saying, 'I don't want those long-haired freaks in my building. We don't want that crap in our place.' "

But the soulless concrete arenas were the wave of the future. Bill Graham's closing the Fillmore West marked the end of the more intimate weekly psychedelic ballroom circuit he had pioneered. The Fillmore clones across the country had all gone the way of the dinosaurs in the new age of rock 'n' roll. Promoters like Don Law in Boston, Larry Magid in Philadelphia, and Arnie Granat in Chicago were now following Graham's ascent to the next rung on the rock-concert ladder.

By 1972 rock 'n' roll had joined the ranks of big business, becoming a significant part of the entertainment industry. Whereas a best-selling album in 1968 needed to sell only 200,000 to 300,000 to be a hit, only four years later there were now at least twenty artists in contemporary music who were selling more than 1 million records.

"The business is so huge," commented Graham. "Eight or nine years ago, there were five million buyers of contemporary music records. Three or four years ago there were ten to fifteen million, today there are twenty-five to thirty million people who buy records."

Rock was now a big-money game, and Graham was maneuvering carefully into a position where he could take as much of the pot as he could. Despite his riding off into "retirement" on a Mediterranean motorcycle tour with friends, followed by a Mexican vacation with his three-year-old son, David, the truth was that Graham's presence in the music business now loomed bigger than ever. Overhauling his production arm of FM Productions and placing it under the control of Barry Imhoff and a nucleus of former staffers from Fillmore West, Graham tightened his stranglehold on the San Francisco concert scene. No longer having to meet the crippling $12,000 weekly overhead at the Fillmore West enabled Graham to be more flexible in booking and take full advantage of the new rock 'n' roll gold rush.

Explaining the ferocious forces that drove him forward continually, Graham told *Melody Maker* writer Derek Jewell: "Success is difficult to put aside if you've smelt the sweetness of it. I'm hooked on it, I guess.

"I wanted to get time at home and at the ranch—peace of mind you know—and I thought maybe I'd write a book or be a movie producer or sail a boat somewhere. But it didn't happen that way.

"Look, supposing [Sir Laurence] Olivier, twenty years ago, respected and admired, went onstage and said, 'I've loved acting, but now I'm going to retire and take up surfing.' It takes a special kind of man to do that, and I couldn't do it."

Five months after closing the Fillmores, Graham came storming out of "retirement" to gross $250,000 in ten days from a string of Bay Area shows, maintaining his position as Northern California's premier promoter. His level of activity can be gauged from just one week in October, when he produced seven shows in nine days, with headliners ranging from Traffic at Winterland to Grand Funk Railroad at the massive Oakland Coliseum. He also maintained a presence in New York by producing four nights of The Grateful Dead at the Felt Forum in December.

Early in 1972, Graham established Winterland as his new flagship auditorium. He paid $100,000 to renew his lease through to the end of the year giving him first refusal rights on the 5,400-seat hall. Although he had to produce shows every weekend at Winterland to cover his overheads, the hall was more than double the capacity of the Fillmore West. He also continued to use Berkeley Community Theater, but now staged his bigger shows in the Civic Auditorium (7,500 capacity), the Cow Palace (14,531), and the Oakland Coliseum (54,000).

There was great amusement in the music business when Graham contradicted his previous opposition to large, impersonal shows and signed a deal with General Electric to produce three concerts to be carried via closed-circuit television to seventy theaters throughout America. Questioned by the *New York Times* about his turnaround, Graham replied succinctly, "I never said that rock was dead, but I think it's moving into another phase, and I expect to be a part of it."

"Consider this my second choice. If it were possible to put performers into each of these towns personally, that would be my first choice . . . There's General Motors, IBM, McDonald's, Sara Lee and rock 'n' roll."

By January 1972, following three years of constant battles, David Rubinson finally had enough of working with Graham and resigned from the Fillmore Corporation. He moved on to become a highly successful independent producer. His taking the recording company with him left Graham to concentrate solely on producing rock concerts. Graham was delighted not to have to "kowtow to the madness of the industry" and take what would be a short-lived break from management.

"Artists rule you with their whims, good and bad," he said at the time. "You wanna know why there are few good managers in rock 'n' roll? Because a manager's life is guided by how his artist feels that day. Hell, I don't wanna take it. I don't *have* to take it."

In April, the long-running feud between Graham and *Rolling Stone* publisher Jann Wenner exploded after the magazine published trenchant feature on Graham's business empire, claiming he was forced to close the Fillmores in order to salvage his hemorrhaging organization. The cover story, titled "Bill Graham Drives His Chevy to the Levee," by staff writer Tim Cahill, sent Graham into a fury. He marched into *Rolling Stone's* downtown San Francisco offices for a marathon six-and-a-half-hour showdown behind closed doors with Wenner and Cahill. Screaming and shouting, he insisted on going through the story line by line, to the amusement of the *Rolling Stone* staff, listening outside.

"He seemed to enjoy having the writer there now and being able to challenge him on every point because he was misquoted here and there," said former *Rolling Stone* writer Ben Fong-Torres.

What particularly angered Graham was the introduction, which pictured him walking through a warehouse after the closing of the Fillmore West, sadly looking over the old props and equipment. It read, "So perhaps in some corner of his mind, Bill Graham could hear The Who, the Airplane, the Dead, as he ran his hands over his collected mementos. He smiled. 'Hello, balloon inflator,' he said, 'Remember me?'

"Bill denied ever saying that and thought it made him sound real stupid," said Fong-Torres." He couldn't believe this so-called rock bible would say this about him because now when he would be going down the street in St. Louis or whatever, some kid would say, 'Oh, look, there's that guy who said, 'Hello balloon inflator. Remember me?' "

The actor in Graham emerged as he kept repeating the balloon-inflator line over and over again, changing his inflections and emphasis each time to prove to Wenner that he could not possibly have said it.

As rock 'n' roll grew from the counterculture to mainstream American culture, a further influx of promoters recognizing the huge financial potentials set themselves up in business. Early in 1972, Frank Russo, a Rhode Island newspaper publisher, moved into concert promotion full time.

"I had promoted shows in college and then gone into newspapers," Russo said. "I started in the concert business by picking up the phone and calling the manager of Blood Sweat and Tears and staging my first concert. At that time there was a tremendous amount of electricity in the rock 'n' roll business. Rock 'n' roll was exciting. Kids went to shows without even knowing who was playing because it was a happening and it was affordable."

After establishing himself as Rhode Island's premier concert promoter, Russo deliberately sought out Bill Graham, whose career he had been following closely.

"We struck a friendship from day one," said Russo. "I learned a lot about the promotion business from him, absolutely. Bill changed things by being very innovative and was not, in my opinion, a person who always thought about making money."

Similarly, in Chicago, young promoter Arnie Granat, who had run the security at the Aragon Ballroom, was already a veteran with just a year's experience promoting concerts with his JAMS organization.

"When I first got into the business, Bill Graham was already the godfather of promoters," said Granat, who is still Chicago's leading promoter."He was the model for all of us young aspiring promoters of that time. Bill was rock 'n' roll. He was Mr. Music."

Granat became Graham's devoted student, gleaning from his mentor the finer points of the concert business. "He embedded in me the qualities he held dear in this business," Granat said. "He was the type of guy who always lived by the credo of not screwing or fucking in business people who were friends. He always held to that 100 percent when it came to us."

Record executive Michael Klenfner, who was one of Graham's closest friends, said the promoter's business philosophy came from the street.

"It didn't matter how much money a guy had to Bill," said Klenfner. "It was what kind of guy he was. Especially in the music business with these guys that made a lot of money, the [David] Geffens, the Ahmets [Ertegun,] the this's, the that's. If the guy was a straight shooter, Bill was with you. If he wasn't, he was a shithead.

"Bill had this theory. You know how 25,000 Frenchmen can be marching and one guy is marching wrong. And the mother says, 'Look at that, 24,999 Frenchmen are marching wrong—my son is marching right. Bill Graham subscribed to that theory. The 24,999 could be marching wrong. And that's what made him brilliant."

Earlier in 1972 when Bill Graham heard that the Rolling Stones planned to tour America that summer, he had few expectations that he would be included considering his well-publicized falling-out with the band three years earlier. But the Stones' British-born tour manager Peter Rudge knew it was impossible to perform in San Francisco without Graham and persuaded Mick Jagger to let bygones be bygones. Jagger agreed on the understanding that he didn't have to talk to the loudmouthed promoter who had blamed him for the Altamont tragedy.

Graham later told *San Francisco Chronicle* columnist John L. Wasserman about his mixed emotions on receiving both the Northern Californian and Los Angeles legs of the Rolling Stones tour.

"I said to myself, 'How could anyone else do it?' And the ego came in, and the vanity and pride and greed and everything else."

Peter Rudge insisted that Bill Graham receive the same contract as all the other American promoters. According to Rudge, Graham was so upset that he had an additional "doctored" contract drawn up so he could boast to his staff that the Stones had cut him the best deal of the tour.

The 1972 Rolling Stones 39 city North American tour in June and July, grossed close to $4 million and was the beginning of Graham's turbulent, often unrequited love affair with the world's number-one concert drawing rock band.

"The Rolling Stones are, in our business, the pinnacle of everything," explained Ben Liss, president of the National Association of Concert Promoters.

"It's like when you have the Kennedys and they appoint you their ambassador to England. That confirmation was so important to Bill over and above financial success. He loved the recognition and the respect that working with the Stones gave him."

Graham produced eleven of the Stones' West Coast shows, which included four appearances at Winterland. Although the Stones were pleased with Graham's presentation, they kept their distance. Bill Wyman says the band still "mistrusted" Graham after their conflicts of the 1969 tour. "You always had to keep your eye on him," explained the Stones bassist.

Despite the initial resentment, Graham managed to win over the Stones with his professionalism and imaginative staging of their shows.

"He did his work very conscientiously, and we suddenly realized that he was a man who was not only a good promoter but a great lover of music, which doesn't always go together," said Wyman.

Jack McDonough believes that the 1972 Rolling Stones tour marked a crucial turning point for Bill Graham, who now demonstrated without a doubt that his shows were in a class of their own. "You needed a generalissimo who could do everything," said McDonough. "Bill was the only one stepping to the fore and saying, 'Okay, Rolling Stones, you want to tour the United States? Who's going to take care of it for you? I can do this for you? I don't believe there was anybody else in the business who knew how to put the pieces together, understood the audiences and the musicians and was like a military tactician in terms of being able to move a campaign forward. The '72 Stones tour proved to the world that rock 'n' roll had reached this level."

In October, Graham starred in a marathon sixty-hour live broadcast on San Francisco station KSAN, reliving his greatest moments at the Fillmore. Aided by cocaine, the elder statesman of rock was in his element. During the electronic fireside chat he recounted his favorite anecdotes while receiving tributes from a long succession of musicians and others who had been instrumental in starting the San Francisco music scene.

The only rain to dampen his parade came from Nick Gravenitis, who told KSAN listeners how Graham had mistreated Janis Joplin before she became a star and had thrown her out of the Fillmore. Graham denied the story angrily, but after the broadcast Gravenitis stood firmly by his story, telling *Rolling Stone,* "Graham will not cop to the fact that he did some ugly shit in his life. His memoirs are gonna be like history books about the Americans and the Indians, written by the Americans."

After the epic broadcast at a celebration at the Fleur de Lys, KSAN's Tom Donahue presented Graham with a framed note from a listener, saying, "Bill Graham may be an asshole but he gave me some of the best years of my life."

Indeed, Bill Graham was making definite efforts to clean up his image. No longer wanting to be known as the ranting, raving mad capitalist, Graham sought to be perceived as a mature statesman of rock, an innovator of what he loved to call "public assemblage." Admitting that he suffered from an image problem, Graham told Derek Jewell, "Okay, whatever negative characteristics I had—if I was an asshole, mean, hard, whatever—then I still have those faults," he explained. "But by going back into the business I think I've grown good characteristics, too. But it's different now; sure, it's different."

San Francisco Examiner's Phil Elwood believes Graham's "belligerent and hostile image" was fast becoming a liability. "The improved Bill Graham image started when Bill decided he had to change from being a screaming entrepreneur on the lip of the stage telling kids to shut up to being the guy who has a little classical string quartet at the end of each evening playing 'Greensleeves,' " said Elwood.

The unlikely architect of Graham's new image came in the guise of a former embalmer from Cincinnati named Zohn Artman. By the early 1970s Artman was working as a secretary for Union Pacific Railroad. Outrageously flamboyant and openly gay, the silver-haired Artman was, at thirty-five, in the midst of a mid-life crisis.

"I really wanted to work with people that were alive," Artman said. "The people I worked with got drunk at lunch and faked it through the afternoon. Now where was that?"

After seeing the movie *Fillmore*, Artman became fascinated with Graham, the "absolute madman," and decided to ask him for a job. At his interview, Graham asked the self-confessed Patti Page addict, who knew nothing about rock 'n' roll, why he wanted to work for him. Artman looked him in the eye and replied, "I'm gay and I have a sense that you wouldn't care." After discussing ethics for three hours, Graham offered him a job. Artman was so overcome by emotion that he broke down in tears. Starting as office manager, Artman soon demonstrated a natural talent for public relations, and Graham made him his personal assistant and put him in charge of his personal publicity.

Making Graham and his operation accessible to the press, Artman carefully cultivated critics, columnists, and influential politicians by developing his legendary lavish backstage hospitality that included more-than-ample supplies of drink and drugs. He also initiated an almost-feudal system of rewards and punishments to effectively control newspaper coverage and stifle criticism.

Explained *San Francisco Examiner* columnist Bill Mandel: "Reporters and critics who need Graham to do their jobs—and do them at the classy, luxurious, addicting level Graham can provide—lavish him with praise and tiptoe v-e-r-y carefully around anything that might offend him."

The *San Francisco Examiner*'s Phil Elwood, whose relationship with Graham was not always an easy one, used to receive lavish gifts. "On my fiftieth birthday Zohn Artman personally delivered a huge framed poster to my house in Berkeley as a gift from Bill," Elwood remembered. "It was a highly valuable gilt-edged 1898 recruiting poster from the Spanish-American War, and Zohn's note said: 'We know your enthusiasm for American history and thought this was a little something you might like.' "

Jack McDonough of *Billboard* said Artman provided his entrée into the Graham organization and finally to Bill Graham himself. "Zohn was very, very skilled at handling the press because he handled human nature," McDonough said. "He understood Bill well and he understood all the things that make San Francisco such a strange and wonderful place."

Operating through the genial Artman, Graham carefully increased his social power and influence in San Francisco. To cultivate the most important people, he gave them and their children free concert tickets. Another highly effective Artman tool to aid Graham's social aspirations was to build him up as a philanthropist, channeling his charity dollars and efforts to the right causes.

Graham also started laying the foundations of his future power base in California by making large campaign contributions to important politicians and judges and befriending them so that he could call in his favors if and when they were needed.

Artman was so effective in his work that Graham soon made him his closest confidant, calling him his "resident wizard." But there was a backlash of jealousy from other Bill Graham employees who despised the openly homosexual Artman and the ease with which he combined his key position in the Graham empire with his role as one of the leaders of the San Francisco gay scene.

For Graham business was booming, yet his private life was at an all-time low. Despite his millionaire life-style, which included a new luxury hilltop house in Mill Valley he named Masada, a ranch in Boulder Creek, and a ski chalet in Switzerland, the divorce from Bonnie had crushed him. He was especially bitter that Bonnie was using the generous alimony she received from him to support her new artist boyfriend in Mexico and regularly bitched to his staff about her "supporting some asshole with all my money."

Concerned about his son David, who was a slow developer and a late talker, Graham took Bonnie to court to try to get full custody of the four-year-old.

"Bill resented not being close to David," said Chris Brooks. "It made him very unhappy."

The court awarded Bonnie custody of David during the school year, allowing Graham access to his son for summer vacations and Christmas.

One night after a particularly exhausting Grateful Dead show, Bill Graham drove out to the Trident Restaurant in Sausalito. Perched on the water's edge, the restaurant is a favorite among the cognoscenti in Marin County and the perfect place to relax. That night Graham was served by a beautiful, raven-haired twenty-four-year-old woman named Marcia Sult. She felt sorry for Graham, who was falling asleep at her table. Even though it was past closing time, she brought him bread and soup and struck up a conversation with him. Saying he was totally exhausted and too tired to drive, Graham persuaded Marcia to take him home. Once in his kitchen, the tough promoter dropped to his knees in front of her without saying a word. Marcia felt Graham's anguished cry from the heart for help and drew him close for comfort. Soon they were embroiled in an affair and Marcia moved into Masada with her young son, Thomas. For the troubled promoter, finding Marcia was a temporary oasis in a desert of work and personal insecurity.

Perhaps one of the few people in San Francisco who had never heard of Bill Graham was a naïve nineteen-year-old college student named Regina Cartwright. Brought up in Beaverton, Oregon, by her mother, a former exotic dancer who told her she was the illegitimate daughter of comedian Lenny Bruce, Regina knew nothing about rock 'n' roll when she answered an advertisement for the job of receptionist at Bill Graham Presents, which paid $80 a week. Having no previous typing or office experience, Regina did not impress Keeva Krystal, who was about to show her the door when Bill Graham came strutting in, in an uncharacteristic good mood. He stopped when he saw Regina and on hearing she was there for the vacant receptionist position, ordered Krystal to hire her immediately. He then disappeared into his office.

"He scared the hell out of me," said Regina, who at the time was studying to be a Lubavitcher Jew. "I asked who this man was and Keeva said, 'That's Bill Graham.' And I said, 'Yes? I didn't read *Rolling Stone.* I had never heard of the Fillmore West. I was that innocent about rock 'n' roll."

Regina soon became the first line of defense at Graham's busy Market Street office, answering the phones and screening unwanted calls. Her new colleagues were intrigued by the shy religious girl who came to work in thick-rimmed glasses with long traditional Jewish dresses modestly covering her arms and legs. But it was her innocence and simplicity that appealed to Bill Graham.

"Bill liked the fact that I had no idea who he was," Regina said. "He kept coming up to me and shouting, 'You don't know who I am?' He couldn't believe it. I remember the first day that I wore my glasses to work, he stopped me and said, 'You look like a young Jewess.' "

Soon after starting her job, Regina began finding a single white flower placed carefully on her desk when she arrived every morning. When she realized that it was being left by her new boss, she became very uncomfortable and didn't know what to do. "I had had very little experience with men," she said. "I didn't know how to handle this kind of advance, especially coming from my boss. All I ever wanted to do for Bill Graham was to do a good job and be the best receptionist he had ever had. But he had more in mind.

"During my first few months, I seemed to get special treatment. I was always placed next to Bill whenever we went out to a restaurant, and when he drove us home I somehow was always dropped off last. That was the beginning of his campaign to get me," Regina recalls.

The other people in the office resented Regina for the extra attention that Graham was giving her. He threw caution to the wind and started chasing his prim new receptionist in full view of the office.

"I was frightened when he started pursuing me and I started dating anybody to put distance between us," Cartwright said. "I eventually became engaged to my rabbi's son as a last resort, and we planned to get married once he finished his studies."

But Bill Graham was not dissuaded so easily. One evening after work, he called Regina into his office and began a conversation that clearly had nothing to do with work.

"He gave me the most romantic, long, flowery speech about him, me, mountaintops, and oceans," Regina recalled. "He told me I was beautiful and pure and kept saying he wished we were the only people in the world. I was amazed. He was my boss, and I didn't know what to do.

"I told him I was a Lubavitcher and engaged to the rabbi's son and he goes, 'No, no, no. I found you. You belong to me. It would be such a waste.' "

After talking nonstop for forty-five minutes, Graham suddenly stopped and looked at her, asking, " 'Well, what do you think?' I looked at him and said, 'So I guess I'm not fired.' He really looked dumbfounded when I left the room.

"I knew he was with Marcia, and I didn't know what to do. He seemed to be so in love with her. I didn't want to break up their relationship, and I wasn't so innocent that I didn't know what Bill wanted from me."

When Graham's favorite nephew, Avi Chichinski, who had befriended Regina in the BGP office, fell fatally ill with bone cancer, she went to visit him in hospital. By this time his doctors had given up hope, and Marcia Sult, who was deeply involved in holistic medicine, had persuaded Avi's mother, Ester, to send the dying youth all over the world trying to find natural cures.

"He begged me to go to Bill and put an end to Marcia's and Ester's quest for yet another painful and useless treatment," Regina said. "He was at the end, and he just wanted to die.

"I said, 'Bill won't listen to me. Why not ask Zohn Artman to talk to him?' And Avi said, 'Don't you know my uncle's in love with you and wants to be with you?' I said, 'No. He's in love with Marcia. They're living together with the boys as a family.' He said, 'No. I know. Believe me.' That was the last time I saw Avi, and he died soon afterwards."

As Graham's infatuation with Regina grew, he sent Marcia to Paris, clearing the way for his assault on his receptionist.

Driven to scale new peaks in concert production, Graham exorcised his Woodstock ghosts in July when he produced a massive rock show at the

Watkins Glen racetrack in upstate New York, drawing a record 600,000 fans. The mammoth outdoor show, starring The Band, The Grateful Dead, and the Allman Brothers Band, was everything that he had once preached against.

"I must be honest and cop to the fact that a lot of things I was putting down predicting what would happen, did happen, and I joined the ranks," Graham admitted. "Basically, what it amounts to is supply and demand."

Two months earlier, he had produced a more modest show starring The Grateful Dead called "Dancing on the Outdoor Green," for 50,000 fans at San Francisco's Kezar Stadium near Golden Gate Park. A second show with Led Zeppelin was a sellout, but when guitarist Jimmy Page was more than two hours late, the angry fans threatened to riot. This led to a protest by the surrounding Kezar neighborhood against any future rock shows.

"Led Zeppelin said they knew the Kezar contract said for them to play at two o'clock," Graham said. "But they say, 'We're going to play at four!' and here I am screaming *'Contract!'* and they say, 'Sorry.' So what can I do?"

On August 5, Graham changed sites to Oakland Coliseum where he presented Leon Russell and Loggins and Messina in a show that would serve as the prototype for his later "Days on the Green" or DOGs as they became affectionately known.

"Bill conceived of his 'Days on the Green' shows as a continuation of his Mime Troupe benefits," said *Performance* magazine's Bob Grossweiner. "He was bringing the free concerts at Golden Gate Park into a context where the bands would be paid to play while retaining that special atmosphere of the old days in the park. In essence the 'Days on the Green' were often more of a selling point than just the acts."

But the ever-restless producer moved back into the national spotlight when asked to produce Bob Dylan's comeback tour. A reclusive enigma, Dylan hadn't toured since 1966, and the legendary star appeared more godlike than mortal. In 1974, rock mogul David Geffen decided to woo Dylan for a major American concert tour and signed Bill Graham to produce what amounted to the Second Coming of Jesus. To persuade Dylan to go on the road, Geffen hatched an elaborate plan using The Band's leader Robbie Robertson to convince Dylan to come out of concert retirement.

"There was a great demand for that tour, and it had been building up," Dylan said.

Graham's ground-breaking 1974 Bob Dylan and The Band tour laid down the rules for the modern rock 'n' roll tour. It was the first full-scale national American tour organized by a single promoter, with forty concerts in twenty-one cities in just forty-three days. The demand for the tour was so great that Geffen estimated that twenty tickets could have been sold for every one available. Graham and his FM Productions technical crew oversaw each detail of the tour, onstage and off, creating a complete touring environment for Dylan's entourage, hiring the luxurious Starship as tour plane and providing a lavish menu of entertainment to keep the musicians amused on the road.

Said The Band's bassist Rick Danko, "We had the Starship with a couple of bedrooms, $200 to $300 bottles of wine—it was a lot of fun."

The seven-week tour played only indoors and was seen by a total of 650,000 people, with no audience larger than 20,000. All the technical aspects were handled by Graham's FM Productions, which lugged $920,000 worth of sound equipment around America to become what Graham called "the Hertz of Rock." FM Productions spent $160,000 alone on designing sound equipment especially for the tour.

"Bob Dylan is the king for me," Graham told late-night talk-show host and sports commentator Bob Costas in 1990. "He is the single greatest poet our industry has ever produced, and on a given night with just his guitar and words, no one even comes close."

Dylan's unique ability to move an audience with his emotionally charged songs provided Graham with the perfect opportunity to add some innovative effects of his own. After touring the first few cities, Graham realized that the audiences were reacting visibly to the "How does it feel" chorus in *"Like a Rolling Stone."*

"The audiences just got into that more and more and by the fourth or fifth chorus in every city everybody just stood up and started taking big breaths." Graham then ordered his crew to turn up the house lights during the song's final choruses so everyone could see each other. "Well, I've never seen anyone do that ever," Graham said.

In July, Graham followed up the Dylan tour by presenting a national stadium tour for Crosby, Stills, Nash & Young. His tour campaign was planned down to the smallest detail from his mission control headquarters where he hung a sign saying, "Yea, though I walk through the Valley of the Shadow of Death, I shall fear no evil: for I am the meanest sonofabitch in the Valley."

The tour's logistics were monumental, on an unprecedented scale. Like a general planning an elaborate battle maneuver, Graham drafted in a mobile cavalry division of six 30-foot semis operated by professional drivers. His crack FM team also laid the foundations for many future superstar tours by designing the first collapsible outdoor stage and roof—it could be broken down in sections and shipped to the next show.

"Our job, when we're on the road, is constantly, constantly checking," said Graham's FM aide de camp, Barry Imhoff. "It's like servicing an airplane."

Graham directed everything but the technical aspects of the tour, for, incredibly, rock's most accomplished producer was not capable of doing even the simplest wiring job and once blew up his Webcor speakers when he plugged them directly into the electric socket by mistake.

"He said from that moment on he decided never to do anything technical again," said Ray Etzer, the former Fillmore hamburger flipper whom Graham promoted to comanage Santana with him. "That pretty much epitomizes his complete respect for those people that could do those things. He ended up having FM Productions with perhaps a hundred different electronic geniuses working for him."

Explaining tour logistics to *Billboard,* Graham said, "In no other area do I put as much faith and trust in others. It's one area where I'm not educated either by street or by school."

The CSN&Y tour would be the industry's biggest-grossing tour to date, and the high-priced tickets reflected the supergroup's draw. At the Oakland Coliseum show, Graham demanded $10 to $15 for what was billed as the largest concert ever in Northern California, drawing more than 80,000 people. In November he took ex-Beatle George Harrison on an even more ambitious coast-to-coast tour. Accompanied by Indian sitar virtuoso Ravi Shankar, Harrison's seventy-one-person entourage required special macrobiotic diets. To cater for their needs, Graham hired a cooking crew and traveling kitchen to accompany the tour.

Graham's three record-breaking back-to-back national tours made more than $22 million, from which Graham and FM Productions cleared $5.5 million. But the tours had run roughshod over the unwritten rules of the concert business, causing a furious backlash from agents and promoters who were terrified that Graham was putting them out of business. The agents feared Bill Graham was setting a precedent for artists to bypass the established agency system, as well as giving his promoter friends a slice of the action in their local markets.

"They didn't like it," explained *Billboard*'s Jack McDonough, "and threatened in return to freeze Graham on upcoming San Francisco–area bookings."

In retaliation, major agents and promoters called Graham on the carpet and ordered him to attend a meeting in a rented Long Island house and defend himself. Present were superagent Frank Barsalona and eighty of the most important agents, promoters, and managers in the music business. At the meeting they insisted he stop promoting national tours and respect the unwritten laws of concert promotion.

"It was a '*Stop Graham*' movement, plain and simple," Graham said. "In a seemingly diplomatic manner, they were telling me, 'Look, what you're doing is wrong because you're eliminating two things that are of the utmost importance for our system to work: the agent and the local promoter.'

"With these artists, it was 'Bill Graham out of S.F. going to town after town with Dylan without an agent and without a local promoter. Bill, look what you're doing to the industry!'

"Finally I said, 'What you guys are saying is that if I continue to do this, you agents will freeze me in San Francisco by booking with my competitors. What you're saying is I shouldn't eliminate my brothers. But these brothers would fuck me out of San Francisco in a minute if they had a Dylan tour.'

"I picked out one of the guys and said, 'Excuse me, you're the promoter for Rochester, New York, right? Right. Pretend I represent Bob Dylan. You want to do our national tour? You cocksucker, are you going to turn it down? What are you guys talking about? You're just envious.' "

After hours of discussion, Graham agreed to pull back on condition that if any other promoter mounted a national tour, the rest of the industry would take concerted action against them.

The meeting ended in an uneasy truce after Graham, in true comic-book style, arrogantly emphasized his enormous clout in the industry with a well-rehearsed drama staged especially for the meeting by some of his old New York actor friends.

"I knew in advance it was going to be a big heavy encounter," Graham told *BAM* magazine. "At about five minutes to three I lit a cigar—I don't smoke cigars—and I'm sitting in the middle of this huge oval table looking pretty cool with my cigar. Four black limousines pull up in front of the house. Everyone in the room is watching this out the window."

The promoters and agents couldn't believe their eyes when five gangsters dressed straight out of the Al Capone era came out of each limo carrying musical instrument cases and strolled up the front walk and came into the meeting.

"The first guy has a violin case, the next guy a viola, the next a saxophone. Perfect. Central casting all the way! They come into the room and walk around the table before lining up against the wall. Everybody is frozen. *Frozen!* I'm watching the faces. They don't know what the hell is going on. There's absolute silence for about thirty seconds and then one of the guys with the cases says, 'Excuse me, Mr. Graham . . . is ev-ery-ting satis-factory?' I took my cigar out, flicked the ashes, and said, 'Thank you, Hugo, that will be all!' On cue these twenty guys take off their jackets and file out of the room. And on the back of their shirts in big letters—BILL GRAHAM PRESENTS.

"The people in the room just *shit!* They couldn't believe it. It was one of the great moments in my life!"

Chicago promoter Arnie Granat says that promoters have a Mafia mentality. "We have territories that we have carved out and try to protect. Mostly people respect them but not always. When they don't you have to fight. It happens. It's almost like the Mafia. Our fights are legendary. Through lawsuits, through threats, through mobs. We've had all types of threats. They've been other promoters who have chosen to come into the ring with us, and we have to defend ourselves. Then it becomes offensive."

Granat believes that Bill Graham could have easily taken over the entire American concert business single-handedly in 1974. "Bill could have done one [national tour] a month," said Granat. "He had all the contacts. He didn't want to because there was pressure from agents, and he thought it was the wrong thing to do."

Six months after the meeting, another promoter tried to emulate Graham by staging a national tour with a major act.

"You know which promoter it was?" asked Graham. "One of the guys who had instigated the 'Stop Graham' movement. I sent a telegram to each of the major agents that said, 'You gave me your word that if anyone did what I had done you would freeze them, but you're not doing that.' That slid by. Six months later, another promoter did it. That slid by.

"About a year ago [in 1978] I said *'Basta!'* I think I'll put a little aphrodisiac in Los Angeles . . . Fuck around a little in Chicago. That's the only reason I do shows now and again in L.A.

"It's never said, but there's an unspoken alliance among promoters. We're all very competitive, we all have our own egos, healthy ones. The guys in Chicago, Denver, L.A., they look at their area like 'It's my turf!' We're all John Wayne. It's like I stay off their turf, they stay off my turf."

The combative promoter also fought his employees, as his shy new receptionist Regina Cartwright found out one day after he offended her with an obscene joke about women.

"I walked out," Cartwright said. "I told him that even though he was my boss, I didn't have to listen to off-color jokes. He just picked up my desk and threw it over in front of everybody. I stood there and said, 'Why did you do that?' Then he turned to me and said, 'I have no idea.' And we both started laughing because it was so stupid."

Later that day, Graham called her into his office and told her that she was the first person who had ever directly questioned his raging temper.

Cartwright recalled, "I told him I was surprised that nobody cared enough about the fact that he always ran around the office screaming and shouting like a crazed madman. He smiled and said, 'No one's ever asked before.' " So I said, 'Why do you do it?' " And he said, 'To intimidate people. Why else?' "

Then he asked her to sit down and watch as he demonstrated the Bill Graham method of intimidation.

"He picked up the phone and called some poor schmuck agent in L.A.," Cartwright said. "He started talking, and within five minutes he was in a full-blown tirade. He had the person on the other end of the line in tears or something. It was just an earth-shattering thing. And he was calmly looking at his watch the whole time while he was yelling and screaming at this poor person.

"It went on for ten minutes and then he screamed, 'I've got to go. Fuck you. I hate your guts,' and slammed down the phone. Then he smiled at me and said, 'That's how it works.'

"He was totally in control of every public tirade that he ever had. It was all an act, but it was the only way he could get people to do exactly what he wanted. It was totally calculated as to how long it would last, what it would be about, and when it would occur. That became his persona, part of the Bill Graham myth."

Yet underneath his raging-bull exterior, Graham was a deeply sensitive man who could be hurt easily and who took offense at the merest slight. He was a bad judge of character, as was shown when he discovered that one of his oldest friends from his New York days, whom he had installed as one of his top executives, had plundered the company to pay for his wife's fur coats and expensive home improvements. Graham felt bitterly betrayed and, on closer inspection of his books, realized that several other employees had been ripping him off.

Indeed, his personal finances were such a mess that it was found he didn't even own Masada; it had never been put in his name. He had to go to court to get his name on the deeds.

After a few months of being spurned by Regina Cartwright, Graham decided he would marry Marcia Sult and flew to the South of France, where she was staying with his son David, to propose marriage. When Marcia asked for twenty-four hours to make up her mind, Graham flew into a fury and took the first plane back to America, effectively ending their relationship.

Now, depressed about his private life, Graham embarked on a string of brief affairs which he termed "hatefucks." He lost himself in his work, often putting in twenty-hour days, but the constant pressures and doubts inevitably built up as he refused to take his staff's advice to take a vacation. To cope with the stress he relaxed with his favorite high-octane hashish brownies and mellower marijuana cookies, which were delivered to him regularly in white bakery boxes by some drug-dealer friends. He had also started regularly snorting cocaine to help him maintain his frantic schedule, viewing the drug as a necessary business tool.

But the side effects of coke made him more unpredictable and volatile than ever. Two years earlier in 1972, the violence which always lay just beneath his surface erupted during a fight with an eighteen-year-old fan outside the front door of Winterland before The Grateful Dead's New Year's Eve concert. In the scuffle, eyewitnesses saw Graham throw the teenager right under the wheels of a passing truck. Seriously injured, the youth was rushed to the hospital with broken ribs and other internal injuries.

"He didn't mean to," remembers Graham's friend, Wavy Gravy, the legendary 1960s scene jester. "Bill tossed him in the street, and the truck went over him. He had to have his spleen removed. Bill was horrified, but at the same time he was really pissed at the guy."

In the summer of 1975, he took Marcia and their sons David and Thomas whitewater rafting in Utah. While they were drifting along, Graham looked up to see an overhead plane skywriting "B-I-L-L C-A-L-L. He immediately rushed to the nearest phone to get the news that Led Zeppelin had canceled its two Oakland Coliseum appearances, in August, which were worth millions of dollars, after singer Robert Plant was seriously injured in a car crash. Canceling the rest of his vacation, Graham flew back to San Francisco and arranged to refund 120,000 tickets at a personal cost of $130,000.

11

Becoming a Star

In February 1975 Bill Graham came to the rescue of the San Francisco School Board when it fell $3 million into debt and was forced to cancel all sports and extracurricular programs. Sports-loving Graham read the news on an airplane to Los Angeles and was furious that the city's children should be deprived of such essential activities. He decided to find a way to fund the programs himself.

Graham's public relations wizard, Zohn Artman, saw the school's plight as a golden opportunity for his boss to become part of the San Francisco establishment. Graham called up his friend, San Francisco Mayor Joseph L. Alioto, offering to stage a superstar benefit to raise the $250,000 needed to save the sports programs. The mayor was delighted, and two weeks later joined the promoter at a press conference to announce plans for SNACK (Students Need Athletics, Culture, and Kicks). Standing side by side with Mayor Alioto, the former Mime Troupe renegade triumphantly told the press that he had persuaded top-draw bands like The Grateful Dead, Paul Kantner and Grace Slick's renamed Jefferson Starship, Carlos Santana, and the Doobie Brothers to play for free to help the schools. And even the Parks and Recreation Department, which Graham had once battled for the right to stage Mime Troupe plays in the park, gave permission to hold the show at Kezar Stadium, leading some cynics to question whether the SNACK benefit wasn't an elaborate ploy for Graham to regain the use of Kezar Stadium for his future outdoor shows. Graham angrily denied the accusation, claiming that his motives were solely philanthropic.

"Maybe I'm making too much of the issue," Graham told the *New York Times.* "But for the last ten years I've made my living off the youth of America. This is my way of repaying them for all they've done for me."

In the weeks leading up to his most elaborate show to date, Graham worked round the clock with his new crack FM team. To broaden the show and address the audience between sets, he invited sports heroes like baseball's Willie Mays, football star Gene Washington, and legendary olympic athlete Jesse Owens. But his greatest coup was in persuading reclusive Marlon Brando to make an unannounced appearance. Graham later boasted that he had talked the great actor into coming during a 3:00 A.M. phone call two days before the show.

As Graham's SNACK benefit became national news, journalists began to question why rock music was bailing out the San Francisco School Board in the first place. Having a reputation for financial mismanagement, the school board became embarrassed that Bill Graham appeared to be doing its job of raising school money. One day before the concert, the board tried to steal Graham's thunder with the bombshell announcement that it had "found" $2.1 million in overlooked funds, more than enough to reinstate the sports programs—the SNACK Benefit was no longer needed. Calling it "a rather strange mistake," Graham pledged the show would go on and accused the school board of undermining his efforts.

On March 23, 1975, the Summer of Love returned to San Francisco when more than 60,000 people each paid $5 to attend a milestone concert headlined by Bob Dylan.

"It was almost as if the gods of rock & roll had decided to smile on the event," gushed *Rolling Stone.* Backstage, Zohn Artman had outdone himself setting up a lavishly catered VIP reception area. The stars were even ferried around their luxury enclosure in white golf carts. The Grateful Dead camp added their own brand of excitement to the hospitality backstage by injecting cans of orange juice with LSD and then handing them out to unsuspecting souls.

The high point of the show came after the Jefferson Starship set, when Bill Graham walked up to the microphone and said, "Ladies and gentlemen, a man who needs no introduction—Mr. Marlon Brando."

As the legendary middle-aged actor walked out onstage, he received a welcome from the rock audience that Graham could only describe as "Nuremberg chanting." In one of his great performances, Brando, obviously moved by his reception, reached out to the crowd and gave a speech worthy of Mark Antony.

"Nobody in history has witnessed an occasion like this," began the actor. "We came here today because some people needed some sports equipment. Some people came to hear the sound. But there's another sound, another sound that we have to listen to—because if we don't listen to it, we're not gonna get it together. It's not my generation—I'm doin' five-o right now—but your generation's gonna catch the shit that my generation and the people before me have laid down for you.

"Now the school system suddenly found a bunch of million dollars, but they didn't need the dough. So the brothers up here have decided we're gonna split the money. Now there are plenty of people that are hurting. The poor people—the white people, the Chicanos, everybody that's been ripped off.

"I'm gonna give five thousand bucks to the show, but that's not gonna help us—we gotta give and give and give and give—we gotta give of our feelings. If we haven't got anything but our feelings, let's give that, 'cause that counts more than every . . . fuckin' piece of money in the world!"

When Brando came offstage, he was crying and seemed mesmerized. Concerned, Graham asked him if he was all right. Brando brushed Graham away, saying he just had to catch his breath and would be okay soon.

Remembered Graham, "Fifteen minutes later, I went over to him again and said, 'Is everything okay?' " He just grabbed my arm and said, 'You know something? Those weren't extras out there.' All of a sudden I realized that because of his profession he never gets to experience this mass adulation that rock 'n' roll stars feel all the time.

"With Brando it's those extras in *Viva Zapata* that are paid twenty-six dollars a day to get on a horse and off a horse, to laugh. They're paid to do that. Well those people gave him something that he just doesn't experience. Imagine what those sixty thousand people did to that man."

Perhaps the only star capable of following Brando's memorable appearance was Bob Dylan, supported by Neil Young and The Band. Dylan brought Kezar Stadium to its feet with a brilliant set, crowning Graham's biggest triumph to date. Quoted by the *New York Times,* a well known music figure said, "Nobody but a presidential candidate could get this many stars together. Nobody has Graham's prestige or force of personality."

The day after the concert, Mayor Alioto called a press conference to thank Graham publicly and criticize the school board for its lack of support. On principle, Graham decided to withhold the money raised until the board proved it needed it, but after being threatened with prosecution for fraud by the San Francisco Board of Supervisors and the State Attorney General's office, Graham grudgingly handed the cash over and received lukewarm thanks from the school board.

Graham viewed the SNACK concert as the first real test of the effectiveness of the organization he had built up since closing the Fillmores.

"From the company's point of view, the SNACK show was very important, when teamwork and organization really counted," he told *Billboard's* Jack McDonough. "The company showed itself to be a magnificently human apparatus. I didn't even believe myself that they could function as well as they did."

Graham's other high spot for 1975 came when The Rolling Stones asked him to manage the western half of their American tour that summer. It was during this tour that the Stones finally dropped their guard and warmed to their old enemy at last.

"We became very good friends in the late 1970s," remembers Bill Wyman. "We did great tours with him."

After one Rolling Stones tour, Graham invited Mick Jagger and his entourage to stay at his Masada, while he was away on business. He came back to find that his home had been trashed, and, to add insult to injury, his whole supply of hash brownies and marijuana cookies had disappeared from the upright freezer.

"Bill called me up in a rage," Regina Cartwright said. "He was screaming that Mick Jagger and 'those fucking animals' will never stay in his house again."

After the incident Graham installed a heavy padlock on his freezer to make sure that nobody else could ever get into it.

"He was so hurt that Mick had such little care or concern for his home that he was almost crying," Cartwright said. "He was hurt in the same way as if your brother had come in and wrecked your house for no specific reason. He was also very upset that Mick and his friends had eaten all of his brownies and cookies."

Now riding on a wave of success, Graham staged the first of his 1976 summer series, *Day on the Green,* at the 54,000 capacity Oakland Coliseum Stadium with an April 25 show called "The British Are Coming." In a stunning set piece, FM Productions built "Bill Graham's Castle" right on the stage at a cost of $17,000. The realistic replica of an English medieval castle was complete with turrets, lookouts, and a union jack flying overhead. The all-British lineup included Robin Trower, Dave Mason, Fleetwood Mac, and Gary Wright. At one point, to the delight of the audience, the Beatles (played by actors) entered the stage over a drawbridge to be welcomed by a trumpet fanfare.

"The 'Day on the Green' concerts were Bill's finest hour," says Phil

Elwood. "They were magnificently produced and made a lot of money for him."

Elwood believes that it was no accident that Graham used the Oakland Coliseum Stadium for his major summer shows; it allowed him to tap directly into the increasing numbers of fans coming from suburban areas outside San Francisco. "I'm sure that Bill did amateur demographic surveys of his audience and realized that the Oakland Coliseum Stadium was perfectly situated to draw people from all over that area," explained Elwood.

The Oakland Coliseum Stadium also provided the perfect opportunity for Graham to fine-tune larger arena shows, concentrating on a single venue so he could iron out all the technical difficulties. During the summer run of the *Days on the Green,* which featured acts like The Eagles, The Doobie Brothers, and The Beach Boys, Graham put Winterland on a hiatus, as the smaller venue would have drawn fans away from his bigger shows and affected his bottom line.

Utilizing Bill Graham's successes, Zohn Artman concentrated on weaving his magic on the Graham image. In June he successfully pitched a major feature on his boss to *People* magazine. Describing himself as "an honest con man" Graham told Middle America about his struggle for success and how his tough childhood had helped him become the country's leading promoter.

"This is a street-instinct business," he said. "That doesn't always mean illegal or dirty. There are honest hustlers, honest con men."

The accompanying photo spread showed the millionaire promoter as a waiter carrying a trayful of drinks up the backstairs for "his rock stars," and in a sexy clinch with "good chum" Marcia Sult who had been temporarily reunited with him.

Asked if he still felt pessimistic about rock since shuttering up the Fillmores, Graham replied, "Rock 'n' roll is our first national music. Jazz was a minority music. But this is America's music. It may not be a political or social force anymore. But it will be around for a long, long time. Don't forget, the rock music industry is a billion-dollar baby. It's not going to fall off the edge of the earth."

When movie director Francis Ford Coppola offered Bill Graham the chance in 1976 to play the cameo role of a sleazy theatrical agent in his new film *Apocalypse Now,* which was about to start shooting in the Philippines, he jumped at the chance. Seeing this as a way of rekindling his acting career and taking a well-earned rest from the music business, he flew to the Philippines to join the film crew.

He arrived in the middle of a typhoon, to find Coppola's project wracked by problems, and he immediately contracted dysentery, losing 17 pounds in two weeks.

"It was miserable," Graham told *San Francisco Chronicle* columnist John Wasserman. "There we were in the middle of the jungle, the hotel was flooded and I moved in with a farm family. No electricity, no dope, no booze, no broads—*nothing.* I slept on the floor, on a mat, with nine kids and some salamanders—sitting in. Yuk.

"The first nights were unbearable. I'm always busy, moving, working, but there was nothing I could do. Days we were out there trying to put the tents up and get the mud out of the way to keep filming—Francis was Genghis Khan, he was crazy; lovely man, but *insane*—but nights I had nothing but me.

"At night all communications stopped. You know, in our life, you can't sleep at 3:00 A.M., you light a joint, you push the button for Randolph Scott, you go to the refrigerator. But there, there was nothing. By the third day I realized that the only thing I had was me. For years it was always The Do—be a busboy, take dance lessons, put on shows—but now, there I was, forty-five years old, lying in a hut in the middle of the Philippines, and the only diversion I had was to look at *me.* I mean, you can sit on an airplane and reflect, or you can sit on the can or in the bathtub. But this was different. Everywhere there was the mirror.

"So I began to think about my family. My real family was part of my youth, which I don't remember, obviously because I choose not to remember it. And both my foster parents are dead now. It's like somebody getting jilted by a girl, and then another, and then another. After a while he's really careful about going out. What happens is that something is taken away from you. I didn't let many things get too close. I'd just build this wall. My family would be what was around me at the time.

"So I began to seriously ask myself about my son, about my family, about what it is that I do. And for the first time on that level I asked myself, 'Why do I say I love my son?' when I go to New York, and he lives outside Philadelphia, and I call and say, 'I wish I could come and see you this weekend but I'm really busy.'

"I ain't that busy. If I really loved my son I'd say, 'Fuck this, fuck Led Zeppelin, fuck the Rolling Stones.' My sister lives in San Francisco and sometimes I go for weeks without seeing her. Why should that be?

"So I kept asking myself, 'Why do you work so hard? Why can't you have closer relationships? What are you afraid of?' I can't say who I am as a result of all that, but I really took a good look. I went through my Jungian primal scream, or whatever you want to call it, whatever you call what you go through.

"And I realized how, in many ways, I've copped out. 'Sis, I wish I had time to visit you' bullshit! I could have made time, but I used the excuse of work, even when I wasn't getting that much satisfaction from it. I thought about my son and the excuses that I use with him . . . my family in general, my private life . . . why don't I have more of a private life?"

Cut off in the jungle, Graham focused his thoughts and attentions on his receptionist, Regina Cartwright. When she answered his calls to the office, he refused to talk to anyone else but her and spent hours at a time confiding his problems on the set.

"He called me every day he was there," Cartwright said. "My phone would be lighting up with all these calls, and I'd ask him who he wanted to talk to. He said he just wanted to talk to me. I said, 'Why me? I'm just the receptionist.'

"He kept telling me about all the craziness that was going on and what was happening to him. Meanwhile I'm to ignore the phones while everybody's yelling at me and getting really mad."

One day a huge bouquet of flowers arrived for Regina from the Philippines with the message, *"Love and Cheers, Bill."*

"If I was unpopular in the office before, now it was even worse," Cartwright said.

Soon after Graham returned from the Philippines, he and Cartwright became lovers, even though he was back living with Marcia Sult.

"He finally seduced me," Cartwright said. "I just got tired of him chasing me, but I fully expected him to dump me after a quick affair and marry Marcia."

Although Graham, who was twenty-five years older than Cartwright, had cast his receptionist in the role of his perfect woman, at the beginning he was not willing to give up Sult completely.

"One of us had to go and he didn't know which one," Regina said. "So Marcia was sent off on another tour of Europe and I moved in with him."

Finally triumphant after two years of chasing Cartwright, the middle-aged promoter became even more obsessed with her once she moved in with him. He saw her as the real-life incarnation of his first screen love, Ava Gardner, and forced her to watch his favorite movie *The Barefoot Contessa* again and again on his giant television screen in his bedroom.

"To Bill I was the barefoot contessa, and he had picked me out of the peasant village to take me to new heights," explained Cartwright, who on Graham's orders left her receptionist job so she could devote herself to him full-time.

"Bill believed that the only reason I was put on this earth was to run into him when I was a kid and be there for him. Sex was his first bond with me. But I soon fell in love with him. He liked to tell me that God had designed my body especially for him and I was the only woman who really knew how to love him.

"We used to have extended lovemaking sessions that would last for hours. He was an unusual lover and at times could be considerate. He wasn't used to making love with a woman he was actually in love with. He had no problems having sex with me, but he had problems dealing with our relationship. He was very inexperienced in loving relationships and in some ways he was like a little boy."

As the new woman in Graham's life, Regina was introduced to his sister Ester, her husband Manny, and the rest of the family. The wealthy promoter liked her on his arm when he arrived at all his concerts but, once there, always left her alone in an empty dressing room reading her favorite poetry, hidden away from any younger men who might show interest. He also refused to allow her ever to be photographed with him in public, saying he wanted to keep her part of his private life.

"Bill would say, 'Stay here and don't get lost'—like I was a little puppy," Regina said. "He would go nuts if any man would dare to talk to me. He had me watched all the time. Once, backstage at Winterland, a British photographer came up to me and asked to take my picture. Suddenly Bill came rushing into the backstage area, and the poor guy was picked up by two Bluecoat security men and Bill literally kicked his tush out of the backstage door into the street."

As Bill Graham's girlfriend Cartwright found herself thrust into the social whirl of the music business. "I was a wallflower," she remembers. "I saw the women in his world as much more socially adept and knowledgeable than I was. And I was very, very shy and I would go to parties and try and find a quiet corner to sit in while Bill worked the room."

After Marcia made her final split from Graham and left to live in Hawaii, pregnant with his baby, Regina enjoyed an idyllic honeymoon period with Graham, who romanced her and introduced her to his rich and famous circle of friends.

"We loved going places," Cartwright recalls. "He'd eat a lot of hash brownies, and we'd go for rides on his sidecar motorcycle. We'd go to the flea market in Sausalito or drive out to Napa and hang out with Francis [Coppola].

"He always said that I was the only person he could just relax around and just be himself and not have to do anything. But of course I never asked him to do things for me. I never even asked him to be faithful."

But soon Cartwright discovered a violent darker side to Graham, the inveterate womanizer, who loved to come home and brag about his conquests. "I know the anatomy of every woman he ever schtupped," said Cartwright. "He told me everything. He called them his hatefucks, so I never felt threatened. When he was done with them, he left it up to me to get rid of them. I was very loyal to Bill and I never questioned him. He told me he was committed to me, and his other sidewomen meant nothing."

When Francis Coppola later invited Graham to stay on his yacht during the 1978 Cannes Film Festival, Regina was furious when he invited a popular Hollywood starlet along instead of her. "Bill told me he needed a celebrity to take to the Cannes Film Festival," said Cartwright. "He didn't feel I had the cachet of being from Hollywood."

Furious at Graham's snub, Cartwright, who had spent $2,000 on a new wardrobe for Cannes, moved out of his home and refused to take his calls for a week. Finally, Graham drove over to the friend where she was staying and begged forgiveness, telling her every last intimate detail of his affair.

The pioneer British band Led Zeppelin was the undisputed number-one album-selling band in the world. On hearing the band was about to tour America in July 1977, Graham went to extraordinary lengths to make sure the group played for him. He invited the band's gargantuan manager, Peter Grant, to a luxury luncheon for two—in the middle of an empty Oakland stadium, knowing that Grant's love of good food was the key to securing Zeppelin.

Branded "one of the most riotous tours in rock history" Led Zeppelin behaved like a band of marauders, plundering millions in their record breaking tour. The trouble started when Grant's 10-year-old son Warren tried to take an ornate wooden plaque with the band's name on it from a dressing-room door. Graham's security guard Jim Matzorkis told him he couldn't have it, cuffing him on the back of the head. Led Zeppelin drummer John "Bonzo" Bonham, who had left the stage during an acoustic number, saw what was going on and told Matzorkis to apologize. As a parting gesture, the burly drummer delivered a massive kick to the crotch of the terrified security guard.

When Grant, a former heavyweight professional wrestler, heard that his boy had been hit, he became enraged and, with his tour manager Richard Cole and his bodyguard John Binden, went in search of the injured guard. Matzorkis had gone into hiding, and when they couldn't find him, they tricked Bill Graham into revealing where he was, promising there wouldn't be any trouble.

Graham took Grant to the trailer where Matzorkis was hiding and they went inside with Binden. "Peter blasted Jim in the face," Graham said. "I tried to stand between them, but Grant forced me out of the trailer and locked the door. My man said, 'Bill. Bill, help me . . .' Matzorkis worked his way to the door while they were hitting him, and he was able to get away. His face was a bloody mess."

Cole, who was standing outside the trailer with one of his security staff, claims Graham sent in an army of twenty guards to rescue Matzorkis.

"I saw these guys coming and I picked up a piece of aluminum tubing from a table umbrella and fought them," said Cole. "A lot of the guys had the special gloves with lead and sand in them." Cole then chased Graham employee Bob Barsotti across the green and over a fence, where he hit him in the face with the pipe.

Later, Zeppelin guitarist Jimmy Page said it was self-defense. "I'll tell you there was a team of guys there with sand in their gloves," Page said. "It was a very hairy scene. If somebody hits you and you hit them back, it's self-defense, init? [*sic*]"

When tempers cooled, Led Zeppelin returned to their hotel and planned their next move. They knew they were in danger of being arrested, but had an ace in the hole as the band was due to play another sold-out show the following afternoon. The band's lawyer called Graham with a veiled threat that Zeppelin wouldn't play unless a waiver was signed to indemnify them from any subsequent police action. Graham put his employee Nick Clainos, an entertainment lawyer, on the case, and Clainos soon discovered that anything signed under duress would not hold up in court. Tensions ran high the next morning when the band arrived at the Oakland Coliseum Stadium for the second afternoon show. Half an hour before Zeppelin as due to play, Graham signed the waiver.

"I think there were two reasons why he signed," Cole explained. "First of all, he didn't want to lose all that money, and secondly, if he had Zeppelin arrested, there would have been a riot and excessive damage. You can't really blame him. It was good business. Anyone would do it.

"In hindsight, we should have known that Graham was a very smart man and got the fuck out of there that night while the going was good."

Chris Brooks, no longer employed by Graham at the time, was a member of the Led Zeppelin entourage.

"Richard [Cole] divided everybody into groups to go in the limos," Brooks said. "We were under strict instructions that as soon as the limos pulled up we should get in quick. We did a motorcade to the Oakland Stadium and immediately after the show we got back in the limos and drove to the city. No hanging out. No nothing."

As soon as Led Zeppelin finished playing, Clainos filed charges to have Peter Grant, John Bonham, Richard Cole and John Binden arrested. According to Cole it was a spy-versus-spy situation, with both sides having paid informants in the opposite camp.

One of Zeppelin's security guards was an ex-police officer whose friend in the SWAT team informed them that the Led Zeppelin four were about to be arrested.

"When we heard what was happening, we phoned to say we were coming down peacefully," Cole said. "Otherwise it could have been a terrible mess if they'd gone in shooting."

Matzorkis and two other Graham staff members filed a $2 million damage suit against Grant, Bonham, Cole, and Binden, who all pleaded innocent. This marked the first time in the history of rock 'n' roll that a promoter had filed criminal charges against a band.

After Led Zeppelin posted bail and caught the first plane back to England, Graham, analyzing the incident, drew a parallel with Nazi Germany. Pledging never to book Led Zeppelin again, he told *Rolling Stone,* "For these people to assume that might makes right takes me back to Germany—and I've blocked out pretty much of my childhood—but that's where they come from. I cannot help but wonder how much of this did, in fact, go on in the past with these people."

The case was eventually settled when Zeppelin's lawyers made a *nolo contendere* deal with the judge, agreeing to pay an undisclosed amount to Graham's staff. That Oakland show in July 1977 turned out to be Led Zeppelin's final performance in America. Not long afterward, the group stopped performing altogether.

As he celebrated his tenth anniversary in rock, Graham was at the zenith of his career. Now approaching middle age, he could look back with satisfaction at all he had accomplished. In 1975 3 million people paid a total of $20 million dollars to see 250 Graham-produced shows in Northern California and an additional fifty in other markets. Bill Graham Presents staged shows in no less than seventeen venues in Northern California and over forty more nationally. Though Graham himself was making millions of dollars a year, much of which he stashed away in Swiss bank accounts through his sister Evelyn Udry, he was also making big money for the rock bands.

Even the previously unbusinesslike Grateful Dead finally acknowledged that his methodical "straight" approach to music had allowed the band to survive and flourish. "He had to turn it into a business," says Grateful Dead drummer Micky Hart. "I mean [otherwise] it would have been on a spiral downhill."

Rock diva Grace Slick was now also beginning to find some redeeming qualities in Jefferson Airplane's old manager.

"I think his reputation is actually a little bit more negative than it ought to be," she said. "Yeah, he blows up. So what, I mean you've got two legs if you don't like it, walk away. And he's got a hot temper. But good lord, the stuff that balances that just takes it way."

An anonymous member of the Grateful Dead family, however, was far less approving, saying Graham was "weird" about money and respect. "He tries to buy as much as he can for as little as he can," said the family member. "He never loses sight that he's in the game to make bread, and God help you if you're in the way of him winning."

Looking back at his career in March 1976, Graham told *Billboard*'s Jack McDonough, "Some of the dreams and fantasies were nice, but I think all of us are much more honest now about the fact that we're business people."

Overall, Graham's relationship with The Grateful Dead was good, and the band affectionately named him their Uncle Bobo. Although it was an ongoing game to surreptitiously dose him with LSD—a feat which drummer Micky Hart later claimed credit—the Dead regarded the prickly promoter as a benevolent older uncle who could always be tapped for cash or equipment.

In March 1978, prior to President Jimmy Carter's September Camp David talks with Egyptian President Anwar Sadat and Israeli Prime Minister Menachem Begin, the Dead decided to go to Egypt on their own peace mission at the same time and asked their Uncle Bobo to buy them a new P.A. system for the trip. The band members made large placards that read "Egypt or bust. PA's a must" and paraded up and down outside Masada in a torchlight parade to catch his attention.

"We said, 'Bill, we've gotta talk to you,' " remembers Micky Hart, who once caught Graham reading a book called *The Art of Intimidation.* "You had to go on the offensive with Bill, or else he would eat you up. He was in his bathrobe, but we sat him down and took the phones off the hook."

When the Dead revealed their intentions of going to Egypt to stop the fighting between Egypt and Israel, Graham sat up with them for six hours discussing the peace plan, but ultimately decided it was too dangerous to get involved with.

"We went to Egypt," Hart said. "But Bill was big enough to know that he was really wrong. He came to Egypt, paying his own way, and on the last of the three nights we played he rented forty horses and forty camels. And when we got off the stage we all got onto camels and horses and rode out into the desert to an oasis. We had tray races around the desert, drinking beers, and Bill enjoyed it with us.

"And so he wasn't so big that he didn't know a good thing was happening, and that really meant a lot to us, 'cause we always liked to enjoy the high times with Bill. And he had one with us that time."

Bill Graham was always looking for new opportunities to diversify out of rock 'n' roll into other areas of promotion. In early 1976 he ventured into the quieter world of horticulture to present a six-day event at the Cow Palace called "Bill Graham Presents the World of Plants Show." FM Productions, which now employed a staff of fifty, outdid themselves by building a 35-foot-high fake volcano towering over a huge tropical lagoon. The volcano came to life every two hours, spewing out clouds of dry-ice smoke to the accompaniment of beautiful grass-skirted hula girls.

The centerpiece of the show was the Bill Graham Pavilion. Complete with sentimental pictures of his parents and family and his treasured Korean Bronze Star, the shrine reflected his new hobby of gardening.

"I thought no one's doing anything with plants," he said. "It's a big thing. It's a big risk, but I'm not going to spend the rest of my life putting on plant shows."

Zohn Artman boasted to *Rolling Stone* that the plant show had netted his boss a cool $105,000 profit and said it could become an annual event. Artman, who was becoming increasingly powerful in the Graham empire, pulled off a major coup when he arranged a major profile of Graham in the *Wall Street Journal* in April 1976. Lauding the promoter as "a hard-driving perfectionist who succeeds because of excellent organizational skills and an uncanny ability to select staff," the *Journal* article elevated Graham to the top ranks of American business.

Describing Graham as one of the last members of a "fast-disappearing breed of immigrant entrepreneurs who have made a fortune in this country," the *Journal* took a hard look at Graham's efforts to diversify his empire by opening a chain of outlets selling concert tickets, posters, and his own line of T-shirts. The article revealed that Graham's FM Productions generated almost $30 million in revenues for fiscal 1975, clearing a profit of $750,000. It claimed that the promoter drew $2,500 a week from the business and personally earned $250,000 annually in commissions from managing Santana and Montrose. He was credited with real estate holdings of $300,000, a further $300,000 in savings, and about $250,000 in stocks.

"He works hard for his money, spending most of his waking hours on the job and sleeping only four or five hours nightly," reported the *Journal*. "Even then work isn't far away."

Even his Washington, D.C., rival Jack Boyle, president of Cellar Door Productions, told *Journal* readers that Graham had the best business mind in concert promotion. "He makes better financial transactions and merchandises his product better than anyone else in the business," said Boyle. "He has the innate ability to get along with anyone when he wants to. And he's the best person I know in hiring great personnel."

Graham hired many key personnel like ace bookers Danny Scher and Gregg Perloff right out of university student-concert management.

"Bill spotted Danny Scher booking jazz shows at Stanford University," said Phil Elwood, who was a friend of Scher's parents. "He told me that the only thing he could do with Danny was to hire him. He was that good."

After carefully hiring the best talent available, Graham had molded his staff into a highly effective machine which he could trust implicitly. With the organization bursting at the seams, the only way for it to grow was to restructure it to allow greater flexibility for expansion into new areas. At a formal press conference and dinner at Masada in winter 1977, Graham announced a major restructuring of his company into a six-division corporation. Placing himself firmly at the helm, as chairman of the board of Bill Graham Presents, Graham appointed five vice presidents to oversee the day-to-day running of the operations. After eleven years, the sheer size of his business forced him to relax his grip on the company reins and delegate more.

"I will no longer put in ninety hours a week," Graham explained. "There's got to be a maniac dictator on top, but there are people working for me without whom there would be no organization. And I feel good about it."

The newly designated divisions consisted of a laser operation/theatrical shop, which supplied Graham-produced shows and rented equipment to outside acts, a booking company and management division, a record company called Wolfgang Productions, a publicity arm, a publishing company named Grajonca Music, a merchandising company called Winterland Productions, an advertising company cheekily named Chutzpah and the recreational Focus on Fitness department with a mission to explore new opportunities for the company.

Graham also promoted his carefully trained team of executives to head up each division with the title of VP and introduced a profit sharing scheme. Danny Scher headed up the booking division; country music-loving entertainment lawyer Nicholas Clainos was put in charge of management as well as the record company and publishing companies; the former Fillmore East security chief Jerry Pompilli became Graham's principal talent scout; Zohn Artman, now proudly bearing the title "Chargé d'Affaires to the Chairman of the Board" ran publicity; and Bill Graham himself headed the Focus on Fitness department.

"We're pretty much like Avis now. Besides producing shows, if you need a sound system or light system or technician—and we have the best—or you need a stage built or a set designed, we can do that, too. There's the management wing, there's the T-shirt and poster wing, there's production, light and sound, trucking . . . it's rather complex, much more organization and logistics than it used to be. I don't like it much, but it's there, and if we didn't do it, somebody else would."

The key Graham-owned company, Winterland Productions, had nothing whatsoever to do with music and would eventually grow into Graham's most profitable revenue earner, supervised by Del Furano, who became one of Graham's most trusted vice presidents. Winterland invented the highly lucrative merchandising side of the rock business, handling the retailing and wholesaling of rock-related merchandise like T-shirts, posters and souvenirs. Already grossing $4 million in 1976, Winterland operated several retail stores in the Bay Area and distributed to more than 1,000 nationally. Among the top bands Winterland had contracts with were Fleetwood Mac, Rod Stewart, Crosby, Stills & Nash and The Doobie Brothers.

To plan the company's restructure, Graham hired outside experts in business and corporate law. "Bill had very good advice for the restructuring," said Phil Elwood. "He elevated five of his employees to vice presidents and gave them commissions as well as a salary. That was the way the lawyers told him it was done."

Like a child with a new toy, Graham loved the idea of his new corporation, which now employed a total of 150 people, and likened it to playing a real-life game of Monopoly.

"The organization has grown so much that it now seems like we're strategists trying to land on five different beachheads at the same time," he told *BAM* magazine just after the restructuring. "I'm sitting in there saying, 'Get the P.T. boats off the merchandising beach; move Broadway to Park Place over in the shop department.' "

Graham was also "going Hollywood" and rediscovering his love of movies and acting. For $5,000 he agreed to stage a rock concert at a stadium in Phoenix, Arizona, to be filmed as part of the new Barbra Streisand/Kris Kristofferson remake of *A Star is Born.* And despite having been paid well by the movie studio, Graham raked in an additional $175,000 by selling tickets to the 50,000 fans arriving at the show as extras.

That Thanksgiving Bill Graham pulled out all the stops to produce The Band's *Last Waltz* retirement concert. His staff provided a four-course buffet-style Thanksgiving feast for the 5,400 people in the audience at Winterland. After the final plates were cleared away the tables were moved out and the music began.

The Band's final performance had a superstar lineup that included Bob Dylan, Neil Young, Joni Mitchell, Eric Clapton, Paul Butterfield, and Neil Diamond. The musicians performed in front of the San Francisco Opera's chandeliered set from *La Traviata.* Backstage, Graham, who had an overall artists' expense budget of $500,000 a year, created a surreal cocaine environment for the performers to prepare themselves for the show.

After his FM designers were instructed to watch Jean Cocteau's surrealistic masterpiece *Blood of a Poet* for inspiration, they designed a totally white cocaine room dotted with dozens of Groucho Marx noses. The room was rigged so that when someone walked in, a tape recorder was triggered, playing sniffing noises. Certainly, the extensive cocaine

Graham, playing an antiwar activist, defends his views to James Caan while Anjelica Huston looks on during a scene from the movie *Gardens of Stone*. (Courtesy Tri-Star Pictures, Inc.)

Bill Graham finally proved himself as an actor in the 1991 movie *Bugsy*, in which he played crime boss Charles "Lucky" Luciano. Here he holds his own in a dramatic scene with Ben Kingsley, who played Meyer Lansky. (Courtesy Tri-Star Pictures, Inc.)

Super promoters Bill Graham and Ron Delsener buried their differences to talk business during the press conference in New York to announce the 1982 ARMS tour (Action and Research into Multiple Sclerosis) to benefit Ronnie Lane, a former member of the Small Faces. (David Allen)

Bill Graham was right by Bob Dylan and Mick Jagger at the superjam, the traditional ending to the Rock 'n' Roll Hall of Fame induction ceremony at the Waldorf Astoria. (David Allen)

Marlon Brando, right, brought his unique starpower to Bill Graham's 1975 SNACK benefit at San Francisco's Kezar Stadium. (Jon Sievert/Michael Ochs Archives, Venice, CA)

Tina Turner and Mick Jagger set the historic 1985 Live Aid alight, but Bill Graham, pictured with his arm raised, called the shots backstage. (David Allen)

Jerry Garcia of the Grateful Dead celebrates after the SNACK benefit with Bill Graham. (Alvin Meyerowitz/Michael Ochs Archives, Venice, CA)

Bill Graham promoted Elton John's first concerts at the Fillmore West and championed his early career to superstardom. Here they are at the Oakland Colosseum in 1975. (Alvin Meyerowitz/Michael Ochs Archives, Venice, CA)

Carlos Santana, watched by his mentor and friend Bill Graham, swaps his guitar for a table tennis paddle. Santana was first discovered during an audition at the Fillmore Auditorium and was later managed by Graham. (Alvin Meyerowitz/Michael Ochs Archives, Venice, CA)

Bono, Bill Graham, Sting, Bryan Adams, and Peter Gabriel at the press conference to announce the 1986 Amnesty International Conspiracy of Hope tour. (David Allen)

Horrified by the spread of crack, Graham organized two Anti-Crack concerts in New York in 1986. Here, at Madison Square Garden, Graham is pictured with musicians who rallied to his cause. (David Allen)

David Crosby, who has been outspoken about his own problems with drugs, is seen with Bill Graham backstage at the Anti-Crack benefit. (David Allen)

Bill Graham's "secret" daughter, Caitlin Cartwright, who was born on December 30, 1988, to his long-time girlfriend, Regina Cartwright. Here Caitlin is pictured during a visit to Graham's home, Masada. (Courtesy Regina Cartwright)

Regina Cartwright in a tender moment during a night out in Manhattan with Bill Graham in 1990. (Courtesy Regina Cartwright)

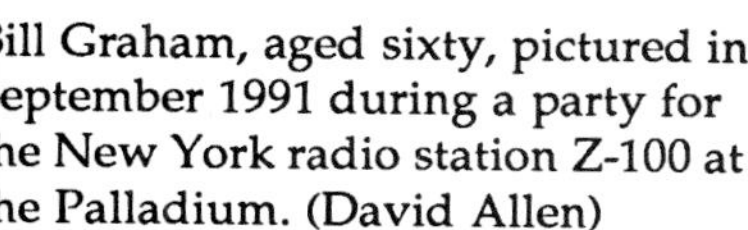

ill Graham, aged sixty, pictured in eptember 1991 during a party for he New York radio station Z-100 at he Palladium. (David Allen)

The tangled wreckage of the helicopter dangling from the top of a 200-foot utility tower near Vallejo, California. The October 25, 1991, crash killed Bill Graham, pilot Steve "Killer" Kahn, and girlfriend Melissa Gold instantly. (AP/Wide World Photos)

In 1992 Bill Graham was posthumously inducted into the Rock 'n' Roll Hall of Fame. Proudly accepting his award were his sisters, Ester Chichinski and Sonja Szobel, and sons, Alex and David Graham. (David Allen)

use by performers and technical staff almost derailed the show with constant arguing between artists and production staff.

By now Graham was heavily into cocaine, snorting it constantly to keep up his prodigious energy level. He used only the purest coke, which was often given to him by The Grateful Dead. Regina Cartwright remembers him once proudly opening up his home safe to show her a huge two-pound rock of cocaine which was so big he had to chip off bits with a knife.

Martin Scorsese, who was directing the *Last Waltz* movie, had raised money from Warner Brothers solely on the box-office potential of Bob Dylan. Throughout the pre-production stage, Graham battled with Scorsese over how his stage show would be presented on film. The Band's leader Robbie Robertson recalls that in the days leading up to the concert, Graham's mood swings alternated between foaming at the mouth, screaming, and being placidly reasonable.

The *Last Waltz* concert went off perfectly until it was time for Bob Dylan to close the show. Minutes before he was due onstage, he announced he had no intention of having his performance filmed for the movie. Panicking, Robbie Robertson called Graham to the back of the lobby to tell him the news, begging him to intervene.

Recounting the story to Bob Costas in 1991, Graham said, "Robbie Robertson said, 'Bill, my God, Bob has changed his mind at the last minute. The wind isn't blowing in the right direction; he's changed his mind.' As artists will from time to time, he's decided that he doesn't want to be filmed.

"So I went up to Bob's room and he didn't want to be filmed because he'd changed his mind. I knew that Martin was filming and that Bob was the key of the film, he's Bob Dylan—the best there is. And Scorsese was somewhat beside himself.

"And I said, 'It's fine, no problem.' And Robbie and the rest of the people there were very much concerned. This great film crew standing by and the instruction was not to film. I said, 'Fine, just let Bob onstage.' "

After introducing Bob Dylan from the stage, Graham went over to the guards, assigned by Dylan's staff to stand by each camera to prevent filming, and screamed, "You Haul" in his most authoritative fashion. Then he ordered the cameramen to begin filming.

Graham explained his rationale for defying Dylan's order and jeopardizing his future relationship with the superstar to Bob Costas, saying: "The worst that could happen is that they would destroy the film and he would never talk to me again," Graham explained. "What's he going to do with me? Not play for me? But look at the situation. How can you not go for that? How many shots like that do we have of capturing magic?"

After the show, Graham was so pleased with how well the show had gone that he tipped each member of The Band $1,000. But Graham's pleasure soon turned to anger and hostility after Robertson and the other members of The Band left Winterland without offering what Graham considered to be enough gratitude. A week later, Graham felt personally insulted by Robertson, who had his road manager convey a message to call the guitarist. Graham called Robertson and had a furious row which he ended by slamming the phone down. The two men never talked again.

Robertson claims Graham never mentioned his problem of not receiving adequate thanks until after he had seen the completed Scorsese movie, which he disliked. Robertson speculated later that it would have taken a huge billboard of thanks to satisfy Bill Graham.

In February 1977, a few months after their final split, Marcia Sult gave birth to Graham's second son, Alex. Once again Graham was too busy to attend and it was left to Zohn Artman to be at the birth and become the baby's godfather. Business now ruled Graham's life, and he was amassing a fortune.

That year *Billboard* estimated Bill Graham had grossed somewhere between $100 million and $150 million in the previous five years—and there appeared to be no end in sight. But privately he was weakening under the intense pressures he lived under, and he had gone into analysis to try and make some sense of his life.

"There's a lot of madness and pressure in concert production," said Graham now 46. "You're rolling the dice for six figures every weekend."

Graham's worsening cocaine problem had started interfering with his work to such an extent that Zohn Artman and a deputation of top management had a showdown confrontation about his drug use.

"Zohn sat him down and said, 'Bill, you have an enormous cocaine problem, and it's really messing up your business,' " says Regina Cartwright, who was at the meeting. "We said, 'Bill it's really horrible. Look what the cocaine is doing to you. You have a terrible temper and no one can deal with you.'

"Bill had a strict rule that any employee found using drugs would be instantly dismissed. No questions asked. He had already fired two women for smoking pot in the ladies' washroom. Zohn pointed out how hypocritical it was for him to have this rule that applied to everyone but him."

Graham publicly agreed to quit using cocaine in the office. He did not give it up, however. He just secretly used it behind closed doors.

12

Punk Wars

The punk-music revolution hit America in 1977, changing the music scene forever. The reign of the psychedelic bands and the excesses of the late sixties and seventies dissipated slowly as the raw energy of New Wave bands like The Sex Pistols and The Clash burst onto the scene.

Punk's earliest advocate in San Francisco was transplanted Los Angeles concert promoter Dirk Dirksen. He came to the city in 1974 and opened an experimental music/theater club called the Mabuhay Gardens in a failing Filipino supper club. Run as a cooperative owned by Dirksen, his staff, and the performers, the Mabuhay fast became an underground alternative to Bill Graham's "corporate" rock shows and the disco craze. Soon the Fab Mab, as it was nicknamed affectionately, had become a hot house for emerging bands like The Nuns, Crime and The Dead Kennedys.

"It was outrageously loud, simple chord progression music," says Dirksen. "The energy was phenomenal."

The first punk band to successfully cross over into the mainstream and ignite the S.F. punk scene was The Sex Pistols. By the beginning of 1977, England's infamous punk band, with charismatic singer Johnny Rotten and free-fall bassist Sid Vicious, had been making headlines in England and the United States for their outrageous behavior and "couldn't give a shit" attitude to stardom. When the Antichrists of punk announced their first American tour in the fall of 1977, Bill Graham jumped at the chance to promote their final show in San Francisco, confident that they would sell out Winterland. But the tour's bookers, Premier Talent, informed Graham that the Pistols' marketing strategy was to play only small, 500-capacity halls and have double the number of people outside running riot and making news to boost record sales. Concerned about the meager profit from such a small venue, Graham resorted to poker tactics. Using Premier's booking agent Bob Regehr as a go-between with the Pistols' fast-talking manager, Malcolm McLaren, Graham pointed out the "thousands and thousands of Pistols' fans" in San Francisco dying to see their punk heroes. He then persuaded McLaren to allow him to test the waters by broadcasting an appeal on KSAN radio to see how many people wanted to see the notorious British band.

A week later Graham called England with the news that 11,000 listeners had sent cards into the station saying they would buy tickets to the show. Delighted, McLaren gave Graham the go-ahead to arrange a Winterland show. Actually, Graham had been bluffing; he had received a mere 412 postcards. In the end, however, the canny promoter proved his point, managing to sell out the Winterland show in just two days. "The truth is never as important as what people believe the truth to be," Graham explained.

By the time the Sex Pistols tour arrived on the West Coast, the dissolute group was on the verge of breaking up, with Rotten openly fighting with their manager Malcolm McLaren as well as his fellow band members.

Taking no chances with the hard-core punk audience expected to attend the January 14 Sex Pistols show, Graham beefed up his security. He also ordered the house lights to be left one-quarter on during the show and stationed bouncers on the balcony with orders to take whatever measures necessary to prevent anarchy breaking out in Winterland.

Graham's old friend Howie Klein had now moved from New York to San Francisco to launch his own punk record label, 415 Records. Instrumental in bringing new bands like Devo, Blondie, and The Ramones to the Mabuhay, Klein managed to persuade his mentor to book his label's band, The Nuns, to open the show. On the afternoon of the show, driving past Winterland on his way to meet Graham and McLaren, Klein saw the members of local punk band Negative Trend waiting outside, trying to hustle tickets for the sold-out show. Klein arrived at the hotel to discover Graham and McLaren locked in a heated argument over the manager's demands that there be an open stage for any punk band that wanted to open for the Pistols.

"Malcolm asked me who the worst punk band in the city was," Klein remembers. "I said, 'Well, I guess Negative Trend is the worst band. They're pretty horrifying.' "

McLaren then told Klein to find Negative Trend and make sure the band was at Winterland that night to play at the show.

Graham absolutely refused to add Negative Trend to the bill, but when McLaren threatened to pull the Pistols from the show, he retracted, under the provision that Negative Trend perform after the Sex Pistols—an offer readily accepted by McLaren.

Returning to Winterland, Klein found the members of Negative Trend still desperately searching for tickets. "Imagine their reaction when I told them to go home and get their instruments because they were going to close for The Sex Pistols," said Klein. "They thought I was lying and it took me ages to convince them it was for real."

By the time the hard-core punk audience began arriving at Winterland, Bill Graham was having second thoughts about booking The Sex Pistols. Later, visibly shaken after seeing several syringes thrown onto the stage during the Nuns' opening set, Graham shrugged his shoulders, saying, "If this is what rock 'n' roll is coming to, I don't know if I want to be a part of it."

Backstage, the Sex Pistols were plotting to give San Francisco a show it would never forget. En route to the stage, Johnny Rotten shouted, "Let's really fuck it up tonight. We'll fuck up these fucking hippies." The evening went from bad to worse, starting with Graham who, offended at comedian Richard Meltzer's sick joke about singer Tony Bennett while introducing The Sex Pistols, personally hauled him offstage.

From the moment they hit the stage, the Pistols did not disappoint their fans. To the thunderous applause of the sold-out Winterland crowd, Johnny Rotten jeered and mocked the audience, who loved it and begged for more. As the pogoing hard-core punks at the front of the stage kept a steady flow of spit raining at the Pistols, Graham looked on helplessly in total disbelief.

Graham, however, had the last laugh after the Pistols finally left the stage, at the end of what would be their final show together. He instructed his staff to start playing *"Greensleeves,"* the traditional signal for the audience to exit a Graham show. When the hapless members of Negative Trend walked out onstage sheepishly, they found themselves looking out on an empty hall.

By the late seventies, punk was firmly on the map, and the Mabuhay was selling out and attracting more than 1,000 kids to every show, and, not unlike Bill Graham's Fillmore Auditorium in the sixties, the Fab Mab became the "in" place to go. One night Paul Kantner stopped in at the Mabuhay to check out the new scene. He was so impressed with the raw energy that he suggested Bill Graham open a new field club in San Francisco to scout new talent. Graham was interested and sent his chief talent scout Jerry Pompili to arrange an audition at the Mab for a newcomer named Eddie Money whom he was interested in signing up.

Graham liked what he saw and determined to take over the punk market by starting his own club. His first move was to poach one of Dirksen's key employees, Ken Friedman, and set him up as an independent promoter, putting on shows around the city. Wisely, Graham kept a low profile in the new S.F. club scene, sending his trusted employee Queenie Taylor to investigate the punk circuit and learn everything she could. Members of the San Francisco punk scene were suspicious of Bill Graham's sudden interest in punk, fearing that he was going to move in and swallow them up. So when Graham announced his first punk music show, the leaders of the scene promptly decided to boycott him.

"We all got together to figure out how to stop this incursion into punk by Graham," recalled deejay Tim Yohannon whose "Maximum Rock 'n' Roll" radio show specialized in punk. "We organized it through word of mouth and fliers, and we persuaded local bands to refuse to play Graham shows."

The boycott was so effective that, unable to find a local band to play, Graham had to import an L.A. punk band called The Screamers for his first punk show at California Hall. As a result, the negative publicity killed box-office sales, and most of the tickets had to be given away. Alarmed at the effectiveness of the community action, Graham decided to appeal directly to the audience, challenging Yohannon to a live radio debate on punk music with a round table of local punk club owners and promoters.

"When I tried to corner him about his real feeling on punk, he was like a sleazy Mafia lawyer," says Yohannon. "But at least I got him to acknowledge that he didn't know anything about punk or its aesthetics."

During the final moments of the broadcast, Graham became very conciliatory and publicly offered to finance anyone who could prove he or she had the know-how to start a punk club in San Francisco. Taking Graham at his word, Yohannon found a site, arranged insurance, and secured a city club permit.

"We called Graham back and said, 'Okay, now we've got a club and we're not a ragtag group and we're ready to start punk concerts.' " Graham just said, 'Fuck off,' and hung up. That's the side of Bill Graham that most people don't see. He made us this grandiose public offer but it was total PR."

Five years later, the former members of Negative Trend had formed a new band named Flipper, finding success in the San Francisco music scene. But they still harbored a grudge against Graham for making a fool of them at the Sex Pistols show and were outspoken in their antagonism.

"I hate Bill Graham's guts," Flipper vocalist and bassist Will Shatter told *Rolling Stone*. "Bill Graham's got his power trips, and that's one of the things we're trying to get away from. We've proved that you don't need people like Bill Graham. You don't need big record companies or heavy agents. You don't need any of the established music-business things."

Graham, delighting in going head-on with the punks and taking the high ground, challenged Shatter to a public debate in October 1983 on the future of the San Francisco music scene. "The first thing I would say to him is, what do you think Bill Graham stands for? Money? Power? Control? Capitalism? I've never met this young man. And I'll tell you something, Mr. Flipper, I would never say that Flipper can't play for us because they're Jews or they're black or they're for the war or they don't like short people. You know why I wouldn't do any of those things? 'Cause I don't know that. You, Mr. Flipper, don't even know who I am or what makes me or this company tick. Nothing gets my juices going more than blind accusations."

Bill Graham first proposed marriage to Regina Cartwright in spring 1981 to give him the marital stability he needed to gain custody of his four-year-old son, Alex, now living in Maui with Marcia Sult. Cartwright's relationship with Graham had become serious, and he was beginning to rely on her more and more.

"He used to say I was the center of his core," said Regina. "I just loved him unconditionally. No other woman would have put up with what I did from him."

Regina refused to marry him just so he could have Alex. When Graham's sister Ester found out about his proposal she was furious, even though Regina had turned him down, and began a campaign to break up their relationship. Since Ester had moved to San Francisco in the early sixties to be close to her brother, she had become a major influence in his life. He relied on her for advice and was one of the few people he would listen to.

"Ester ruled his personal life and for some reason he was really scared of her," Regina said.

To placate his sister, Graham shipped Regina off to France for a few months while Ester fixed him up on dates with women she regarded as more suitable marriage partners. Soon Graham grew tired of his sister's matchmaking and flew to Paris, offering to buy Regina a house in Los Angeles, just an hour's plane commute away from San Francisco.

"He wanted to shuttle and balance all his women for his convenience," Regina said. "He couldn't have me in San Francisco because of Ester, but I refused to move to Los Angeles at any price."

Finally Graham allowed Regina to move to New York and set her up in an apartment on Central Park South, finding her a job with his friend, financier Stephen Greenberg. He continued their affair long distance, moving in with her whenever he came to New York.

"We were virtually a married couple when he was in New York," said Regina, whose favorite pet name for him was Beej. "He used to introduce me as his wife wherever we went and whenever he took me on his trips to Europe."

Their sex life was obsessive and intense and Regina was available for him whenever he wanted her while he was in New York. "Bill would call me up at 2:00 A.M. and just come over," Cartwright said. "When he arrived I'd be fully made up and dressed in something sexy. I did whatever he wanted because I was in love with him. I felt it was loyalty to be there when he needed me."

Throughout their relationship, Graham refused to use—or to allow Regina to use—any contraception. As a result, Regina suffered a series of pregnancies which ended in miscarriages.

"I couldn't use the pill because I had high blood pressure," Cartwright said. "Bill always insisted that I remove any birth-control device I wanted to use, and if I wouldn't, he'd take it out himself. He said he wanted me in my pure state."

Regina was also suffering from severe anorexia as a result of Graham's obsessive demands that she keep the slim body with big breasts that he loved so much.

"I was in my mid-twenties and I was buying my clothes in the preteen section and having the tops let out," Regina recalled. "If I weighed 115 pounds he called me fat and told me to go on a diet. So I would. I usually weighed anywhere from 95 to 105 pounds, which was 20 pounds less than my healthy weight. If the man you love continually tells you you're too fat and grabbing whatever chubbiness and folds you have, what can you do?

"He was oblivious to the way women think and feel. I think my anorexia was part of the reason I had seven miscarriages with Bill."

Their relationship was full of double standards. If Graham was free to bed any woman he wanted, it was a different story for Cartwright.

"He had me watched," she said. "If I was even seen in the company of a male in New York, Bill would call me up the next day from anywhere in the world and say, 'Why were you with so-and-so at Danceteria?' More often than not, I was with my girlfriends, anyway."

But there were good times for Regina in New York when the famed promoter dropped his public face to become the sensitive father figure she had fallen in love with. At these times they got close and Graham would let down his guard, telling her about the secrets of his life and the cutthroat music business.

"Bill told me a lot of things about the industry and his private life to clear his conscience," Regina said. "I know where all the skeletons are hidden. There were some very scary things about Bill in our relationship, and his confidences were among them."

Baring his soul to Regina one night, he revealed the real Bill Graham.

"He told me he had created Bill Graham," Cartwright said. "Somebody had dubbed him the P. T. Barnum of rock 'n' roll in the early days, and he decided to really be Bill Graham. He never believed that he was who he was. I mean, he never really was that person. He was always a frustrated actor, and it was a role that he would assume every day and put down at night. It was not who he was when he hung around the house. I was one of four people in his whole life who really knew who he was."

At one point Regina asked why he never smiled for the camera and always looked so deadpan serious. He explained that it was a trick he had learned in his acting days and felt it was his most effective pose.

"I told him he looked ridiculous," Regina recalled. "He looked like Heathcliff on the moors. After that he was always trying to smile and developed his official smile for the camera. He was such a phony in public, but he was so good at it that nobody ever knew."

Although Graham was one of the richest men in show business, he rarely bought new clothes and often looked like a tramp. One day when she was unpacking his suitcase during a New York visit, Regina found all his ancient underwear and socks were tattered and had holes in them.

"I said, 'Bill you're a real mess,'" she remembers. "I took him to Charivari and told them, 'Do this man!'"

Recognizing Graham, the delighted store staff closed the expensive clothing store as Regina spent $5,000 fitting him out in fashionable new designer clothes.

"Bill had never spent so much on himself in his whole life," said Cartwright. "He ended up framing the $5,000 check, which hung in his office for many years."

Early on in their relationship Regina asked him why money was so important to him.

"He had a plaque in his office saying *It's not the money—it's the money,*" she said. "Bill asked me once what I thought it meant. At the time I was still his receptionist and, thinking that my job depended on my answer, I said it means never having to worry about where your next meal's coming from. He said to me, 'No one has ever understood that statement but you.' "

Ever since his childhood during the Holocaust, Graham had developed a love affair with food, his weight continually fluctuating between 170 and 220 pounds. He would go on eating binges, pile on the pounds, and then go on a cocaine bender to lose them again.

As the undisputed king of American concert promotion, the flamboyant impresario had now scaled every peak of rock 'n' roll but his relentless ambition to climb further knew no boundaries. In 1978 he felt ready to launch himself on the world stage and make history by producing the first ever rock 'n' roll concert behind the Iron Curtain. His chance to organize a rock festival in Russia came a couple of years earlier when he was contacted by Russian film producer Dimitri DeGrunwald, whose current Soviet-backed film contrasted the differences in nineteenth- and twentieth-century Soviet life. As an integral part of the film, he asked Graham to stage a July Fourth rock concert in 1978 for 250,000 people in Leningrad's Palace Square. After obtaining security clearance from the U.S. State Department, Graham spent two years secretly working to get the unprecedented project off the ground and managed to personally negotiate the first major corporate rock sponsorship by persuading Levi Strauss to commit $300,000 toward the concert. On top of that, Graham sold the recording rights to CBS.

DeGrunwald was in charge of liaison with the Soviet authorities, who seemed to be cooperating on every level. A month before the show, everything was going smoothly. Graham had signed up Santana, The Beach Boys, and Joan Baez to perform alongside three Russian acts. When he announced the history-making concert at a lavish press conference in his offices on June 14, the countdown to the show was already well under way. Air tickets and hotel rooms for Graham's entourage had been booked, visas obtained, and six trucks full of sound-and-light equipment were en route from London to Leningrad.

"This is an awesome project for us," Graham explained to the press. "The greatest musical event undertaken in the world today."

"My family came from Eastern Europe, so this project is emotionally pleasing for me also. If I had the choice of being on the first spaceship or of going to Russia to do this concert, I would go to Russia."

By the following day, Bill Graham's Russian festival was national news; the promoter was hailed as an inspirational hero crusading for peace. Unfortunately, the Russian government had not been warned about the conference, and DeGrunwald was ordered to Moscow and told the show had been "postponed" due to "historical imprecisions" in the film script.

Taking on the Russians, Graham called the official Soviet reasons for postponement "bullshit," saying it was an insult to his intelligence. He aggressively launched an angry stream of cables at Russia pleading his cause, and enlisted the help of Senator Edward Kennedy and multimillionaire Armand Hammer, the chairman of Occidental Petroleum, who had more than fifty years' experience in dealing with the Russians. Hammer personally interceded on Graham's behalf with Soviet ambassador to the United States Anatoly Dobrynin. But when the Russians adamantly refused to allow the concert, a disappointed Graham pledged to stage a concert on Soviet soil whenever the Soviet government would give their permission.

"I will always be ready to go," he said. "This is not waiting to get stadium availability in Detroit. This is fucking Russia. This is not the moon. I mean, this is bigger than the moon. There's nobody up there to change."

Meanwhile, America was falling into a deep recession, and for the first time ever, concert ticket sales were down. Bill Graham and the other concert promoters were alarmed, fearing the bubble had burst. It looked like the end of the spectacular outdoor extravaganzas which had netted them millions of dollars.

Hit by low ticket sales in the summer of 1978, Graham was forced to move his second "Day on the Green" show indoors to a smaller 14,000-seat hall. Nationally the pattern was just as bleak. Denver promoter Barry Fey canceled a Fleetwood Mac concert due to low sales, and Arnie Granat's JAM Productions sold only 46,000 tickets for a show in

Chicago's 60,000-capacity Comiskey Park Stadium. New York promoter Ron Delsener claimed that the novelty of the expensive big outdoor shows, which cost $12.50 to $15.00 a head, had worn off, and that audiences now preferred indoor concerts in smaller halls with better sound and cheaper tickets.

"You can't do too many of these [festival] shows," said Delsener. "After the fourth or fifth the kids say, 'Hey, this is bullshit.' "

Premier agent Barry Bell's philosophy on the blockbuster shows was that "Stadium concerts can be very lucrative but they're a big gamble."

Even the smaller 5,000- to 10,000-seat halls were suffering, and on New Year's Eve 1978 Bill Graham closed Winterland, announcing that he would now concentrate on artist management.

Graham's management arm was by now a major part of his overall operation; it represented a stable of artists that included Santana and Eddie Money, a new signing who was fast becoming a headliner. But Graham's major coup was in persuading the enigmatic Belfast cowboy, Van Morrison, to come out of retirement and sign with his company, Wolfgang Management.

Graham officially relaunched Morrison's career with the singer's first public appearance since the *Last Waltz* at a tiny 100-seat San Francisco club called Sweetwater in August 1978. The show was unannounced, and the audience was mainly music journalists and people in the business.

Afterward, Graham said that he was delighted to be managing Morrison. "Without sounding melodramatic, the chance to work with one of the main innovators in music today is a privilege, not a challenge. I already know that he's a major artist; our job here is to make the public aware of it."

After releasing Morrison's comeback album, *Wavelength,* Graham sent the nervous musician on a national tour chaperoned by Zohn Artman. But Graham's relationship with the equally temperamental Irish singer was short-lived when Morrison lost his temper with his new manager and told him to fuck off.

"Bill beat up Van Morrison in an alley in New York," Regina Cartwright recalls. "He came back home to me with scratches all over his neck and back, and I thought he'd been with a woman. He told me that Van Morrison had told him to fuck off, so he had to beat him up. It didn't matter who you were, you never told Bill Graham to fuck off, as Van Morrison discovered."

Explaining his new emphasis on management, Graham said that it allowed him more creativity than live concerts because bands now traveled with their complete stage show ready to be assembled at each site, leaving the promoter little influence on the show.

Wolfgang's vice-president, Nick Clainos, by now the most powerful of BGP's five vice presidents and the man behind Graham's new push into management, told Jack McDonough, "My goal is to make management as high profile in this company as concerts."

Despite closing Winterland with his traditional Grateful Dead New Year's concert, Graham had no intention of cutting back on live concerts. Rock concerts were changing yet again, and Graham was positioning himself to be in the right place at the right time.

Yet many observers now believed that Graham's hold on the Bay Area concert business was beginning to slip. An in-depth analysis of San Francisco rock by *Variety* in July 1979 found Graham's position in the Northern California market had weakened. Blaming "reasons not totally under his control," *Variety* cited the current disco and country-and-western boom as the main reasons for his decline. "Also to be considered in the examination of the Graham mini-erosion is the lack of boffo rock acts for use in his once-awesome *Day on the Green* concerts," said *Variety*.

Graham's archenemy James Nederlander posed the biggest single threat. Nederlander operated the Los Angeles Greek Theater and four other major sites across the country making him the largest talent buyer in the U.S. and one of the few promoters working on Graham's national level. Specializing in booking middle-of-the-road pop and family entertainment, Nederlander beat out Graham for an exclusive contract on the 8,000-seat Concord Pavilion in Concord, California, which Graham had sought as his replacement for Winterland. In the three years it had been open, the Concord had been most profitable when Graham had produced ten lucrative shows at the Concord in 1978. When Concord City Council awarded the whole 1979 season to Nederlander, Graham was livid and called a press conference to complain. Among the major hitters who rallied to Graham's side in his battle with the council was San Francisco's new mayor, Dianne Feinstein, whom he had been cultivating carefully.

"I've never experienced anything like this," declared the outraged promoter during a press conference in his offices. "What I attended in those city council chambers was a kangaroo court."

Graham's other danger came from Roy DuBrow of Morningsun Productions, who staged shows in downtown San Francisco's beautiful art deco 2,200-seat Warfield Theater. But even though Graham looked vulnerable to attack, *Variety* warned that he should not be written off just yet.

"This plethora of new promoter action should not delude aud-arena operators into the belief that Graham is fading away," said *Variety*. "When he has the acts, he still knows how to fill and spill. But the fact is that Graham has company from every direction now that rock is rocky."

If concert grosses were on the decline, Graham's Winterland merchandising arm, run by Del Furano, was now grossing a steady $10 million a year and remained his main profit center. Handling logoed T-shirts, baseball caps, and tote bags with a range of clients that included Bob Seger, Ted Nugent, Cheap Trick, and Fleetwood Mac, Winterland was changing the financial face of rock 'n' roll.

"The figures are awesome," Graham declared, discussing his departure into the rag trade. "In the midst of this economically bad period, the kids are spending money like you wouldn't believe on products associated with their favorite groups. It's very big business."

To illustrate this point, the 18,500 fans who attended a Journey concert at the L.A. Forum each paid on average $4.33 at the show for shirts and other items of band memorabilia.

In late 1979, when DuBrow pulled out of the Warfield Theater after experiencing a disastrous season, Graham immediately moved in to take over the 2,200-seat former vaudeville theater. Signing Bob Dylan to play a series of concerts at the Warfield, Graham announced that he would stage eight to ten shows a month there from now on.

Now on a roll, Graham also fulfilled his longtime ambition of owning a nightclub by buying the 600-seat Old Waldorf. Recognizing a new trend where audiences would pay top dollar to see top bands playing in an intimate nightclub atmosphere, Graham realized that this was the future direction of rock. The Old Waldorf also provided the perfect site to compete with the small punk clubs like Dirk Dirksen's Mabuhay Gardens. The Fab Mab had introduced all the New Wave bands to San Francisco, and Dirksen's championing of such bands as Madness, Blondie, Talking Heads, Devo, The Cramps, and Black Flag helped them become established in the city.

Not long after Graham moved into the Waldorf, Dirksen discovered that the bands no longer wanted to play for him and were going over to Bill Graham, who could offer more money for their services.

"Performers are great prostitutes," Dirksen said. "There's very little loyalty in that sense. At that point all those acts like Talking Heads started showing up at the Waldorf to play for Graham, and to my dying day I will say that wasn't by sheer coincidence."

Howie Klein, the man who coined "New Wave" as a more acceptable name for punk, says that the bands liked Bill Graham because he ran a more professional operation. "Dirk Dirksen did the best he could," said Klein. "The bands would start off at one level, and as they got more popular, they would want to move up to the next."

Although he was happy to book punk bands, Bill Graham hated the raw, stripped-down music with a vengeance. "The mechanicalness in the music induces mechanical dancing. It seems to be a hiding of, rather than an expression of, what you feel," Graham said. "Too much of what I hear is asensual. There's no contact in the dancing. There wasn't in the sixties or seventies, true, but people looked at each other. But with pogoing there seems to be no communication at all."

At the beginning of 1984, now directly controlling every level of the Bay Area concert scene, from his 600-seat Waldorf Club to the 54,000-seat Oakland Coliseum, Graham moved to stamp out all opposition. Wielding his power aggressively, he started trying to force booking agents to restrict acts from playing for rivals so he could starve out his opposition.

"He's the bully on the block," said club owner Bobby Corona, who sued Graham for $6 million alleging unfair competition and malice in 1984. "And I'm tired of walking across the street to stay out of his way."

Corona accused Graham of trying to destroy his Keystone Club by using intimidation and offering financial incentives to artists including Mink DeVille, James Brown, Captain Beefheart, and Junior Walker to break their Keystone contracts and play for him instead. Corona claimed that Graham Presents employee Harry Duncan threatened Junior Walker's agent, warning that BGP would not book the saxophone-playing star, whose hits include "Roadrunner" and "Shotgun," for larger shows if he didn't break his Keystone contract. Not wishing to upset Graham, Walker broke the contract and performed for Bill Graham.

Godfather of Soul James Brown who already had been signed and paid a deposit to play three Keystone shows, was offered more money by BGP's Duncan to play for Graham. As a result, Corona had to pay Brown extra money for him to play. Corona also accused Graham of intimidating the jazz-rock band Dixie Dregs into canceling a Keystone show in Palo Alto by threatening not to allow them to play the more important San Francisco market.

Wanting to avoid a public court hearing into his business affairs, Bill Graham agreed to pay Corona $22,500 in a secret out-of-court settlement in which he did not admit any liability.

Another competitor, Tom Bradshaw, whose 450-seat Great American Music Hall was in direct competition with the Old Waldorf, also accused him of poaching acts.

"Graham will do anything for a buck," Bradshaw told the *San Francisco Business Journal* in December 1982. "He doesn't do any research or development, but just skims the cream off the top. He sits there waiting for an act to do well on my level and when the act is ready to move on to a larger hall, he moves in."

The majority of Graham's rivals didn't dare publicly confront the powerful promoter, fearing indirect reprisals through booking agents. Although he was highly respected for his business efficiency, nearly everyone in the San francisco music industry had their own story of how Graham had abused them in one way or another.

To diversify from rock, Graham brought legitimate theater to the Warfield with a revival of *Ain't Misbehavin'* and had announced plans in July 1980 to present the stage version of the popular *Rocky Horror Picture Show* in the near future.

Challenging the Nederlander Organization, Graham told the *San Francisco Chronicle* that he was expecting trouble with his move into legitimate theater. "We're in a competitive business," said the promoter. "But that's the nature of the game. If somebody came into this town and said they were going to start putting on big rock shows, you can bet I'd be the first to clench my fists and shout 'You'd better get up early in the morning.' "

On December 3, 1979, the greatest single tragedy at a rock concert since Altamont occurred when 20,000 fans poured into Cincinnati's Riverfront Coliseum for a Who concert, and eleven people were crushed to death. The many hard-core Who fans had arrived for show, which was promoted by the Electric Factory, hours early to secure good positions as near the stage as possible in the stadium which had festival seating, meaning that there were no fixed seats.

The Who was doing their sound check at 6:30 P.M. when an estimated 8,000 excited kids began lining up outside the main entrance. The crush increased steadily as more and more fans arrived in the parking lot and crowded onto a bridge, the only way into the stadium. At 7:00 P.M., when The Who finished its sound check, the pressure on the kids in front was intense, with people at the back yelling, "One, two, three, push!" Five minutes later, when four out of the sixteen doors were finally opened to the surging crowd, it was too late to avert the oncoming tragedy.

The huge crush from the back was literally bodyshattering. Some unfortunate fans were smashed up against the doors; others were forced off their feet and carried horizontally through the crowd. Amazingly, all through the horrific nightmare, the ticket takers remained at their posts, attempting to inspect tickets. More than an hour later, the full extent of the tragedy was realized when eleven bodies were carried out among the many injuries.

Electric Factory's Cal Levy, who promoted the show, told *Rolling Stone*, "Hey, I'm no Bill Graham, okay? I just think that when all the facts are known, all the reports are completed, that it will show that there was a combination of things that brought about an uncontrollable situation on that plaza."

In the aftermath of the tragedy, Bill Graham was sharply critical of the promoter's security and stated that it could never happen at one of his shows.

Describing the Cincinnati concert nightmare as one "where people were forced to act like cattle," Graham told the *San Francisco Chronicle* why his shows were safe. "Pre-planning is mandatory," said Graham. "You must avoid the domino reaction. All you need is one or two people to push the panic button and the chain reaction starts."

Although Bill Graham still supported festival seating, the official City of Cincinnati report into the tragedy did find fault, declaring that it should be banned from all future indoor events.

As the recession deepened, the concert business became tougher and tougher for promoters, who were forced to lay off staff and cut back their operations. Angrily denying there would be any layoffs at BGP, Graham was livid when one of his upper management suggested issuing pink slips after the "Day on the Green" concert of the 1980 summer season lost "a bundle of money" when only 35,000 people turned up at the Oakland Coliseum Stadium when it needed 45,000 to break even.

"Basically," said Graham, "We're seeing the first time since the sixties that a combination of recession and cost of living has come with such force that it's unbalancing our music industry."

"We're living in a time where the music fan, after he or she has finished paying the everyday bills, is now left with a smaller amount of money. Never before has this fan had to be so choosy."

As hard-hit record companies began to reduce financial tour support, the rock bands reacted by demanding higher percentages from promoters to offset their added expenses on the road.

"In the early 1980s the deals changed dramatically," explained promoter Frank Russo. "It started to be an eighty-twenty split at the net. So you take all your fixed expenses, including the band's sounds and lights, deduct that off the gross, and split the rest eighty-twenty."

Atlanta promoter Alex Cooley blamed the outrageous demands of David Bowie, during his "Serious Moonlight" tour, for changing the concert business forever.

"The first person to go to a new way of pricing was David Bowie," Cooley said. "The business was horrified by it. Most of the major promoters had worked with Bowie at that point and then he'd gotten very big and the deal came down—'It's an eighty-five–fifteen.' It caused a furor. It was the first time that I remember anyone squeezing a deal to the point of what I considered ridiculous."

Strict antitrust laws made it illegal for promoters to act together in a concerted effort to fight Bowie's and other artists' demands. There were heated telephone calls and informal discussions at trade shows among promoters, but ultimately they were powerless to act together.

Cooley said that once Bowie set a precedent, all the other artists followed suit. "Acts talk amongst themselves and say, 'We got X dollars out of this situation, you only got Y,' " said Cooley. "So the guy that got Y goes back to his manager and says, 'Why aren't you doing your job? Why aren't you getting me as much as so and so?'

"Then the artist hires an accountant and a lawyer to watch his manager, and it becomes a circus with each of them trying to outdo the other and cut harder and harder deals. It's just a cycle that gets started."

Cooley says that the booking agents are also under intense pressure to drive the best deal possible at the expense of the promoter.

"They have to squeeze every nickel out of a deal," said Cooley. There's one person, who shall remain nameless, who says that if a promoter walked out of a building with any profit, he didn't do his job right. I think that kind of attitude is very short-term. Get every nickel right now and to hell with tomorrow."

As the promoters were squeezed harder and harder in the 1980s, many started resorting to other more questionable methods to make up their losses.

"When a group performs in a hall they rent four walls, a floor, and a ceiling," Bob Grossweiner explained. "The rest they pay for."

Bill Graham's favorite trick was to have a potted palm tree on stage for every show for which he charged the artist $15. During a roast for FBI's Ian Copeland, the emcee carried out the potted palm onto the stage, handed it to Copeland, saying, "Here you are. You finally own it." Later that night, Copeland got drunk and urinated over the tree.

"Promoters actually have a tough time," explained music business expert Donald S. Passman in his book *All You Need to Know About the Music Business*. "If they lose, they can lose big, but as acts get more successful they squeeze them and limit the promoter's upside. The result is a friendly game of 'hide the pickle' that promoters routinely play in rendering statements of how much has been earned."

Many artists employ tour accountants to "count the house," using clickers to ensure that the promoter's figures are accurate. Festival seating makes it easy for promoters to fake attendance figures.

Vinnie Fusco used to routinely count the house when he represented Bob Dylan and Janis Joplin. "I'd find discrepancies and I'd bust them," he said. "I'd say, 'Where's the fucking money? I counted the gig.' "

Passman says that "greedy" promoters have developed systematic methods of "adding" expenses over the years: "Crasser promoters have been known simply to create phony invoices for various items. A more sophisticated example might be that the promoter advertises so much in the local paper or radio station that they get a 'rebate' at the end of the year. In other words, if they spend $100,000 for ads on a radio station, the station gives them back $5,000 at year end. This doesn't show up on each individual invoice, and thus the shows are charged for the full amount.

"The interesting part is that everyone knows pretty much what the promoters are doing, and thus there is this little 'waltz of the toreadors' while your agent negotiates how much the promoter can steal from you. Because everyone knows what expenses really are, they are accepted amounts of stealing, and it's bad form for (a) the promoter to steal more than is customary, or (b) the artist to 'catch' the promoter and not allow the accepted level. So in this bizarre netherland, everyone reaches a happy compromise."

Fusco says that he caught one promoter overstepping the line by actually stealing the band's musical equipment to resell. "That was happening a lot. All of a sudden, after the third band gets robbed, you realize that the promoter is doing it."

For years the promoter's extra "expenses" went unchecked and it would take another decade before the authorities would move in and bring indictments against several promoters for stealing millions of dollars from some of the biggest acts in rock 'n' roll.

13

Gimme Shelter

In 1980 the Rolling Stones were preparing to go back on the road for a world tour and needed a new tour manager to replace Peter Rudge. The world's greatest rock 'n' roll band, as they liked to be known, wanted to clean up by playing an unprecedented forty-city arena tour and gross a record $35 million. The Stones' business team drew up a shopping list of promoters, including Bill Graham, Barry Fey of Denver, and New Jersey's John Scher, summoning them all to New York for a round of interviews.

Graham, with his experience of staging successful national tours for Bob Dylan, George Harrison, and Crosby, Stills, Nash & Young, seemed to be the logical choice for the job. But when he arrived in New York to meet with Mick Jagger and the Stones' business representatives, he was unusually nervous. Over a two-week period, Graham ardently wooed Mick Jagger through the singer's beloved Upper West Side Japanese sushi restaurants. Treading carefully, like a timid suitor on a first date, Graham told Jagger his life story and his philosophy of rock music. He assured the singer that if he was lucky enough to be given the tour, he would stay out of the spotlight and not upstage the Stones. Jagger was impressed with Graham's professional approach but remained noncommittal, keeping the eager promoter hanging by a thread for weeks before finally agreeing to hand over the complete 81/82 World Tour.

"Bill came up with the best offer and we thought, 'Let's go for it,' " said Rolling Stones bassist Bill Wyman, who was kept closely informed of the situation. "He seemed to have become much more established and much more organized than he was before."

Working for an undisclosed percentage of the net profit, a euphoric Graham dropped everything and worked full-time organizing every aspect of the Stones tour. Graham found himself in the enviable position of not only being tour director, but handling all the merchandising, staging, and design, as well as promoting all the West Coast dates. But working with the Rolling Stones meant far more than money to Bill Graham; it helped satisfy his craving for acceptance and acknowledgment. The ragged Holocaust survivor had finally made it to the imperious position of being the prime minister to the traveling court of the biggest rock band in the world and could now wield tremendous influence and power in every branch of the music business. Everyone now wanted a slice of what promised to be the most lucrative tour in history, and the only way to get it was to go through Graham. Like a latter-day Svengali, Graham jealously guarded the band members and, while they were under his control, he carefully vetted anyone who came into contact with them.

To whip the Stones back into musical shape, after being off the road for three years, Graham rented Longview Farm in the wilds of Massachusetts for rehearsals. While Graham roamed around the farm with his notepads and charts, finalizing logistics and setting up the tour, the Stones dusted off their instruments and got back into playing with each other again. The time Graham spent hanging out with the Stones in the calming Massachusetts countryside was one of the happiest periods Graham had ever known, both creatively and personally.

Earlier that year he had embarked on an affair with his personal assistant Jan Simmons and had shipped Regina Cartwright, who was yet again pregnant with his baby, off to his sister Evelyn in Geneva, where she had another miscarriage.

Although mostly working twenty-hour days, Graham seemed happy and relaxed, often joining Jagger for his daily jog so he could update him on the tour's progress. Graham still viewed himself as a hired hand and was careful not to get overly familiar with the Stones in case it backfired on him. But he soon found himself having to act as a go-between for Jagger and Keith Richards, who at the time were barely speaking to one another.

Graham built an entire organization around the 1981 Rolling Stones stadium tour. By far the most ambitious ever attempted, the logistics for forward planning were awesome. The forty-city tour used four staging systems that were transported around America on thirty-five semi-trucks.

One of the biggest problems facing Graham, however, was a master forger who threatened to flood America with counterfeit Stones tickets. The counterfeit tickets, which had first appeared at the Grateful Dead's 1980 New Year's Eve concert, had been increasing in number at every show. Soon there were tens of thousands of fake tickets being sold for each Bill Graham show.

"A counterfeiter relates to the demand," Graham told the *San Francisco Sunday Examiner*. "It's like cigarettes during the war."

To prevent the forged ticket from circulating, Graham had a "counterfeit-proof" ticket designed, which he claimed was impossible to copy. He also posted a $10,000 reward for the arrest and conviction of the counterfeiter.

From his illustrious position as tour director, Graham carefully selected which promoters received a lucrative slice of the action too, enabling him either to secure future favors from friends or to punish his enemies. The first concert of the tour, at St. Morgan's Cove in Worcester, Massachusetts, went to his old Rhode Island promoter friend Frank Russo. "Bill always took care of me," said Russo. "And it was a great show."

Graham cocooned the Stones in a luxurious environment while they traveled around America, simulating an exotic tropical island getaway backstage, complete with palm trees and Astroturf.

"He made it look like Hawaii," said Bill Wyman. "He really did go out of his way to make us comfortable and look after us. He ran a good ship.

"I remember playing table tennis backstage with him. We'd go to dinners and things afterwards and do all sorts of things. He'd always be available if you needed him for anything, if you needed to sort something out and it was a problem.

"Even personal things—he would always be around and available to have a chat with or sort something out for you, organize something. He was very, very good in that way," Wyman recalled.

To Bill Graham, a Stones tour was nothing less than taking the reigning kings of rock 'n' roll on a royal tour on par with that of any legitimate monarch. For the duration of the tour Graham's nagging insecurities and self-doubts could be put on hold. To Graham, the power and the glory of masterminding the Rolling Stones tour was as deep as being in love.

"No other group has ever made me feel that way," Graham told *Details* West Coast editor Roger Trilling. "Challenging, hard work, logistical madness, but so rich. Every city was the capital of rock 'n' roll for that day.

"They're great performers. Mick and Keith fronting the band. That's rock 'n' roll. That's the essence of the street rock 'n' roll statement."

Everything went smoothly for the first few East Coast shows, but as the tour swung west toward Graham's home territory, the promoter's ego suddenly took over. He started a campaign to persuade the Stones to play a single show at his new 600-seat Old Waldorf Theater as a personal tribute to him in his home base. Jagger and other Stones refused, feeling the Waldorf was too small and there was nothing in it for them. When *San Francisco Chronicle* columnist Warren Hinckle printed rumors about a possible Stones gig at the Waldorf, Graham panicked, fearing that if Jagger saw the story he would suspect Graham of planting it. When Graham spotted Hinckle a couple of days later, during the Stones' Seattle show, he personally set his security guards on the writer.

"That was a goddamn nasty thing you wrote about the Old Waldorf. You really are an asshole," Graham screamed as his guards physically threw Hinckle out of the King Dome.

Journalists in San Francisco were horrified by Graham's treatment of Hinckle. *San Francisco Examiner* columnist Bill Mandel launched a stinging attack over the next three days in a series of hard-hitting columns titled "The Truth About Bill Graham."

"Graham is the absolute emperor of rock impresarios, and like an emperor, his whims are law," penned Mandel, who told readers that he, too, had been physically attacked by Graham at a Philadelphia concert some years earlier.

"Graham, however, is his own judge, jury and executioner. There are no stockholders to please, no voters to charm. 'The public' is his constituency and when you're presenting the Rolling Stones or any top rock group, 'the public' lines up 24 hours early to vote for you. Graham alone rules, and there's no court of appeal."

But Graham's power was not absolute when it came to the Rolling Stones, as he discovered when the Stones' tour accountants caught him stealing hundreds of thousands of dollars from the band during his two San Francisco shows.

"Something happened on the eighty-one tour," explained Bill Wyman. "We found that he was fiddling on one of the gates. We found a discrepancy. He was running one gate without keeping a record of it, so all the money going into that gate was going into his pocket without us knowing about it. We found out by pure chance. Our business people told us that if they hadn't been so sharp we would have been short of quite a few hundred thousand dollars. It was a big lump of money. We're talking about six figures, and that's a lot of money. And it destroys your faith in someone that you've slowly built up after being distrustful of them in the beginning."

Wyman said that the Stones felt disappointed in Graham and couldn't understand why he would risk millions of dollars and his future relationship with the band for comparative peanuts.

When the Stones' tour accountants confronted Graham about taking the money, furious arguments erupted between both parties before he agreed to return all the money to the band. On the surface, the tour continued as if nothing had happened, but within the Stones' camp, Graham was a marked man.

"Our people really watched him like a hawk," Wyman said. "And they did find things. It left quite a nasty taste in our mouth. He spoilt his whole track record for us in one moment. It was such a shame. The shame was we found out, I suppose."

After getting caught by the Stones, Graham maintained business as usual for the rest of the tour and acted as if nothing had happened. On December 4th he threw a huge celebration party for the Stones and 500 specially invited guests on the *President* riverboat in New Orleans. To make sure everything went off perfectly, he recruited local concert promoter Adolph Ringen to arrange the lavish $50,000 affair, which included a sixteen-course gourmet meal prepared by famed chef Paul Prudhomme. Champagne and cocaine flowed freely during the four-hour party and at one point Rolling Stones' Ron Wood and Charlie Watts got up on stage to jam with the Dirty Dozen Brass Band.

The U.S. leg of the tour wound up on December 19 at Hampton Roads, Virginia, and in the new year, Graham moved to London to coordinate the European part of the tour due to start in May. To launch the tour, he arranged for the Stones to play a surprise one-off gig for just 400 people at the 100 Club on Oxford Street. Under Graham's direction, six posters were put up outside the club, saying "Tonight, The Rolling Stones." The first 350 people who turned up got a once-in-a-lifetime chance to see a vintage Stones' three-hour set in the intimacy of the tiny basement club where the band had started its career three decades earlier.

"It was just like a commando raid—in and out. Perfect," boasted Graham.

The two-month European tour took the Stones through England, Holland, Germany, France, Spain, Italy, and Switzerland—and they only played soccer stadiums and arenas. Using London as his base of operations, Graham and his team executed the tour's logistics and planning. While in Europe, Graham became engaged to his personal assistant, Jan Simmons, to the anger Regina Cartwright.

"Bill's explanation was that Jan put a gun to his head," Cartwright said. "Bill told me that she had bought the engagement ring, picked a wedding date, and even sent out engraved invitations to everyone in the business."

At the last minute, Graham called off the wedding and spent what would have been his wedding night on December 17, 1982 making love to Cartwright at New York's Helmsley Palace Hotel. Even though she had been "jilted" by Graham, Simmons went back to work for him.

"When Bill came back to me, I had a lot of trouble dealing with the fact that he kept Jan on as his secretary," said Cartwright. "I found it difficult to sleep with a man who continues to have his ex-fiancée as his secretary."

Soon afterward, after a big fight with Graham, Simmons left BGP to start working for the Grateful Dead organization.

When Graham and the Stones parted company in late 1982, the promoter had all but forgotten the "discrepancy" at the West Coast concert. He felt confident that he had become an indispensable part of the group and was now the official Rolling Stones tour director.

As the economics of the rock 'n' roll tour market worsened, Bill Graham decided survival lay in diversifying into other areas of entertainment. His decision was prompted by the current lack of available bands who had the draw of the Rolling Stones or Led Zeppelin and could sell out the big shows. Using his monopoly of the Bay Area, he started screening major boxing matches on satellite closed-circuit linkups to eight Northern California venues, presented "Sesame Street Live" at the Cow Palace and even promoted dance shows by Twyla Tharp. Prompted by his country-and-western–loving lieutenant, Nick Clainos, he also planned a major move into country-music concerts.

Although Graham had pledged not to fire anyone during the hard times, he made a cruel exception of his "resident wizard," Zohn Artman. The colorful public-relations guru of BGP was caught using cocaine at the office, and Graham fired him on the spot—even though the promoter himself was still using it secretly behind closed doors.

"Bill had a very serious problem with cocaine and God knows what else during the first ten years of our relationship," said Regina Cartwright. "It got to the point where he would not do it around me. He'd go into the bathroom, turn on the water, and I'd hear, 'Ssssnnnffff.' And he'd come walking out trying to look innocent. And I'd say, 'Bill, you did it!' And he'd deny it like a little boy."

A few years later, when Artman contracted AIDS, Graham felt so guilty about firing him that he sent his old PR man and a friend on a first-class, all-expense-paid railway tour of Europe on the Orient Express.

Although he ultimately dreamed of becoming a modern-day Sol Hurok, able to present a variety of entertainment, from classical ballet to ice shows, Bill Graham never strayed far from rock. When rock lover and cofounder of Apple computer, Steve Wozniak, decided to put up $12.5 million toward presenting a major rock festival over the three-day Labor Day weekend in 1982, he turned to the legendary promoter for help.

Wozniak, who used to be a Fillmore West regular as a youth, loved rock music and had long dreamed of one day staging his own music festival featuring his favorite groups. Now that his Apple computer had made him a multi-millionaire he decided to indulge his fantasy but had no knowledge of the music business.

"We were having trouble booking groups, and we approached Bill and asked if he would book bands and manage the stage," said Wozniak. "I put everything in his hands and said I would trust him."

Graham agreed and mobilized his team for what the idealistic Wozniak called the US Festival—a name indicative of a deliberate move away from the "me" generation. To run the festival in the San Bernadino Hills, the 31-year-old computer genius set up a company called UNUSON (Unite Us in Song), recruiting his staff from EST followers.

"The problem was that I didn't even know that the people that I hired were from EST," Wozniak explained. "They brought in this one woman to lead them in séances before business meetings. I was rather shocked myself."

While the UNUSON staff held frequent meetings to discuss the spiritual meaning of the festival, Graham's crack BGP troops were building a huge 300-foot by 67-foot space-age stage surrounded by 50-foot video screens and a 30-foot Diamond Vision screen for night viewing. Among the bands signed by Graham were The Police, The B-52s, Talking Heads, The Grateful Dead, The Kinks, Tom Petty and the Heartbreakers, Fleetwood Mac, and Santana.

The day before the show on September 2, Graham, having been up all night coping with last-minute problems, was called into a 7:00 A.M. group-meditation meeting.

"You could tell Bill was going crazy standing there holding hands," remembers San Francisco deejay Bonnie Simmons, who was with Graham at the US Festival. "They get all the way through relaxing your body, and the man who's leading the meditation service says, 'All right, now, we've had some problems in people getting along between the various forces putting the show together. I want everyone to close their eyes and imagine that they have a little notepad in their mind. And then I want you to take the little pencil that you have in your mind and write down the names of all the people that you've had disagreements with or problems with, or just feel tense about in this room, on the bit of paper. Then I want you to rip the little piece of paper off the pad in your mind and crumple it up. And when you've done that you can open your eyes, and everyone will feel better.'

"So a couple of minutes go by and everybody opens their eyes. The meeting is breaking up, and Bill is still standing there with his eyes closed. We said, 'Come on, Bill, we can go now.' Bill goes, 'Ssssh. I'm still writing.' "

Things went from bad to worse when Graham's well-trained professional staff began feuding with Wozniak's rank amateurs. Finally a frustrated Graham decided to take over control of the US Festival from Wozniak, claiming that the estimated 300,000-person crowd, each of whom had paid $37.50 for the three-day festival, was being placed in danger by bad organization.

"It scared the hell out of me," said Graham. "Our company had to work around the clock, undoing everything that they'd done."

Once the festival began, Graham started getting more and more angry, and soon he was right at the end of his tether. Having almost lost his booming voice from shouting, he was exhausted and confrontational. "Bill's ready to punch somebody out," said a friend of his.

The straw that broke Graham's back came when Kinks leader Ray Davies refused to go onstage until after sundown, for a better position in the show.

Wavy Gravy recalled, "Bill, simply and eloquently, picked up the [Kinks'] manager's Mercedes with a forklift and held it over the lake until the band wisely took the stage."

On the final day of the festival, Graham was completely in command, with his troops running everything from the pressroom to backstage security. When a cheerful Wozniak turned up at his festival with a bunch of his friends to watch the show backstage, Graham denied them access.

"You can't hang out backstage with 2,000 of your friends," Graham later explained to the *San Francisco Chronicle*. "There were trucks and equipment all over the place. Someone could have been hurt."

Calling Wozniak a "nobody who wanted to be somebody," Graham said, "It got to the point where he thought he was the new king of Siam. He felt he was the leader of all those people. He was saying, 'I did this' rather than saying, 'My money bought this.' "

Totally humiliated, Wozniak fired back at Graham, saying, "Bill Graham is full of shit. These are my friends. I made their guest passes on my own computer. What do you mean they can't come backstage? This is my show. I paid for it."

But Graham had an even bigger surprise in store for Wozniak. As the festival's climax, Wozniak had planned a historic satellite link up with a Russian rock band in Leningrad to play for the American crowd.

"This had never been done," said Wozniak. "This was a historic first when perestroika was just starting."

With his recent Russian disappointment still fresh in his mind, Graham was loath to allow this young upstart the chance of upstaging him by holding the first US/Russian rock event. When the satellite pictures started coming over, Bill Graham started sulking, refusing to cooperate.

"We put it up on our screen and Bill was supposed to go up to the microphone and announce this historic first," Wozniak remembers. "I ran across the stage, and he was looking at some monitors and saying, 'This is really being faked from a studio in Southern California.'

"He didn't believe it, so I had to go up to the microphone and announce to the crowd that we were making history."

At that point Graham pulled the plug on the satellite transmission, leaving Wozniak speechless.

After the festival, the battle between the two men continued. The computer millionaire fired Graham, calling him "unprofessional." The promoter claimed that Wozniak had been "duped" and "manipulated" by his staff.

"Wozniak has talent, but he's a wealthy, lucky simpleton," raged Graham. "That's the price he paid for sitting in a room all the time with wires, metal, and ions. He never learned anything about the street. He never played half-court basketball. He never learned about life."

When Graham returned to San Francisco from the US Festival he embarked on a no-holds-barred offensive to enlarge his empire well past

Northern California—as far afield as Las Vegas, Honolulu, Salt Lake City, and Boise. In the first half of 1983 he broke all the unwritten rules of the business by moving into his rivals' territory and promoting shows in Los Angeles, Sacramento, San Jose, and Monterey at will, daring the local promoters to challenge him.

"We're aggressive in getting word out that we're willing to expand," Graham explained to *Billboard*'s Jack McDonough. "If there's a promoter who's good and knows his area well, we'll work with him."

In late 1983 Graham secretly started making plans to return to New York and resume promoting there for the first time in twelve years. Ever since closing the Fillmore East in 1971, Graham always considered New York his own, believing that he could move back and start promoting again whenever he felt like it.

"New York is something that you don't get out of your system," he said. "It is awesome beyond any other community, and so challenging. Both the positive and the negative. To have a New York audience enjoy an artist, to have a New York audience get off on an event is an enormous thing. It's the most challenging audience in the world."

But when Graham attempted to return to the New York concert scene, he was blocked effectively and kept out in the cold.

Launching his campaign by setting up an office/apartment in Manhattan, Graham first poached one of New York promoter Ron Delsener's key employees to run it. Arranging meetings with Delsener and his main New York rival, promoter Jerry Brandt, he offered to buy the Ritz on East 11th Street from Brandt. When turned down, he offered to copromote concerts with him. In order to neutralize Graham on the spot, Delsener acted swiftly by setting up his own deal to coproduce shows with Brandt.

"It's clear that Bill is out in the cold. So far," wrote the *New York Post*. "The rock and roll scene is like the Mafia—everybody has his territory."

"Ron Delsener moved up strongly when Bill moved out, and New York became almost his exclusive territory," said Sid Bernstein, himself having made an unsuccessful attempt in the late 1970s to regain a foothold in New York promotion.

Since completing the Rolling Stones tour Graham had become restless, missing the twenty-four-hour excitement of working with the band. By this time Bill Graham Presents was running day-to-day operations itself, leaving its restless chairman in a constant search for exciting new projects to relieve his boredom and absorb his ceaseless energy. When asked to set up the first touring benefit show in December 1983 to raise money for former Small Faces bassist Ronnie Lane, who had been stricken with multiple sclerosis, he jumped at the chance. The ARMS tour (Action and Research into Multiple Sclerosis) brought together superstars Eric Clapton, Jimmy Page, Jeff Beck, Charlie Watts, Bill Wyman and Joe Cocker.

Phil Elwood incurred Graham's wrath when, without Graham's permission, he dared to mention the upcoming ARMS Tour in his *San Francisco Examiner* column. "I had essentially intruded on his territory," said Elwood. "He wanted to announce the Ronnie Lane Benefit Concert his way, and Bill felt I had lowered the high level that he had established. That was his privilege, but he didn't have to blow up at me in that way.

"All I said was, 'Bill, I think you're overreacting.' He could get pretty profane. My wife picked up the phone during the argument, and she told me to hang up on him." But Graham's anger never lasted long, and when Elwood saw the promoter at a show the following week, Graham was friendly, acting as though nothing had ever happened.

Graham's love-hate attitude seemed to reach into almost every aspect of his life, allowing him to become a master of the Orwellian concept of doublethink—being able to hold two opposing views at the same time while believing them both to be true.

Explained Michael Ahern, the former stage manager for the Fillmore East and many his later Graham shows; "One of the most interesting things about Bill was that with total truthfulness and complete conviction he could say whatever, and believe whatever, he wanted to at a specific time, and think that it was the truth for the moment he was saying it. Whether it was or not. He could say things and believe them, and they wouldn't be true."

This gift for unconscious doublethink had always provided the promoter with a built-in advantage at any negotiating table.

Bill Graham was now grossing $100 million a year and had turned himself into a star, recognized instantly wherever he went. He had produced more than twenty thousand concerts in his nineteen-year career, and just how powerful a force he had become in the music business was demonstrated when he was honored with a celebrity tribute. His friend, San Francisco Mayor Dianne Feinstein, issued a proclamation making September 29, 1984, Bill Graham Day in San Francisco, commending his "truly stellar abilities" and thanking him for his "enthusiastic public spirit."

The printed program's official list of personal tributes to Graham reads like a Who's Who of the music business, including paid advertisements from Atlantic Records' Ahmet Ertegun, Fleetwood Mac, and the William Morris Agency. Graham's own FM Productions immodestly took out its own tribute, stating, "One of the biggest rock stars of all time cannot sing, dance or play an instrument. A Tribute to Bill Graham who showed the world what staging is all about."

The centerpiece of the star-studded evening, emceed by comedian Howard Hesseman and "Saturday Night Live's" Father Guido Sarducci Don Novello, was the screening of a special one-hour filmed tribute to Graham that featured personal messages from Mick Jagger, Keith Richards, Bob Dylan, Eric Clapton, Pete Townshend, Elton John, Grace Slick, and others. To underscore Graham's enormous stature in San Francisco, the film featured Mayor Feinstein reading the entire proclamation declaring "Bill Graham Day," as well as many of his employees, introduced as "Bill Graham's Gang," delivering glowing tributes to their boss.

Donning a tuxedo for the occasion, Graham sat impassively in the audience throughout the three-hour show as the procession of mostly sycophantic tributes were shown on a huge screen above the stage at the Marin Veteran's Auditorium. But his old anger surfaced during a video message from his former Concord Resort boss, Irving Cohen, who called the impresario a "hippie."

" 'That man is a *chozzer,*' spat Graham, employing a Yiddish term for an ungrateful selfish pig," noted *San Francisco Chronicle*'s Joel Selvin. "He may have been smiling when he said it, but the anger was still real after all these years."

Following the film there was live entertainment by Jerry Garcia, Paul Butterfield, Carlos Santana, and Rick Danko, who all dedicated songs to Graham. Later, at a private party in a nearby warehouse, guests from the top echelons of the music business and San Francisco society joined Graham in a sweaty demonstration of mambo dancing when Tito Puente and Carlos Santana jammed with the Tower of Power—a perfect ending to the almost-feudal tribute by his music fiefdom.

Bill Graham thrived on celebrity and was thrilled when the world's biggest superstar, Michael Jackson, requested that he become national tour consultant for the 1984 Jacksons' Victory Tour. In his meeting with the Jackson family business advisers, Graham asked them to draw up a four-page, single-spaced proposal on involving the black community in the

San Francisco part of the tour. Graham then brought in Frank Russo to promote the international legs of the tour. But the Jacksons' father, Joseph, did not like Graham's concept of how the tour should be run and promptly dropped him and Russo in favor of the electric-haired boxing promoter, Don King, and Chuck Sullivan, who came out of the world of pro football and knew nothing about music promotion. The Jackson camp accused Graham of being "too egoed out," and there were blatant accusations of racism against the "men in the gray flannel suits" from King.

Replying to the allegations, Graham told *Rolling Stone,* "Your ego, as best as I know what ego means, is a feeling that you have a particular gift for something."

In December 1985 Graham launched a bitter attack on King and Sullivan, accusing them of ruining the Jacksons' 1984 tour by overcharging the public with record ticket prices of $28.

"Everybody lost," Graham said. "The show lost, the public lost, and Michael Jackson lost . . . You want to talk about ego? I really don't know the fight game, Mr. King, or the business you're in, Mr. Sullivan. But I know you spat on the public and you spat on the artists."

Russo claims to have been edged out as the Victory Tour's international promoter after refusing to comply with "unethical demands."

"It wasn't the brothers, and the parents were fine," explained Russo. "It was the people around them, the people in control of their business end. So what could have been one of the greatest tours of all time turned out to be one of the sorriest. It was terrible."

But motor-mouthed Don King had the last word on the Victory Tour, for which the Jacksons split a reported $40 million.

"I promoted Michael Jackson's Victory Tour—went right out the chute and put together the biggest concert tour in the history of mankind," King boasted to *Playboy*. "People around Michael said, 'Hey, King has no experience in this business. He didn't have his apprenticeship. He doesn't know all the little nuances and the little languages that go along with this business.' Well, this was not amateur night in Dixie."

Performance magazine's Bob Grossweiner believes that Don King exploited the Jackson family and produced a tour travesty. "The Jacksons were snowed in by Don King," he explained. "Don King did nothing except collect two million dollars and promote himself and his boxing. They paid Sullivan and all those other people—everyone was getting a percentage. That's why the ticket prices went sky-high up to twenty-eight dollars. The Jacksons had all these people that had suckered themselves in and they had to pay off."

Bill Graham used his experience with the Jacksons to jump into his favored diatribe about the dynamics of art and money. "I feel sad for the country," he told *BAM* magazine. "The Jacksons may have made all of this money, but it could have been so much more. Why is money always such a domineering power?

"The Jacksons . . . it's almost an industrial show. No body heat. I would have told the Jacksons, 'You give whatever money you would give to me to charity.' I'd like to prove to them that they could have gotten the results they got, moneywise, and so much more, so much more."

Bill Graham might have lost the Jackson tour, but he was tightening his grip on the Northern California concert scene. In a mysterious turnaround, Concord City Council, which only two years earlier had sued Graham, was now inviting him to run its lucrative Concord Pavilion shows. In a complete about-face, it refused to renew its contract with the Nederlander Organization, fueling rumors that the powerful promoter had called in some political favors. Concord Mayor Steve Weir explained, "Nederlander had a weak year in 1984. It was time for us to give Graham a chance."

The tireless impresario was also starting construction on his long-dreamed-of Shoreline Amphitheater in Mountain View, located halfway between San Francisco and San Jose. The 15,000-seat amphitheater, which was to be carved into a seventy-acre landfill, would cost $20 million. But just before ground breaking, Graham ran out of money and turned to Apple computer genius Steve Wozniak to bail him out.

"I was the one that saved the whole project. He wasn't going to make it and I came up with a three-million-dollar investment," said Wozniak, who claims that Graham's organization tricked him out of his money by craftily wording the contract so the loan accumulated interest on paper but nothing had to be repaid for at least thirty years.

"I'm really disappointed at my lawyers and accountants for not spotting that loophole which was built in by the Bill Graham organization," says Wozniak. "I basically lost three million dollars down the drain. I don't expect I'll ever see it based on the fact that I haven't seen a cent yet.

"His people knew what they were doing and although my people had decent credentials, they didn't catch this kind of trick. I really didn't get anything back for it except my box seats."

Later, when Graham ran into further financial trouble building Shoreline, the local Mountain View City Council averted a last-minute catastrophe by floating an $8 million emergency loan for him. Socialite Ann Getty gave another $1 million.

The theater was finally completed in June 1986 after a series of expensive setbacks that jinxed the project and almost brought it to a standstill.

14

After the Fire

As Bill Graham prospered in the concert business through the seventies and eighties he started to rely more and more on his favorite sister, Ester, and almost never made a decision without consulting her first. Ester, who was seven years older than Graham, lived with her husband, Manny Chichinski, just a short drive away from Masada in the house he had given them on Corte Madera Avenue. The six-foot-tall iron-willed matriarch of the Grajonca family became Graham's substitute mother, a rock to lash himself to in a stormy sea of insecurities. Every day Ester would drive over to Masada and stock her brother's fridge with her homemade gefilte fish and matzo-ball soup so when he came home late at night he could heat it up for a home-cooked meal.

"Ester was both a mother and a sister to Bill," said Hinda Langer, whose husband, Josef, was Graham's rabbi. "There were many, many levels of relationship between them."

Graham spoke to Ester every day, and along with Regina Cartwright, she was his closest confidante, one of the few people around him strong enough to withstand his withering temper.

"Ester wasn't afraid to speak her piece," said Rabbi Langer. "If she felt her brother had to hear something, she would let him hear it. Ester could hold her own with anyone."

Ester kept house for Graham, supervising the staff at Masada and even cooked his favorite kosher meals for his dinner parties and business meetings. "She loved to feed her brother and take care of him," said

Rabbi Langer. "Whenever he came back from a trip, he would go straight to Ester for some of her heart-and-soul cooking. He considered her cooking the best cuisine that existed."

Ester was a Lubavitcher, an ultra-religious branch of orthodox Judiasm whose members practice the Chabad philosophy, and she encouraged her brother to join as a way of finding peace in his troubled world. Having built up a childhood resistance to Judaism when his stepfather continually tried to get him to go to synagogue, Graham was still skeptical about religion. In fact, he always referred to Jews by the derogatory term of "Yids" and hadn't shown the slightest interest in being a Jew before. Graham's first direct contact with Chabad was in 1975, when the Berkeley Chabad asked him to build a Chanukah menorah in Union Square, he agreed instantly and dispatched a team from Bill Graham Presents to construct the giant mahogany menorah. At the official unveiling on the first night of Chanukah, Graham was on the stage for the lighting ceremony, but refused to light the first candle, saying, "Surely you can find a better Jew to do it."

Graham's first public association with Judaism caused a backlash of resentment against him, with many accusing him of using religion to enhance his stature in the community.

"People look at it as a crude object. It's money," he countered. "Honestly, to be straight, I put it there because I think it's a good worthwhile thing, as a human being, as a Jew."

Reconciling how he could align himself to Chabad without being a practicing Jew, Graham once admitted, "In my quiet time I feel bad about it, I feel some shame. Somebody might say, 'Bill you're a hypocrite.' But I say no, because I still feel part of the faith, part of the religion even though I should be more involved."

"I'm saying if I don't get myself more involved in the religion, *me*, what can I do to make it possible for others."

Graham liked to stay impartial, so when the Union Square Association hired his company to build a psychedelic Christmas tree at the other end of Union Square, Graham was only too happy to oblige. The Bill Graham menorah lighting became an annual event in the city, but the busy promoter's involvement in the religious side of Chabad stopped there. Rabbi Josef Langer, who was Graham's friend and main link to Chabad, kept inviting him to come to one of his open Sabbath services. After years of making excuses, Graham finally accepted Langer's invitation to be guest speaker for the sabbath meal on Friday April 27, 1979. Thrilled with securing such an illustrious guest, Langer decided to advertise the

Sabbath service using a flier with a picture of Graham and some of the famous rock bands he had been associated with. As the busy promoter was away on a business trip to Europe, Langer went ahead and posted the flier around San Francisco on his own initiative.

"Well, I got a phone call from Bill in Europe and he read me the riot act," said Rabbi Langer. He said, 'Josef, I'm coming this time, but you never, ever call on me again. This is it with us.' And he slammed down the phone. I was devastated. I didn't know how I could rectify it.

"On the night of the event, when Bill walked into Chabad House, my stomach was full of butterflies. I went up, and I didn't know whether I should shake his hand and hug him. We embraced and I said, 'Well, Bill, what can I say? I'm sorry.' And he said, "Don't mention it.' "

At the Sabbath meal, which was prepared by Ester, Rabbi Langer mischievously decided to break the ice and make his guest of honor feel more relaxed by having him reprise his old job as a waiter. "I put a towel over his arm and gave him a tray, saying, 'Bill, you're not going to sit at the head of the table tonight. You're going to sit with the people, but before that, you're going to serve them.' "

Graham loved the idea and started serving the 150 guests with his favorite, matzo-ball soup with a piece of flanken (short rib) in it. After the meal, Graham was in fine form as raconteur, telling story after story about his adventures in rock 'n' roll until 3:00 A.M.

"Ester finally had to pull him out by his shirttails," said Rabbi Langer. "I walked him to the car and we embraced and he looked at me and said, 'Josef, when are we going to do it again?' "

Bill Graham made his first and last public stand as a Jew when President Ronald Reagan announced in April 1985 that he was making an official visit to the Bitburg Military Cemetery, where members of Hitler's SS were buried. Graham was furious when he learned that the president was proposing to honor the very men who had murdered his family. Forty years after surviving the Holocaust, Graham found himself face to face with all the powerful emotions of fear and hate which had decimated his childhood.

"He was very upset about Bitburg," said Regina Cartwright, who was with Graham in New York when he first heard about the Reagan visit. "Elie Wiesel called him, and they met to talk about what they could do to protest the visit. Before he went, he ate two marijuana cookies to clear his head."

When Graham returned home to their East 64th Street apartment, he was very emotional and ate an extra-strong hash brownie to try and calm down.

"He decided he was going to fire Ronald Reagan," Cartwright said. "That's how stoned he was. I told him he couldn't fire the president, and he got angry with me, screaming, 'I can do anything I want.' "

Graham spent fourteen hours drinking cups of coffee and telling Regina about Nazism, tearfully reliving his nightmarish journey through the Holocaust.

Cartwright remembers, "He became that little boy again when he told me how his sister Tolla had died at the roadside. I could see that he was reexperiencing it again. He was crying when he finished the story and he said, 'The minute I saw you, I thought you looked like Tolla.' "

On his return to San Francisco, Graham embarked on a one-man crusade against President Reagan. Organizing a protest rally in Union Square, he enlisted the support of San Francisco Mayor Dianne Feinstein and State Assembly Speaker Willie Brown. To publicize the rally and his case against Reagan, Graham took out a full-page advertisement in the *San Francisco Chronicle* on April 26, 1985. Headlined "A Personal Plea," the ad castigated the president for the visit, accusing him of visiting Bitburg merely to thank German Chancellor Helmut Kohl for supporting his pet "Star Wars" theory.

The plea read: *"The President's rationale on this issue suggests a tragic mentality, for it implies that the Holocaust horrors are a part of the past, and should be forgiven and forgotten. Impossible. Many of us fortunate enough to have come here from Europe to live in peace cannot forget and will not forgive.*

"As the most prominent representative of our country, our President has no moral right to pay his respects at the graves of murderers. He must find ways of fulfilling his political mission other than by condoning genocide."

The only signature to the plea was "Bill"—in the superstar manner of a Madonna or a Prince.

Graham planned the Friday noon rally on April 26 with all the attention to detail that he accorded on his concert spectaculars. There was a VIP stage at one side of Union Square for the speakers, politicians, entertainers, and leaders of religious organizations, and his staff handed out black armbands to the 200 people who turned out, many bearing swastika-stamped posters of Reagan. Right at the back of the stage sat Graham's sister Ester, offering her support.

"This is not a Jewish issue, but an issue of worldwide morality" Graham told the rally.

The emotional rally was addressed by Mayor Feinstein and a series of Holocaust survivors who told of their experiences in the concentration camps, pleading with Reagan to cancel his visit to Bitburg. But Graham was very disappointed in what he considered a low turnout and did not hesitate to accuse San Franciscans of apathy as he boarded a plane to London after the rally for a meeting with Boomtown Rat Bob Geldof to discuss staging a global TV spectacular called Live Aid to benefit famine-hit Ethiopia.

In a predawn raid, just hours after Reagan's Bitburg visit on May 5, two Molotov cocktails were hurled through the windows of BGP's 11th and Howard Street offices, burning it to the ground. The fire resulted in $1 million of damage and almost total destruction of Graham's priceless collection of rock 'n' roll memorabilia and of the only remaining picture of his parents. Flames from the four-alarm fire soared 100 feet into the sky from the single-story brick warehouse which had served as Graham's headquarters since 1972.

With Graham vacationing in the South of France at the time of the fire after his London Live Aid meetings, his second-in-command, Nick Clainos, took control of the clean-up operation. As the news of the fire spread, stunned BGP staff arrived one by one in total disbelief to see the smoldering rubble that had been their office.

"It's something that Bill built from the beginning that's now nothing but a memory," said a tearful employee sifting through the debris. "There's nothing tangible to show for it, which is a real shame."

"This office was a museum," said BGP vice president Gregg Perloff. "You have more than eighteen years of rock 'n' roll here. Original posters, letters, props, news clippings. All the slides, photographs, and negatives from every concert. All gone. You can't put a price on that."

As soon as the San Francisco Fire Department established that the fire was arson, theories immediately began to be constructed as to who was responsible. Despite a call to a local TV station from "a Nazi soldier" claiming responsibility, BGP dismissed the obvious link to Graham's Bitburg protest.

"He's been controversial for years and years," said Sherry Wasserman, his box-office manager. "I don't think what happened with that has anything to do with the fire."

And veteran West Coast syndicated columnist Herb Caen noted that the arson could have been the work of many people: "Graham has made a few other enemies and probably gets as many threats as anybody in town."

Various theories in San Francisco had Bill Graham torching his own offices to prevent the IRS from investigating him, while others believed it to be the work of angry trade-union members trying to teach the promoter a bitter lesson for daring to move into trade-show production. But Graham, who heard about the fire when he checked into his office the next day, only to be told by an answering-service operator, "I'm sorry, the offices are closed. Bill Graham burned up last night," had no doubts who was responsible.

"This happened a day after Ronald Reagan's visit to Bitburg," said a weary Graham after a twenty-hour flight from Geneva back to San Francisco. "I don't think there's any doubt about the connection. If anybody doubts that anti-Semitism exists . . . it does."

Despite offers from Jerry Pompili and David Rubinson to flush out the arsonists Haganah-style from the bars of the Richmond District, Graham seemed tired and uncharacteristically restrained, saying that he didn't want to escalate the violence. Mayor Feinstein rallied to his side, posting a $10,000 reward for information leading to the arrest and conviction of the firebombers. Describing the fire as "a deep personal tragedy for Bill Graham" which is "shared by all of San Francisco," Feinstein was careful not to lay the blame on neo-Nazis.

Later, in a press conference during which he led reporters through the charred remains of his office, Graham donned a hard hat and adopted a Churchillian stance as he addressed the national television crews.

"What we lost is nothing, compared to South Africa, Ethiopia, the campuses around the country," he said bravely. "We lost some proof of events, happenings, and personal belongings. It's a shame that any price has to be paid for the right to speak."

Away from the cameras, Graham became more emotional, saying, "I don't write. I don't paint. I don't sing. I don't perform. That was our gallery. That was our statement. That was our company's work, our art."

He then departed to the comfort and security of his sister Ester, who, as always, remained firmly in control of her feelings. "We've been through this before, and we're all still here," she counseled.

It was business as usual for Bill Graham Presents, which, without missing a beat, went ahead with a Julian Lennon show the night after the fire at the Warfield Theater and moved into temporary offices near Fisherman's Wharf within the week.

But inside, Graham felt emotionally raped, thrown back into his Holocaust nightmare, and he started floundering.

"Bill took it terribly," said Hinda Langer. "With Bitburg, Bill made his first major stand as a Jew, and he was retaliated against so violently that I'm sure it caused him a tremendous amount of conflict. Who wants to be a target?"

Graham was never the same again after the fire. His great fear that everything he had built up over the years could be taken away from him had been proved true. First the Rolling Stones had lost their hard-won respect for him and thought him dishonest, and now the fire had exacerbated his insecurities, causing him to lose perspective and direction.

"There's no question about it," says Joshua White. "He was a self-destructive person. But he didn't do it in ways that were obvious. It was more subtle than that. There was that kind of macho posturing between him and the artists. He got into some kind of subtle piddling match with all kinds of people.

"In the late 1980s people would always tell me how Bill was impossible to work with and how crazed he'd become. That could easily have been from the effects of cocaine," White said.

And the numbing effects of cocaine-induced paranoia on Bill Graham nearly derailed Bob Geldof's Live Aid.

In the aftermath of the fire, Bill Graham edged into a deep depression. In June 1985 he described hearing a "dark voice" in his head questioning everything he did, telling him the fire had somehow been sent to punish him. There seemed to be no escape from the torturing voice. At night things worsened. Graham, an insomniac all his life, was unable to sleep at all, spending every night alone in his house, working and wrestling with his demons. In a desperate effort to silence them with sleep, he turned to the then-popular new sleeping drug Halcion.

"There were times when my head was underwater for *such* a long time. I was gagging," he said. "In the ensuing years after the fire, there were no intervals. There were no rehab periods. Only madness and new projects and more and more work."

He was also deeply troubled about his longtime relationship with Regina Cartwright, who finally had decided to break free from Graham that summer.

"The sad thing about Bill and me was that I did not remain a teenager," Cartwright said. "Over the years I grew up, but he never really changed. He knew something was wrong with him in that a normal man who is in love with a woman does not want to fuck everything than prances in front of him."

To try to repair the relationship Graham took Regina to Maui that summer to see his eight-year-old son, Alex. During the visit he decided the young boy was becoming too effeminate and again asked Regina to marry him so he could gain the boy's custody and provide a male role model.

"Bill had always virtually ignored Alex," said Cartwright. "He would always do things with David, but Alex was usually left out during his visits to Masada. Now he feared his son might become gay, and he suddenly started taking an interest. He told me, 'No son of Bill Graham will ever become a *feygeleh.*' I told him that this was no reason to marry me, and that's when things between us started to go wrong.

"The pressures of our relationship just got too much for me. I had no identity. I basically made a decision that I wanted to have a man who didn't run around with every woman that came along and then expect me to clean up the mess for him in the fall."

So Regina began dating a young New York promoter who fell in love with her and proposed marriage. When Graham found he had a rival, he immediately flew to New York begging her to return and marry him.

"It was a very sad time for us," Cartwright said. "I was going to leave him and I did, in a certain way. Although I broke off my engagement and returned to Bill as his lover, we were never the same again after 1985."

As the heartbroken promoter's spirits sank lower and lower he started using more and more cocaine, which made his behavior unpredictable and erratic. He had also discovered the new "designer drug" Ecstasy, a drug whose effects were like a combination of speed and LSD, and was taking it regularly. He loved the way the drug prolonged lovemaking for many hours and once tried to force Regina Cartwright to take a hit for a marathon sex session.

"Bill literally tried to jam a capsule of Ecstasy down my throat," Cartwright recalled. "He said it made sex great. I told him that I thought our sex life was great as it was."

Never having heard of Ecstasy, Regina insisted on calling her psychiatrist to find out whether she should take it. When her doctor heard what Graham was trying to do, he asked to speak to him. "He chastised Bill and threatened to have him arrested if he forced me to take it," Cartwright said. "Bill backed down."

Graham's increasing drug use during this period was starting to affect his professional life. His attention span was becoming so short that his staff was finding it harder and harder to get him to concentrate for more than a couple of minutes at a time, in meetings.

Since his initial meeting with Bob Geldof in London in May 1985, where he was recruited to produce the American half of Live Aid, Graham had done virtually nothing. The English end was well under way, with Geldof securing Wembley Stadium and lining up blanket TV coverage on the BBC. Geldof was becoming increasingly frustrated by the American impresario's apparent lack of interest in the benefit concert.

"Bill was for weeks badly shaken," Geldof wrote in his autobiography *Is That It?* "Live Aid was not the consideration uppermost in his mind."

Finally Geldof and Electric Factory promoter Larry Magid arranged for the U.S. show to be held in the 90,000-seat JFK Stadium in Philadelphia. But still the distracted Graham dragged his feet, not willing to commit himself entirely to Live Aid and not even convinced that the concert could be pulled off.

Hedging his bets, Graham told a reporter, "Assuming it comes off well—and it's hard to say now—it will have the largest viewing audience of any entertainment project that I know of."

As the performers began to appreciate the potential global reach of Live Aid, they started calling Graham to offer their services. But Graham, often drugged out, was hostile and rude to them. Kris Kristofferson, who volunteered to play a set, pulled out angrily after Graham deliberately refused to cooperate with the singer because he didn't want him to play. Country superstar Willie Nelson also lost interest after becoming disillusioned by Graham's negative attitude.

But the biggest blow to Geldof was losing Paul Simon—whom he considered key to attracting other stars to join Live Aid—because the singer did not like Graham. "Paul Simon rang," Geldof remembers. "He was being messed around [by Bill Graham] and he was upset. Every time he phoned anyone over there to get things organized, he met a blank wall. He thought the whole thing was a mess. He felt that people were being deliberately obstructive to him and, as he and Bill didn't get on, had decided to pull out."

Graham was also finding it impossible to work harmoniously with the vital television side of Live Aid. As concert producer, he felt that the live show should take precedence over the telecast and refused to compromise his concert staging for the needs of television. He took an instant dislike to Mike Mitchell, who had been brought in to produce the complex satellite telecast. Mitchell, who had helped Peter Ueberroth organize the 1984 Summer Olympics in Los Angeles and played a indispensable part in arranging the complete fourteen-hour MTV telecast and three-hour ABC network special on Live Aid, thought Graham was deliberately trying to "screw" him and come close to a breakdown dealing with him.

"Bill hated the idea of MTV," said Joshua White, who had moved into television, to become a producer, after the Fillmore East. "He wouldn't cooperate with them and did not handle them well."

White believes that Graham's underestimation of the growing power and enormous influence of MTV in the late 1980s, was a fatal mistake in his career. "Bill didn't understand that MTV in the mid-eighties was just as important and as dynamic as The Grateful Dead and Jefferson Airplane had been twenty years earlier," said White.

Graham disliked having to compromise music in order to fit the small screen and MTV.

"You can't bottle the Grateful Dead," he told journalist Roger Trilling in 1991. "There was no television until I was seventeen. Today with 24 channels and cable and video stores people have become much more isolated. There's much less communial entertainment and communial joy."

As Live Aid drew nearer, Geldof became seriously concerned that Graham's negative attitude could jeopardize the whole project by alienating artists. "Bill Graham was still distracted," Geldof said charitably. "Whenever any of the people who had said they would play contacted his office, he was giving out the feeling that the whole situation was confused and that nothing was really going to happen."

Graham told Regina Cartwright that their volatile breakup was the reason for his difficulties with Live Aid. "Bill was deeply disturbed," Cartwright said. "He told me that he was unable to work and put together the concert of his life. He said it was my fault. And I couldn't help it. I wasn't being a bitch, I was just trying to hang on to myself and my identity."

Finally, three weeks before Live Aid, a frustrated Geldof flew to New York with English promoter Harvey Goldsmith for a showdown with Graham and found the situation even worse than he had feared.

"We met in New York with Bill Graham's people and with the staging crew," said Geldof. "They had not put the tickets on sale, they didn't have a final bill of artists organized, and they had even lost the plans for the circular stage which had been sent to them three weeks before."

At an eleventh-hour crisis meeting with city officials in Larry Magid's Philadelphia office, Graham suddenly realized that Live Aid was workable and became his old self again, delivering a brilliantly impassioned speech on its behalf. To bring the reenergized Graham back up to speed, Geldof flew two members of Goldsmith's London stage crew to Philadelphia to work with the American crew.

As the idea of Live Aid gained momentum and captured the public's imagination, the show took on major proportions as the world's leading rock stars joined the cause. Mick Jagger, Bob Dylan, Tina Turner, Phil Collins, and David Bowie all offered to play, but the concert took on a sense of history when the surviving members of The Who and Led Zeppelin decided to get back together for one-off sets for Live Aid.

"Suddenly Bill Graham was fired with enthusiasm," says Geldof. "And I began to understand his reputation."

Working the phones, a newly motivated Graham weaved his magic and recruited Madonna, Joan Baez, and Judas Priest for the show. Suddenly Live Aid was a major international news story, and a delighted Bill Graham stepped into the spotlight to become its enthusiastic U.S. pitchman.

"The word is mammoth. Everything's mammoth," gushed the promoter to his hometown *San Francisco Chronicle*. Two weeks before Live Aid, without giving any prior notice, Graham put tickets on sale on the east coast. All 90,000 were snapped up within five hours. He then threw himself into organizing the complex logistics which would see thirty-five of the world's top rock acts set up and play on the JFK Stadium stage in just fourteen hours. Using a 200-strong crew, Graham erected a massive rotating double stage, where one band could set up as another was playing. In keeping with the charity status of the show, Graham ordered a spartan no-frills backstage and banned performers from using limos.

Explaining the historical significance of Live Aid, Graham said, "In terms of logistics, Live Aid is on a continuum with Woodstock. At Woodstock, which was both the watershed of the sixties counterculture and a clear message that rock had become big business, there was no precedent for putting on a show for so many people. By contrast, Live Aid is a controlled situation that demonstrates just how much rock has become entwined with the mass culture.

"On one hand, it's two concerts filled with so many superstars that everybody has to be hustled on and off the stage. At the same time, Live Aid is also a single worldwide broadcast designed to inspire people to give money to fight African famine. The trick will be stitching them together from two concerts on two different occasions."

As the global show started becoming the media event of the decade, ABC-TV executives decided to invite President Reagan to Philadelphia to enhance their coverage. When Bill Graham heard that his hated enemy had been asked to appear, he erupted into a passionate fury, threatening to "do something to get arrested" if Reagan showed up.

"Whatever is beyond hate is what I feel for that man," he said, the horror of his office fire still fresh in his mind. "I should get over it, but I don't know if I ever will."

Graham knew he had to pull something out of the hat when Bob Geldof, threatening to eclipse him, pulled off a major coup by securing promises from Prince Charles and Princess Diana to attend the London show.

"I couldn't get it out of my head," said Graham. "A week before Philadelphia, I thought, 'What is our royalty?' Then I called Jack Nicholson and, thank God, Jack came through and started the whole day off by walking on the stage in front of 105,000 people and saying, 'Hello, world.' "

Right from the very start of Live Aid, as the temperature in Philadelphia soared into the high nineties, Graham fought a pitched battle with MTV's timing demands, refusing to make any compromises in his stage presentation to accommodate coverage. Determined, as always, to start the show on time, Graham disregarded the fact that the first TV host, actor Elliott Gould, was in the middle of announcing the opening act on camera, when he ordered the first band to start playing.

"If you fuck up the beginning of Live Aid on TV and start the concert before Elliott Gould has finished, you've fucked it up forever and it's on tape," said Joshua White. "For the ninety thousand people gathered at JFK Stadium, the concert started on time, but for the half a billion people watching around the world, it's a mistake. And he never made that connection."

Dressed for battle in a T-shirt, frayed shorts, and heavy boots, Graham, who was also stage-managing the spectacle as well as producing it, was a blur of frenzied activity all day. When he wasn't directing the complex stage operations and making sure that the bands kept to their appointed twenty-two-minute sets, he was upsetting Mitchell and the other TV producers by refusing to give an inch to fit their tight scheduling to accommodate the on-screen announcers. He seemed to take a cruel delight in deliberately throwing them off balance by shifting emcees and changing the script without any warning.

"Bill just never understood that this was bigger than him," said White. "His ego wouldn't let him do that. These were changing times, and television was important. MTV changed the whole future of the music business, and he was powerless to stop it. If anyone should have understood that, Bill should have. And he didn't. And it proved to be most unfortunate for him."

During Madonna's raunchy set, her future husband, actor Sean Penn, suddenly walked out onstage. When a furious Bill Graham ordered him off the stage, the unpredictable actor pulled out a gun and held it to the promoter's head. As the security men overpowered Penn, the gun went off, sending the stage staff diving for cover.

"Bill was very frightened by that," said Regina Cartwright. "It was the closest that anyone had actually come to hurting him since the Korean War. Bill told me that Sean Penn actually had his finger on the trigger and was ready to fire."

The Live Aid concert on July 13 was a triumph of transatlantic organization, taking rock music to a new global level with more than sixty acts being seen by billions of music fans in 170 countries. "Perhaps Bill's greatest day was at Live Aid in Philadelphia," said Graham's former Winterland stage manager Patrick Stansfield. "He plotted, schemed, cajoled, squeezed and stitched together the seconds and minutes throughout the day."

Meanwhile back in San Francisco after the concert, the Bill Graham publicity machine was hard at work projecting the promoter as the real power and inspiration behind Live Aid. "The real hero of the affair was Bill Graham," wrote *San Francisco Chronicle* pop critic Joel Selvin in his review of the concert. "He conquered mind-boggling logistics and the rigid demand of the television script to produce an efficient, smooth concert that barely ran a minute over schedule throughout the fourteen hours."

Two days after the concert, Graham viewed the videotapes of the MTV coverage in New York and went into a rage. He called a press conference in New York in which he launched a scathing attack on Music Television. "A bunch of pricks" was how Graham described MTV. "I couldn't believe what I saw," roared the promoter, who said he had problems with the station's "attitude, consciousness, and greed. It's not that much different from the bootlegger who stands outside the building hawking a shirt."

Graham's bitterly antagonistic attitude against MTV would prove to be a major handicap in his career, as the station transformed the business of rock music and he found himself an anachronism, unable to fit into the new age of video rock.

Months after Live Aid, Bill Graham summed up his experience, saying, "I would never talk about Live Aid in detail, even when I get to heaven, because no one would ever believe me."

All through the rest of the summer and fall of 1985 Graham and Regina Cartwright continued to work at their troubled relationship. In an attempt at a reconciliation, he invited Regina's family to join his at the annual Christmas festivities at Masada. While she was staying there, he shared one of his biggest secrets with her. In the guest room of the house, which had once been owned by the lawyer Jake Erlich, there was a huge built-in safe sunk into the foundations.

"He opened up the combination lock, and there were all these stacks of thousand-dollar bills," Cartwright said. "I'd never seen so much money in my life. He told me proudly that after twenty years he had four million dollars in his home. Four was his lucky number, and that was his symbol of success."

Calling it his entertaining stack, Graham said he would raid it every time he needed some ready cash to go on a trip, but was always careful to replenish it to $4 million on his return.

Tensions ran high throughout Christmas as Regina's mother, brother, and sister met with a frosty reception from Graham's disapproving sister Ester, who did not approve of her brother's relationship. Ester was also angry when Graham insisted that Regina prepare the Christmas dinner, even though she was on crutches after a skiing accident. When the meal was served in the dining hall off the huge kitchen, Regina's mother Adele desperately tried to make conversation to break the uncomfortable silence.

There was little Christmas cheer as the Graham and Cartwright families and friends Steve and Roseann Kahn took their positions after the meal by the large Christmas tree, the children having gone upstairs to their rooms.

"You could have cut the atmosphere with a knife," said Regina. "Everybody, except the Kahn's, were glaring at my family and it was very uncomfortable. At one point my brother and sister left to take a walk just to get out of the room—it was that bad. Bill and Ester just sat there silently staring at us, and he had a really weird smile on his face. It was eerie because he never relaxed that smile. He was stoned on something and it frightened me."

At one point the promoter's youngest son Alex, aged 8, who was visiting from Hawaii, sat down at the piano to play some classical music he had been learning.

At the precise moment Alex struck the last note of the piece his older half-brother David came into the room, and Ester rose to her feet to declare, "This is Bill's true son." It came as such a shock to Alex that he burst into tears and ran out of the room.

"It was the cruelest thing I ever saw," Regina said. "There's this terrible coldness within that family which always chilled me to the bone. Bill's the best of the adults of that family, and you can extrapolate from that."

After completing Live Aid, Graham focused on the Bay Area with the opening of Shoreline. Owned by a limited partnership, the futuristic amphitheater was directly controlled by Bill Graham Enterprises. Naming his loyal lieutenant Nick Clainos as president to oversee his vast $100-million-a-year empire, Graham was now ready to embark on the next stage of his career.

Clainos, who like Graham favored the shouting phone approach to business, had a huge empire to take care of. As well as the concert division, the corporation now included a food and beverage company called Fillmore Fingers, artist management, a publishing company and an inactive record label, a nightclub division, two Punch Line comedy clubs (one of which was run by Graham's sister Ester) and a film and television division. Graham had sold off half his highly successful Winterland merchandising division, which now grossed $50 million a year by itself, to CBS, and now owned the rest with a group of shareholders.

The future looked good for Bill Graham's summer concert business with the *San Francisco Chronicle*'s pop critic, Joel Selvin, confidently forecasting Graham's "biggest season ever" with a potential box office bonanza of more than $15 million.

Privately, Graham was furious after discovering that his new Shoreline Amphitheater had been built on landfill, creating pungent odors which could blow directly into the audience whenever the winds were coming from the wrong direction.

"He blamed me for Shoreline," Regina Cartwright said. "He phoned me up in New York one night to tell me how upset he was at me for buying a multimillion-dollar toxic-waste dump."

The very next morning Graham flew to New York on the red-eye and drove straight to their new East 64th Street town house to bawl her out in person at 7:00 A.M.

"He hadn't even walked into the house and he started screaming at me from the doorway," she said. "He was shouting, 'The fumes are envolving me.' Not enveloping but envolving. He said it stunk and was making everybody throw up. He accused me of driving him so crazy that he wasn't in his right mind and couldn't make a proper business decision anymore."

After spending thousands of dollars to stop the foul smells by covering the nearby dump with cement, Shoreline opened to great fanfare in June 1986, its ghostly white twin tent peaks looking like the "world's largest brassiere" according to the *San Francisco Chronicle.* BGP vice president Danny Scher, who had overseen Shoreline from its inception, boasted, "It's the largest tent of its kind in the world. Not only does it protect the stage and the amphitheater from wind, but it's an architectural statement. It's a symbol. You can see it from miles around."

Bill Graham, who joked that he would have to get a day job if Shoreline failed, launched Shoreline's first season with an array of major acts from Bob Dylan and The Grateful Dead to Bill Cosby, Julio Iglesias, and Hank Williams, Jr.

Shoreline was soon to become a major profit center for Bill Graham as it established itself as one of the Bay Area's leading entertainment venues.

15

The Conspiracy of Hope

Amnesty International, an organization committed to protecting human rights, was little known in America in 1981, when Jack Healey landed the job as its executive director in the United States. The twenty-fifth anniversary of Amnesty was on the horizon, and the forty-eight-year-old former Franciscan monk and Southern Africa Peace Corps worker was looking to make an impact and put the organization on the American map. A rock 'n' roll fanatic since his teenage years in Pittsburgh, Healey, a self-confessed juvenile delinquent before taking the cloth, decided that rock music would be his medium to deliver the Amnesty message to mainstream America.

Not knowing anything about the business side of rock, Healey met with various promoters to discuss how to utilize rock on behalf of Amnesty. Denver promoter Barry Fey suggested a "torture train," which would carry the flags of offending nations across the country in a bid to embarrass them. Riding on board would be rock bands and musicians who would play whistle-stop shows in towns and cities along the way.

Healey liked the idea of a traveling rock show and in 1982 took the idea to Bill Graham, whom he had long admired. Healey struck a powerful nerve in Graham's social conscience when he told him about the Amnesty mission for human rights. Healey remembers, "Finally Bill said,

'Well, if you get the talent, I'll do the show.' And that was it."

A few months later, en route to an Amnesty International meeting in Finland, Healey stopped off in Dublin to meet U2's singer Bono and manager Paul McGuinness at their Windmill Lane offices. The human-rights activist, who had been impressed by Bono's passion when he had seen U2 at Madison Square Garden, struck a chord with McGuinness. He moved him with examples of Amnesty's work for human rights and then asked U2 to use its superstar power to help the organization "break out into the open." McGuinness knew intuitively that U2 would rally to Healey's cause and scribbled a note giving U2's total support and commitment to the tour and urging other bands to join in. The letter served as the catalyst which would help Amnesty raise $4 million and triple its U.S. membership during the tour.

Healey also got a commitment from Sting and, fired with enthusiasm, arranged a second meeting with Graham at his San Francisco office to ask him to fulfill his promise and produce the tour. To Healey's consternation, Graham now seemed unresponsive. When the disappointed charity organizer accused Graham of not being committed enough to Amnesty as an institution, the paranoid promoter misheard and threw a tantrum.

"He thought I meant that he should be committed to a mental institution because he was crazy," Healey said. "He started screaming at me, 'You think I'm crazy?' I figured I might as well up the ante, so I said, 'Well, you are crazy if you don't help us.' We got into a terrible shouting match, and I knew that I had his attention. I then went into him full force in front of his whole office. It was unbelievable. Bill's always an explosive character, but the bottom line was that he loved Amnesty and he took care of us."

The Conspiracy of Hope tour, named by actor/director John Huston in a video he had made on behalf of Amnesty International shortly before his death, really started gaining momentum after Bono recruited Peter Gabriel and Lou Reed. Jackson Browne and Joan Baez enlisted, and Bill Graham persuaded the Neville Brothers to round out the bill. Graham and Healey decided to take the Conspiracy of Hope tour to six cities, starting in San Francisco and then on to Los Angeles, Denver, Atlanta, Chicago, and winding up with a star-studded climax in New York. Working closely with Graham planning the tour, Healey soon found himself plunged into the internal politics of the rock business.

"This is the hardest job I've ever had in my life," said Healey. "The rock 'n' roll industry is a schmooze community. They like talking to each other a lot with very little paperwork. We're the opposite. We like a lot of paper and little talking."

During the year of preparations for the tour, Graham and Healey became very close. They realized that they had a lot in common. They had both been raised on the street and abided by its rules. One night they walked through the streets of Manhattan talking about their lives. Healey was genuinely moved as the hard-bitten promoter opened up his heart to him, confiding how difficult he found it to reconcile his huge success with his tragic childhood. Punctuated by long emotional silences, Graham told the former priest how long-forgotten fragments of his past had started coming back and haunting him since his offices had been set on fire.

"When we were walking along, he was completely disoriented," Healey remembers. "He'd tell me about his nightmares and then shut up for a whole block. It was just too painful for him. He did not know how to handle it. I'm used to that because I meet victims of torture who can't bring it back either. The pain threshold is so high, so dangerous, that it brings back trauma. I clearly saw that with Bill.

"He told me all about growing up. Losing his sister. The camp. Floating in a boat. He told me how excited he was when he found his sister Ester after the war and how she always made matzo-ball soup for him when he was feeling bad."

As they paced Manhattan, Graham talked about his obsessive hunger for success, which had robbed him of so many parts of his personal life. "Bill wanted to make it to prove that he was as good as anybody else," said Healey. "That was part of his trauma of being targeted by the Nazis. They made you feel that you were shit and you can't do anything. You want to prove that you can do anything. That, to my mind, was the total motivation for Bill Graham, and also one of the reasons that I was so disappointed in him."

The Conspiracy of Hope tour began on June 4 in San Francisco's Cow Palace in Graham's home territory before heading south to Los Angeles where it "went Hollywood" with star presenters like Madonna, Sean Penn, and Jamie Lee Curtis and a special performance by Bob Dylan and Tom Petty and the Heartbreakers. At the show Graham gave Healey an envelope containing a check for all the expense money that Amnesty had given him, saying that he was donating BGP's time to the tour.

Everything went smoothly until Bill Graham lost his temper with journalist Rona Barrett, who was covering the tour with an ABC-TV camera crew, and threw her off the tour plane. Healey first heard about the incident when a reporter telephoned him for comment on the story which could have proved devastating to the tour.

"I went to Bill and he just said she was too Jewish," Healey remembers. "I thought it was really hilarious with Bill being Jewish, and I didn't know what to say. He was mad at her, but he wouldn't tell me why. He just said it was a joke and I wasn't supposed to ask anymore. I let it go."

As the tour progressed through Denver, where it played to a half-empty arena, lost $600,000, and headed east, the tension grew, with ongoing battles between the management's of U2 and Sting over who would close the show. Sting's manager, Miles Copeland, was at bitter odds with Graham and Healey throughout the tour after he refused to allow the superstar singer to take part in a lucrative live show from Giant's Stadium for MTV. This led to a series of angry meetings between all parties with the result that Copeland finally backed down and allowed the MTV broadcast to go ahead.

But between the battles on the tour, Graham still delighted in the music that was being played. Graham's close friend, Michael Klenfner, was on the tour with Graham and saw both sides of him.

Klenfner recalled, "To stand on stage in the middle of a war when he's been fighting on an Amnesty tour and all of a sudden Sting gets up there and does a set. And Bill's just yelled at four hundred people, taps you on the shoulder and goes, 'Wow, did you hear that bass line?' That's all, you know that was him.' "

By the final show on June 15 at New Jersey's Meadowlands Stadium, which Graham was coproducing with local promoter John Scher, you could have cut the tense atmosphere with a knife. Graham, who was using ecstasy throughout the tour, was seething all day and lashed into stage manager Michael Ahern who was setting up the stage show.

The volatile promoter's next victim was John Scher, who had decided to leave the stadium to take his father out for a birthday meal before the show.

"Bill exploded John for leaving the stadium, screaming, 'Get the hell outta here,' " said Healey, who was an eyewitness to the fight which escalated into a bitter ongoing feud between the two promoters.

Later that night, Graham, Healey and Scher were to be photographed together by *Rolling Stone* magazine to accompany a major feature on the tour. Graham was determined to punish John Scher by leaving him out of the photograph, so he called Healey and told him that the photo call had been changed to an hour earlier.

"I asked Bill why we were going an hour early, and he told me I'd see in a minute. As we were leaving after the photograph had been taken, we saw John Scher walking in, expecting to be photographed. Bill had avoided having John in the photograph, and after that they had a rivalry."

Although Bill Graham was diametrically opposed to the synthetic video world of MTV and kept his distance, ironically he found himself the recipient of the station's 1986 Lifetime Achievement Award in the summer of 1986 for his work on the Amnesty tour. When he was called up onstage at that year's MTV Video Awards, he was gracious and told the millions of viewers about his latest project, an anticrack concert in New York. Many saw his interest in tackling crack as a self-serving public relations exercise to help him regain control of the New York concert market. But Graham maintained that his decision to fight crack came after revisiting his old Bronx neighborhood with two high-school friends who still lived there and seeing how it had become overrun with drugs.

"What I saw was an epidemic far beyond my imagination," he said. "It was a twilight zone. If you showed me pictures of it, I would have accused you of making it up. I couldn't imagine how bad it was. My friends would point to buildings . . . 'They manufacture crack there . . . they collect money there.' They'd point to whole blocks that are too dangerous even for the police to go into."

He coopted his old friends New York *Daily News* journalist Pablo Guzman and salsa concert promoter David Maldonaldo and called a meeting of leaders in the music industry and politics to brainstorm over breakfast at Manhattan's Carnegie Deli for a solution. Guzman, who had been a friend of Graham for eleven years, was now having trouble dealing with the unpredictable promoter.

"Soon after Bill comes on board the Live Aid ship, I gave him a call," Guzman recalled. "In classic form, Bill gets on the phone and proceeds to tell me off. Forget about years of friendship. Forget about a mutual love of salsa. Forget about the times [twice] I helped the guy put together Latin jams at the end of Santana gigs. I mean, before a 'hello,' this guy comes on yelling."

Guzman, still a staunch Graham supporter who constantly found himself having to defend the vitriolic promoter to fellow critics who "hate his guts and artists who would gloat at his funeral," agreed to work with Graham on the anticrack benefit.

At a New York City Hall press conference in August 1986 Graham outlined plans for two major concerts on October 31 and November 1, to be called "Crackdown on Crack," to raise $200,000 to fund a drug-fighting agency. The first show at Madison Square Garden would star pioneer rappers Run-DMC supported by the Allman Brothers Band, Crosby, Stills and Nash, and Santana. The lineup for the following day in the smaller Felt Forum would be Latin stars Tito Puente, Eddie Palmieri and Willie Colon. An enthusiastic Mayor Ed Koch, embracing Graham during the press conference, ordered every church in New York City to ring its bells at noon on the first day of the benefit.

But when the $25 tickets went on sale, Graham had miscalculated the draw of the bands and sales were slow. "I'm baffled," Graham admitted. "I may have made a mistake. I might be living in the wrong time thinking that the show would sell out. It's an awesome musical event."

Finally, "Crackdown on Crack," which was held amidst allegations from Graham that "factions" in the Latin and black communities were not pulling together, was a huge disappointment. It raised only $44,000, which was used by New York's Board of Education to produce antidrug videos.

After the failure of the Crackdown on Crack benefit, Graham was finally having to face that he wasn't infallible and he just might be losing touch with the MTV generation, which was now in the driving seat of rock. Former big draws like Santana and the Allman Brothers no longer ensured ticket sales. Now the public wanted to see only the new breed of good-looking video stars at the big shows.

"Video revolutionized our world," Graham sighed. "You no longer have to tour from a club level, to the theater level, to the bigger level. Madonna came along and so did Michael Jackson. The first time Madonna ever went across the country, she was already a superstar. So when you make it now, you can make ten million. You can make twenty million. There are probably fifty groups today that make more money than The Beatles. Why? Because it's so huge."

Now 55, Graham was too old to relate to the new hip MTV generation and was also having to accept the inevitable effects of the aging process. He was inconsolable when he discovered that he was no longer as virile as he had once been and in a dramatic moment in 1986 he wrote Regina Cartwright:

"I'm sorry. Save yourself—trust my love for you. I just can't trust your passion and lust—It's not for me—hasn't been since November—You enjoy sex—But it doesn't have to be me anymore—But for me it's been only you—Always—& that's my problem."

In March 1987, Graham took his sisters Ester and Rita to Israel on an emotional trip to see Carlos Santana play a special concert at the real Masada site.

"It's impossible to describe the awesome power of Masada," Graham wrote to Regina Cartwright. "Every member of Santana band and crew came along by bus and I rented a jeep for Ester, Manny and myself. We all went thru the old city of Jerusalem, drove to Masada and walked to the very top of Masada.

"Santana played the most inspirational show of his life at the foot of the great wall—10,000 went kosher bananas—my outlook on life is enhanced forever."

But Graham's positive attitude did not last. On his return to America, his self-doubts and frustrations continued to spill over into his professional life. Always used to getting his own way, he now refused to take no for an answer. He reverted back to the lonely, bitter child he had once been in the playground at DeWitt Clinton High and refused to participate in any project where he couldn't dictate the rules as in the case of his birthday party plans for the Golden Gate Bridge.

With the fiftieth anniversary of the famous bridge coming up in May 1987, Graham pledged to throw his adopted city a spectacular four-hour birthday concert in its honor starring homegrown bands like The Grateful Dead and Huey Lewis and the News. Promising to raise the money for the celebration himself, Graham stood back from the limelight, telling the *San Francisco Chronicle,* "The star of the day is the Golden Gate Bridge. I have crossed it between 20,000 and 25,000?, and every day is different. Every day is a hit."

Graham wanted to close the bridge to traffic for a day and estimated that 2 million people would walk across it on the way to his concert. But his anger was sparked when the bridge authorities opposed closure, fearing it would cause a nightmarish traffic jam in Marin County. When Graham found out that the birthday committee was planning to invite his detested enemy, President Reagan, as a guest of honor, he was livid. During a three-hour public meeting during which the bridge board's transportation committee put off making a decision on making the bridge a pedestrian way and asked Graham to pay for the celebration's insurance, Graham threw a tantrum.

"I'm out!" he shouted at the committee. "You want me to carry my own insurance, stage the events, take great risks, work for free, and then disregard my professional opinion. We are not some bull in a stable ready to be ridden. Do you think we should sit there and say, 'We are ready to participate in your scheme, oh great ones?' " The Golden Gate Bridge party went ahead on May 24 without Bill Graham, proving he was not indispensible for organizing San Francisco music events.

Now, after a run of failures, Graham was unexpectedly handed his long-sought dream of staging the first official rock 'n' roll concert in Russia, a full decade after his last attempt to bring live rock behind the Iron Curtain. He received a call from a group called the American Peace Walk Committee that was organizing an antinuclear walk from Leningrad to Moscow. They invited him to stage a concert at the finish line. Under the new regime headed by Mikhail Gorbachev, the buzzword was "glasnost" and the official line now supported bringing Western rock to the Soviet Union. Graham was so excited that his dream now seemed feasible under the new leadership that he immediately dispatched his personal pilot and close aide Steve "Killer" Kahn on a reconnaissance mission to Moscow.

Never wanting to provide front money from his vast fortune for his non-money-making projects, Graham again turned to computer tycoon Steve Wozniak for help. "Bill called me up one day and said he had the chance to put on the first ever concert in Russia," Wozniak said.

Appealing to Wozniak's sense of history, Graham told him time was of the essence and that the event, to be held on American Independence Day, would help cement peace between the United States and the Soviet Union.

"So I said, 'Sure. I'll help support it,' " Wozniak said. " 'What do you need?' Bill said $500,000 and I said okay. It was all done in one phone call."

Dubbed the "Walk and Roll Summit," the show, to star Bonnie Raitt, Santana, the Doobie Brothers, and James Taylor, was uncertain until two days before the official announcement as the promoter traded frantic telegrams to Moscow, finalizing arrangements with Russian government officials. During the final preparations, Graham was dosed with LSD during a Grateful Dead show in Ventura. While he was still at his sister Ester's house he was given the news that the Russian show had been postponed to July 6. Returning to earth immediately and fearing a replay of his last abortive attempt at a Russian concert, Graham raged on the phone to the Soviet officials, "Do you think we are animals in the zoo? We won't do the show. That's it." Later, after his sister Ester came to the rescue and calmed him down with a bowl of her chicken soup, Graham got back on the phone and arranged to find another site which wasn't booked for July 4.

"I pushed the button," declared an excited Graham a couple of days later on his way to Moscow to organize the concert. "They've never had anything even closely resembling this in Russia. It's outdoors . . . It's free and it's in Moscow—on the Fourth of July."

Reflecting on the political implications of bringing live rock concerts to Russia, Graham said, "I am not qualified to comment on the Russian's motivations, but in this arms race, nobody's winning and it's costing millions of dollars. We are taking advantage of an opportunity to make a statement on their soil to have these artists who have supported the antinuclear movement make that statement from the stage in Moscow."

Pulling together the giant show, where 200,000 young Russians were expected to crowd into the Izmailovo Stadium, was a staggering feat crossing many national borders. The roofed stage came from Budapest, the lights from Stockholm, and the elaborate sound equipment was flown in from London. Graham also constructed a backstage gourmet restaurant for his American party and refused to allow the Russian generals to come in and eat there if they didn't have the necessary access passes.

On the day of the concert, the Russian authorities were taking no chances. Bill Graham and his BGP team arrived to find the stadium completely surrounded by uniformed Red Army troops with the militia patrolling outside with menacing German shepherd dogs. Inside, dark-suited KGB men prowled around and sensing trouble, the American promoter took control, calling his liaison officer, Mr. Fedosev, to a meeting to lay down some ground rules and threatened to stop the show unless they were met.

"There were to be no weapons inside the stadium and no uniforms," Graham remembered.

When the Russian authorities attempted to renege on an earlier promise that the audience be allowed on the field in front of the stage and posted a solid line of uniformed soldiers on line with the mixing board 50 feet in front of the stage, the fearless promoter took on the Red Army and held it to a Mexican standoff.

"I said, 'The show won't go on. I won't have these musicians play if there's nobody in front of the stage.'

"By this time forty thousand people were in, but all behind this line. And they thought they'd won. I said, 'You don't seem to understand. This show is not gonna happen unless these people are allowed to move up. We're not going to have this big demarcation line.'

"And five minutes before [the official start of the show] they wouldn't move and I wouldn't move. I said, 'There is no show. We'll go back home.' And finally, through an interpreter, the security man said, 'Well, we can't move them up now, because they'll trample over each other.' "

With an interpreter, Graham, brusquely defying the Red Army chiefs, came down from the stage and walked over to the soldiers who were sitting cross-legged in front of the stage, creating a human wall between the audience and the fans. Instructing his interpreter to tell the soldiers to copy him exactly, Graham sat down and started sliding toward the stage a foot at a time, followed by the wall of soldiers, and the audience. He finally stopped his epic journey right in front of the stage, got up, and signaled the show to begin.

"If the authority doesn't seem to make sense to me, I'll challenge authority and defy it, up to a point," he explained.

The six-hour show went on as planned and introduced the Russian fans to live rock 'n' roll, Bill Graham–style.

"It was just one of the steps that made the people of the two countries feel a similar bond," said Wozniak, who flew down to the show with some of his friends. "I saw the music, and I talked to the performers. Bonnie and Carlos Santana, in particular, really had it in their hearts to do some good for the world."

From Russia Bill sent Regina Cartwright a card expressing his feelings for her after the success of his landmark show. "I feel so small and humble," Graham wrote. "I seek peace of mind & love for us all—mainly you—Je T'Embrasse—Love & Cheers, Bill."

Bill Graham finally made his long-threatened new assault on New York in 1987. He directly attacked John Scher, his old enemy from the Conspiracy of Hope tour, using Jerry Garcia as his weapon. The two promoters had a long-standing arrangement to divide The Grateful Dead, with Scher promoting the band east of the Rockies and Graham to the west. But Graham shattered the truce when he persuaded Jerry Garcia to do a series of solo performances at the Lunt-Fontanne Theatre on Broadway.

"It was a devastating blow to John," says *Performance* magazine's Bob Grossweiner. "He had done everything with The Grateful Dead in the East, but Bill was trying to win back New York, and Scher was an archenemy. There was a lot of bad blood between them because of The Grateful Dead."

Bill Graham was at the Lunt-Fontanne Theatre every night for the seventeen Garcia shows in October 1987 and made his electric presence felt. He brought an eight-man BGP crew to New York to supervise the staging, and his beefed-up security staff were under orders to throw anyone out who tried to tape the shows. He was recording them for future release. Every night Graham waited outside the theater on 46th Street, hoping to catch an illegal T-shirt seller or a ticket scalper. When he did, he pushed them out into the street, hurling abuse in vintage Graham style.

Garcia fan Joe Pipe was smoking a joint during one show when Graham punched him in the back and started haranguing him. Pipe, who was also recording the show on tape, secretly captured Graham in the midst of a classic tantrum.

"You don't know about no smoking, right?" screamed Graham at Pipe as Garcia's electric band played *"I Shall Be Released."* "You don't see the sign. You didn't hear the announcements. You don't give a flying fuck about anybody, do you? We could get our fucking license taken you fucking asshole. Put that out and keep that out. You don't know any better, do you?"

After his successful Broadway run and frontal attack against John Scher in his home territory, Graham was delighted. Calling the shows "a-once-in-a-lifetime experience," Graham boasted to *Performance,* "In all, it was an absolutely joyous event for the parties involved."

But the boyish-looking promoter from New Jersey stood his ground against Graham, firing back in the pages of *Performance* in full view of the whole concert industry: "The last several years of dealing with Bill has left a bad taste in my staff's mouth and has clearly brought into focus that Mr. Graham and I have somewhat different styles in promoting."

Criticizing Graham's $30 ticket demands, Scher accused Graham of meddling in New York and helping to feed the cancer of the union's exorbitant demands without having to worry about the consequences. Claiming Graham was irresponsibly attempting to muscle back into the New York market in a "Kamikaze-like manner" Scher took the veteran promoter to task over his business ethics.

Graham's reply to Scher's attack came in a letter to Don Waitt, the publisher of *Performance*. Refusing even to mention Scher by name, the furious Graham accused "the man" of taking "his laundry into the public arena."

"The man attacked my character, my professional abilities and my intelligence, and he did so publicly," wrote Graham. Defending his honor, Graham said he cared about New York where he had an office, adding that he had merely offered Jerry Garcia "the opportunity to express himself in a legitimate Broadway theater."

The other concert promoters were alarmed by the growing hostility between Graham and Scher and feared an all-out promoting war between the two. That summer Graham and Scher declared a temporary cease-fire to join thirteen other promoters in Philadelphia to discuss forming a trade association to improve communication between promoters.

"It was similar to the Cold War, where the Russians would meet the Americans in Helsinki," explained Ben Liss, who later would become the association's executive director. "They felt that a more healthy dialogue could take place in a closed-door setting amongst colleagues rather than in the public forum."

With many promoters losing big money that summer with unsuccessful tours like the disastrous heavy metal tour "Monsters of Rock," promoters were also getting worried and decided that they must pull together if they were to survive. Evening Star's Danny Zelisko spoke about the problems promoters faced negotiating with the superstar bands like U2 and The Rolling Stones: "You get up to fifty pieces of paper of *what else* you're going to do [for the act]. "Promoters need to draw up their own rider. We need more harmony in negotiating deals . . ."

On December 5, 1988 the North American Concert Promoters Association (NACPA) was officially set up in Washington, D.C., without Bill Graham, who did not attend the meeting. The seven promoters elected to the board of directors were John Scher, Frank Russo, Brian Murphy, Don Law, Larry Magid, Jack Boyle, and Jules Belkin. Ben Liss was appointed executive director.

Explaining Graham's absence, Liss diplomatically told *Performance*, "The founding members list only represents who was in Washington, D.C. Prior obligations kept some promoters away. There were a number of people not present who have expressed interest . . ."

When Bill Graham and twenty-six of his fellow promoters held their first meeting behind closed doors in Fort Lauderdale, Florida, in December, they found they were powerless to take any concerted action because of the tough anti-trust laws against price fixing. With their lack of teeth, the NACPA eventually became nothing more than a select social club for promoters with a high membership fee.

"They can't talk dollar signs," said Bob Grossweiner of *Performance* magazine. "They can't coalesce and say, 'So-and-so wants a one hundred thousand dollar guarantee. Let's all pass.' That violates the antitrust laws. There really isn't that much else they can do."

Although their hands were tied from taking concerted action, there was widespread alarm in the business about the current decline of the concert industry with fewer artists able to sell out stadiums, and those that could not wanting to tour.

During the mid-eighties, major bands like Def Leppard and Bon Jovi were making so much money from album sales that they could no longer even be bothered to go out on tour. Inevitably the music began to suffer as the bands got lazy, only touring every four or five years, merely content to release the occasional live album to fulfill contractual obligations.

By the late 1980's the few acts that could sell out a stadium knew their worth and started squeezing the promoters even harder, making the 90/10 split a fact of promoting life, with Bruce Springsteen even managing to secure a 95/5.

"The price is dictated by the star," Graham said. "There's this constant pressure that's put on the promoter that says, 'Look, I don't need you,' and it's true. The big acts can get almost anyone to promote a show for them."

But even a big-name act no longer guaranteed a sellout, and one mistake could mean a six-figure loss for a promoter. Several could put him out of business.

"We roll the dice and we roll them all the time," explains the soft-spoken Atlanta promoter Alex Cooley. "There should be some risk/reward ratio, but it's got skewered out of all proportion. The acts are guaranteed profits, and we're sitting here without any guarantees of anything.

"In the long run it keeps us betting on the small acts because we have to figure a show down to the bottom line and if it's questionable we pass. It stops a lot of acts from working."

Cooley says that as the concert business became tougher from the end of the 1980's into the early 1990's, some promoters, agents and managers started becoming too greedy.

"Get every nickel today and to hell with tomorrow is a very short-term attitude."

Bill Graham agreed, saying, "Does the greed factor of man play havoc in our industry? Oh, God, yes."

Frank Russo said he became so disillusioned with the concert promotion business that he eventually sold out to Boston promoter Don Law at the beginning of the 1990s and got out.

"When I first got started, it was a very fair sport with the bands and promoters literally partners," he said. "But the fairness changed as the industry grew and grew. Business managers now have more control of the acts than the actual managers. Our association had a lot of positiveness, but unfortunately, with the covenants that it was working with, it couldn't be as successful as it would have liked to have been.

"In the last two or three years, the business has changed terribly. People's words don't mean as much as they once did. A lot of people have, what I call, selective amnesia: in making deals, keeping their words, changing their minds."

Russo blames MTV and pay-per-view television for the decline in concert attendance.

"Why go and spend twenty dollars for a concert when you can go and rent something or watch MTV for almost nothing?" he reasons. "At the beginning many people thought that MTV would have a positive effect on the industry, but it has turned out to be detrimental. Because a number of great artists can't get on MTV because they are not video material, the ones that are have really taken the bite out of live concert appearances. So the patron becomes lazy and the artists get too much exposure. Pay-per-view has also had a major negative effect. For twenty-five dollars or thirty dollars you can stay home and invite four or five friends to watch the shows for five dollars each. You get to see the same concert that you would have schlepped out to a stadium for a fraction of the price."

As life got increasingly tougher for promoters they were forced to find new ways to compensate for their losses. One virtually untapped area with a huge potential was the new practice of adding service charges to boost ticket prices. When Bill Graham had begun staging concerts twenty-five years earlier, the promoter paid ticket agencies to distribute tickets at their face price. As the promoters' profits started falling in the early 1980s, they began to make up for the losses by shifting ticket-distribution costs onto the public.

Through the 1980s the main player in the huge multimillion-dollar ticket market was Ticketron. As the pioneer of computerized ticket selling, Ticketron was responsible for introducing a new customer convenience by selling tickets in retail stores and over the phone. In 1975 an ambitious former roller-derby promoter, Jerry Seltzer, using start-up capital provided by friends and relatives, started an agency in Northern California called BASS (Bay Area Seating Service). Seltzer's BASS was a small but aggressive operation and probably would have stayed that way without the intervention of Bill Graham, who wanted to become involved in ticket distribution.

"BASS didn't make the big time until it got Bill Graham's business," Seltzer said. "Graham gave us credibility."

There has been much speculation on the exact details of Graham's involvement with BASS, which remain shrouded in secrecy, one of the best kept secrets in the concert business. Graham always denied having a share in the company, but it has been reported that BGP receives a "kickback" of up to 50 percent of the service charges that BASS make on selling his shows, which would be worth millions of dollars in additional revenue every year.

When Jerry Pompili was asked how much Bill Graham Presents receives from BASS, he replied, "It's none of your business."

The third force in ticket distribution was TicketMaster, a small company, once likened to a "hungry and aggressive band of rebels," that didn't make a dent in the business until 1982, when it was acquired by Fred Rosen, a former Catskills stand-up comic turned attorney. Backed by powerful Chicago real-estate billionaire Jay Pritzker, in less than a decade, Rosen transformed his computerized ticketing service from a small $1 million-a-year ticket business to America's preeminent ticket distributor, selling $1 billion of tickets annually.

By the mid-1980s, the outspoken Rosen was fast becoming the Napoleon of the ticket business, with a well-planned state-by-state buy-out campaign of local distributors. The sole exception to his national ticket takeover was Northern California, where he recognized the enormous clout of the Bill Graham–supported BASS operation. There he sought a friendly alliance.

"They're not stupid," said Larry Morse, a legislative aide for California State Senator Milton Marks, who attempted to rein in BASS-TicketMaster with legislation some years later. "They understood that they did not need to do battle with Bill Graham."

So in 1986 BASS joined forces with TicketMaster to effectively carve up California: BASS would handle tickets in Northern California, and TicketMaster would take Southern California. This alliance allowed BASS to tap into TicketMaster's advanced computer software and use its logo. Although there was no cross-ownership, the new name of the company operating in Northern California became BASS-TicketMaster.

According to *Performance* magazine, the truce allowed TicketMaster to lock up the lucrative Northern California market "with the considerable clout of Bill Graham" in its corner. After the alliance, Rosen told *Performance* that he felt the price of concert tickets was "way underpriced" and left little doubt he planned to change things.

"How come a concert is only sixteen-fifty?" Rosen asked. "One reason is that groups don't want the ticket prices higher; they feel they owe it to their fans."

Pointing out that the public is quite willing to pay higher prices to ticket scalpers and brokers, Rosen pledged to take that extra money back and put it in the hands of promoters and facility owners. "That extra money escapes the system and doesn't inure to the benefit of our industry," said Rosen.

Stating that the realistic price of every concert seat should be $25, Rosen explained, "Nobody ever paid more for a ticket than they wanted to. The scalpers prove it every time."

Over the next five years Rosen would prove true to his word, introducing stiff service charges that would double the cost of tickets to every American music and sporting event.

In early 1988 Regina Cartwright became pregnant by Bill Graham for the eighth time. After years in therapy, Regina had conquered her anorexia and was in good shape and healthy. This time she did not miscarry and looked forward to a successful pregnancy to make Bill Graham a father again at fifty-seven. Regina's pregnancy presented Graham with a major problem since he had lied to his sister Ester, telling her that he had given up his affair with Regina two years earlier. Scared to admit he had been lying to his sister, he ordered Regina to abort their baby immediately. She refused emphatically.

"I was determined to have my baby," Cartwright said. "He had a fit because this one was a healthy pregnancy, and Bill wanted me to have an abortion. I understood why he wanted me to have an abortion, but I didn't see Ester and other disapproving people as a reason to kill our child. He was so concerned that his sister Ester would find out."

Two days after finding out about the pregnancy, Graham cooled down and took Regina to an expensive New York restaurant to celebrate their new baby. He promised to stand by her on the condition that the baby remained a closely guarded secret, even to her psychiatrist.

16

Whipping Post

As the eighties drew to a close, Bill Graham found his world crashing down all around him. Although he was still the undisputed heavyweight of concert promotion, most of the top bands like U2 and Bruce Springsteen disliked him and did not like working with him. Yet Graham did not realize just how badly he had alienated the bands until he was effectively blocked from producing the Human Rights Now! tour for Amnesty International in 1988.

The 1988 Conspiracy of Hope tour had been so successful in placing Amnesty International firmly on the American map that Jack Healey decided he now wanted to take his message of peace around the world in a traveling rock 'n' roll caravan. The worldwide tour would also mark the fortieth anniversary of the signing of the United Nations General Assembly's Universal Declaration of Human Rights.

Fired with enthusiasm, Healey quickly recruited Sting and Peter Gabriel for the tour and then added newcomer Tracy Chapman and African superstar Youssou N'Dour. Healey then asked Bill Graham to produce the tour.

Healey recalls, "I told Bill who we had on the bill and he said, 'You still need a steak.' You don't have a steak. That was to be Bruce Springsteen. To Bill's mind, Bruce was steak and the others were salad and vegetables. So he sent me after Springsteen."

Springsteen, now the world's biggest white rock 'n' roll star, was just finishing up his record-breaking Tunnel of Love tour. Still not fully comfortable in the rock business, Healey knew the odds were firmly stacked against his landing Springsteen for the Amnesty tour. In 1986 Springsteen had turned down Bono's invitation to join the Conspiracy of Hope tour, and Healey also knew that Springsteen's manager, Jon Landau, was not even on speaking terms with Graham, who had cursed him out from the stage when he first started managing the superstar. But behind the scenes Healey had an ally in superagent Frank Barsalona, who at that time was also not speaking to Graham. Barsalona approached Springsteen and found that he was interested in joining the tour but had strong reservations about Graham's being in charge.

"Essentially my instructions from Frank were that while there may be differences between the Springsteen camp and Bill, they wanted to play for Amnesty and not do a Bill Graham tour," Healey said.

Barsalona told Healey he would have to run the tour using Graham as his deputy, or Springsteen wouldn't take part, and Healey was given the unenviable job of breaking the news to Graham. "It was a terrible night for Bill when I told him," Healey remembers. "He was very upset. We went out on the street, and he said to me, 'What happened? I don't know why this is going on.' "

The former monk then tried to lighten the blow to Graham's ego, saying that he shouldn't take Springsteen's snub too personally.

As if to prove Springsteen wrong, Graham pushed himself into the Amnesty project of planning a major tour in third world countries which had never seen rock music before and had no facilities for it. He estimated it would cost $22 million to fly the six bands in two separate 747's for the six-week tour. Reebok Athletic Shoes, which was enjoying a record year, agreed to underwrite the whole tour for up to $10 million, and Graham's staff started working on the budget. But when Frank Barsalona saw the completed budget breakdown, he was appalled at the expense and told Healey it would look bad for rockers to be traveling in such luxury on a charity tour.

"Frank and I decided that really in the best image of the human-rights movement we wouldn't waste a dime," said Healey. "We would make it as spartan as we could get away with. We wanted to loudly say across the world that we represent starving people. I didn't like Bill's budget. I'm not saying that it was irresponsible, I'm saying it was different."

After the budget, Healey soon found himself at odds with Bill Graham over almost everything. Still reeling from his rejection by Springsteen, Graham had his own vision of the Human Rights Now! tour. There were bitter clashes between Graham and Healey over where the tour should play. Poring over his world atlas, Graham dispatched his staff on reconnaissance missions to New Delhi and Costa Rica and inspected the Ivory Coast personally.

Accusing Amnesty of playing it safe with concerts in New York, London, and Toronto instead of taking the rock message to places like Costa Rica, Abidjan, and New Delhi, Graham threatened to expose the organization to the press unless it agreed to his itinerary.

Said Graham: "Well, for one reason or another, certain acts and certain members of the executive committee of Amnesty said, 'Well, this looks too difficult. Let's not go there."

Jack Healey says that Graham failed to take into account Amnesty's internal politics, which necessitated staging concerts to aid recruitment in key areas.

There was also trouble when both Graham and UK promoter Harvey Goldsmith started negotiating separately with their own contacts to bring the Amnesty tour to Russia. "It was sheer anarchy," Healey says. "We were all confusing everybody in the Soviet Union, and it all broke down."

But the real explosions happened after Bruce Springsteen agreed to join the tour, with the proviso that his stage crew would be used instead of Bill Graham and Michael Ahern. To add insult to injury, Bill Graham was told to stay away from the press conference where the singer would make his official announcement. Springsteen, who was touring in Sweden, was flown to London for the press conference, which made headlines around the world, while a gloomy Graham sunk into a drug-induced depression and spent three days sulking in Amnesty's London office.

"It was Springsteen's commitment that made the tour possible," said Michael Ahern, the tour's original stage manager. "He moved it into another league of visibility."

Once Springsteen agreed to tour, his crew took over, leaving little for Ahern and Graham to do. The superstar's advisers drafted a new "frugal" budget and his stage manager George Travis was given the same title as Ahern, who soon bowed out. As the tour planning progressed, Graham become more and more difficult to deal with as he secretly retreated into the world of the drug Ecstasy.

"I did not know how to handle Bill Graham," Healey admits. "He was as tough as nails. Bill had never been a deputy to anyone in his life, and he never accepted that I was in charge. Remember, he's the biggest promoter in the world at that time, and it was the biggest tour in the history of the world. And Bill wanted to be in charge.

"Many times on that tour, he said, 'Fire me, Jack. Fire me.' I wasn't going to fire Bill Graham. I loved him. It was just sheer agony for six weeks."

Ex-*Rolling Stone* music editor James Henke wrote the official book on the tour and saw the problems firsthand. "Bill was a very strong-willed person and wanted to do things his way, and the Springsteen people likewise," Henke said. "I'm sure he felt that when the Springsteen people came in they took over a lot of his responsibility because of how big a star Springsteen was. So I'm sure, given Bill's ego, that did not make him too happy."

Former Graham employee Lee Blumer worked on both Amnesty tours and was close to both Graham and Healey. "They're two characters out of a book," Blumer said. "They are both charismatic leaders, and I don't think there is ever room for two charismatic leaders in the same game. They both have completely different styles, and Jack is really used to running his show and Bill is used to running his show. It was strange. They would kill each other."

To try and restore peace to the tour, a decision was made by Amnesty leaders and Springsteen's camp to get Graham out of the way, so he was sent to New Delhi to organize the Indian concert.

"They didn't want me talking to the press about what was going on behind the scenes on this tour," Graham said later.

Dejected and humiliated, Graham reacted by making grand gestures and being deliberately overgenerous, offering Healey anything he wanted to help the tour. He consulted his atlas constantly for new places to play and tried to offer constructive advice whenever possible. But the inherent violence in Graham's nature was never far away and surfaced at the slightest provocation.

The Los Angeles show had been scheduled for the night of Yom Kippur, causing an outcry from the city's largely Jewish music community. Healey immediately agreed to change nights, but Graham was furiously combative, holding fast to the scheduled date and threatening to go public. Healey remembers, "Bill said, 'Fuck 'em! I want to fight.' " And the concert went ahead as scheduled.

In Argentina there was a discussion of how many cameras should be used on the official tour film. The film crew wanted to use twelve, but Bill Graham started arguing for fifteen.

"I hadn't a clue how many cameras were need to shoot it," says Healey. "So I finally said, 'Well, how many cameras does Bruce use on a shoot?' They said twenty-one, so I said 'Well, we're twenty-one, thank you.' Bill loved that decision. He loved deciding that way. I could have sat there and argued between twelve and fifteen and said thirteen and made everyone unhappy. I accidentally made Bill happy because I didn't know and Bill didn't either. I was always in that spot."

In good spirits after the show in Rio, Graham wrote a card to Regina Cartwright, telling her he'd "reached new heights of energy beyond belief."

But things came to a head in India, with Bill Graham almost coming to blows with Healey. They arrived to find that the concert sponsor, the *Times of India,* was having its 150th birthday and attempting to use the Amnesty concert as its official celebration. The situation escalated dramatically when the newspaper's publisher attended the concert and was chased into the stands by one of Graham's security men, who beat him to the ground, ripping off his press credentials.

"The next day we were on the front page of the *Times of India,*" Healey said. "I had to organize a three-hour press conference to explain things. Bill got mad at me over it. He put his fists up and wanted to slug it out with me. I managed to diffuse things by saying, 'Bill, we're both men in our fifties. Have you any idea how silly we are going to look going at each other like this?' "

Yet Graham's problems in India were not reflected in a card he sent Regina Cartwright the day after the concert: "We created an allegiance with the stadium personnel and townspeople to such a high communal level of spirit and mutual respect that all of India will never forget last night . . . I've never felt more tired—yet never felt more rewarded for my work."

After the tour, Graham was furious with Healey and disillusioned with Amnesty, saying he was "saddened" and "exhausted." Citing the unparalleled high level abuse of power in Amnesty International, Graham said, "I really don't want to always yell at the world that I am right and they are wrong."

Graham came off the tour spiritually and mentally broken. He had increased his daily dosages of Halcion and, along with the Ecstasy he was taking, his mood swings were alarming.

"Bill spent the worst six weeks of his life on that tour," Healey says. "I was personally so beat up on the tour that I took a commercial flight back to New York as I couldn't face traveling on the tour plane since I was so worn out from the tension."

In his customary style, Graham refused to take Healey's phone calls after the tour and cut him off as if he had never existed.

"I saw Bill once after the tour. I was coming down a flight of steps and he came out of a door and headed towards me. I said, 'Hi, Bill.' He just stared at me and kept on walking. I felt terrible. I loved the man."

After the frustration and pressure of the Amnesty world tour, Bill Graham plowed head on into his backbreaking schedule like a man possessed. To many, the middle-aged promoter seemed indestructible, punishing his body with drugs and a traveling work schedule that would have taxed a man half his age. He laughed at the idea of jet lag and, coming off the Amnesty tour, he flew from Buenos Aires to Melbourne to see Mick Jagger perform—via New York, San Francisco, and Hawaii—in a nonstop thirty-eight-hour flying binge.

He was now taking double his dosage of Halcion on top of all the other drugs, and the awful side effects from the sleeping pill began taking their toll. Even his trusted staff tried their best to avoid him by staying out of his way.

In mid-March 1988 on a flight from Denver, Graham wrote to Regina: "I'm going home. I live alone. I sleep alone. I feel alone and I'm deeply in love with you. I'm not going anywhere. I'm back out here in the real world trying, really trying to deal with the joy of my imagination and the horror of reality." Another letter, calling her his "physical and passionate mate," said he still desired her but admitted he was a "beaten man."

On December 30, 1988, when Regina Cartwright gave birth to a healthy baby girl she named Caitlin, at a Manhattan hospital, the bottom fell out of Graham's world. He came to New York to see his new daughter when she was six weeks old, expecting Regina to go to bed with him as usual, and for the first time she refused.

"Bill could never accept the end of our sexual relationship after I became pregnant with Caitlin," said Cartwright. "It was as if something basic and primitive which made him a man had been torn away from him and he blamed me."

The once-energetic promoter, always on the move, now seemed slow and lethargic; he appeared to have grown old overnight. The lines in his face etched themselves deeper into chasms, and his thick hair was now completely gray. Bill Graham was behaving like a lovesick teenager and was so distracted by Cartwright's sexual rejection and by becoming a father again that he could no longer focus on work and was fast becoming a liability to his lieutenants who now ran BGP. In frustration, Graham continually lost his temper with his staff at the office. No longer was there the inside wink and nod during a theatrical tantrum; now his temper was for real—he wasn't playing around.

The BGP staff were much relieved when Graham announced he was leaving day-to-day business and had a new project in mind. He had decided to relive some of his triumphs of the past by reopening the Old Fillmore Auditorium to replace his Wolfgang Nightclub, which had burned down the year before.

"Bill's very excited," said David Mayeri, general manager of the company's nightclub division, AKG, Inc. "He'd like to put the original Fillmore posters from the sixties on the walls and set up an exhibit of rock-and-roll memorabilia, making it a little museum."

Covering the walls with his favorite pictures from the early days, Bill Graham had become the Phantom of the Fillmore, returning to haunt the site of his first breakthrough shows a full generation earlier. To convey the flavor of the old hall to the new rock fans, he mounted a complete series of vintage posters in the upstairs lounge. He also reinstalled his famous barrel of free apples in its old place at the top of the stairs and rehired his old poster artists to create new Fillmore posters for his next generation of shows, which kicked off with the English soul singer, Terence Trent D' Arby.

A nostalgic Graham reminisced to *San Francisco Chronicle*'s Joel Selvin about returning to the Old Fillmore. "That's the joint where we were able to do things like Lenny Bruce with the Mothers of Invention, the building where we did The Byrds with two one-act plays by LeRoi Jones. That was the magical era where we put things on the public didn't ask for."

Fully aware of the commercial possibilities of the Fillmore artwork, with the current fashion resurgence of the sixties, Graham ordered Jerry Pompili to catalog his vast collection of posters, T-shirts, backstage passes, and other rock paraphernalia with a view to arranging lucrative licensing deals.

"I'm not going to put them on cornflake boxes," explained the former Fillmore East head of security. "But this archive is huge, and it eats up a lot of money. This is one way to get a little of it back."

Yearning for the old days, Graham had also started dropping into the Concord Resort, the scene of some of the happiest times of his youth. Often arriving in his private plane with his son David, pilot Steve "Killer" Kahn and a girlfriend in tow, Graham loved to sit and reminisce about old times with his friend Jack Levin, who was now assistant maître d'.

"He used to call me to get a reservation," Levin said. "I couldn't wait to see him, and I loved sitting and bullshitting with him, while he was having dinner."

Levin used to lay on a special meal for him featuring his favorite foods. "And could he eat!" said Levin. "Instead of seating him at a small four-seater, we used to put him at a larger table to hold all the food. Honest to goodness, when he came here, he used to eat like the Russians were in Monticello."

In May 1988, estranged Rolling Stones Mick Jagger and Keith Richards resolved their differences and decided to record a new album and go out on the road for their first world tour since 1981. When Bill Graham heard about the Jagger/Richards reconciliation, he was overjoyed and couldn't wait to be back running the Rolling Stone bandwagon. He took it for granted that he would be the band's promoter and started doing the preliminary spadework for the tour without consulting the Stones.

The only member of the Stones who had reservations about going out on the road for what was to become the Steel Wheels tour was Bill Wyman, who was occupied by his love affair with eighteen-year-old model Mandy Smith, soon to be his wife. Determined that nothing would derail his Rolling Stones tour, Bill Graham started a campaign to make sure that Wyman got back in the Stones saddle and didn't rock the boat.

"I didn't want to tour," Wyman says. "Bill rang me three or four times from California and says, 'Come on, you've gotta do it.' He was one of the people who helped talk me into it."

But while Graham was mobilizing his forces for the tour, veteran Canadian promoter Michael Cohl, who runs Concert Productions International (CPI), started pursuing the Stones aggressively in the fall of 1988. Cohl offered to handle the entire tour, giving the band a huge percentage of between $65 to $70 million, much of the money up front. He would shoulder the whole financial risk in return for collecting the potentially enormous net profits from each show, where tickets would sell for $28.50. The convivial shaggy-haired forty-one-year-old promoter spent the next few months flying between his Toronto base, New York, and the Caribbean getting to know the Stones and their business advisers and gaining their confidence.

When Graham heard from the Stones' American business adviser, Joe Rascoff, that another promoter had made an attractive bid for the tour, he was alarmed. Rascoff refused to reveal who the other bidder was and told Graham he had ten days to make a counteroffer. Feeling wounded that the Stones would even consider working with another promoter after his great work for the band, Graham called up the top three promoters in the business who had the clout to pull off a Rolling Stones tour.

Michael Cohl received a telephone call from Graham saying he was researching the potential for a Stones tour with promoters. Cunningly, Graham then told Cohl that he had heard that "somebody who is remaining nameless" was also in the running and he'd feel like a "schmuck" discussing ideas with him if he happened to be the competitor.

"So I thought for about half a second and said, 'Well, then you shouldn't be discussing it with me,' " said Cohl. "And then he said, 'Well, I take it that you're the other bidder?' And I said, 'You can take it that I've made a bid and I don't know if I'm *the* other bidder or one of many. The fact of the matter is that you shouldn't be discussing it with me because yes, I am trying to get the tour.' "

According to Bill Wyman, Graham was never in the running for the Steel Wheels tour after the band had caught him stealing from them on the 1981 tour. "It had left quite a nasty taste in our mouth and so when we had the chance of doing the eighty-nine tour and he came up and proposed to do it, we did not take him on to do the tour. So that was a shame, really," explained Wyman.

Although the Rolling Stones had no intention of giving Graham the tour, Mick Jagger still put him through the humiliation of flying to Barbados with Nick Clainos to make an official presentation to himself and the band's business advisers.

The Stones finally agreed to Cohl's offer, which paid them $70 million up front before they even picked up their instruments. When Graham heard he had lost out to Cohl, he was devastated that Mick Jagger, whom he had considered a close friend, could go with another promoter, especially after BGP had worked on his solo tour to Japan and the Far East the year before.

In his despair and humiliation, Graham went on the defensive, attacking the group and Michael Cohl in the press. "They allowed themselves to be purchased by someone who put up a whole pile of bullion," he complained.

Accusing the Stones of "going to bed with an abacus, to sleep with numbers," the heartbroken promoter added, "I wanted to dance again. I didn't think they would do that. The basic disappointment was that they chose to work with someone else for reasons that I understood, but didn't expect. They're a great diamond to cut, and she's a beautiful woman to dance with, and I thought we were very good partners in that sense."

Bill Wyman believes that Graham knew full well the real reason why he wasn't hired was because of the financial "discrepancy" on the 1981 tour but could never admit it.

"He had taken it for granted that he was doing [the Steel Wheels tour], so when he found that he wasn't it was even more of a shock than just putting in a bid that was turned down," says Wyman. "He'd already accepted the fact that he was doing it. I think that's the thing that hurt him most."

The bassist, who officially left the Stones in 1992, after thirty years, says that even if Graham had been in contention, his offer of $30–35 million was so far below Cohl's blockbuster offer that he believed it showed Graham had "a lack of faith" in the Stones.

"We thought Michael Cohl's bid was too confident, but it turned out to be no more than normal. Bill Graham's come up with this offer and that offer. But it never approached the offers we had from the other people."

Mick Jagger was under no illusions, saying, "Of course we're doing it for the money. People get highly paid in rock 'n' roll. That's why it's so attractive. It's like boxing."

Cohl believes that losing the Rolling Stones tour led Graham into an identity crisis. "That whole thing with number one is such a strange thing, isn't it?" he said. "People have told me that it was almost a macho thing where it became a sign of his existence. A definition of who he was and all of a sudden it was bang, gone. It was like 'My God, they've taken away who I am.' "

The Rolling Stones rejection, coming so soon after Regina Cartwright's sexual one and coupled with the drugs he was taking, was the final straw, sending Graham over the edge and into a tailspin. For the first time in his life, he was unable to work and had trouble even thinking. Suicidal and desperate, he saw three separate psychiatrists, each of whom, in turn, refused to treat him after his abusive behavior.

"I have never in my life, ever, had any problem with just focusing," Graham said. "I'd go mad sometimes, but I never lost the ability to read the compass. If it was more than the Stones, I don't know what else it was.

"I had some trouble sleeping because I was out on the Amnesty tour and trying to do my work. There was so much pressure and I started taking Halcion which I didn't know was a killer. Then, right after the Stones thing happened, I went to see a psychiatrist. And if anybody would have told me somewhere down the line that you're going to someday sit down with a guy and talk to him about your problems, me? I don't talk to anybody. I know how to handle. I look in the mirror and I talk to me. Who's to say what it would have been like without him, but I went through a lot of pills—morning pills and midday pills, Prozacs and lithiums and classes and sessions and depressions. I checked myself into the clinic. I couldn't face anybody for a weekend."

"I was afraid of him when he took Prozac," recalled Regina Cartwright. "He became murderously manic."

For three months Graham was unable to function and stayed in a darkened room at Masada for days at a time taking drugs and becoming what he termed an "absolute TV junkie." He spent as much as six hours a day pouring out his heart to Regina Cartwright on the telephone in addition to writing desperately sad rambling letters to her about his "madness" and his "self-loathing."

"Dear Regina,

"Last night was the worst. Even I can't have these demons haunt me and not tell you—I'm going mad—I've tried and tried to explain that those problems have possessed me all my adult life before I met you—And you became my savior—I became a full man with you—I fulfilled your needs and mine as well . . ."

In another letter, twenty-four-pages long, written in 1988, Graham describes himself and Regina as "two misfits who love each other."

Bill Graham's final public humiliation was a *Rolling Stone* story claiming that he had carelessly let the $70 million Rolling Stones tour slip through his fingers. He felt he had been publicly branded a loser for the first time in his career and could not handle it at all.

NACPA executive director Ben Liss was so concerned about Graham that he wrote a personal letter to try to cheer him up. "I told Bill that this is what life is about," said Liss. "Sometimes you succeed and sometimes you don't. I told him, 'You've got to pick up and move on. You have so many talents and so much to offer.' "

Visiting his psychiatrist three times a week, Graham started to gain some insight into why his life had broken down and started coming to grips with his Halcion addiction.

"The crusher was the Stones decision," he said. "But then I realized what had led up to it. The fire, Live Aid, my relationships with women. It had already begun taking its toll during Amnesty International. My strength has always been confidence in myself and my faith in my abilities. But now I felt almost powerless."

Analysis showed him that he had never faced up to the serious personal problems left over from his tragic childhood. He began to confront his deeply buried "survivor's guilt" over his older sister Tolla who had died in Marseilles in 1941. And he began to see how his problems and insecurities had driven him into relentless work as an escape. Though he would never regain his old fire and passion, he slowly he began to rise out of his depression and start functioning again.

Much of Graham's healing process came from accepting and developing close bonds with his new daughter, Caitlin. Whenever he was in New York, he would visit Regina Cartwright and act the doting father, determined to give her the early fatherly love his two sons had been deprived of. He also supported Regina and Caitlin monthly with a personal check of $13,000 to cover all their expenses.

"She was his deep, dark secret," Cartwright said. "But he insisted he be involved in every single major or minor decision in her life."

Although Regina never allowed him to share her bed after the birth, Graham still did not give up hoping that she would change her mind and resume their sexual relationship. Now nearly sixty, Graham sent Regina a cassette tape of his favorite Santana song *"I Love You Much Too Much"* over and over again, with the message, "This is us."

The man who unseated Bill Graham as the leading promoter in the concert business in 1989 began his career by starting a strip joint in Ottawa called Pandora's Box. The club, which was constantly being busted by police in 1967 for permitting an immoral act in public, made nineteen-year-old Michael Cohl and his four partners $100,000 in its first six months. Almost every day the girls would get busted, and Cohl, who then had hair down to his waist, would bail them out of jail at noon and have them back onstage performing by five o'clock.

Cohl considered his strip club experience a "confidence builder," and after selling the club fifteen months later he used his share of the profits to move into concert promotion in the early 1970s. His first show, with country singer Buck Owens at Toronto's Maple Leaf Garden, bombed and Cohl lost his shirt. But the young Canadian refused to give up, borrowing money from friends for his next show, which was called Beggar's Banquet, with Poco, Sha Na Na and Melanie. That show was a success, and Cohl was on his way.

In 1973 he ousted Toronto's top promoter Martin Onrot and gained control of the Maple Leaf Garden by forming a partnership with Bill Ballard, the son of the stadium's majority owner. With a third partner,

David Wolinsky, they formed Concert Productions International Inc. (CPI). Unlike Graham, Cohl decided not to compete with his fellow promoters and formed alliances instead to set up national tours through Canada. "Michael thinks like a chess player, always a thought ahead of someone else," says a former employee.

By the early 1980s, Cohl was the Canada's premier promoter, producing live music concerts, plays, and sporting events. He then started down a Canadian path parallel to Bill Graham's in the United States. Using Graham's Winterland as a model, Cohl entered the lucrative merchandising arena in 1984, buying an established company called Brockum for $3.4 million (U.S.). He immediately started chasing Winterland by offering more and more money to rock stars for their licensing rights.

Michael Cohl became a major player when Labatt Breweries bought into his company for $25 million, creating the much more powerful BCL—Ballard, Cohl, Labatt. Explained Labatt Brewing Group president, Sid Oland, "We see the entertainment business as a communications business. When you grow up in the beer business, you become involved in the communications business. You need communications, like advertising, to sell beer."

When Graham was snubbed by the Stones, he declared an unofficial war on both the band and its new promoter Michael Cohl, deliberately playing up the beer connection. Hell-bent on revenge, he embarked on a one-man public-relations battle against them, bad-mouthing them in the media and criticizing the staging of the tour at every opportunity.

"I do think the precedent set by the Rolling Stones is very negative," Graham told the industry trade paper *Amusement Business*. "It took away from many promoters a relationship and a share in the money. Many had to work for much less. Another party gets a share."

Some local promoters were furious when they were initially offered a flat fee of $25,000 by Cohl to stage the Rolling Stones in their markets. Eventually, however, they were able to negotiate separate deals.

Boston promoter Don Law angrily rejected the show offered to him, allowing his rival Frank Russo to move in. "We're just very happy that CPI has chosen to include promoters across the country as part of the deal," Russo said. "We have negotiated out own deal with Michael, and CPI was very fair to us."

As a consolation prize, the Stones had made Graham their local promoter for their two shows at the Oakland Stadium, but he absolutely refused to take a backseat in his home turf to Michael Cohl's BCL, and defiantly billed it as a Bill Graham show. "It is important to me that others are not credited for our work," Graham explained to *Performance.* "We haven't been in this business for twenty-five years so that others can take bows that belong to our staff. We don't work for someone else."

The Stones were the hottest ticket in America—TicketMaster computers were hardly able to keep up with the incredible demands. In San Francisco the 112,000 $28.50 tickets (with a $5.50 TicketMaster surcharge) were snapped up in under five hours. Tickets were selling on the black market for as much as $450.

Graham went to extraordinary lengths to place his personal stamp on the San Francisco shows and give the impression they were Bill Graham concerts. He mounted a high-profile campaign to stop people standing on chairs during the shows, spending $6,000 of his own money to outfit every usher and security guard in his company-designed T-shirt with a caricature of the Stones and the message "Please don't stand on the seats."

Applauding Graham's campaign, *Amusement Business* magazine's Linda Deckard wrote, "That's what Graham calls 'promoting.' He considers BCL's role that of an agent for this tour." Asked by Deckard if he would have paid $70 million for the Stones like Cohl, Graham answered cavalierly, "It's not an impressive figure. We figured it's about the profit from 2.7 billion T-shirts. I would have put up that kind of money."

However, careful not to alienate Mick Jagger and The Rolling Stones completely, Graham built a special backstage tent complete with incense, candles and four beautiful masseuses, labeling it "Stones Crew Only." "That was my own dollar," he boasted later.

When Michael Cohl brought the Rolling Stones to the Oakland Stadium for the first show he felt himself walking into a "high noon" situation with Graham. "It had the potential to be nice and friendly or icy cold and strange," he said. "I went to the stadium determined to be friendly and civil to Bill, and I hoped that was going to be his attitude. I wasn't going to criticize him, and I assumed it was going to be civil and businesslike. But Bill never even came in the dressing room and couldn't even bring himself to say, 'Hi.' "

At one point in the concert, Cohl found himself face to face with Graham in a room. "It was one of those icy cold situations," he remembers. "I'm four feet away, and I looked him straight in the face and said, 'Hi, Billy, how are you?' And he looked away. So I didn't force it. I got the message. We'll let everyone else deal with it. Good-bye."

During the first night's show in San Francisco, Bill Graham wouldn't talk to Mick Jagger and Keith Richards, but he finally came to the dressing room on the second night to wish them good luck.

"It was sour grapes and it was really bizarre," said Cohl. "I kept reading his fantastic quotes [in the press]. I found it somewhat shocking when he says things like, 'Well they went with the calculator.' Which is what he always used to call me. The abacus. At the end of the day, I wasn't a fan of Bill Graham. He doesn't know me from Adam. He wouldn't know if I was married or not, have any kids or if I spend forty-eight hours a week working for charities. He doesn't know anything about me. He frankly doesn't know anything whatsoever about my business practice. But in his own narrow-minded view of the world, he thought he knew a lot."

A couple of weeks before the Rolling Stones were due to bring in their landmark Steel Wheels tour without Bill Graham, a major earthquake hit the Bay Area. To Graham the mammoth quake was the epiphany that helped him refocus. He toured Watsonville, which had suffered some of the worst damage, and, looking at the young people who had been made homeless, was reminded of his own exodus from the Nazis.

"Those are the faces that you see on the refugees," he told *Performance* magazine's Jane Cohen. "I had this pain in my stomach that I couldn't understand, didn't understand. We were all in the office. We were all safe. No major damage—except that I had lost the Fillmore and another building.

"Later I went running in the country and I realized what it was. Some of us at one time or another think about, 'Oh, my God, I'm going to die. I'm in an avalanche, in a car wreck or I'm in a war.' But I realized the thing that got stuck in my gut was the fact that moment at 5:04 P.M. all of us in Northern California thought about dying."

Fired with a new lust for life, Graham started organizing a massive three-city benefit for victims of the earthquake. The quake hit just before the Rolling Stones were due to play the Oakland Stadium, and it was touch and go whether the quake-damaged area would be safe in time for the Stones' show.

"Thank God the Stones were able to play their dates as scheduled," Graham said. "Afterwards I was able to get my thoughts back into full gear onto the Earthquake Relief benefit."

Taking back command of his company, Graham mobilized his troops to organize three separate concerts. They had just two weeks to get their technical crews together, get waivers from the FCC for the live TV and radio coverage from KQED public radio and television stations, and agreement from the notoriously difficult labor unions.

Nearly fifty acts agreed to play, including Crosby, Stills, Nash & Young, Bonnie Raitt, Los Lobos, the Steve Miller Band, Aaron Neville, Grace Slick, and Paul Kantner. Graham used his clout to persuade more than 100 companies in the Bay Area to provide their services free with full union support, and announced he was personally donating $1 million from his own pocket to match the first $1 million raised from the event.

But when the *San Francisco Chronicle* refused to donate free advertising to the cause, Graham publicly took the newspaper to task in the trade magazine *Performance*. "The only sad thing, which is a reminder of what greed is all about, the only newspaper in San Francisco refused to take an ad. The *San Francisco Chronicle*, of which we've been the biggest client for twenty-five years, insisted on charging us $14,800 for two ads. That's what a monopoly is all about—no feelings—no compassion."

Following his coup of persuading Marlon Brando to appear at the SNACK concert and Jack Nicholson at Live Aid, Graham now invited the legendary comedian Bob Hope to come to Earthquake Relief. Hope decided to appear at the Cow Palace show after joking from a TV studio that it would be hard for him to leave his golf game.

"When he walked onto the stage at Oakland, you'd think it was water dropped on a very thirsty mass," Graham remembered. "They adored him."

Backstage, even the rock stars were in awe of Hope and insisted on having their photographs taken with him. David Crosby was so shocked when he suddenly found himself in front of his childhood hero he gasped, "Bob Fuckin' Hope" as he shook the octogenarian comedian's hand, prompting Graham Nash to quip, "Hope and Crosby—together on the same stage again."

"Onstage he couldn't speak for five minutes, they applauded him so loudly," Graham said. "He told the public he was thrilled to be there to receive their affection. He walked off the stage. He went backstage and he said, 'Can I see you in the dressing room?' He takes me in and closes the door, grabs my arm and he said, 'I'm eighty-six years old. I've been in this business for sixty-four years. I have never felt this warm and close with my audience. I have never felt such love and devotion. I can't tell you, Bill, how thrilled I am to be here.' And Bob Hope has pretty much seen everything. Then we took him back to the airport and he says, 'Let me see, I don't know how to say this, but I hope to say it right—where's our next gig?' "

Earthquake Relief raised more than $2 million, including Graham's donation, and areas were set up at each of the three shows where food and clothes could be donated.

Bill Graham may have been left down for the count by the Rolling Stones, but after Earthquake Relief he was back on his feet, fighting and lashing out at friends and enemies alike.

17

His Last Bow

In July 1990, Bill Graham launched a venomous attack on the Rolling Stones during a speech to music industry leaders at the New Music Seminar in New York. Without mentioning them by name, he accused the Rolling Stones of "being involved with the morally corrupt" and condoning the legal scalping of millions and millions of dollars' worth of tickets.

Graham's speech formed the hub of a major expose in *Rolling Stone* magazine about the $300-million-a-year ticket scalping business headlined "Ticket Rip-off—While Music Business Insiders Make Millions from Various Scalping Scams, The Fans Are Getting Screwed." The story attacked the Steel Wheels tour and used it to illustrate ticket scalping. Written by reporter Michael Goldberg, who had also penned Bill Graham's twentieth anniversary tribute in *Rolling Stone* in 1985, the story alleged that BCL deliberately held thousands of tickets from shows that somehow found their way into scalpers' hands. BCL was accused of withholding the best tickets for a Canadian company called Event Transportation Systems (ETS) which arranged travel packages to Stones' concerts. Widely quoted throughout the story, Graham announced he was starting a group called Californians Against Ticket Scalping to campaign for federal legalization against scalping.

Replying to the *Rolling Stone* article in *Performance* magazine, BCL accused "unnamed individuals" of planting the story because of sour grapes at not being involved in the Rolling Stones' tour and strongly questioned its credibility.

A few weeks before the annual meeting of the NACPA, just after *Performance* magazine anointed Michael Cohl as its promoter of the year for his work with the Steel Wheels tour, Bill Graham shocked the concert world by announcing he was leaving the association. In a stinging attack on most of his fellow promoters, singling out John Scher and Michael Cohl, Bill Graham finally seemed to have gone too far.

Describing the Steel Wheel's tour as a "sad commentary" on how his colleagues constantly stab each other in the back for profit, he said he could no longer belong to the promoters' organization, NACP.

"Some kick each other, maim others, hurt others emotionally," railed Graham.

Singling out his arch enemy John Scher for special mention, Graham accused him of deliberately sabotaging his son David's band Blues Traveler on a New York tour for revenge.

"There are some promoters in our business who want to beat, they want to conquer," he stormed. "They've got Napoleonic attitudes."

Then Graham rounded on almost everyone in the concert business, complaining that too few had called to offer him sympathy after his offices had been destroyed in the earthquake.

"They're not worthy of my friendship," he raged to *Performance* magazine's Jane Cohen. "When there's no earthquake they try to burn me and when there is an earthquake they don't care about me. I feel very sad for those people. They're not worthy of my sitting next to them."

But despite all Graham's posturing and complaining, the Rolling Stones 1989–90 tour of North America, Japan, and Europe broke all records, drawing 6.2 million people to 110 shows and grossing $250 million. Some 3 million fans went to 60 North American shows, generating $90 million in ticket sales alone. There was a valuable sponsorship deal with Budweiser as well as the sale of TV rights for a pay-per-view special of the final concert in Atlantic City for a further $7 million and a Fox TV network special. But the real money came from merchandising, which generated a reported $40 million and helped take Michael Cohl's cut somewhere between $12 and $15 million from the North American portion of the tour, easily breaking Bill Graham's biggest take for a tour and making Cohl the new number-one promoter.

The savvy Canadian promoter took merchandising to a new peak by creating the Rolling Stones Rockware, a line of clothing manufactured and sold by Brockum, a company Cohl had built up to be Winterland's biggest rival. Designed by British designer Lance Yates with input from Mick Jagger and Charlie Watts, the designer-style collections featured the band's famous tongue logo (designed by Andy Warhol) on T-shirts, bandannas, sweatshirts, tank tops, jams, and a leather jacket (which retailed for $450).

"The Stones have been a breakthrough in merchandising," said Allen LeWinter, Brockum's vice president of sales and marketing. "We're aiming one collection to the fans who've grown up with the Stones such as classic T-shirts, etcetera and another group is aimed at the twelve- to eighteen-year-olds, including jams and all-over printed T-shirts."

The collections were bought by major department store chains Macy's and J. C. Penney's, which built in-store Rolling Stones boutiques featuring a video of the band in "active wear for the rock life-style." Many felt that the ultraslick merchandising campaign was an insult to rock 'n' roll. *New York Newsday* labeled the Steel Wheels corporate support as "crass, even by today's standards." Defending the Stones, Keith Richards maintained, "I don't see how a piece of fabric hurts the music. You don't have to buy a T-shirt, but I don't mind making a bit on the side. I've got a large family to support."

But all the criticism over the tour's exploitation was soon forgotten once the Rolling Stones strutted out onstage to play better than they had for years with a newfound fire and energy. The critics unanimously praised the brilliance of the Stones, and as the concerts got better and more successful, Bill Graham became angrier and more vocal in his criticism.

The tour's production coordinator, Michael Ahern, who had started his career at the Fillmore East, said that even Bill Graham could not control how the Rolling Stones performed. "They are the Rolling Stones and without him they performed even better than they did with him in 1981," he said. "Not getting the Rolling Stones probably wasn't nearly as upsetting to him as having the tour be really successful," said Ahern. "If the tour had failed, it probably wouldn't have bothered him a bit."

Bill Graham was still passionately idealistic for the sixties, and it was an idealism that led him to embark on a brand-new career in Hollywood. In 1989, before his disappointment with the Stones, Graham returned to Hollywood as a big-time movie producer after using his influence and connections to put a proposed feature film on Jim Morrison and The Doors back on track. Graham was first asked in 1983 to act as a go-between between the estates of the singer and of Morrison's late girlfriend, Pamela Courson, which were both withholding permission from the project. After smoothing things out, Graham decided to get involved in what he envisaged as an uplifting story of the idealistic 1960s seen through the story of The Doors. He put up $50,000 of his own money and become joint partners with BGP president, Nick Clainos, and fledging Israeli producer Sasha Harari and hired three-time Oscar winner Oliver Stone to direct. But after the movie was finished and Graham saw Stone's focus on the dark side of rock 'n' roll as embodied by Morrison, he disowned it. "Creatively, it was probably the biggest disappointment of my career," said Graham, who got billing as the 1989 film's producer. "I made a drastic mistake in not challenging the choice of director."

Calling Stone's film "sensationalistic" and "exaggerated," Graham attacked the director for not having any affinity or respect for the sixties and blamed himself. "I'm just sorry I was weak at the time," said Graham, explaining that he had selected Stone in the midst of his depression. "I wasn't as strong-minded or as strong-willed as I usually am about any project of that scope. I made a mistake.

"I don't mean to be harsh, but the fabrication hurt me. It made Jim Morrison and the group out to be totally gone. That once he achieved some fame he was gone ninety percent of the time. No. Rarely was he uncontrollable. What we didn't get was the joy and the hope of those times and today's youth, through that movie, will not get what I hoped they'd get through that picture."

In early 1990, director Barry Levinson, who had first met with Graham to discuss directing *The Doors,* was casting his new film, *Bugsy,* a movie about gangster Bugsy Siegel and the creation of Las Vegas starring Warren Beatty.

"It's a very strange thing," said Levinson. "I was looking at a picture of Lucky Luciano, and there was one particular shot that reminded me of Bill. And he doesn't look like Lucky Luciano, but this one particular shot from this angle just reminded me of Bill Graham."

Levinson asked Graham to fly to Hollywood and read for the role but was not overly impressed with his performance and asked the promoter to go home, learn the lines, and become more comfortable with the part. Disillusioned with the music business and now devoting most of his time to organizing charity events, Graham saw a new career in movies opening for him as he neared sixty—a second chance to achieve his lifetime dream of being a movie star.

But when he started rehearsing his part with his new girlfriend, Melissa Gold, he found he could not remember lines. "They were scary, scary days," Graham said. "I sat up there with Melissa and realized that I had no retentive memory."

Graham confided his fears to his old friend Peter Coyote at a San Francisco fund-raiser for the Holocaust Oral History Project. "He was horrified," remembered Coyote. "He hadn't acted in thirty years."

Coyote suggested Graham take acting lessons to prepare him for his role and put him in contact with, Harold Guskin, a professional acting teacher in New York.

"Bill was perfect casting for Lucky Luciano," says Guskin. "He was charming, interesting, and brilliant. After I got to know him, I said, 'I know you're well respected, but I have a feeling that you know what the killer part of Lucky Luciano is all about.' And he laughed. He's a tough guy."

As he prepared for the role, carefully researching Luciano and organized crime, Graham began identifying with the gangster. "There were distinct similarities," said Graham, who had Guskin move into Masada for two weeks of intensive rehearsals.

Graham and Luciano both had arrived in America as young children and had lived in ethnic areas where they learned the rules of the street in order to survive. Where Graham gambled with the other kids for pocket money, young Charles Luciano ran a protection racket, charging the Jewish kids a penny a day.

"He finally came across this one guy who wasn't gonna pay, and he started beating him up." said Graham. "It was Meyer Lansky. And he couldn't believe this guy fought back, and said, 'Holy shit. Come on my side.'

"My first memory of life in America was getting my head kicked in for being a Jew. Not having any protection."

But Graham was especially intrigued by the close parallels between the inner workings of his company and Luciano's organized crime syndicate. Said Graham, "There was one thread that runs through: his relationship to the people around him. That fascinated me. That with the inside circle, once you got in his *famiglia* through all the years, nobody fucks with anybody. It's tough enough out there. In here, no keys, no locks, it's open, it's just pure, and it's very tight and strong. If anybody inside fucks with anybody else on the inside, Charlie stops it. Charlie doesn't allow it.

"I can honestly tell you that that's exactly the way I run the company. I don't use brutality, but there's some strong energy that I put out. There are times I'd like to be looked at as a benevolent dictator in this company, which I try and run very much as a commune. I have no partners and I get the most. The others live well, but not as well as me."

The first of Graham's two key scenes comes when his character Lucky Luciano loses his temper with Bugsy Siegel for being over budget in the construction of Las Vegas's first casino. In order to get the scene right and tap into his rage, Guskin told Graham to remember the anger he'd felt at the Fillmores when an artist had arrived late for a gig.

"He suddenly opened up," said Guskin. "All of a sudden he was roaring and I thought, 'Jesus, he's really back there.' Then I realized that rage was with him all the time, just below the surface, and probably popped up daily. And he'd go at you and then I'd notice that he'd look around to make sure that he hadn't actually hurt anybody. There was nothing vicious, but that rage was really there. I think that was one of the things that made him so powerful and anytime he wanted to, he could just tap into it, and I'm sure it took over eventually even when he didn't want it to. I think he saw it as his weapon."

When Graham flew to Hollywood in his personal jet, he was delighted to find he had a star dressing room, with his name on the door, right between Warren Beatty's and Ben Kingsley's rooms. But despite his outside bravado, he was scared to death of falling on his face in such distinguished acting company and actually got stage fright for the first time in his life.

"He was physically sick because of nerves on the first day of filming," said Guskin. "Warren saw what was happening and came running over to Bill and was very deferential. Warren really treated him like he was the man."

The complicated scene in which Graham had a part takes place during a top-level meeting of crime bosses. It is one long, continuous moving shot around a big table as a furious Luciano calls for Bugsy's execution. "This was the kind of shot you just couldn't set up," said Guskin, who watched the filming from an off-the-set vantage point. "The camera was moving and Bill had to eat his food and talk in one long monologue. It could totally throw you. Barry explained the setup, and I'm watching Bill go, 'Oh, gee. How am I going to get through this?'

"Warren kept talking to him about how to deal with everything. He said, 'You move here and you think about the food and don't worry about the lines. Just think about the food and the lines will take care of themselves.'

"He actually worked him through the whole thing. It was a beautiful gesture. Warren and Bill just worked the scene out together. Barry Levinson backed off and let them do it and then did the final touches. I think Warren had enormous respect for Bill."

Levinson said Graham had truly proved his excellence as an actor by carrying the scene. "He was right on the money," Levinson said. "We didn't have to do a lot of takes or try to piece it together later. Bill had that thing where he really knows how to control the room and to control people. He could just suddenly take charge."

One night after filming, Graham told Levinson about his early days in New York and his love of the Latin music clubs and the mambo. He suggested that Levinson use the music and dance as background for a pivotal scene where Lucky Luciano throws a big party in New York Harbor to celebrate his deportation. Levinson loved the idea and invited Graham to dance the mambo for the scene. A delighted Graham agreed on condition that the studio fly in his friend and regular dance partner Carmen (Cuca) Leon to perform with him.

"Bill called me up and as a joke asked me if I knew anyone who would be interested in dancing the mambo in *Bugsy* with him," remembered Leon, who first met the promoter ten years earlier through her cousin Michael Carabello, Santana's original drummer.

"I said, 'Excuse me! You're talking to her.' "

Graham's sensuous mambo scene with Leon took two hours to shoot and perfectly captured his love of Latin dance. "Bill was a great dancer. He was smooth and had a Fred Astaire air about him," said Leon, who used to be a professional dancer in New York. "It was his dream come true to be dancing the mambo for Hollywood. He was relentless. He wouldn't give up, and he danced with all his heart and soul. You can see it in his expressions in *Bugsy.*"

When he viewed the early rushes from *Bugsy* in the fall, Graham was thrilled by his performance. "He called me because he had seen a couple of his scenes while he was doing some loops and he was very excited," Levinson said. "We had a great conversation, and I remember that he was so pleased to see himself in a nice role in a movie. I think that Bill basically accomplished everything that we wanted in that role. He was able to provide the power so you could understand the strength of these people. You can never underestimate them. They're formidable.

"I think Bill would have made a terrific character actor. He certainly could have done a number of roles that not a lot of actors could handle. It's hard to say how great an actor he could have been, but he certainly had a real credibility and an interesting persona." When Bugsy was released in late 1991 Bill Graham's powerful performance was acclaimed by the critics.

During his two weeks of filming, Graham maintained his demanding business schedule, making sure that he attended every show he produced. To get him around the Bay Area, he had formed a corporate offshoot called Fillmore Express which boasted a helicopter and a company jet, both at Graham's disposal. He loved the power of having a helicopter at his personal disposal, and where other people would drive short distances, he would have pilot Steve "Killer" Kahn fly him. Masada became a regular landing pad for his helicopter, much to the annoyance of his neighbors, whose lives were being made a misery by the noisy takeoffs and landings at all hours of the day and night. Even his old Concord Hotel buddy Jack Levin pleaded with Graham to cut down on his flying, which he considered dangerous.

"One time he came with a fella named Killer, who he introduced as his pilot," Levin remembered. "I said, 'Billy, are you crazy flying with a guy called Killer!' I was always against him flying so much, so I used to say to him, 'You bought a plane, you're flying here, you're flying there. Aren't you big with driving?' "

Graham claimed flying was far safer than driving and used to tell Levin, "You hop in a plane and pssss—you're there."

In January 1991, when Graham turned sixty, he became very depressed and concerned that he was becoming old and his body was starting to fail him. Hardly suffering a day's illness in his life, he realized that he no longer had the strength of his youth and could not accept it.

"He was very upset," Regina Cartwright said. "It was a big thing to him, and he told me he was having trouble thinking and eating. I think it was the natural aging process and he was beginning to experience the slowdown that men get when they reach sixty."

Since his daughter's birth Graham had made a point of regularly visiting her in New York and had even invited Regina to bring Caitlin to stay with him in Masada in 1990. While they were there, a relaxed Graham fussed over his baby daughter and even brought her into his office one day to proudly show her off to the staff without admitting he was the father.

"Bill recognized his temperament in Caitlin, and they really became very close during our stay at Masada, said Cartwright. "He loved having a daughter and was making a real effort to let her know he was her daddy."

At the end of 1990, Bill Graham and his fellow concert promoters forecast a long cold winter freeze in the business as the country entered the worst recession since the 1930s. By the following summer, promoters from coast to coast were alarmed by falling ticket sales.

In June 1991 Graham was forced to cancel a major summer tour with the Jerry Garcia Band, the Allman Brothers Band and Crosby, Stills & Nash due to lack of interest.

"So much more of a worker's dollar goes toward a ticket these days," Graham lamented. "The bottom line is, 'Where am I going to put my bucks?' "

At the beginning of October, Bill Graham admitted business was off 30 percent to 40 percent from the year before. "This is the first bad year rock 'n' roll has ever had," Graham said. "Every major promoter in this business has made money for the last twenty-five years that I know of. I have never had a losing year, ever. The phenomena of rock 'n' roll has always been that somehow people found money to buy tickets. Somehow the recessive character of our country, this year, affected rock 'n' roll."

Graham laid the blame on sky-high ticket prices for driving away the kids who could not afford $100 for a couple of tickets. "The only way the price can come down is if the star and the superstar's prices come down. Who makes the final decision? The artist. We've had an amazingly difficult summer, and I'm going to do nothing but work harder than ever to convince artists, through their agents and managers, to charge us less so we can charge the public less."

There were fewer and fewer major tours available for promoters. The stakes became huge, with some unfortunate promoters losing millions of dollars on unsuccessful tours, including Whitney Houston's ill-fated 1991 tour.

Bill Graham now also pulling away from active promotion to concentrate more and more on staging benefits. He was also busy campaigning for his Californians Against Ticket Scalping organization. As the main backer of a bill to make ticket scalping illegal in California, he accompanied the Grateful Dead's Bob Weir and BASS-TicketMaster's Jerry Seltzer to address the California Senate Judiciary Committee in Sacramento on April 30, 1991. Before testifying, Graham didn't mince his words, telling reporters, "These guys are fucking the public."

After eloquent speeches from both Graham and Weir, a special amendment was introduced by a union group to deflect action away from the ticket scalpers and onto TicketMaster. The service charges levied by TicketMaster, now running at 25 percent or more, had become the grounds of a class-action lawsuit against the company, the allegations being that it "arbitrarily" fixed prices and that Bill Graham Presents received "secret rebates."

As the hearing suddenly turned against TicketMaster, Weir broke ranks with Graham and Seltzer to launching a stinging attack on Fred Rosen and TicketMaster, accusing them of using strong-arm tactics to stop The Grateful Dead from selling tickets to their devoted fans through the mail. "He's trying to crowd us out of the market," said Weir as he revealed that The Grateful Dead was planning to sue TicketMaster.

A couple of months later, San Francisco Senator Milton Marks's bill to cap service charges to 15 percent was defeated in its first committee hearing. Many saw it as the result of the behind-the-scenes power of Bill Graham calling in political favors.

"Bill Graham's name strikes terror into a lot of people who are involved in the legislature," said Senator Marks's legislative aide, Larry Morse. "It was impossible to move a piece of legislation over his objections."

In October 1991 Bill Graham had become secretly engaged to his new love, Melissa Gold, who had moved in to Masada. Melissa's former husband, the novelist Herbert Gold, ran into the couple at a party given by Norman Mailer at Tosca in San Francisco and had an emotional talk with his longtime friend Graham.

"They were having a love affair," said Gold, who has three children from his marriage to Melissa. "I talked to Bill about her, and I know he cared about her. He was going through a bad time, and I think that was appealing to Melissa in some way. She was a helping person, and she was generous with her desire. If she saw people that were suffering, she wanted to do something if she could. I wished them luck."

With his impending marriage to Melissa, Graham had also decided to move Regina Cartwright back to San Francisco with Caitlin so he could be closer to his daughter as she grew up. He offered to buy her a house, provide a maid, and pay all expenses if she agreed. When she refused, he became angry, giving her an ultimatum: either move west by April 1, 1992, or he would seek custody of Caitlin when he married Melissa and cut off all Cartwright's financial support.

"It was his way of punishing me," said Regina. "I wasn't going to live in his life-style and let my daughter be exposed to the world of rock 'n' roll like his sons had been. He said he still loved me and that I was the only woman for him and wanted us to be together. I knew he was marrying Melissa, and when I told him how pleased I was, he got really angry. He just wouldn't ever leave me alone."

Looking back over his life in a poignantly revealing interview at

Masada with journalist Roger Trilling on a beautiful fall day in late September, Graham speculated on what he might have done if he had not fallen into rock promotion.

"If I had my life to live over, there are one or two things I've thought about," Graham said. "I would have studied differently and tried to get into politics in one of two jobs: to be the mayor of New York City, from the printing strike, to the subway strike, to the garbage strike, it's a hell of a life. I could possibly have done some good things to stop, what is to me, the beginning of the decay of the capital of the world, New York. I've always thought about being mayor of New York because what a way to go out—because you can never win, you can't beat it, but what a challenge.

"And the other job would have been to get into politics and my platform would be very simple: to have Northern California secede from Southern California. We are two different planets. You *feel* things up here and you *feel* things down there. We live in two different worlds. Our goals are different.

"If anyone were to say, 'What is the basic difference between the sixties and the nineties?' Most of us had hope then. Now most of us may have *individual* hope, but for the planet? It's a survivalist state of mind. That's the big difference."

Like millions, the good-hearted sixties clown Wavy Gravy heard about the helicopter death of his longtime friend Bill Graham through news reports on early Saturday morning, October 26, 1991.

"Bill Graham dead. It didn't compute," said Wavy. "I always believed he was invincible. That somehow he would kick death's ass—'Yo, death, outta here.' And death would sheepishly shuffle off in quest of more meek and mortal fare.

"I turned on the television and switched to CNN, where the impossible imposed itself upon the pulsing blue dot. Bill's demise seemed to be big news. The CNN announcer described the high winds and heavy rains which caused Bill's helicopter to crash into an electro tower. An image of the wreck intractably in the side of the tower burned into my brain as the disembodied voice of the announcer droned on, 'All parties were instantly electrocuted. Bill Graham, his pilot and friend Steve 'Killer' Kahn, and close companion Melissa Gold.' At that moment of impact several nearby towns were left without power. The date was October 25, 1991. Bill Graham was sixty years old."

As news of his death filtered through America, millions of rock fans and the entire American music business fell into shock and disbelief.

The *San Francisco Examiner* devoted most of its Sunday newspaper to Graham tragedy. "If Elvis Presley was the king, Bill Graham, the nonpareil Bay Area music impresario who died in a helicopter crash Friday night, was certainly the emperor," read its front-page story. "Rock 'n' roll, which has a cruel tradition of taking its royalty prematurely, has lost its most powerful reigning monarch."

Calling Bill Graham "The embodiment of the modern San Franciscan," Mayor Art Agnos of San Francisco paid tribute. "He had a deep reverence for our history and tradition and unlimited energy for contributing to the betterment of our community and the entire world."

A week later, more than 300,000 rock fans paid homage to Bill Graham at the first free concert in Golden Gate Park in more than a decade. The Grateful Dead, Santana, and Crosby, Stills, Nash & Young were among the bands who turned up to play at Graham's final concert, which was organized by Bill Graham Presents.

Carlos Santana, who described Graham as his "best friend and brother," told the audience how the promoter had called him the night before he died, saying, "Stay well, my friend." "Just the way he said it," Santana said. "Maybe his mind didn't know, but something inside him did."

Comedian Robin Williams mused on what Graham would do in heaven with the array of legendary musicians he would be able to work with.

"I wonder if Bill's in heaven organizing a show," asked Williams to the delight of the audience. "He's up there saying, 'Hey, Elvis, you're on next.' "

Epilogue

In the months after Bill Graham's death it was business as usual at Bill Graham Presents amidst much industry speculation over its chances of long term survival without its mighty leader. It was left to Paul Kantner to succinctly sum up the situation when he observed how the Macedonian empire had collapsed after the death of Alexander the Great.

Stepping onto the BGP throne, Nicholas Clainos, who had been appointed the executor of Bill Graham's $35 million estate, moved fast to assume complete control. Graham's eldest son, David, now 24, found himself relegated to making public appearances and giving speeches that recalled his father's achievements. In January 1992, David and his shy sixteen-year-old half-brother, Alex, both flew to New York to attend their father's induction into the Rock 'n' Roll Hall of Fame and accepted his posthumous award.

Within weeks of his death, Bill Graham's long-awaited autobiography in collaboration with author Robert Greenfield, which was already six years in the making, was placed on the front burner with Nicholas Clainos personally renegotiating the contract terms with publisher Doubleday.

But despite its "show must go on" attitude and the company's ambitious announcement of plans to build a huge new $20 million 30,000 seat amphitheater in Benicia, California, all was not well within the Graham organization. BGP was coming apart at the seams as top executives vied for power. Eventually the private squabbling spilled onto the pages of the *San Francisco Chronicle* in April 1992 when pop music critic Joel Selvin reported an acrimonious staff meeting where fifteen executives suddenly announced a planned buy-out of the company from the Graham estate. In his column, Selvin quoted a mystified David Graham, who had been groomed by his father to one day take over the company, as commenting, "I don't understand the legality of this."

At one point in the chaotic meeting someone asked who was now the president of Bill Graham Presents, prompting two executives to reply in unison,"I am." The meeting finally ended with an executive (unnamed in Selvin's column) being led from the room after he became infuriated by the barrage of employee questions.

But the top management at BGP moved fast to exert damage control. Vice-president Stan Feig circulated an internal memo urging all staff to complain to the *Chronicle* about the story. After a quarter of the 45-strong company voiced their anger to the *Chronicle*, Selvin printed some of their comments in his column the following week, wryly noting, "Obviously there is no shortage of unity among the troops."

But BGP could not muzzle its malcontents forever. On May 24, 1993, at Marin County Superior Court, fifteen BGP executives led by Nicholas Clainos staged an attempted buy-out of the organization worth $4.75 million. Ironically, and quite legally, Clainos as the Graham executor was also officially the seller of the company he was attempting to buy. Under the terms of the offer agreement David and Alex Graham would share a ten percent interest in the new company with an option to buy a further ten percent.

Now moving into the open with her own bid for the company, top BGP executive Queenie Taylor, who had worked for Bill Graham for almost twenty years, tried unsuccessfully to stage her own buy-out with financing from Bill Graham's two sons. When they refused to cooperate, Taylor was left out in the cold. Commented Joel Selvin, "It looks as if deposed Bill Graham Presents executive Queenie Taylor will play thorn in the side to her former colleagues."

Taylor's reply was to challenge BGP by setting up her own company in direct competition with BGP and booking acts at the Maritime Hall on Freemont Street. But she was aced out of the game when her old company simply outbid her when she tried to book Jellyfish and X for her first two shows. Undaunted, Taylor defiantly pledged to stage her own 1993 New Year's Eve rock 'n' roll celebration in San Francisco.

As 1993 draws to an end, the future of Bill Graham Presents looks uncertain. On the sidelines some of the world's largest entertainment conglomerates are flexing their muscles ready to buy the company and absorb it into their own faceless multinational empires, something Bill Graham would have abhorred.

Notes and Sources

General

Most of the research for this book was gathered through personal interviews. The list of those interviewed may be found in the acknowledgments.

My greatest sources of primary research material were the New York Public Library and the Lincoln Center Libraries. I also received invaluable assistance from the archives of the YIVO Institute for Jewish Research in New York, especially from Leo Greenbaum and Marek Web.

The following books were used for secondary research. In places where books have been either reprinted or updated, I list the most recent copyright in the edition consulted for research.

BRANDELIUS, JERILYN LEE. *The Grateful Dead Album.* New York: Warner Books, 1989.

BROMBERG, CRAIG. *The Wicked Way of Malcolm McLaren.* New York: Harper & Row, 1988.

DALTON, DAVID. *Janis.* London: Calder & Boyars and Nel, 1972.

DAVIS, R. G. *The San Francisco Mime Troupe: The First Ten Years.* Palo Alto, Cal.: Ramparts Press.

DRAPER, ROBERT. *The Rolling Stone Story.* Mainstream Publishing, Great Britain, 1990.

DUNPHY, EAMON. *Unforgettable Fire.* New York: Warner Books, 1988.

ELIOT, MARC. *Rockonomics.* New York: Citadel Press, 1993.

FLIPPO, CHET. *Everybody Was Kung Fu Fighting.* New York: St. Martin's Press.

GELDOF, BOB and VALLELY, PAUL. *Is That It?"* New York: Ballantine, 1988.

GLEASON, RALPH J. *The Jefferson Airplane and the San Francisco Sound.* New York: Ballantine Books, 1969.

GRAHAM, BILL, and GREENFIELD, ROBERT. *Bill Graham Presents.* New York: Doubleday, 1992.

GRAVY, WAVY. *Something Good for a Change.* New York: St. Martin's Press, 1993.

GRUSHKIN, PAUL. *The Art of Rock.* Cross River Press, 1987.

McDonough, Jack. *San Francisco Rock.* San Francisco: Chronicle Books, 1985.
Marsh, Dave. *Born to Run.* Omnibus Press, 1987.
Monk, Noel E., and Guterman, Jimmy. *Twelve Days on the Road. London: Sidgwick & Jackson, 1992.*
Passman, Donald. *All You Need to Know About the Music Business.* New York: Simon & Schuster, 1991.
Perry, Charles. *The Haight Ashbury: A History.* New York: Vintage Books, 1985.
Phillips, John. *Papa John.* New York: Dell Books, 1987.
Smith, Joe. *Off the Record: An Oral History of Popular Music.* New York: Warner Books.
Spitz, Bob. *Barefoot in Babylon.* New York: Norton, 1989.
NME—Rock 'N' Roll Years. London: Hamlyn Books, 1992.
Shapiro, Harry, and Glebbeck, Caesar. *Electric Gypsy.* London: Heinemann.
Taylor, Derek. *It Was Twenty Years Ago Today.* London: Bantam Press, 1987.

Notes by Chapter.

PRELUDE

The phone call to Regina Cartwright came from my interviews with Regina Cartwright.

Information that Bill Graham had gone to the Concord Pavilion to make peace with Bob Brown is from interview with Bob Grossweiner.

The warning to Steve Kahn not to fly and his final conversation with Concord air controller Steve Ingebretson came from the National Transportation Safety Board Accident, File # LAX-92-A029.

Background on the backstage dinner and conversation is from article in the *San Francisco Chronicle,* 10/28/91.

Conversation in the car back to the helicoptor is from van driver Dan Johnson of the Concord Pavilion.

Expert analysis of the final flight is from Tom McConnel of the Valleja Helicopter Rescue.

Information on his future discussions for a TV show is from Roger Trilling's interview with Bill Graham for *Details,* October 1991.

ONE. BEGINNINGS—GETTING TO THE U.S.A.

Background on Bill Graham's early childhood came from Foster Home Bureau files and a translation of the Escort Notes, 9/26/41. I also made use of an interview with Bill Graham in Jack McDonough's *San Francisco Rock* for additional material on his early life.

Graham's stealing expeditions in Paris and his witnessing the Battle of Paris came from the escort's notes in the Foster Home Bureau files.

"Everybody moved south . . ." Roger Trilling's interview with Bill Graham for *Details,* October 1991.

Details of Tolla's death came from my interviews with Regina Cartwright.

Physical descriptions of Graham are from his temporary passport issued by the American Friends Service Committee, 8/10/41.

The story about the stray bomb hitting the convent he was in came from *Performance* magazine, 12/22/89.

Background on *Serpo Pinta* voyage and his reception at dockside came from standard operating procedures laid down for German refugee children by the Foster Home Bureau.

Details of Graham's difficulties in adapting to Pleasantville and his wild behavior are from a letter dated October 6, 1941, from the Foster Home Bureau's Director of Placements Lotte Marcuse to her superior Elsie L. Heller.

Information about his adoption by the Ehrenreichs is from a letter from Marcuse to Robert Lang, executive director of the U.S. Committee for the Care of European Children.

The payment to the Ehrenreichs of $25 a month and the ensuing rivalry between Billy and Roy Ehrenreich comes from Foster Home Bureau Quarterly Supervisory Reports.

"To them I wasn't a Jew . . ." is from *Chabad Journal,* 1983.

Statement that there was no chance of finding any of Graham's family alive is from a letter dated 11/15/44 from the Committee for the Care of European Children.

Information regarding Billy's tantrums and fits of anxiety and his psychiatric report are from the Foster Home Bureau Quarterly Supervisory Reports, 3/5/43 and 6/29/43, prepared by caseworker Marjorie Davis.

The decision not to take Billy away from the Ehrenreichs and placing him in the care of the authorities is from a Foster Home Bureau report, 1/4/49.

Background on his search for role models comes from Roger Trilling interview with Bill Graham for *Details,* October 1991.

Information on the search for his family came from reports from the Foster Home Bureau.

Details of Graham's early jobs are from a Foster Home Bureau report by caseworker Elaine Steinman, 12/2/47.

Graham's growth from "frightened little boy" to "friendly young man" is from USNA Summary, 1/4/49.

Details on Graham's pursuits at DeWitt Clinton High School are from the school's 1949 high school yearbook.

TWO. GOING OFF TO WAR

Information on Graham's embarrassment at earning $10 a week and details of job at Davidson's is from Foster Home Bureau report, 1/30/50.

Details about Graham's army court martial in Korea are from Roger Trilling's interview with Graham for *Details,* October 1991.

Story about Pearl's death when Alfred Ehrenreich told Graham that Roy was also adopted came from Graham interview in *Chabad Journal,* 1983.

Background on Alfred Ehrenreich remarrying and the acrimony between Graham, Roy, and their new stepmother is from an interview with Frank Ehrenreich.

"I guess you did not know . . ." Lotte Marcuse letter to Graham, 10/3/50.

Background information on Graham's days working at the Concord and his crap games is from interviews with Jack Levin and Irving Cohen.

"I organized the greatest crap games . . ." article in *Pacific Sun,* 6/26/75.

Information about Graham's studies with Lee Strasberg's Actor's Studio are from Roger Trilling's interview with Graham in *Details,* October 1990.

THREE. THE SAN FRANCISCO MIME TROUPE

Background information about Graham's time at Allis-Chalmers is from profile of Bill Graham headlined *"The Producer of the New Rock"* in the *New York Times Magazine,* 12/15/68.

Information on the San Francisco Mime Troupe operations, Graham's work and the Mime Troupe bust are from interviews with Peter Coyote, Jim Haynie and R.G. (Ronnie) Davis and also from Davis' book *The San Francisco Mime Troupe: The First Ten Years.*

Howard Hesseman's story about Bill Graham is from an interview for KSAN Radio's Fillmore special broadcast, 10/29/72.

Background on the Family Dog is from interviews with Chet Helms, Alton Kelly and Ralph J. Gleason's book *The Jefferson Airplane and the San Francisco Sound.*

Information on the first Family Dog dance is from Charles Perry's *The Haight Ashbury: A History.*

Graham's deal with Charles Sullivan to get the Fillmore for $45 a night came from interviews with Jim Haynie and Alton Kelly.

"The Mime Troupe Benefit . . ." is from *Rolling Stone's* 20th anniversary tribute to Bill Graham.

Interview with Paul Kantner about the First Mime Troup Benefit is from an article in the *San Francisco Chronicle/Examiner, 12/8/91.*

"We expected a few hundred people . . ." is from article in *Rolling Stone,* 8/23/80.

"Here were these filmakers . . ." is from Ralph J. Gleason's *The Jefferson Airplane and the San Francisco Sound.*

"What I saw was an adventure . . ." comes from *An Oral History of Popular Music* by Joe Smith.

The story of Graham sidestepping the Musicians Union is from interviews with Jim Haynie.

Graham's confrontation with Luria Castell is from Ralph J. Gleason's *The Jefferson Airplane and the San Francisco Sound.*

Background on the Trips Festival is taken from Charles Perry's *The Haight Ashbury: A History.*

"He found Himself . . ." is reprinted from Wes Wilson's *Off The Wall* magazine #2, 1991.

The Trips Festival critique by mr. jones is from the *Daily Cal,* 2/3/66.

Information about Graham finally taking over the Fillmore is from Ralph J. Gleason's *The Jefferson Airplane and the San Francisco Sound.*

FOUR. BIRTH OF THE FILLMORES

"What's their draw? . . ." comes from interview with Chris Brooks.

Background information about Graham's early lack of knowledge in rock music and his business methods comes from interviews with Chet Helms.

"We had unpleasant times . . ." Ralph J. Gleason's *The Jefferson Airplane and the San Francisco Sound.*

Background on the growth of the hippie scene and Bill Graham's battle to win a dance license for the Fillmore comes from Charles Perry's *The Haight Ashbury: A History* and Ralph J. Gleason's *The Jefferson Airplane and the San Francisco Sound.*

Information on the demands of the Musicians Union comes from interviews with Jim Haynie and Alton Kelly.

Background on Bill Graham's arrest at the Fillmore is from interviews with Jim Haynie and from Ralph J. Gleason's *The Jefferson Airplane and the San Francisco Sound.*

Description of Bonnie MacLean is from *The Art of Rock* by Paul Gruskin.

Information about the Fillmore's early finances and his skirting of fire regulations comes from interviews with Jim Haynie.

The comparison of the Avalon and the Fillmore as dancehalls is from an interview with Peter Albin of Big Brother and the Holding Company.

Accusations that Graham turned his Fillmore security force into a private army come from *KSAN*-Radio's Fillmore Tribute, 10/29/72.

Graham's early drug use is from interviews with Jim Haynie.

Information on Graham confiscating dope from dealers and giving it to musicians is from his interview with Roger Trilling for *Details,* October 1991.

Graham's ill-treatment of Janis Joplin is from interviews with Nick Gravenitis and Julius Karpen.

The story of Graham hiding in a closet to overhear what was being said about him is from interviews with Nick Gravenitis.

Background on the race riots that brought the National Guard into the Fillmore district is taken from Ralph J. Gleason's *The Jefferson Airplane and the San Francisco Sound.*

Information on the development of poster art is from interviews with Chet Helms, Wes Wilson, and Alton Kelly.

Wes Wilson's final poster lampooning Bill Graham as a snake holding a dollar sign between its teeth is Fillmore poster #62.

Bill Graham's negotiation with Matthew Katz is from Ralph J. Gleason's *The Jefferson Airplane and the San Francisco Sound.*

Graham's declining relationship with Jefferson Airplane during his management comes from KSAN-Radio's Fillmore Tribute, 10/29/72.

The story of Spencer Dryden's firing from the Jefferson Airplane is from an interview with Marty Balin.

FIVE. THE SUMMER OF LOVE

Background on the hippie scene in Haight Ashbury is from *The Haight Ashbury: A History* by Charles Perry.

"The burgeoning Howard Hughes of the dance scene," is from *The Rolling Stone Story.*

Information and background about Monterey comes from an interview with the festival's organizer and publicist Derek Taylor and his book *20 Years Ago Today.*

"There was a definite rivalry . . ." is from *Papa John* by John Phillips.

Insight into the backstage activities at Monterey comes from Marc Eliot's *Rockonomics* (Citadel Press, 1993).

Bill Graham's introduction to the early blues artists, his explanation of "draw," and his analysis of promotion being a "tough business," illustrated by the Ike and Tina Turner story is from his interview on KSAN-Radio's Fillmore Tribute, 10/29/72.

"I'm a New Yorker . . ." comes from *Jazz & Pop* magazine #8, 1969.

"Oh, he likes us now . . ." is from *Janis,* by David Dalton.

Graham's description of Janis Joplin and his story about the Charlatan's late arrival at his shows are from KSAN-radio's Fillmore Tribute, 10/29/72.

Graham's attitude to LSD comes from an interview in *Crawdaddy* magazine, May 1969.

"We thought he was a demented man . . ." is from KSAN-Radio's Fillmore Tribute, 10/29/72.

"The first people . . ." is from KSAN-Radio's Fillmore Tribute, 10/29/72.

The Jeff Beck story and Graham's treatment of the *Time* magazine reporter are taken from Bill Graham's interview on KSAN-Radio's Fillmore Tribute, 10/29/72.

"The flowers wilted . . ." is from *The Fillmore Movie.*

SIX. GETTING DOWN TO BUSINESS

Background on the O'Keefe concert arrangements is from interviews with Joshua White and John Morris.

Larry Magid's promoting history is from his profile in the *Philadelphia Inquirer,* 2/28/88.

Jack Boyle's setting up of Cellar Door is from a story in *Performance,* 3/10/89.

"I met Bill over a bowl of soup . . ." is from an article in *Performance* magazine, 2/7/92.

The New York *Daily News story on the early Fillmore East is dated 6/30/68.*

SEVEN. LAYING DOWN THE GROUND RULES

Bill Graham's interview with *Variety* is dated 12/13/67.

Grossman's "secret" visit to the Fillmore East is from *Rockonomics* by Marc Eliot (Citadel Press, 1993).

The explanation of the network of the early network of touring venues and background on Frank Barsalona and his setting up of Premier Talent comes from *Born to Run—The Bruce Springsteen Story* by Dave Marsh.

Information about the early splits between promoters and bands is from interviews with Bob Grossweiner of *Performance* magazine.

Background on Fillmore grosses is from a profile of Bill Graham in the *Wall Street Journal,* 4/9/69.

"He was a supreme shark . . ." is from an interview with Carlos Santana on National Public Radio's *Morning Edition* broadcast, 2/12/93.

The "How to argue and win" credo is from "Remembering Bill Graham" on KRON-TV, 11/14/91.

"The Fillmore Neighborhood became a battleground . . ." is from Roger Trilling's interview for *Details,* October 1991.

Details of the Grateful Dead's and Jefferson Airplane's short-lived tenure on the Carousel is from *The Grateful Dead Album.*

Graham's trip to Ireland to secure the Carousel is from Roger Trilling's interview for *Details,* October 1991.

"It was a historic gig . . ." is from KSAN-Radio's Fillmore Tribute, 10/29/72.

"Bill was screaming like a maniac . . ." is from KSAN-Radio's Fillmore Tribute, 10/29/72.

The story of Bonnie MacLean finding Graham in bed with a sixteen-year-old groupie is from interviews with Regina Cartwright.

"My wife is a human being . . ." is from *Rolling Stone,* 4/7/72.

"When trying to make it . . ." is from article in the *Wall Street Journal,* 4/9/69.

Background information on David Rubinson is taken from *San Francisco Rock* by Jack MacDonough published by Chronicle Books, San Francisco, 1985.

"The city has developed a better music industry . . ." is from *Billboard,* 11/29/69.

"Bill says I run the place . . ." comes from article in the *New York Times Magazine,* 11/15/68.

"Dictatorship without timeclocks . . ." is from a 1971 story in the *Village Voice.*

"I'm the best . . ." comes from article in the *New York Times Magazine* 11/15/68.

Background on the Motherfuckers and interviews with spokesman Ben Morea and Kip Cohen are from *Rolling Stone,* 2/15/69.

The story of Graham's defence of the Fillmore East against the Motherfuckers is from his interview with Roger Trilling for *Details,* October 1991.

EIGHT. WALL STREET GOES WOODSTOCK

The business analysis of Bill Graham and rock 'n' roll is from the *Wall Street Journal* article *"Pop Music Explosion: Rock and Bankroll,"* 4/9/69.

"Making money is of course an important thing . . ." is from *Variety*, 3/17/71.

"He screwed Chet . . ." is from a Michael Bloomfield interview broadcast on KSAN-Radio's Fillmore Tribute, 10/29/72.

"Did I take advantage . . ." is from KSAN-Radio's Fillmore Tribute, 10/29/72.

"This is America . . ." is from an interview in *Jazz & Pop* magazine #8, 1969.

Background information on the San Francisco Light Show strike is taken from interviews with Chet Helms.

"Chet runs this place on a dream . . ." is from article about the strike in *Rolling Stone*, 9/6/69.

"It was one of the ugliest things . . ." is from an interview with Ralph Gleason broadcast on KSAN-Radio's Fillmore Tribute, 10/29/72.

Information about drugs backstage at the Fillmore is from interview with Philip Elwood of the *San Francisco Examiner*.

Background on the groupie scene is taken from *Rolling Stone* magazine's special on groupies, 2/15/69.

Background information on Woodstock is from the book *Barefoot in Babylon.*

Band grosses for Woodstock were supplied by Michael Lang.

Information about the *Rolling Stones'* 40-page rider is taken from Graham's interview on KSAN-Radio's Fillmore Tribute, 10/29/72.

Background information about the *Rolling Stones'* concert is taken from Jerry Hopkins' story in *Rolling Stone*, 12/13/69.

NINE. ROCK 'N' ROLL GROWS UP

"It was a tragedy . . ." is from the book *NME—Rock 'n' Roll Years.*

"I will not do 90/10's . . ." is from article in *Melody Maker*, 1/5/74.

Patricia Kennely's defense of Bill Graham is taken from her column in *Jazz & Pop*, June 1970.

"We've always been fond of Bill . . ." is from interview with Pete Townshend in *Melody Maker*, 6/4/71.

Variety magazine's criticism of musicians' behavior is from an article dated 9/17/69.

"That's why this business . . ." is from Ralph J. Gleason's *The Jefferson Airplane and the San Francisco Sound.*

The story about Jimi Hendrix's 1969 New Year's Eve concert is from an article in the *Pacific Sun*, 6/26/75, and from the book *Electric Gypsy.*

"Bill was a very passionate man . . ." is from Carlos Santana's interview broadcast on National Public Radio's "Morning Edition," 2/2/93.

Graham's dispute with Roland Kirk is from a *Rolling Stone* article dated 12/13/69.

The argument with Miles Davis is from a column by Alfred G. Aronowitz in the *New York Post*, 3/18/70.

The Buddy Rich story is from Bill Graham's interview on "Later with Bob Costas" broadcast in 1990.

The background on Paul Baratta's coup for Winterland is from articles in *Rolling Stone*, 2/21/70 and 10/1/70.

Information on Graham's battle to keep his empire together is from article in *Rolling Stone*, 4/27/92.

"The economics got so it was madness . . ." is from story in *Melody Maker*, 1/5/74.

"Janis, like everybody else . . ." is from *Rolling Stone* tribute to Janis Joplin, 10/29/70.

"If one butcher shop does good business . . ." is from a Graham interview published in *Billboard*, 11/14/70.

"After a time I get sick . . ." is from article in *Melody Maker*, 11/14/70.

"Bill is a strange man . . ." is from *KSAN*-Radio's Fillmore Tribute, 10/29/72.

"Right now there is a struggle going on . . ." is from interview with Bill Graham in *Variety*, 1/6/71.

"The stars know . . ." is from article in *Newsday*, 1/30/71.

Background about Bill Graham berating staff is from a story in *New York Post*, April 1972.

Background on Bill Graham's business empire is from *Rolling Stone*, 4/27/72.

The story about Sol Hurok asking Graham to produce shows at the Metropolitan Opera House and his subsequent altercation with Jon Taplin is from an article in *Down Beat*, 6/10/81.

Clive Davis's reply to Graham's assertion that rock was dead was printed in *Variety*, 6/2/71.

Background on Howard Stein and the attack on him by Bill Graham is from story in the *New York Post*, 6/4/71.

Information on Winterland fans being dosed with LSD during a Grateful Dead concert is from a story in *Rolling Stone*, 8/5/71.

"What am I . . . some kind of fly-by-night slob? . . ." is from *Variety*, 6/9/71.

"It's a strange feeling . . ." comes from the *New York Times*, 6/29/71.

David Rubinson's accusation that Bill Graham faked telephone scenes in the *Fillmore* movie were carried in a story in *Rolling Stone*, 11/23/72.

The story about the difficulty Graham had in getting approval from the Grateful Dead for their scenes in the movie is taken from interview with Graham broadcast in KSAN-Radio's 1972 Fillmore Tribute, 10/29/72.

TEN. GOING NATIONAL

The statistics about American rock audiences are from article in *Variety*, 7/26/72.

"No upholstered place wants acid rock . . ." is from story in *Variety*, 7/19/72.

"The business is so huge . . ." is from KSAN-Radio's Fillmore tribute, 10/29/72.

"Success is difficult to put aside . . ." is from article in *Melody Maker*, 1/5/74.

Details of Graham producing seven shows in nine days are from story in *Rolling Stone*, 4/27/92.

Bill Graham's plan to close-circuit three shows to 70 theaters in the U.S. are from news story in the *New York Times*, 2/21/72.

"There's General Motors . . ." is from a *Variety* interview with Graham, 5/17/72.

"Artists rule you with their whims . . ." is from an article in *Melody Maker*, 1/5/74.

Ben Fong-Torres' story about Bill Graham's closed-door session with *Rolling Stone's* Jann Wenner and Tim Cahill is from KRON-TV's "Remembering Bill Graham" tribute, 11/14/91.

Bill Graham's reaction to getting the 1972 Rolling Stones' tour is from John L. Wasserman's column in the *San Francisco Chronicle*, 7/4/77.

The story of Bill Graham's 'doctored' contract is from *Bill Graham Presents*.

"Bill will not cop to the fact . . ." is from story in *Rolling Stone*, 11/23/72.

"Okay, whatever negative charactistics . . ." is from Graham's interview with Derek Jewell in *Melody Maker*, 1/5/74.

Background information on Zohn Artman is from article in the *San Francisco Examiner*, 11/5/78.

"Artman smoothed the sometimes rocky road . . ." is from *San Francisco Examiner's* writer Bill Mandel's column, 5/27/84.

"Reporters and critics who need Graham . . ." is from *San Francisco Examiner's* writer Bill Mandel's columnist, 10/20/81.

Background about payoffs to politicians and judges is from interviews with Regina Cartwright.

Information on Graham's complaints that Bonnie MacLean was supporting her new boyfriend with his money and that David Graham was a late-talker is from interviews with Chris Brooks.

Details of David Graham's custody and Bill Graham's meeting with Marcia Sult is from *Bill Graham Presents.*

"I must be honest and cop to the fact . . ." is from article in *Melody Maker,* 8/21/76.

"Led Zeppelin said they knew . . ." is from article in *Melody Maker,* 9/1/73.

Background information about the Bob Dylan tour is from article in *Billboard,* 11/2/74.

"Bob Dylan is the king . . ." is from Bill Graham's interview on "Later with Bob Costas" broadcast by NBC in 1990.

"Our job . . ." is from article in *Billboard,* dated 11/2/74.

"He said from that moment on . . ." is from KRON-TV's "Remembering Bill Graham" broadcast, 11/14/91.

"In no other area . . ." is from *Billboard,* 11/2/74.

The story about Bill Graham being brought to task for organizing national tours is from his interviews in *BAM,* 1/19/79 and 9/21/84.

Details of Graham's string of affairs he called "hatefucks" is from interviews with Regina Cartwright.

Background on Bill Graham pushing a fan under the wheels of a truck is from interviews with eyewitness Peter Brandt and Wavy Gravy.

ELEVEN. BECOMING A STAR

Background on the SNACK concert is from story in the *New York Times,* 3/24/75, and an article in *Billboard,* 3/26/75.

"It was almost as if the gods . . ." is from SNACK review in *Rolling Stone,* 5/8/75.

The story about Marlon Brando being overwhelmed by his reception is from Bill Graham's interview on *"Later with Bob Costas,"* broadcast on NBC in 1990.

"Nobody but a presidential candidate . . ." is from article in the *New York Times,* 3/24/75.

"The company showed itself to be . . ." is from *Billboard,* 3/13/76.

Background information on FM Productions' set pieces for DOG concerts is from the *Wall Street Journal,* 4/21/76.

"This is a street instinct business . . ." is from *People,* 6/16/75.

Background on Graham's experiences in *Appocalypse Now* are from his interviews with John L. Wasserman in his *San Francisco Chronicle* column, 7/11/77, and Jack MacDonough's *San Francisco Rock.*

Background about Led Zeppelin's fight with Bill Graham is taken from an interview with Richard Cole.

"Peter blasted Jim in the face . . ." is from story in the *New York Post,* 8/16/77.

Jimmy Page's defense of Led Zeppelins from an interview carried in the *San Francisco Chronicle,* 1/11/78.

Information that Bill Graham stashed money in Swiss bank accounts through his sister Evelyn Udry is from interviews with Regina Cartwright.

"He had to turn it into a business . . ." is from a Mickey Hart interview on *KRON*-TV's "Remembering Bill Graham" broadcast, 11/14/91.

"I think his reputation . . ." is from Grace Slick's interview on *KRON*-TV's "Remembering Bill Graham" broadcast, 11/14/91.

"He tries to buy as much as he can . . ." is from *Wall Street Journal* profile on Bill Graham, 4/21/76.

Background on the Grateful Dead's Egypt trip is from a Mickey Hart interview on *KRON*-TV's "Remembering Bill Graham," 11/14/91.

Background information on the "Bill Graham's Presents the World of Plants Show" is from story in *Billboard,* 3/13/76.

Analysis of Graham's finances in 1976 is from *Wall Street Journal* profile on Bill Graham, 4/21/76.

Background on the restructuring of Bill Graham Presents is from article in *Billboard,* 10/9/76.

Information on Winterland merchandising is from story in the *San Francisco Chronicle,* 7/4/77.

"The organization has grown . . ." is from a Bill Graham interview with *BAM,* 1/19/79.

Bill Graham's cocaine use is from interviews with Regina Cartwright.

"There's a lot of madness . . ." is from *Billboard,* 3/19/77.

TWELVE. PUNK WARS

Background on history of punk in San Francisco is from interviews with Dirk Dirksen and Tim Vohannon.

"The truth is never as important . . ." is from Graham's interview with Roger Trilling, October 1991.

Background information on the Sex Pistol's U.S. tour and their final appearance at Winterland is from the books *Twelve Days on the Road* and *The Wicked Ways of Malcolm McLaren.*

Information on Bill Graham's attempts to promote punk music are from an interview with Dirk Dirksen and Tim Yohannon.

"I hate Bill Graham's guts . . ." is from article in *Rolling Stone,* 10/13/83.

Background on Bill Graham's unsuccessful bid to produce a rock concert in Russia is from an article in *Rolling Stone,* 8/10/78.

"This is an awesome project . . ." is from the *San Francisco Chronicle,* 6/15/78.

Background on the effects of the 1978 recession on concert promotion is from article in *Rolling Stone,* October 1978.

Industry speculation on Bill Graham's slippage in the concert promotion business is from *Variety,* 7/18/79.

Graham's cultivation of Dianne Feinstein is from interviews with Regina Cartwright.

"I've never experienced anything like this . . ." is from *Billboard,* 1/13/79.

"This plethora of new promoter action . . ." is from *Variety,* 7/18/79.

"The figures are awesome . . ." is from *Billboard,* 6/28/80.

"He's the bully on the block . . ." is from the *San Francisco Chronicle,* 4/7/84.

Background information on alleged intimidation by Bill Graham Presents on musicians and the Keystone Club is taken from court papers from the Superior Court of California—County of Alameda, 1984.

Details of Graham's out of court settlement with Bobby Corona are from the settlement agreement dated 6/26/86.

"Graham will do anything for a buck . . ." is from the *San Francisco Business Journal,* 12/6/82.

Background on Graham's plans to bring legitimate theater to the Warfield is from the *San Francisco Chronicle*, 7/23/80.

Background on the Cincinatti Riverfront Coliseum tragedy is taken from the book *Everybody was Kung Fu Fighting*, a story in the *San Francisco Chronicle*, 12/5/79, and the official City of Cincinnati report.

Background into the worsening recession and loss of income by promoters is from the *San Francisco Chronicle*, 7/23/80.

The story about Ian Copeland comes from interviews with Bob Grossweiner.

THIRTEEN. GIMME SHELTER

Background on the setting up of the 1981 Rolling Stones tour is from interviews with Bill Wyman and Frank Russo and the book *Bill Graham Presents*.

Information about Graham's affair with Jan Simmons and their proposed wedding are from interviews with Regina Cartwright and Chris Brooks.

"A counterfeiter . . ." is from article in the *San Francisco Examiner*, 8/30/81.

"No other group . . ." comes from Graham's October 1991 interview with Roger Trilling for *Details*.

The story about Graham throwing Warren Hinckle out of Seattle's King Dome was published in the *San Francisco Chronicle, 10/17/81.*

"Graham is the absolute emperor . . ." is from column by Bill Mandel in the *San Francisco Examiner*, 10/20/81.

Details of the Rolling Stones secret concert at London's 100 Club are from story in the *New York Post*, 6/3/82.

Background on Bill Graham's plan to diversify out of rock to counter the recession is from an article in *Billboard*, 8/8/81.

The story of Graham sending Zohn Artman to Europe is from interviews with Regina Cartwright.

"You could tell Bill was going crazy . . ." is from Bonnie Simmons' interview broadcast by KRON-TV's "Remembering Bill Graham" tribute.

"It scared the hell out of me . . ." is from the *San Francisco Chronicle*, 9/10/82.

"Bill's ready to punch . . ." is from the *San Francisco Chronicle*, 9/6/82.

"You can't hang out . . ." is from the *San Francisco Chronicle*, 9/10/82.

"Bill Graham is full of shit . . ." is from the *San Francisco Chronicle*, 9/6/82.

"Wozniak has talent . . ." is from the *San Francisco Chronicle*, 9/10/82.

"We're aggressive . . ." comes from *Billboard*, 7/23/83.

"New York is something . . ." is from story in the *New York Post*, 4/9/87.

Story of Graham being blocked from returning to New York is from the *New York Post*, 5/21/84.

Background on the September 1984 tribute to Bill Graham is from the official event program, the *San Francisco Examiner*, 10/1/84, and the *San Francisco Chronicle*, 10/1/84.

The Jackson camp's allegations of Bill Graham being "too egoed out," are from an article in *Playboy*, May 1988.

Bill Graham's attack on the handling of the Jackson's Victory tour are from article in *Rolling Stone*, 12/19/85.

Report that the Jackson's split $40 million is from the *New York Daily News*, 5/16/86.

"I promoted Michael Jackson's Victory Tour . . ." is from Don King's interview in *Playboy*, May 1988.

"I feel sad for the country . . ." is from Bill Graham interview in *BAM*, 9/21/84.

Background on Concord City Council's decision to award the new contract for the Concord Pavillion to Bill Graham Presents is from the *San Francisco Chronicle,* 10/17/84.

FOURTEEN. AFTER THE FIRE

Background information about Bill Graham's relationship with his sister Ester is from interviews with Rabbi Josef Langer and Mrs. Hinda Langer.

Graham's attitude to Judaism is from his interview with Mrs. Hinda Langer published in the *Chabad Journal,* Winter 1983.

"This is not a Jewish issue . . ." is from the *San Francisco Chronicle,* 4/27/85.

Background on the destruction of the Bill Graham Presents offices is from coverage on *KPIX-TV*, the *San Francisco Chronicle*, *Performance*, *Bill Graham Presents,* and the *San Francisco Chronicle's Datebook.*

Information about Bill Graham's growing addiction to Halcion is from interviews with Regina Cartwright and Graham's interview with Roger Trilling in *Details,* October 1991.

"There were times when my head . . ." is from *Bill Graham Presents.*

Background information on Bob Geldorf's problems with Bill Graham during the setting up of Live Aid is taken from Bob Geldorf's autobiography *Is That It?* Ballantine, 1988.

"Assuming it comes off well . . ." is from a Bill Graham interview in the *Houston Chronicle,* 7/3/85.

"The word is mammoth . . ." is from the *San Francisco Chronicle,* 6/7/85.

Background on logistics of Live Aid show in Philadelphia is from *Performance,* 7/26/85.

"In terms of logistics . . ." is from *USA Today,* 7/11/85.

Bill Graham's threat to get himself arrested if Ronald Reagan attended Live Aid show is from a story in *Mother Jones,* January 1986.

"I couldn't get it out of my head . . ." is from *Performance,* 12/22/89.

Story of Sean Penn pulling a gun on Graham is from interviews with Regina Cartwright.

"The real hero of the affair . . ." is from the *San Francisco Chronicle,* 7/18/85.

Bill Graham's condemnation of MTV after Live Aid is from articles in *Variety, the San Francisco Chronicle* and *Bill Graham Presents.*

"I would never talk about Live Aid . . ." is from story in the *San Francisco Chronicle,* 11/10/85.

Background on Nicholas Clainos' promotion to president of Bill Graham Presents is from article in *Amusement Business,* 4/12/86.

Background on the opening of Shoreline is from a story in the *San Francisco Chronicle,* 6/3/86.

FIFTEEN. THE CONSPIRACY OF HOPE

Background to the Conspiracy of Hope tour is from an interview with Jack Healey, and an article in *Rolling Stone* in 1986, and the book *Unforgettable Fire* by Eamon Dunphy.

The story about Miles Copeland is from *Bill Graham Presents.*

Bill Graham's use of Ecstasy during the Conspiracy of Hope tour comes from interview with Regina Cartwright.

Background information about the Crackdown in Crack concert comes from the *Los Angeles Times,* 8/27/86 and the *New York Times,* 8/26/86.

Pablo Guzman's comments about Bill Graham were published in his *New York Daily News,* 9/16/86.

"I'm baffled . . ." is from article in the *San Francisco Chronicle's Datebook* section, 10/29/86.

"Video revolutionized our world . . ." is from Bill Graham's interview with Roger Trilling, October 1991.

Background information on the ill-fated concert to commemorate the 50th anniversary of the Golden Gate Bridge comes from stories in the *San Francisco Chronicle,* 2/13/87 and 3/26/87.

Background on Bill Graham's 1987 Russian concert is from an interview with Steve Wozniak, an article in the *San Francisco Chronicle,* 6/24/87 and *Bill Graham Presents.*

The descriptions of the Moscow show come from Bill Graham's interview with Roger Trilling, October 1991.

The Bill Graham/ John Scher battle of words was carried in issues of *Performance* in late 1987 and early 1988.

"You get up to fifty pieces of paper . . ." comes from article in *Performance,* 12/9/88.

"There are fifteen or twenty promoters . . ." is from Bill Graham's interview with Roger Trilling, October 1991.

Bruce Springsteen's 95/5 split comes from an interview with his first manager, Mike Appel.

"The price is dictated . . ." is from Bill Graham's interview with Roger Trilling, October 1991.

Background information on BASS comes from an article in the *San Francisco Chronicle,* 3/26/90.

Jerry Pompili's quote, "It's none of your business" is from a story in the *LA Reader,* 5/22/92.

Background information on Ticketron and Fred Rosen are from articles in the *Wall Street Journal* 6/19/91, and *Performance,* 7/18/86.

SIXTEEN. WHIPPING POST

Background information that Bill Graham was disliked by U2 and Bruce Springsteen comes from an interview with Jack Healey.

"We must penetrate . . ." comes from Roger Trilling's 1991 interview with Bill Graham, October 1991.

Bill Graham's deepening depression and his escalating useage of Ecstasy and Halcion comes from interviews with Regina Cartwright.

"They didn't want me talking to the press . . ." is from *Bill Graham Presents.*

"I really don't want to always yell . . ." is from the book *Bill Graham Presents.*

Background on the side-effects that the drugs were having on Graham is from an article in the *San Francisco Herald,* 3/11/88.

Information on Bill Graham reopening the Fillmore is from the *San Francisco Chronicle,* 1/18/88.

"That's the joint . . ." is from story in the *San Francisco Chronicle,* 4/24/88.

"I'm not going to put them on cornflake boxes . . ." is from the *San Francisco Chronicle* 5/8/88.

Background information on the Steel Wheels Tour is from an interview with Bill Wyman.

Information on Michael Cohl's campaign for the Steel Wheels tour is taken from interviews with Cohl and an article in the Canadian publication *Report on Business,* 1990.

Bill Graham's "abacus" quote and his disappointment at not being given the Steel Wheels tour is from Roger Trilling's interview with Bill Graham in *Details,* October 1991.

"Of course we're doing it for the money . . ." comes form *Rolling Stone,* 9/7/89.

Information that Bill Graham saw three different psychiatrists comes from interviews with Regina Cartwright.

"An absolute TV junkie . . ." is from *Bill Graham Presents.*

"The crusher was the Stone's decision . . ." is from *Bill Graham Presents.*

Background on Bill Graham's survivor's guilt is from interviews with Regina Cartwright.

The sketch of Michael Cohl's career comes from interviews with Cohl and and a profile of him published in *Report on Business,* 1990.

"I think the precedent set . . ." comes from an interview with Bill Graham in *Amusement Business,* 12/16/89.

Reaction by promoters on the handling of the Steel Wheels tour is taken from an article in *Performance* 8/11/89.

"It is important to me . . ." is from an interview with Bill Graham in *Performance,* 11/17/89.

"We haven't been in this business for twenty-five years . . ." is from *Amusement Business,* 12/16/89.

Background information on the earthquake benefit comes from cover story in *Performance,* 12/22/89.

The story of the meeting between David Crosby and Bob Hope comes from Bill Graham's interview with Bob Costas broadcast on "Later with Bob Costas" in 1990.

SEVENTEEN. HIS LAST BOW

The background on the business side of the Steel Wheels tour comes from articles in *Forbes,* 12/2/89, *Rolling Stone*, 1/11/90.

Information on Brockum and Steel Wheels' merchandising is from *20/20,* July 1990.

"We're aiming . . ." is from the *Toronto Star,* 8/24/89.

The story of Bill Graham's attack on the Rolling Stones at the New Music Seminar is from *Rolling Stone*, 11/1/90.

BCL's reply to the *Rolling Stone* article was carried in *Performance,* 11/16/90.

"His company and my company . . ." is from *Performance,* late 1989.

Background information for *The Doors* comes from Bill Graham's interview with Bill Graham for *Details,* October 1991.

"I'm just sorry I was weak . . ." is from Bill Graham's interview on *"Later with Bob Costas"* on NBC, 1990.

"Those were scary, scary days . . ." comes from Bill Graham's interview with Bill Graham, October 1991.

Bill Graham's comparison between himself and Bugsy Siegel comes from Bill Graham's interview with Bill Graham, October 1991.

Bill Graham's analysis of the effects of the 1990 recession on concert promotion comes from articles in *Amusement Business,* 6/24/90, and the *New York Daily News*, 12/5/90.

"This is the first year for rock 'n' roll . . ." is from Bill Graham's interview with Roger Trilling, October 1991.

"These guys are fucking the public . . ." is from the *San Francisco Weekly,* 4/17/91.

Background information on the California Senate Judiciary Committee meeting is from the official tape of the meeting.

Wavy Gravy's reaction to Bill Graham's death is from an essay in his book, *Something Good for a Change,* which he read to me during our interview.

"If Elvis was the king . . ." is from an article in the *San Francisco Examiner,* 10/27/91.

Carlos Santana's reaction to Bill Graham's death comes from *USA Today*, 11/4/91.
"I wonder if Bill's in heaven . . ." is from the *Los Angeles Times*, 11/4/91.

EPILOGUE

The Bill Graham Presents staff meeting is from the *San Francisco Chronicle*, 4/17/92.
Stan Fieg's memo comes from the *San Francisco Chronicle*, 4/26/92.
Details of the attempted buy-out of Bill Graham Presents are from an article in *Performance* magazine 6/4/93 and the *San Francisco Chronicle* 5/18/93.
Queen Taylor's unsuccessful buy-out attempt is from an article in the *San Francisco Chronicle* 7/19/93.

Index